A China Program Book

UNIVERSITY OF WASHINGTON PRESS
Seattle and London

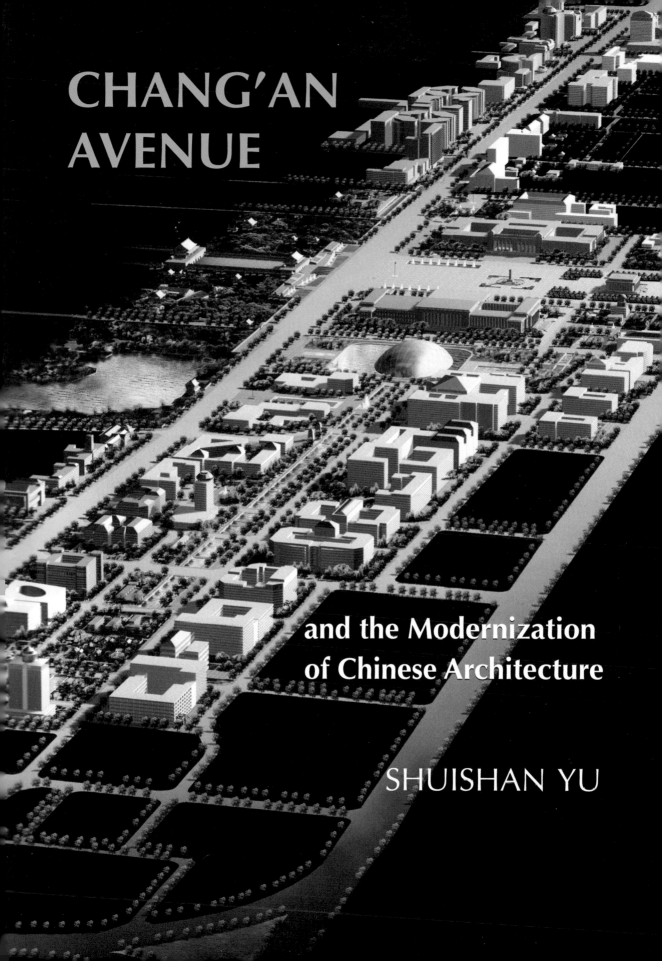

CHANG'AN AVENUE

and the Modernization of Chinese Architecture

SHUISHAN YU

ART HISTORY
PUBLICATION INITIATIVE

This book is made possible by a collaborative grant from the Andrew W. Mellon Foundation.

This book was supported in part by the China Studies Program, a division of the Henry M. Jackson School of International Studies at the University of Washington. A publication grant from the Department of Art and Art History at the Oakland University contributed toward editorial and production costs of the book.

© 2012 by the University of Washington Press
Printed and bound in China
Designed by Veronica Seyd
16 15 14 13 12   5 4 3 2 1

University of Washington Press
PO Box 50096
Seattle, WA 98145-5096, USA
www.washington.edu/uwpress

Library of Congress Cataloging-in-Publication Data
Yu, Shuishan.
    Chang'an Avenue and the modernization of Chinese architecture / Shuishan Yu. — First [edition].
        pages cm — (A China program book/Art history publication initiative)
    Includes bibliographical references and index.
    ISBN 978-0-295-99213-6 (hardback)
    1. Chang'an Jie (Beijing, China).   2. Symbolism in architecture—China—Beijing. 3. City planning—China—Beijing.   4. Architecture and state—China—Beijing.   5. Beijing (China)—Buildings, structures, etc. I. Title.
        NA9053.S7Y8 2013
        720.951'156—dc23   2012027784

In memory of my mother, SHI SHUSHENG 石淑生,

and to my father, YU HONGJING, 于洪经

Contents

Acknowledgments

THIS BOOK was developed from my PhD dissertation under the guidance of professors Meredith Clausen, Madeleine Yue Dong, Marek Wieczorek, Daniel Abramson, and Yomi Braester within the Department of Art History at the University of Washington. I thank them all for giving advice, sharing insights, and providing resources for my research, a true intellectual benefit that I can still feel strongly today. Professor Clausen deserves special thanks for bringing me to the "New World" twelve years ago and being my source of inspiration ever since. Without her criticism and encouragement I would have never made it through my studies in Seattle. She remains the most reliable support for my research and, as an advisor, a model for my academic career.

I received financial support at different stages during my research and writing. The initial research for an article was supported by the Hsiao Fellowship from the Henry M. Jackson School of International Studies at the University of Washington. After the committee and I made Chang'an Avenue the subject of my graduate studies, my fieldwork and archival research in China were made possible by a variety of scholarships offered by the same university, including a Pell Scholarship, two Parnassus Endowment Scholarships, two Nordstrom Awards, a School of Art Award Scholarship, and a graduate school fellowship. My writings developed gradually into a manuscript in the form of a series of summer projects supported by the Faculty Research Fellowship from Oakland University. A publication grant from the Department of Art and Art History at Oakland contributed toward editorial and production costs of the book at a time of universal economic stringency. I am grateful to all of the above-mentioned institutions for their generosity.

This book would not have been possible without the help of numerous scholars, friends, and colleagues. In the United States, professors Bob Mugerauer, Vikram Prakash, Jerome Silbergeld, Martha Kingsbury, Patricia Failing, Brian McLaren, Frank Ching, and Alex Anderson took time to meet and share with me invaluable comments on the project. Professor Nancy Steinhardt gave me the opportunity to present the initial article on Chang'an Avenue at the Society of Architectural Historians annual meeting and offered me advice for revision. And professor Jeffrey Cody made critical comments on an article based on the first chapter. I thank them all for their help and encouragement. I also want to thank professors Patricia Ebrey, Cynthea Bogel, Robin Wright, Susan Casteras, Christopher Hallett, Karen Mathews, Rene Braveman, Christopher Ozubko, Steven Harrell, Zhi Lin, Paul Scotton, Henry Matthews, Susan Platt, Debra Caplow, and Trina Lyons for offering me opportunities to work with them in a variety of teaching and research fields, a priceless experience in my academic career.

In Beijing, professors Zheng Guangzhong and Hu Rongrui took time to talk with me about their experience of planning Chang'an Avenue. In his design studio, professor Wu Liangyong answered my questions about contemporary Chinese architecture and cities. I also benefitted from discussions with professors Chen Zhihua, Peng Peigen, Zhao Bingshi, Shi Qing, Guo Daiheng, and Lü Zhou on a variety of occasions. Lin Zhu provided me with new material she had just published about her late husband, Liang Sicheng. Fu Xinian, Yang Yongsheng, Cui Kai, and Xin Min Hua (Isabel Xia) met and shared with me their insightful observations about and extensive knowledge of modern Chinese architecture and urban development. I am grateful to them all. In Paris, Jean-Paul Olivier and Patricia Casse helped me to schedule an interview with Paul Andreu and Francois Tamisier, who generously met me for two hours around midnight during the busiest time of their work on the National Grand Theater in Beijing. I thank them with all my heart.

I am indebted to professors Li Daozeng and Xu Weiguo at Tsinghua University, and to Zhou Qinglin of the China Architecture Design and Research Group, Mao Shiru and Lu Xinzhi of the China Architecture and Buildings Press, and Fan Xue of the *Architectural Journal* for helping me with copyright issues and allowing me to use their images. Historical data and access to archives were provided by Liu Zhixiong, Liu Zonghan, Fu Qingyuan, and Ma Qinglin of the National Bureau of Historical Relics; Cui Haidong, Wen Bing, and Zhou Xuliang of the China Architecture Design and Research Group; Zhang Lixin of the Capital Planning Bureau; Liu Yu, Li Chunmei, Zheng Zhuyin, Li Qiuxiang, and Liao Huinong of the School of Architecture at Tsinghua University; and my former Tsinghua classmates Zhao Tian and Hua Li. I thank them all for their time and kindness. I especially want to thank my friends Xu Lei and Shang Yan, who generously offered me hospitality whenever I made a visit to Beijing and whose companionship made my long fieldwork so much more enjoyable.

I would like to thank Lorri Hagman for guiding me through the publication process and for her insightful suggestions on preparing the final manuscript. Before her, Ann Fenwick copyedited an earlier version of the manuscript. And still earlier, Lenore Hietkamp and MaryEllen Anderson helped to improve my prose. I have also benefited from two anonymous reviewers of the manuscript, whose comments were constructive and thought provoking. I would like to thank professor David Goldfield for his advice on an article I wrote five years ago that is relevant to this book, and the two anonymous readers of that article manuscript for their comments. I also thank my friends and fellow graduate students at the University of Washington, especially Gayle Clemans, Molly Malecki, Marvin Anderson, John Szostak, Tamaki Maeda, Robert Mintz, Stephen Salel, Eun-Boo Kim, Steve Bunn, Dickson Preston, and Catherine Barrett, for inspiring discussions and shared memories in teaching and study.

I have benefited from professor Wu Hung, whose casual comments during a symposium in Seattle many years ago first drew my attention to Chang'an Avenue. Professors Delin Lai, Zhu Jianfei, and David Bachman shared with me their new scholarship on modern Chinese architecture and history. Professor Susan Shih-shan Huang shared with me not only her new work on Chinese art but also valuable information on publication procedures. I thank them all for their help and support.

I am grateful to my colleagues at Oakland University for creating an invigorating intellectual and creative environment. Andrea Eis, chair of the Department of Art and Art History, and John Cameron, late professor of Medieval Art, have provided me with the best support one could hope for. I thank Susan Wood, Janice Schimmelman, Bonnie Abiko, Carl Barnes, Tamara Jhashi, Claude Baillargeon, Richard Stamps, Linda Benson, and John Corso for their intellectual inspiration, and Dick Goody, Vagner Whitehead, Susan Evans, Sally Schluter Tardella, Lynn Galbreath Fausone, and Cody VanderKaay for their friendship and moral support, which sustained me through the process of completing the book. Iola Adams and Claire Cooper did all of the manuscript copying and mailing throughout the publication process, and Lisa Ngote and Karen Ferri scanned many images for me. My thanks for your continued help.

I would like to thank Jim and Carol Young and the Dickerson family in Seattle for helping me to conquer my cultural shock more than a decade ago, when I first left China and stepped onto American soil, and for their friendship ever since. I would also like to thank my many friends in China, especially Jie Ke, Cui Fengxia, Zhan Yang, and Tian Kai, whose welcome and hospitality made a variety of Chinese places my home again after years of living in the United States.

Special thanks go to my parents, whose love and understanding allow me to travel as far as my dreams carry me. To them, and especially to my late mother, I dedicate this book. My parents-in-law, Liu Jisong and Liu Guozhen, made every effort to enable me to work without worries. Without them taking care of my baby, I would have had much less time for writing and doing research. And, finally, I thank my wife, Lingyun Liu, for her companionship, unwavering support, and love, and my daughter, Angela, who brought so much joy to our life.

A Note on Language

Modern Chinese pinyin romanization is used throughout this book to represent the pronunciation of Chinese names and terms. English equivalents are used wherever possible, with occasional exceptions—such as Tiananmen (literally, "Heavenly Peace Gate"), which is well known worldwide by its romanized pinyin name. Readers may refer to the glossary for English, pinyin, and Chinese-character equivalents of all significant terms used in the text.

Chang'an Avenue
and the Modernization
of Chinese Architecture

Introduction

On January 8, 1976, Premier Zhou Enlai of the People's Republic of China (PRC) died in the Beijing Hospital near historic East Chang'an Avenue.[1] On the morning of January 11, Zhou's body, in a white hearse followed by a hundred-car motorcade, was driven from the hospital to Babaoshan Crematorium near the terminus of West Chang'an Avenue. A million people lined Chang'an Avenue proper as Zhou's hearse passed by, paying final farewell to the premier.[2] That evening, Zhou's ashes were escorted back along the same route and placed in the Cultural Palace of the Working People, the former Imperial Ancestral Temple of the Ming and Qing dynasties on the north side of historic East Chang'an Avenue. Silent and respectful crowds, stretching more than twenty kilometers on either side of the avenue between Babaoshan and the Cultural Palace of the Working People, observed the return of Zhou's ashes. Thousands of people stood in chilly fog for hours along the section of the avenue near Tiananmen Square. For the next three days, Zhou's ashes were displayed in the main hall of the temple, where hundreds of thousands of people paid their last respects. Toward the evening of January 14, escorted again by a procession of one hundred vehicles, Zhou's ashes were borne along and then across the avenue to the Great Hall of the People, the largest and most important of the Ten Great Buildings constructed for the tenth anniversary of the People's Republic of China in 1959. There, public homage continued. An official memorial service was held on January 16, and after that, the ashes were moved once more along Chang'an Avenue to the Babaoshan Revolutionary Cemetery.[3]

Three months later, on the eve of the Qingming Festival, a traditional Chinese memorial day for paying homage to deceased ancestors, thousands of people gathered spontaneously around the Monument to the People's Heroes in Tiananmen Square to the south of Chang'an Avenue to pay homage once again to the deceased premier. They brought wreaths and banners and turned the monument into an unauthorized memorial for Zhou and a beachhead for criticism of those currently in power. The next morning, after discovering that their tributes had been removed by the police, people began protesting in the square and along the avenue. The confron-

Forbidden City dominated the city and separated the avenue into two disconnected halves; after the revolution, Chang'an Avenue cut through the imperial north-south axis at its heart. To the north was the historic Imperial City and Forbidden City; to the south, the Communist Tiananmen Square was constructed.

Modernism, especially in its avant-garde form that is hostile to tradition,[7] cultivated a sense of historical awareness and legitimized its historicity on the basis of chronic uniqueness. On one hand, the present should be different from the past; on the other, the future should be different from the present. The present was singled out by the cult of the "new."[8] Modernity is the center, extending in both directions, into past and future. At the intersection of modernity and tradition, and extending into infinity in both directions, Chang'an Avenue was a perfect metaphor for this linear characterization of the chronology of modernity. While modernity sliced through the ideological boundary between past and present, Chang'an Avenue did this physically.

There are other definitions of modernity in architecture, both formal and value based.[9] What makes modernity a specific historical phenomenon, however, is the awareness of one's historicity. Modernity creates a boundary between past and present. Being modern is not a natural chronological extension of the past, but a self-conscious breaking away from it. The past is comprehensively defined as "tradition." Both the modern and the traditional are products of modernity. In the discourse of twentieth-century Chinese architecture, "modern" was also discussed as a contrast to "national." A satisfying architectural product should be a balance of both "national" and "modern." While "national" (*minzude*) was a positive term and belonged to the present, "traditional" (*chuantongde*) was a neutral term and belonged to the past. As Mao once stated, essence and dross existed in both Chinese and foreign traditions.[10] The difference between "national" and "traditional," however, was never really defined. By confronting both, Chinese modernity imperceptibly blurred the boundary it had previously created between past and present.

An Independent Unit for Academic Inquiry

Arguably the most famous boulevard in China, known as the "Number One Avenue in the Divine Land,"[11] Chang'an Avenue deserves an academic inquiry in its own right. It has expanded both in length and width since the collapse of the Qing Empire, and became the new east-west axis of the socialist capital by the end of the twentieth century. The avenue, together with Tiananmen Square, its most renowned portion, is the largest public space for political ceremonies in China and the place where many of the most important historical events of postimperial China (1912–present) were staged. During the Republican era (1912–49), Chang'an Avenue was the main theater for political protests against those in power.[12] During the PRC era (1949–present), however, it mainly became the stage on which the Communist authorities displayed power and propagated new national mythologies, especially during PRC anniversary celebrations on October 1.[13]

Chang'an Avenue, lined with a continuously expanding series of government buildings and projects of major political significance, was also the primary national showcase of socialist achievements after 1949. Since most national ceremonies during the PRC era were staged along this thoroughfare, the façades of the avenue became the architectural images most closely associated with the way China was perceived abroad and the way the "motherland" was thought of by different ethnic groups in China. As a result, Chang'an Avenue became a prototype for urban planning and a catalyst for the transformation of major Chinese cities. The development of the avenue into a new east-west axis for the Chinese capital provided a model, a revolutionary gesture in urban planning, a breaking away from the identity of the imperial periods. Other Chinese cities followed Beijing, developing main avenues for public ceremonies that cut through historic urban centers and lined up central squares and major monuments.

As the nation's most important public space, both practically and symbolically, Chang'an Avenue was endowed with political significance, received paramount attention from the Chinese architectural profession, and became a prototype that influenced architecture and urban planning in cities throughout China. In the economic sphere, locations closer to the avenue are more privileged than other spots on the same longitude. Many real estate companies include a map of their properties in their advertisements, using Chang'an Avenue as a reference point. Being in the vicinity of the avenue is a major advantage in the current real estate market.

As a unit for academic inquiry, Chang'an Avenue offers a link between urban study and architectural history. While the discipline of urban history studies entire cities, architectural history studies individual buildings. The former largely focuses on the evolution of the macroscopic structure of a city, and, as a result, elicits only a blurred picture of the particular details of how urban fabrics change. In contrast, the latter, with its focus mainly on separate structures, achieves only a fragmentary understanding of how these contribute to overall change in urban space.

In an effort to overcome this dilemma, scholarly attention was recently given to the street as a link between the macroscopic history of a city and the microscopic history of individual buildings. Some of the issues raised in these studies are directly relevant to Chang'an Avenue in twentieth-century China, for instance, Spiro Kostof's analysis of the Haussmannian or Mussolinic "aesthetics of demolition" and the association of "urban conservation" with nationalism,[14] Greg Castillo's discussion of socialist realist aesthetics as reflected in the reconstruction of Moscow's Gorki Street in the 1930s,[15] and Zeynep Celik's treatment of the street as a space for ritual and ideological engagement.[16] Limited in their length and detail, these articles on urban streets are confined to the change of large-scale urban fabric and lack specific discussions of individual structures.

This book, on the other hand, is solely dedicated to Chang'an Avenue, the only thoroughfare in Beijing that runs through the entire city, and whose development has contributed most to the urban transformation of the Chinese capital in the twentieth century. The avenue also offers the largest and most concentrated collection of significant architectural projects in the People's Republic of China. Examining changes in the urban fabric more closely and selecting some monuments as highlights for in-depth discussion will reveal how the construction of individual buildings contributes to the bigger picture. The approach here lies between the traditional disciplines of urban history and architectural history. By focusing on Chang'an Avenue, a thoroughfare of monuments connecting different parts of a city, this study aims to construct a "tectonic joint" for these two disciplines and to promote better understanding in both fields.

The Chang'an Avenue case also provides an opportunity to create a link between cultural history and architectural history. The study of Beijing has been focused on two approaches. One emphasizes the cultural and political significance of urban space and the evolution of architectural symbolism; the other emphasizes specific professional strategies or methods in the urban development of the capital city. The former treats architecture and urbanism as part of cultural and political history; the latter treats the city and its built environment mainly as a design problem and as the history of various solutions that have been offered. The debates surrounding every significant national monument on Chang'an Avenue make it a perfect candidate for a cultural study of architecture. Historical contextualization in the study of specific objects will be a useful tool in the excavation of different layers of meaning of the avenue's architecture.

While cultural studies of imperial Beijing offer a sociopolitical framework,[17] new research on Republican Beijing lays the foundation for understanding the city's urban environment before the dramatic transformation during the socialist period. Delineating the city's responses to various sociopolitical changes in the first half of the twentieth century, these studies reveal that Republican Beijing was a mixture of old and new,[18] and that "old Beijing" prior to "liberation" was not as old and traditional[19] as discussions during the PRC era assumed. Some publications in Chinese provide indispensable historical details on changes in city life and urban spaces before 1949.[20]

Scholarship on PRC era urban culture focuses on Tiananmen Square as a symbol of political transformation.[21] Wu Hung's study of the political history of Tiananmen Square monuments explores how architecture and urban space acquired meanings and how the meanings changed due to the changing cultural political contexts.[22] Studies on the post-Mao era (1976–present) explore the impact of increased commercialization on urban life and spatial organization.[23]

Rich in historical details about changes in Beijing's urban life and material culture, these studies mainly treat architecture and urban development as footnotes for cultural and political history. The built environment of Beijing serves mostly as a neutral backdrop for historical dramas, both grand events and ordinary lives, rather than as an active participant in them. Although it advances our understanding of the symbolic meaning of urban space in modern Chinese political life, scholarship on PRC Beijing frequently equates the creation of a political space to the representation of Mao's will. However, regardless of the original intentions of the authors, scholarship on the pre-Communist city helps to romanticize "old Beijing."[24] Most of this scholarship has ignored the voices of architects and city planners. The Communist urban strategy was often quickly condemned as a failure of CCP leaders' personal tastes or as their blind enthusiasm for the Soviet model,[25] and the urban plans produced during the PRC era have seldom been seriously studied.

A cultural historical approach to architectural history does not treat architecture simply as architectural sociology. Arnold Hauser is to some extent correct when he says that art has its own specific problems to solve beyond its social commitments.[26] Heinrich Woelfflin's tradition of stylistic analysis, Friedrich Hegel's *Zeitgeist*, and Alois Riegl's concept of *Kunstwollen* are useful tools as long as they are not treated in a teleological sense to claim the universality of aesthetic values. Although there is no gender-neutral or universal art-historical knowledge, there are standards for art and architecture in a given time and society that are the targets of artists, both as ideals to reach and as conventions to break. It is precisely the relative independence of art and architecture from politics and ideology that makes it possible to look to their relationships for a better understanding of a culture.

Scholarship dealing directly with twentieth-century Chinese architecture has provided some basic information on specific development strategies and on changes in the built environment in Beijing. Some offer basic facts about and brief introductions to the significant architectural projects of the first fifty years of the PRC era, as well as outlines of the political backgrounds and architectural policies during different periods.[27] Others record key moments in the history of Beijing city planning and contain the major drawings of each successive design.[28] A leading figure in both design practice and academic study in Chinese urban planning, Wu Liangyong focuses on specific development strategies, especially in dealing with the historical city of Beijing, a theory he calls "organic renewal."[29] These studies, written mostly by practicing architects and urban planners, are important for the rich professional detail and broad reference coverage they provide. However, focusing on physical structure and operating within a framework for which the built environment remains mostly a design problem leave little space for critical historical exploration and cultural political analysis.

This book offers a cultural and political history of Chang'an Avenue through detailed analysis of individual buildings and of specific design problems in planning. Chang'an Avenue is the creation of architects as well as politicians, of city planners as well as profit seekers. Politics clearly played a central role in the development of the avenue and in the urban transformation of Beijing. However, political instructions and government-generated cultural guidelines have to go through architects and engineers to be implemented. For a balanced picture of socialist Beijing, it is important to integrate the Chinese Communist Party's political agenda as part of the architectural discourse and not treat architects' debates as merely a footnote to Mao's casual comments.

Modernism, Modernity, and Modernization

The issue of modernity is the theoretical core of this book. Modernity is used here to refer to the defining character of a modern culture in a broad cultural-political sense. Being modern means having a constant awareness of tradition as opposed to "modern" and a belief in the progressive nature of future development. Chinese modernity in the twentieth century is an ever-updating project, a self-conscious replacement of "modern" with "modernization" to create an unself-conscious historical continuity, as evinced in the endless attempts to complete Chang'an Avenue.

Modernism as a mainstream architectural style has recently been criticized. Some argue that architectural modernism is an artificial construction of a group of architects, historians, and critics that eliminates all other practices from their self-promoting historical narration.[30] Others propose replacing the concept of "modernism as a paradigm of style" with "discourse of modernism" as a methodological model to resolve the analytical problems and incoherencies in current discussion of twentieth-century architecture.[31] Such a replacement shifts modernism from a style to an ethically grounded material practice. If the concepts of modernism versus traditionalism or modernism versus regionalism are false polarizations in the West, the transplantation of these concepts to China is more problematic. Thus "modernism" as used in this book is also only of discursive value. It offers a common ground for Chinese architectural modernity to take shape and a rhetorical base for ever-updating modernization to take place.

New scholarship on Beijing and modern Chinese architecture focuses on the issue of modernity. An analysis of imperial Beijing within a cross-cultural theoretical framework of power and subjectivity sheds new lights on the north-south axis of the ancient capital.[32] The application of tradition versus modernization, or essence versus form, makes it possible to create a master narrative on modern Chinese architecture, simultaneously entailing more critical evaluation.[33] Case studies with different analytical approaches contextualize modern Chinese architectural practice within a global theoretical and practical framework and explore an alternative modernity to the Western model.[34] Studies on the contemporary built environment in China highlight the uniqueness of the Chinese architectural modernity, such as the work unit as an urban form.[35]

Modernity in Chinese architecture has other unique features in comparison with its Western counterparts. For instance, significant architectural works have been created collectively since 1949 and often bear no individual creators' names. As Henri Lefebvre has pointed out, the boundaries between social product and artistic work are not always clear, and an artistic work does not have to be associated with the uniqueness of individual creation.[36] While the Chinese socialist stance is quite akin to some of the avant-garde movements in early twentieth-century Europe, the latter were criticized at the time as bourgeois. This is not the only contradiction and inconsistency in the discourse on Chinese architectural modernity, which will be revealed through a deconstructionist[37] reading of materials—buildings, drawings, and archival documents—generated by the historical entity known as "modern China."

The modern China is ever changing. So are the spaces and activities along Chang'an Avenue. While the revival of the north-south axis accompanying the fanfare of the 2008 Beijing Olympics distracted some attention from Chang'an Avenue, the recent installation and removal of the Confucius statue[38] in front of the National Museum to the south of the avenue signaled the continuing struggle over the control of public space. The history of Chang'an Avenue and the modernization project in Chinese architecture that it represents provide a physical and conceptual framework for understanding of these events.

Chapter One

The History of Chang'an Avenue in an Urban Context

"Chang'an" means "eternal peace," or "long peace" in a more literal translation, but the word will immediately remind the Chinese of two of their most powerful dynasties: the Han (202 BCE–220 CE), from which the Chinese ethnic majority acquired its name (Hanren), and the Tang (618–907 CE), from which the overseas Chinese communities derived their collective identity (Tangrenjie).[1] Both the Western Han Empire (202 BCE–9 CE) and the Tang Empire had the city of Chang'an (modern day Xi'an) as their capital, and both dynasties represent past golden ages of Chinese political power. Thus the roots of the name Chang'an Avenue stretch far into China's imperial past.

Chang'an Avenue during the Imperial Era

"Chang'an" was first used as the name for the major avenue in front of the Imperial City in the early Ming dynasty (1368–1644), during the first fifty-three years of which Nanjing was the national capital. Located on the north bank of the Yangtze River some 1,000 kilometers south of Beijing, Nanjing had served as the imperial capital for many southern regimes before the Ming: Wu (229–80), Eastern Jin (317–420), Song (420–79), Qi (479–502), Liang (502–57), Chen (557–89), and Southern Tang (937–75). None of these regimes unified China. Compared to the powerful and prosperous Han and Tang, with Chang'an as their capital, these dynasties were politically weaker, territorially smaller, and short-lived. When the first Ming emperor, Zhu Yuanzhang (the Hongwu emperor, r. 1368–98), finally chose Nanjing as the main capital of his unified Chinese empire, he was concerned about inauspicious associations with these previous ephemeral dynasties. Therefore the new walled quarters for palaces and central government—also known as the Palace City (Gongcheng) and the Imperial City (Huangcheng), respectively, as later in Beijing—were constructed at the southeast corner of Nanjing to avoid overlapping with the palace sites of former regimes.[2] This might also be why the major street in front of the Imperial City was then named Chang'an Avenue, in hopes of a "long peace" and to create auspicious associations with the long-lasting and glorious Han and Tang dynasties.

13

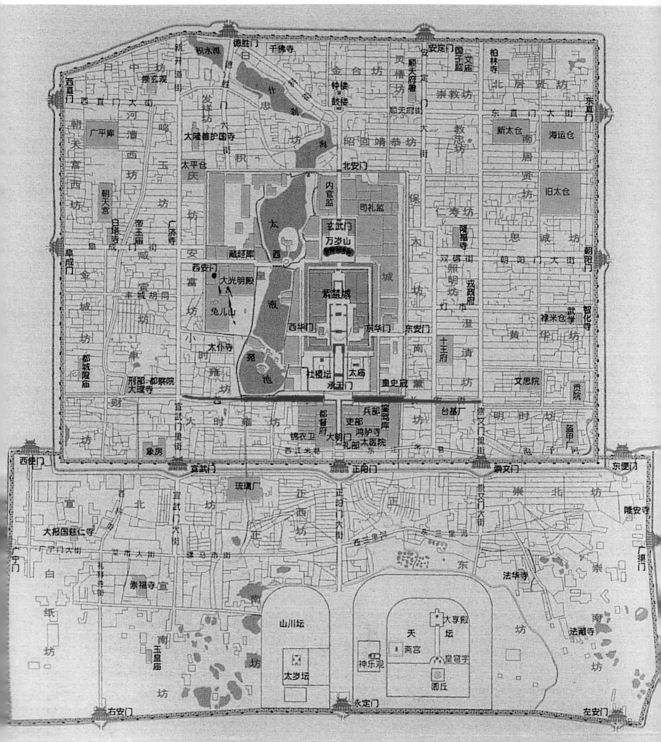

长安街街廊

In 1416 the third Ming emperor, Zhu Di (the
Yongle emperor), decided to move the capital to
Beijing, the site of the previous Yuan dynasty (1271–
1368) capital Dadu (Great Capital). Construction of
the new capital started in 1417 and was completed in
1420. Although the new Ming capital partially over-
lapped with the Yuan Dadu and followed its north-south axis, the layout of Ming Beijing replicated the dynasty's capital Nanjing, including use of the name Chang'an
Avenue for the streets in front of the Imperial City. The Beijing of 1420 had three
layers of city walls: the Inner City (Neicheng) with nine gates,[3] the Imperial City
inside the Inner City with four gates,[4] and the Palace or Forbidden City inside the
Imperial City with four gates.[5] In 1553 walls were constructed to the south of the Inner
City to define an Outer City (Waicheng),[6] adding a fourth layer of walls with seven
gates[7] to Ming Beijing. The entire city was dominated by a 7,500-meter-long north-
south axis. Running from Yongding Gate (Gate of Permanent Stability) at the south
end of the city to the bell tower in the far north, it lined up not only the main gates of
the Outer City, Inner City, Imperial City, and Palace City but also other major imperial monuments.[8] This layout persisted for centuries (fig. 1.1). The Manchu rulers of
the Qing dynasty, which followed the Ming in 1644, made no major physical changes
to the general plan of Ming Beijing or to Chang'an Avenue.

Apart from its central location, Chang'an Avenue during the Ming and Qing
dynasties was no different from the other major thoroughfares in Beijing. At that
time, however, two separate avenues existed, divided by the Imperial Tiananmen
Square.[9] On the western side of the square, from West Three-Arch Gate (Xisanzuomen) to Xidan (named after Xidanpailou, West Single Memorial Archway) lay
the historic West Chang'an Avenue. On the eastern side of the square, historic East
Chang'an Avenue ran from East Three-Arch Gate (Dongsanzuomen) to Dongdan
(named after Dongdanpailou, East Single Memorial Archway).[10]

Imperial Tiananmen Square itself consisted of three squares (fig. 1.2). In the center
was the T-shaped space directly in front of Tiananmen Tower, bounded by Tiananmen
(Heavenly Peace Gate) in the north, Great Qing Gate (Daqingmen)[11] in the south, Left
Chang'an Gate (Chang'anzuomen) in the east, and Right Chang'an Gate (Chang'anyoumen) in the west. Two smaller wing squares separated central Tiananmen Square
from the two avenues: the east wing square, between Left Chang'an Gate and East
Three-Arch Gate, and the west wing square, bounded by Right Chang'an Gate and
West Three-Arch Gate. Walls enclosed all three squares. Imperial Tiananmen Square,
together with the Imperial City behind it, blocked more than two-thirds of the east-
west communications in the Inner City of Beijing.

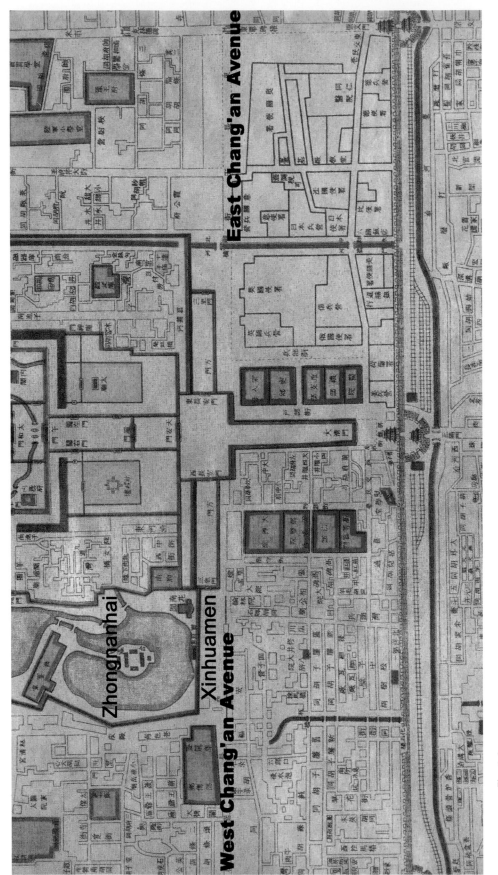

East Chang'an Avenue

Zhongnanhai

Xinhuamen

West Chang'an Avenue

Fig. 1.2

Fig. 1.2. Tiananmen Square, East Chang'an Avenue, and West Chang'an Avenue during the late Qing dynasty, detail of *Xiangxi Dijing Yutu* [Detailed map of the imperial capital], a map of Beijing published in 1908. *Map in the public domain.*

Historic East and West Chang'an Avenues had different functions and symbolic meanings in imperial China. According to the Daoist "five elements" (*wuxing*) theory, east belongs to the element of wood and is associated with spring, growth, and life, while west belongs to the element of metal and is associated with autumn, decay, and death. While historic West Chang'an Avenue was mainly associated with punishment, military power, and authority, its eastern counterpart was more associated with business, civil power, and celebration. On the west side of the Thousand-Pace Corridor (Qianbulang)—the southern part of T-shaped Imperial Tiananmen Square—next to historic West Chang'an Avenue, the Ming dynasty built the headquarters of the Five Armies and the Jinyiwei (secret police force), and the Qing dynasty built the Ministry of Punishment (Xingbu), Imperial Procuratorate (Duchayuan), and the Imperial Prison (Qintianjian). On the east side, next to historic East Chang'an Avenue, both the Ming and Qing dynasties built the Ministry of Rites (Libu), the Ministry of Revenue (Hubu), the Ministry of Civil Office (Libu), the Ministry of Public Works (Gongbu), and the Imperial Hanlin Academy (Hanlinyuan).[12]

Every three years, an imperial announcement written on yellow silk with the names of those who had passed the imperial examination was carried out through Left Chang'an Gate and posted in today's East Chang'an Avenue; and every autumn, convicts awaiting execution were led through Right Chang'an Gate and knelt along the west side of Imperial Tiananmen Square for their final trial and sentence. From these events, popular names for the gates evolved. Left Chang'an Gate was known as the Dragon Gate (Longmen), or Gate of Success, while Right Chang'an Gate was called Tiger Gate (Humen), or Gate of Peril.[13]

The civil-military dichotomy that divided East Chang'an Avenue from its western counterpart was further strengthened by Beijing citizens' different opinions about the areas east and west of the north-south axis in general. The saying in Beijing that "the east is rich and the west is aristocratic; the south is humble and the north is poor" suggests that most of the merchants lived in the east city, while most of the princes, dukes, and other Manchu aristocrats lived in the west city, and that many inhabitants of the south city were from the lower classes, while those in the north were poor Manchus.[14]

After the Second Opium War in 1860, part of the area south of historic East Chang'an Avenue became foreign concessions of Western powers. After the Boxer Rebellion in 1901, the entire area between today's East Chang'an Avenue proper and the southern wall of the Inner City became foreign concessions.[15] Thus East Chang'an

Avenue also became associated with diplomacy, Western influence, the larger world, and, later, with Western imperialism and China's past humiliations.

Chang'an Avenue during the Republican Era (1912–1949)

After the Qing Empire collapsed in 1911, the two Chang'an Avenues were gradually unified. The unification and spatial reconfiguration of the avenue during the Republican era, however, were less about change in the physical environment than about the way urban space was used. In other words, the changes were more symbolic than physical, more about "software" than "hardware." Throughout the Republican era, new facilities, such as electric street lamps and tramlines, were added to the avenue, but its length and width remained unchanged from imperial times.

In 1912 Beihai, the northern part of the former imperial garden west of the Forbidden City, opened to the public, while the central and southern parts, located north of Chang'an Avenue and known as Zhongnanhai, became the presidential palace. A new south entrance to Zhongnanhai, called Xinhua Gate, Gate of New China, was opened onto the avenue. During the Ming and Qing dynasties, this structure had been a freestanding two-story pavilion just inside the imperial garden's south wall. At that time, it was known as Baoyuelou, the Tower of the Precious Moon. The Republican regime changed this freestanding structure into a gate by opening the ground floor and modifying the garden walls (fig. 1.3), which are now connected to the sides of the structure instead of screening the front of it.[16]

On January 1, 1913, the first anniversary of the Republic of China, the government under Yuan Shikai removed the doors in the East and West Three-Arch Gates and the Right and Left Chang'an Gates and demolished the walls connecting these gates.[17] This created a passageway that connected the two avenues for the first time, and common Beijing citizens were now able to walk from one directly to the other.[18] However, two separate streets still existed, along with the four gate towers marking the borders between Imperial Tiananmen Square and the historic Chang'an Avenues.

In October 1914, the former Altar of Soil and Grain (Shejitan) opened to the public as the "Central Park" of Beijing. During imperial times, the altar was a sacred place, where the emperors performed annual duties of sacrifice to the gods of soil (she) and grains (ji). The tradition of constructing an Altar of Soil and Grain in the imperial capital as a national symbol and legitimizing device for the mandate of the emperor as the "Son of Heaven" can be traced as far back as the Zhou dynasty (1046–256 BCE).[19] During the Ming and Qing dynasties, the Altar of Soil and Grain, together with the Imperial Ancestral Temple (Taimiao) on the other side of the north-south

axis, was closed to common Beijing citizens. The
Imperial Ancestral Temple remained a private preserve of the former Qing imperial family well into the
1920s. After the founding of the Republic of China in
1912, however, both sites were gradually opened to
the public.

Fig. 1.3. Gate of New China
(Xinhuamen), built in 1758 as
Baoyuelou, opened as a gate
in 1912. *Photograph by author.*

Before the Republican capital was moved to Nanjing in 1927, the main person in
charge of these urban changes in Beijing was Zhu Qiqian. Born to a family that had
close connections with many powerful Qing officials, Zhu first became minister of
communications, then minister of interior in 1912 during Yuan Shikai's presidency.[20]
In addition to unifying Chang'an Avenue and converting the Altar of Soil and Grain
into a public park, Zhu also supervised the Zhengyang Gate renovation project and
many road and railway construction projects in Beijing.[21]

The transformation of Chang'an Avenue in the early years of the Republican era
was characterized by the adaptation of former imperial urban spaces for civic use and
the protection of the Old City's original urban texture. Imperial structures inside the
former Altar of Soil and Grain were carefully preserved and rebuilt for public enjoyment. Preservation efforts extended even to the old cypress trees planted at the begin-

ning of the Ming dynasty, when the altar was first built. Ten years after the Central Park project, Zhu lamented,

> The nice trees in the former forbidden areas are lush, green, and undamaged after all of these revolutionary changes, and we can still rest under them after hundreds of years. Seeing these trees again, the vicissitudes of an old nation and the rise and fall of regimes become vivid, which makes me sad and full of emotions. Today, the task of reconstruction and preservation does not belong only to the government, but also to the people. Indeed, the garden of old trees has much in common with the spirit of self-discipline. I sincerely hope that our countrymen will love and protect them and will not let our descendants sigh and reproach us [because we didn't care for these cultural relics].[22]

The former imperial monuments, with their forbidden spaces, suddenly became the cultural heritage of the people and the embodiment of national spirit. Physical changes were minimal. All that was needed was a change of name and function. In 1925, when Sun Yat-sen died in Beijing, his body was temporarily placed in the main sacrifice hall of the former Altar of Soil and Grain. In 1928 Chiang Kai-shek defeated the Beiyang warlords and relocated the Nationalist capital to Nanjing. Beijing was renamed Beiping (because the *jing* in Beijing means "capital"), and Central Park was renamed Zhongshan Park in honor of Sun.[23]

After the revolution in 1911, the last Qing emperor, Puyi, was allowed to continue to live in imperial style in the Forbidden City. As the place where the remnant Qing court continued to make ritual sacrifices to its ancestors, the Imperial Ancestral Temple remained part of the palace holdings. In 1924, after general Feng Yuxiang evicted Puyi from the palace, the Forbidden City became the Palace Museum, and the former Imperial Ancestral Temple was opened as the Peace Park.[24] In 1928 the park was closed and the halls of the former temple became part of the Palace Museum.[25]

While major structures on Chang'an Avenue did not experience much physical change after the fall of the Qing Empire, monuments symbolizing China's former humiliation by Western powers did. In 1900, Western countries with concessions on East Chang'an Avenue moved troops into Beijing to protect their citizens during the Boxer Rebellion. This, in turn, placed considerable military pressure on the Qing court. On June 20, 1900, German ambassador Clemens von Ketteler was killed by a Manchu military officer at Dongdan, near the eastern end of historic Chang'an Avenue. This incident was followed by the invasion of China by an international force composed mainly of troops from Japan, Russia, Britain, the United States, and France. After the suppression of the Boxers, as part of the indemnities imposed on China by the Western powers, a three-bay marble memorial archway called the Ketteler-Denkmal was erected at the location where the ambassador died. An apology from Emperor Guangxu was inscribed in a horizontal board over the central bay of the gate in English, French, Latin, and Chinese, a source of a galling shame and humiliation to many Chinese. After the defeat of Germany in World War I, the Ketteler-Denkmal was dismantled and in 1919 was reconstructed in Central Park on the other side of Chang'an Avenue and renamed Memorial Archway for the Victory of Justice (Gongli Zhansheng Fang).[26] Germany's defeat in World War I had given China an ephemeral hope of national revival and the end of foreign humiliation.

Another major change was the incorporation of modern technology. In 1924 tram rails were laid along the avenue. During the period from 1924 to 1948, three parallel tramlines, Lines One, Three, and Five, ran between Tiananmen Tower and Tiananmen Square.[27] This modern technology cut across the 7,500-meter-long imperial north-south axis at its very center.[28]

In the 1941 Beiping[29] urban plan, prepared during the period of Japanese occupation (1937–45), new residential areas in the western and industrial districts of the eastern suburbs were envisioned on either side of the Old City, and Chang'an Avenue was planned as the major connection between them.[30] Although the avenue was not yet physically extended, between 1937 and 1939 openings were made in the city walls where the future extension of the avenue would meet the borders of the Inner City. The western opening was called Chang'an Gate (today Fuxing Gate, or Gate of Revitalization), and the eastern opening was called Qingming Gate (today Jianguo Gate, or Gate of National Construction).[31] After the Japanese surrendered, the Nationalist government hired Japanese technical personnel to prepare a new general plan for Beijing in 1946. The resulting plan was not very different from the 1941 Japanese plan, and no major physical change was made to the avenue (see fig. 6.10).[32]

Chang'an Avenue remained short, divided, fragmented, and not perfectly straight throughout the Republican era. The avenue turned several times between Xidan and Dongdan. Although no longer impassable at Imperial Tiananmen Square, the eastern and western parts of the avenue were still spatially separated by the four intervening gate towers. In fact, four sections of the street, with different names, were referred to in general as Chang'an Avenue. The section in front of Zhongnanhai was called Fuqian Street, and the section between Tiananmen Square and Nanheyan was called East Three-Arch Gate Street. Historic West Chang'an Avenue referred only to the approximately 800-meter-long section between Xidan and Fuyou Street, and historic East Chang'an Avenue was only about a kilometer in length between Nanheyan and Dongdan. The two historic Chang'an Avenues were more than two kilometers apart.[33]

Physical Expansion after 1949

The physical unification and expansion of Chang'an Avenue did not occur until after the founding of the People's Republic of China (PRC). On October 1, 1949, when Mao Zedong stood on the rostrum of Tiananmen and proclaimed the founding of a New China, the space he looked out over was not very different from imperial times, except that it was now filled with people and flags. The parade of military formations along the avenue still had to pass through arches in the gate towers and temporarily disappear from his sight. Flags had to be tilted in order to fit under the arches. As Tiananmen Square became the main political public space of New China, and as national and revolutionary ceremonies proceeded with increasing frequency along the avenue, reconstruction of the thoroughfare became inevitable.

As mentioned earlier, the four sections of historic Chang'an Avenue—historic West Chang'an Avenue, Fuqian Street, East Three-Arch Gate Street, and historic East Chang'an Avenue—did not form a straight line. Not even two of them lined up perfectly. While the other three sections had only slight turns, historic East Chang'an Avenue was about 100 meters south of the other sections. In 1950, in an effort to straighten the avenue in preparation for a mass parade celebrating the first anniversary of the People's Republic of China, a fifteen-meter-wide parallel street was added to the north of historic East Chang'an Avenue, in line with East Three-Arch Gate Street. At the same time, a street of the same width was created to the south of East Three-Arch Gate Street, in line with historic East Chang'an Avenue. Thus, on the east side of Tiananmen Square, historic Chang'an Avenue had two parallel lanes, separated by tramlines and large areas of greenbelts, giving rise to the nickname "Green Boulevard." During the reconstruction of the avenue in 1950, the East and West Three-Arch Gates were demolished, along with the two memorial archways.[34]

In August 1952 the Left (east) and Right (west) Chang'an Gates were also torn down to further open the avenue for public communication and as a parade ground for the third anniversary of the People's Republic of China on October 1.[35] In 1954 the last two imperial monuments marking the separation of Chang'an Avenue, the Western and Eastern Chang'an Archways, were removed for reconstruction in Taoranting Park.[36] For the first time, East Chang'an Avenue and West Chang'an Avenue were fully connected.[37]

Changes were then made in the avenue's width and surface, some in preparation for another National Day celebration. In 1955 West Chang'an Avenue was expanded to a width of between thirty-two and fifty meters. Before that, the widest section of the avenue, a stretch of 2.4 kilometers between Dongdan and Zhongnanhai, measured only fifteen meters. The asphalt and crushed stone road pavements were replaced with asphalt concrete. A decision was also made that, before the tenth anniversary of the People's Republic of China in 1959, the two lanes of East Chang'an Avenue would be merged to form a road with a width of between forty-four and fifty meters.[38]

West Chang'an Avenue was extended to Fuxing Gate in July 1956, and East Chang'an Avenue was extended to Jianguo Gate in July 1958. Before that, between Xidan and Fuxing Gate were two alleys, each five meters wide, and between Dongdan and Jianguo Gate were many small alleys of similar width. To make straight extensions thirty-five meters wide, matching the width of the original sections,[39] about 2,500 bays[40] of courtyard houses were demolished in 1956 and a further 3,000 bays more disappeared in 1958, a total of roughly 2,000 buildings.[41]

Elaborate changes occurred in 1958, in preparation for the People's Republic of China's tenth anniversary celebration in 1959. Tram rails in the middle of East Chang'an Avenue were removed and the greenbelts were paved. The two lanes were merged to form a wide, open passageway. The width of the central section of the avenue between Nanchizi and Nanchang Street (about one kilometer in length) was expanded to eighty meters and was called Grand Parade Road.[42] The original plan had called for an even more ambitious expansion, to a width of 120 to 140 meters.[43] The 391.9-meter-long section in front of Tiananmen Tower was paved with granite blocks. Two rows of elaborate columned streetlights were added to the sides of the road, along with white poplars, elms, pines, and willows. At nightfall, "the lamps formed two long dragons of endless golden lights" along the avenue.[44]

The thoroughfare also expanded rapidly in length after the mid-1950s. When compared to an early twentieth-century map, a 1950 map of Beijing shows the two historic Chang'an Avenues virtually unchanged. In a 1957 map, however, the western extension already reaches the Shijingshan District, the contemporary west end of Beijing's east-west axis. The eastern section, however, remains almost the same length as before 1949, creating a very unbalanced image of the avenue on the two sides of the north-south axis. A symmetrical image would soon be restored. A 1972 map shows the eastern extension reaching far enough to match its western counterpart, transforming the avenue into a true thoroughfare for the entire city. As early as 1966, the avenue reached its current length of 40,000 meters, from Tongxian country in the east to the Shijingshan District in the west.[45]

With Chang'an Avenue cutting through the entire urban area of Beijing and expanding in both length and width, cross traffic became a problem for the maintenance of its image as a wide, open, and straight road, a visible metaphor for China's bright socialist future. Before the late 1970s, traffic crossed the avenue on the same level as the street itself. Since 1980, crossings have been carefully planned and controlled. Bridges and tunnels, including subway station tunnels, were built to make the avenue an unimpeded thoroughfare.[46] However, no bridge was built over Chang'an Avenue proper, in order to avoid blocking the grand vista of the parade route. No ground-level crossing is permitted along the Grand Parade Road between Nanchizi and Nanchang Street. Pedestrians must walk through tunnels, and vehicles must detour to cross the central section of the thoroughfare. Along the avenue proper, both stopping and left turns are banned for vehicles. Crossing on foot is difficult given the width of the street and the few existing pedestrian crosswalks.[47]

Between 1998 and 1999 Chang'an Avenue underwent further, comprehensive renovation in preparation for the fiftieth anniversary of the People's Republic of China. The section between Dongdan and Jianguo Gate was widened from thirty-five to fifty meters, thirty meters for motor vehicles and seven meters on each side for nonmotorized vehicles, with three-meter interval belts. Along Chang'an Avenue proper, pedestrian lanes on both sides were widened to six meters, and along the Chang'an Avenue extensions, all of the pedestrian lanes were widened to five meters. Along historic Chang'an Avenue and Tiananmen Square, sidewalks were paved with granite, and in the sections from Xidan to Gongzhufen and from Dongdan to Dabeiyao, they were paved with colorful concrete tiles. Tiananmen Square itself was paved with granite tiles, and two green areas of grass and trees, each 30 meters wide and 160 meters long, were added to decorate its east and west sides. Pipes and wires were buried underground. Along the entire avenue, traffic signs, billboards, shops, and dustbins were reorganized, repaired, and renovated; green areas were increased; and benches were added. Upon completion of this renovation project for the fiftieth anniversary in 1999, the avenue was claimed to be "unprecedentedly more beautiful and neat."[48]

Planning

Although the two original Chang'an Avenues were united almost immediately after the fall of the Qing Empire, plans to reshape Chang'an Avenue and Tiananmen Square were carried out only after the founding of the People's Republic of China. In four major stages, each with different functional emphases, the 1950s, the 1960s and 1970s, the 1980s and 1990s, and the early twenty-first century, the political elements of the plan became weaker and weaker, while increasing attention was paid to the cultural dimension. "Function" was always the claimed focus, but its meaning differed from phase to phase—political, cultural, humanitarian, or environmentalist. One constant remained: economy was never mentioned, although commercial development has been crucial since the 1980s.

The issue of a comprehensive plan for Chang'an Avenue was first raised in late

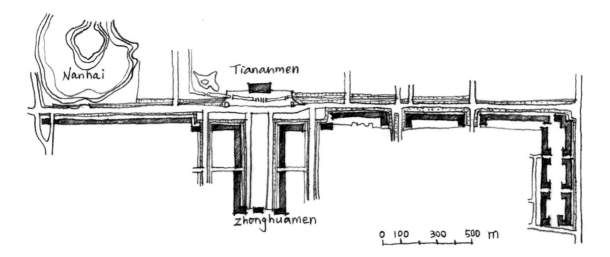

Nanhai

Tiananmen

zhonghuamen

0 100 300 500 m

1949 and early 1950 by Soviet advisors[49] who came to assist the new Communist regime's reconstruction of China, a country torn by more than a century of constant warfare and social unrest. These advisors argued that a new government center should be developed along the avenue, with Tiananmen Square as its focal point (fig. 1.4). Many Chinese

Fig. 1.4. Soviet advisors' proposal for the reconstruction of Chang'an Avenue, 1949–50. *Drawing by author, modified from Dong Guangqi,* Beijing guihua zhanlue sikao, *374.*

architects and scholars opposed such a plan, including Liang Sicheng, the most renowned Chinese architectural historian of the twentieth century, and Chen Zhanxiang, a British-trained urban planner invited to Beijing by Liang.[50] These two were the authors of a famous alternative vision for the reconstruction of the capital, the Liang-Chen Scheme.[51]

While the specific strategies for the urban renovation of Beijing remained unsettled, the headquarters of branches of the new government were constructed along the avenue, including new buildings for the Ministries of Public Security, Textile Industry, Fuel Industry, and Foreign Trade in 1951. One of the major arguments in favor of concentrating these government buildings along the avenue was that the former training ground for foreign troops in the concession area on historic East Chang'an Avenue was the only unoccupied space in the Old City.[52] This explanation, however, did not answer the question of why the new government center had to be located in the heart of the Old City at all, an issue that Liang and Chen had raised.

The motivations for developing Chang'an Avenue instead of constructing a new center outside the Old City were revolutionary ideology and national pride, as well as practical concerns. Ideologically, Chinese revolution in the twentieth century defied the preservation of the old; practically, the new regime needed not only an area for

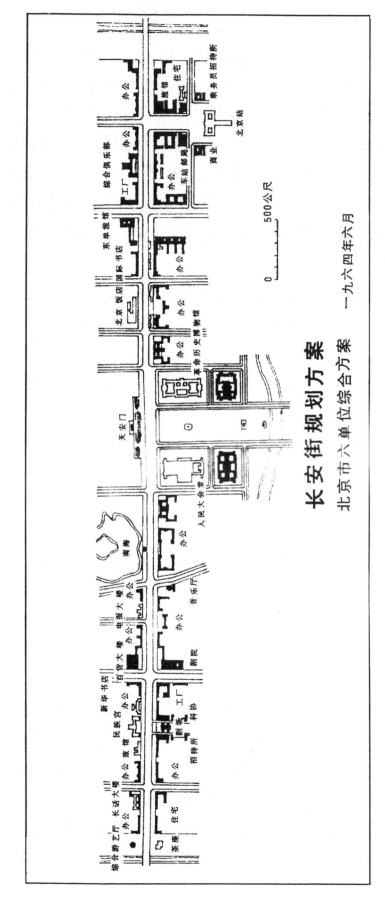

长安街规划方案

北京市六单位综合方案　　一九六四年六月

Fig. 1.5

buildings but also a space with an architectural frame for the display of power. The avenue fulfilled all of these purposes handsomely. As the parade ground for the annual National Day celebrations, it became the route along which the majority of the Anniversary Projects of 1958–59, also known as the Ten Great Buildings, were concentrated. While drawings from the 1950 Soviet plan show that all of the proposed new buildings were on the south side of the avenue, near Tiananmen Square, most of the new construction for the tenth anniversary was on the north side, which would allow the avenue to be developed into a major showcase with monumental buildings on both sides. Widening had another practical purpose. It would allow airplanes to take off or land on the avenue during an emergency. Preparation for war was still a major concern for architects and urban planners in China in the 1950s.

If the first attempt at avenue planning in the 1950s was still part of a general project to renovate the capital, the second stage in 1964 was a well-organized project aimed only at the avenue itself. For the first time, Chang'an Avenue proper, from Fuxing Gate on the west to Jianguo Gate on the east, was planned comprehensively as one urban unit, to be lined with monumental structures on both sides, most of which were official and cultural complexes, with some commercial and service buildings located predominantly on the east side (fig. 1.5).

The original motivation for this round of planning, however, was to fill the vacant spaces left by the unrealized Anniversary Projects of 1959. The 1958 plans called for most monuments for the tenth anniversary to be constructed on Chang'an Avenue and its extensions.[53] Two of the originally planned buildings were not completed. The old buildings on these sites, one on the east side of Fangjin Alley at the eastern end of East Chang'an Avenue proper, the other at the northeast corner of Xidan on historic West Chang'an Avenue, however, were cleared away. In order to fill the empty space on the avenue, six major architectural and urban planning units in Beijing—the Beijing Municipal Planning Bureau, the Beijing Institute of Architectural Design and Research, the Institute of Industrial Building Design, Tsinghua University, the Research Institute of Architectural Science, and Beijing Industrial University—were invited by the municipal government to prepare planning proposals, in a process chaired by vice mayor Wan Li. Experts from all over the country were called on to review the drawings and models provided by different institutes. Finally, a comprehensive design by all of the participants, including the six Beijing units mentioned above and five leading architects from the provinces, was submitted to the municipal government.[54]

During this 1964 planning process, the issue of architectural consistency along the avenue was raised for the first time. Not only was the entire thoroughfare now considered as one single unit for urban development—the redline for the planning area covered both sides of the avenue, from Fuxing Gate to Jianguo Gate—but also the guiding principles emphasized the necessity for a unified urban space along the thoroughfare. It was a prerequisite that the overall arrangement of buildings along the avenue should be "continuous, rhythmic, and complete," and that the skyline of the avenue's elevation should be "simple and clear." The heights of all of the buildings were to be between thirty and forty meters. Abrupt height changes were to be avoided, with the exception of four points: Dongdan, Xidan, Jianguo Gate, and Fuxing Gate, the major intersections on and the eastern and western ends of Chang'an Avenue proper. Another guiding principle specified that the avenue as a whole should exemplify "grandeur, beauty, and modernization." "Nationalization must be based on modernization, absorbing valuable experiences from a variety of cultures—foreign or Chinese, ancient or modern—as a way to make buildings simple, decent, and bright."[55] The relationship between the avenue and the main north-south axis was also specified: the number of north-south axes intersecting with Chang'an Avenue was to be limited in order to maintain the prominent status of the main axis through Tiananmen Square.

Like the first stage of planning in the 1950s, the third stage in the 1980s and 1990s was also part of the general planning for the whole city. In 1982 a new Master Plan for the Municipal Construction of Beijing was drafted, and this was approved by the Chinese Communist Party (CCP) Central Committee and the State Council in July 1983. The following spring, the Capital Planning and Construction Committee convoked leading units[56] in the field to compile a new master plan to further flesh out and update the 1982 plan. Experts and professors in various fields, from city planning to architectural design, from historical preservation to sculpture, were invited to revise and combine the proposals. The comprehensive plan was released in December 1985. In August 1985 the Height Limitation Plan for Buildings in Beijing was enacted by the Capital Planning and Construction Committee and the Beijing Municipal Planning Bureau.

The future of Chang'an Avenue envisaged in these proposals was not very different from that of the 1964 plan (fig. 1.6). However, some general ideas in the previous plan were made more specific. For instance, three secondary north-south axes were added to intersect the avenue and parallel the main axis. These were located at Xinhua Gate and the Minority Culture Palace on West Chang'an Avenue, and at the Beijing Railway Station on East Chang'an Avenue. These plans also offered more details on height restrictions: buildings between Xidan and Dongdan were not to exceed thirty meters, and buildings west of Xidan and east of Dongdan were not to be higher than forty-five meters. Squares to facilitate traffic were planned for the four major intersec-

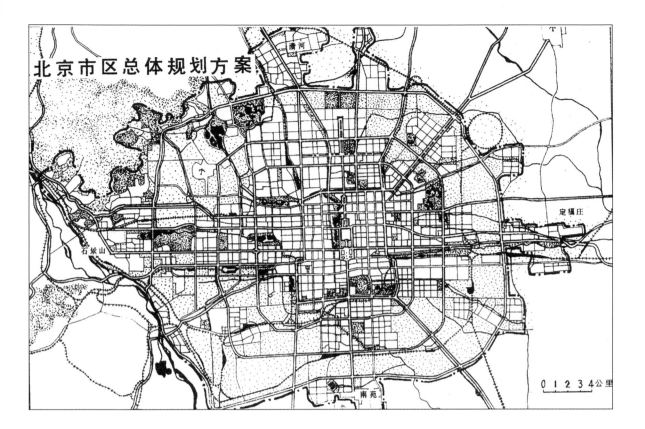

北京市区总体规划方案

tions at Dongdan, Xidan, Jianguo Gate, and Fuxing Gate, and the subway from Jianguo Gate to Fuxing Gate was to be completed as soon as possible.[57]

Fig. 1.6. Beijing master plan, 1982. *Reproduction from Dong Guangqi,* Beijing guihua zhanlue sikao, *389. Courtesy of CABP.*

Also in August 1985, a report on the planning scheme for Tiananmen Square and Chang'an Avenue was submitted to the CCP Central Committee and the State Council. A major change in the 1980s proposals was their new emphasis on the civic and commercial (rather than the political) roles that the square and the avenue should play. Large green fields were planned to cover some key spots,[58] and green space was to appear between every two buildings. In general, green areas were to be located evenly along the avenue. These proposals customarily required the future square and avenue to be grand and solemn. Yet everyday requirements for living, sightseeing, and recreation were also addressed. Commercial and service facilities were envisaged at the intersections of the Front Gate, Wangfujing, and Xidan. The ground floors of the buildings along the avenue were all to be open to the public. The underground area to the north of Tiananmen Square was to be used for parking lots, small shops, and service facilities. More service facilities were to be provided along the sidewalks.[59]

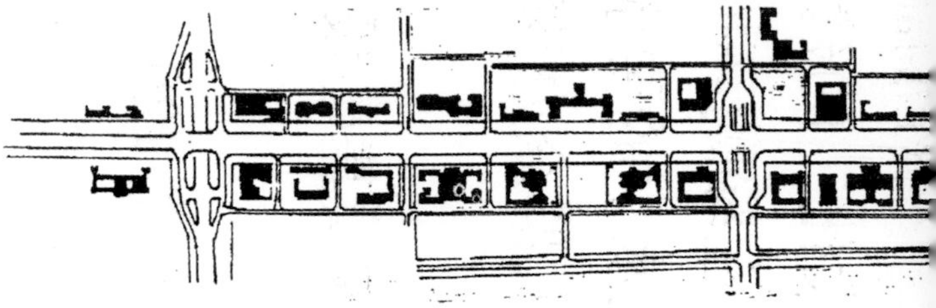

Fig. 1.7. Chang'an Avenue plan, 1985. *Reproduction from Dong Guangqi,* Beijing guihua zhanlue sikao, *402. Courtesy of CABP.*

Another departure in the planning schemes of the 1980s was the emphasis on the preservation of the "style of the old capital" (*gudu fengmao*). Traditional buildings and imperial structures were formerly treated as obstacles to modernization and were demolished to make way for the expansion of the avenue and the square. In its response to the 1982 scheme, however, the CCP Central Committee and the State Council pointed out, for the first time since the founding of the People's Republic of China, "Beijing is the capital of our country and a renowned cultural historical city. Urban construction in Beijing should reflect the historical cultures of the Chinese peoples, revolutionary tradition, and the unique style of a socialist capital. Historical cultures should be preserved and developed, and new creations should be encouraged."[60]

Stylistically, the 1985 Chang'an Avenue planning scheme was dramatically different from both the Soviet plan of 1949–50 and the 1964 comprehensive plan. While Chang'an Avenue in the two previous plans was framed mainly by long straight blocks, in the 1985 plan, these were mostly replaced by complexes with courtyards (fig. 1.7). This had been advocated strongly by Liang Sicheng and the Tsinghua University teams in every round of planning but had never won out before. This stylistic change signals recognition of Liang's approach to the reconstruction of Beijing. It was also a result of the increase of historical preservation in the 1980s, which Liang, had he lived, would have supported enthusiastically.

In 1991 the approach of the new century and the opening of the second fifty-year planning period of the capital led to a new revision of the 1983 master plan. As a replacement for the previous planned economy, Deng Xiaoping's "socialist market economy" policy took root in the 1990s and was also reflected in city planning. Foreign investments and financial organizations were allowed to appear on the avenue. In addition to the 1980s definition of Beijing as the "political and cultural center," the future of the city was now officially characterized in terms of a "globally famous historical capital and modern international metropolis."[61]

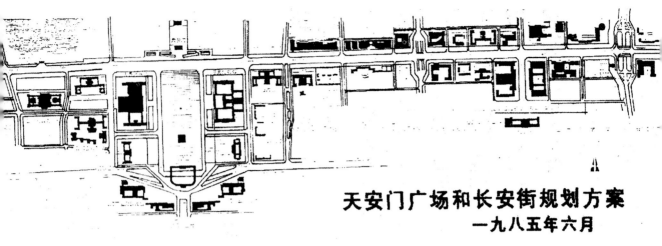

天安门广场和长安街规划方案
一九八五年六月

The fourth stage of avenue planning in 2002 constituted the most comprehensive study of the avenue to date, covering its historical development, its present condition, and the preparation of planning concepts for its future. Like the third planning stage in the 1980s and 1990s, this round was initiated by the Capital Planning and Construction Committee and was divided among several leading institutes, which were almost exactly the same as those in the 1980s planning.[62]

Like the 1950s and 1960s planning, the motivation for the planning in the twenty-first century was to fill in the gaps on the avenue. According to the Beijing Urban Planning Committee, the municipal leaders of Beijing had raised the question of how to create a strategic vision for the completion of the ten unoccupied sites along the avenue. "This is to say," the committee revealed, "the leaders requested us to complete Chang'an Avenue with buildings on both sides before 2009." The "gaps" along the avenue needed to be filled, even without an understanding of what to fill them in with. In fact, the task for the planners was exactly to study "strategies on how to fill the ten unoccupied sites along Chang'an Avenue."[63] The avenue simply needed to be "completed" to facilitate great spectacles during major cultural and political events, this time, the twenty-ninth Olympic Games in 2008 and the sixtieth anniversary of the People's Republic of China in 2009.

The report for the 2002 project named Chang'an Avenue the "Number One Street of China" and "the east-west axis of Beijing city," which "plays an important and special role in the nation's political and cultural activities and which represents the image of the Chinese capital and the whole country."[64] Although the avenue had become the de facto east-west axis since the 1950s, and its status as such was mentioned in materials from previous documents, the 2002 appraisement was the clearest statement yet of the symbolic power this avenue possessed for Beijing and China.

Most of the report was dedicated to such practical issues as how to offer a more artistic and functional urban space with more efficient traffic circulation and better service along the avenue (fig. 1.8). The symbolic significance of the avenue, however, was hinted at in the assessment of its present condition and suggestions for its ideal future. In the section titled "Analysis of Architectural Functions," the authors complained that the avenue was losing its character as a political and cultural center. There were too many commercial and banking buildings along the avenue, and too few dedicated to culture and services. The report also suggested reducing commercial advertisements on the thoroughfare and replacing them with billboards promoting public welfare and publicizing cultural affairs.[65]

Fig. 1.8. Computer-generated images for future Chang'an Avenue, Research and Planning Project for Chang'an Avenue and Tiananmen Square, 2002. *Reproduction from Chang'anjie: Guoqu, xianzai, weilai, 265. Courtesy of Zheng Guangzhong and Zhao Tian.*

Compared to previous Chang'an Avenue plans, the guidelines for future development in the 2002 project added two principles that reflected a new orientation in twenty-first-century Chinese architecture: environmentalism and humanism.[66] On a theoretical level, the environmental principle aimed to improve the natural environment through sustainable design and ecological balance in urban development; the principle of humanism required more consideration of the lives of common people instead of focusing solely on state ideology. On an operational level, for the environmental principle, the 2002 plan proposed expanding green fields and adding more water surface along the avenue; for the principle of humanism, it suggested opening the lobbies and ground floors of all buildings along the avenue to the public so that everyone could use service facilities, such as washrooms. The 2002 plan also suggested adding more public toilets, seats, benches, and souvenir pavilions along the sidewalks to provide more public services and comforts.

The 2002 guidelines also reiterated four other principles that had been fully or partly emphasized in previous plans: (1) basing development upon existing conditions, (2) preservation, (3) function, and (4) art. The principle of basing development upon existing conditions admitted that both great achievements and great problems had resulted from the preceding fifty years of construction, and held that future development should take this as its starting point. The principle of function emphasized the significance of Chang'an Avenue, together with Tiananmen Square, as a political and cultural center, and called for improvements in services for both the people and the central government. The principle of preservation reiterated the obligation to protect and reutilize historical buildings and neighborhoods. Finally, the principle of art demanded that the "Number One Street of China" be on a par with

the great avenues of other world capitals. This required that the avenue have functionally sound construction, convenient communication, modern facilities, a beautiful and splendid image, a pleasant space and a human scale, rich cultural content, deep traditional flavor, and unique Chinese character.[67]

The most detailed design in the 2002 planning was the central office district (*zhongyang bangongqu*) on the south side of West Chang'an Avenue proper. The form of the plan, as well as the choice of this area for in-depth design, was a legacy of the controversy over the status of the avenue in the 1990s, when there were two different views on the east-west axis of the Chinese capital. One view, advocated by city planner Chen Gan, maintained that the avenue already had been and should continue to be developed as the east-west axis.[68] The opposing view was upheld by architect Zhao Dongri, who characterized the avenue as *xuzhou*, a "void" or "false" axis, an empty passageway with monuments only along its sides. Zhao called for the construction of a "real" or "solid" axis (*shizhou*) to the south of the avenue, an axis with monuments directly on it, comparable to the ancient north-south axis with its monuments Tiananmen Tower and the Forbidden City. The area Zhao proposed for the construction of this east-west axis was between the avenue and today's Qiansanmen Street, with Tiananmen Square at the intersection of the east-west and north-south axes. The east-west axis of monuments in Zhao's proposal extended westward from the Great Hall of the People on the west side of Tiananmen Square, and eastward from the Museum of Chinese Revolution and History on the east side of the square.[69] In the 2002 plan, the central office district has it own axis, with monuments and water surfaces directly on it. The axis also started from the Great Hall of the People, with the nearly completed National Grand Theatre as the second monument on it. This axis, however, covered only the west section of Zhao's original proposal. It was also much shorter than both the avenue and the north-south axis, and thus represented a compromise between Chen's and Zhao's views.

In spite of changes in ideology and the guiding principle, the motivation for the development of Chang'an Avenue has remained the same throughout the PRC era: to fill in the "gaps." The 1949 Soviet plan proposed to fill the gaps around the former concession area; the 1964 plan tried to fill the two gaps left by the Anniversary Projects in 1959; and the 2002 project aimed to fill the "last" ten gaps. This chronology suggests that new gaps were produced as soon as old gaps were filled. In fact, such "gaps" were more conceptual than physical. They were the products of changes in ideology and guiding principles, discrepancies in the ideal "completions" of different periods. The gaps were also about public façades—a concept imported from the West when the Chinese first began to grapple with the issue of architectural modernity.

The Changes of Chang'an Avenue's Façades

The concept of a façade as the main public image for a building was foreign to traditional Chinese architecture, which stressed an open courtyard, a void, rather than solid built structure. The Chinese courtyard was enclosed by walls on all sides, and from the street the only clue as to the status of a building complex or its inhabitants was the main gate, usually located in the south wall. The individual buildings that defined the courtyards each had a "face"[70] and a "back." The "face" had large windows and doors and was often elaborately decorated, while the "back" was usually just a plain solid wall, sometimes with small high windows in the upper part. The "face" almost always looked inward to the courtyard, leaving the "back" to the public urban space. Usually a single story structure, the "face" remained concealed from the street (see fig. 6.12).

In traditional Chinese architectural illustrations, buildings were often represented either by sections or by axonometric drawings, but rarely by elevations.[71] The earliest extant drawings of architectural façades in China were those for the Western buildings in the Yuanmingyuan, one of the major summer palaces of the Qing emperors. The concept of using façade in a public space to indicate architectural significance was a result of China's encountering the West.

Chang'an Avenue Façades before 1949

Before 1949, historic Chang'an Avenue was an architecturally traditional street framed mainly by walls and gates. Before 1860, during the Ming and Qing dynasties, the central section was framed by the walls of the Imperial City to the north and the walls of the various government ministries to the south. Historic East and West Chang'an Avenues were bordered on both sides by walled residential compounds, punctuated by shop fronts and temples. The avenue façades were low and predominantly single-story.

In 1860, after the Second Opium War in 1860, foreign embassies were constructed around the area of East Jiaomin Alley to the south of historic East Chang'an Avenue. They were mostly one- or two-story masonry buildings within walled quarters, each for a different country. Although designed and built mainly by Westerners, their main façades all faced inward and away from public urban spaces, following the Chinese convention. After the Boxer Rebellion of 1901, foreign concessions expanded to occupy the entire area between historic East Chang'an Avenue and the south walls of the Inner City, as well as part of what is now Tiananmen Square. The entire 120–hectare legation district was walled and guarded like a medieval castle,[72] physically

Fig. 1.9. The model of the Old City of Beijing made in 1949, showing the legation quarter with its military drill grounds. *Reproduction from* Chang'anjie: Guoqu, xianzai, weilai, *46. Courtesy of Zheng Guangzhong.*

and administratively "a city within a city," as the Chinese called it. Inside the legation district were embassies, residences, clubs, post offices, and military camps. The peripheries of the legation district were cleared as military drill grounds for foreign troops and as polo fields for Westerners. Now surrounded by large areas of open space, historic East Chang'an Avenue completely lost its façades (fig. 1.9).[73]

During the Republican era, some multistory buildings appeared on historic Chang'an Avenue, such as the Capital Municipal Administration Office across from Zhongnanhai and the Beijing Hotel of 1917 on the north side of historic East Chang'an Avenue. On the whole, however, historic Chang'an Avenue was still dominated by walls and one-story buildings. The few tall colonial-style façades rose above the continuous horizontal red walls and gray roofs like "cranes standing among chickens," as some contemporaries put it. After Zhongnanhai was converted from an imperial garden into the presidential seat in 1912, the Tower of the Precious Moon, formerly a pavilion inside the garden, became an entrance façade. At the same time, a long unbroken wall with brick patterns of Western baroque motifs was constructed along the south side of the avenue to hide the shabby courtyard dwellings from the view of the Republican leaders. Much of the façade of historic West Chang'an Avenue was reduced to an endless screen of gray brick (fig. 1.10).

Another significant post-1911 change in the avenue's façades was a direct result of the opening of previously restricted imperial areas. After the walls surrounding Imperial Tiananmen Square were demolished, Tiananmen Tower, the former south gate to the Imperial City and just one of many gates on the north-south axis of Beijing, was singled out as a façade. This new façade was immediately accorded political prominence. Huge portraits of both Sun Yat-sen and Chiang Kai-shek had hung above the central arch before the Communist takeover, conflating a political face with an architectural façade. As a whole, however, the avenue façades remained low and fragmented throughout the Republican era (fig. 1.11A).

Fig. 1.10. Walls facing Zhongnanhai across historic West Chang'an Avenue, 1910s. *Photograph by author.*

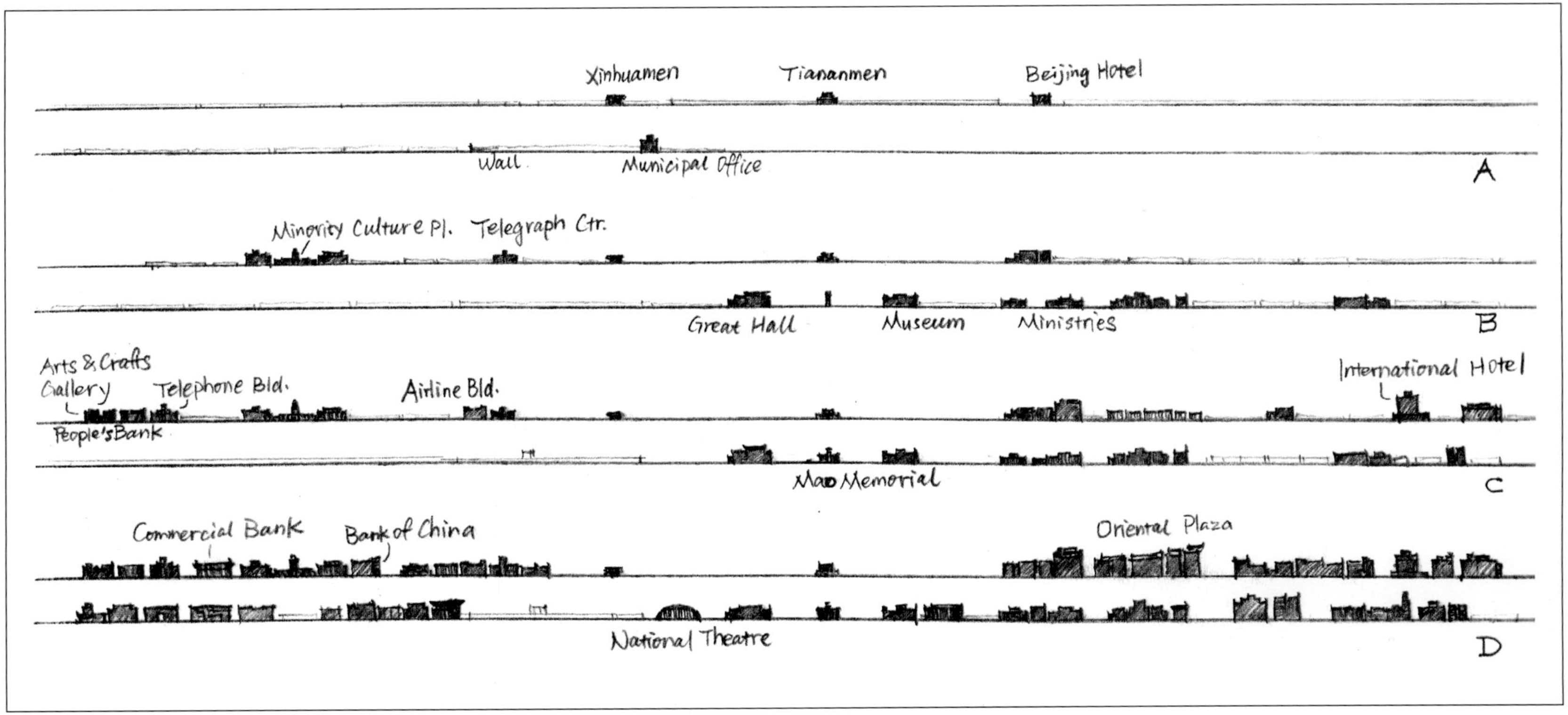
Xinhuamen
Tiananmen
Beijing Hotel
Wall
Municipal Office
A
Minority Culture Pl.
Telegraph Ctr.
Great Hall
Museum
Ministries
B
Arts & Crafts Gallery
Telephone Bld.
Airline Bld.
International Hotel
People's Bank
Mao Memorial
C
Commercial Bank
Bank of China
Oriental Plaza
National Theatre
D

Fig. 1.11

Fig. 1.11. The changing façades
of Chang'an Avenue proper (top:
northern façade; bottom: southern
façade): A. 1910s–40s; B. 1950s–60s;
C. 1970s–80s; D. 1990s–2010.
Drawing by author.

Chang'an Avenue Façades after 1949 and the National Identity of China

During the PRC era, Chang'an Avenue emerged as an urban thoroughfare filled with monumental façades. Almost every new decade's impending national anniversary was preceded by a major round of planning and construction, always with the same aim: to "relatively complete Chang'an Avenue." During this time, to complete meant to fill the gaps among previously finished monumental façades and to replace the low walls of traditional courtyards with modern edifices. Within about half a century, the avenue was transformed from a fragmented street lined mostly with single-story courtyard residences into an endless straight thoroughfare framed by massive symmetrical façades.

The transformation of the avenue's façades can be seen as the unrolling of a collaged scroll depicting China's ongoing search for national identity during the twentieth century, first as a member of the socialist bloc during the 1950s and 1960s, then as a Third World developing country in the 1970s and 1980s, and, finally, since the early 1990s, as a regional power guided primarily by nationalist ideology. Each period left its own section in the scroll. When the multistory buildings filled the gaps among the single-story residential courtyards, the single-story courtyards became gaps. As the height of buildings along the avenue kept rising, each period filled old gaps and produced new ones for the next generation, until laws were finally passed to impose height control. In the end, the two façades formed a pair of long screens, illustrating China's changing national identity in a variety of architectural styles (fig. 1.11B, C, D).

The 1950s and 1960s. The first large gap along Chang'an Avenue to be filled after 1949 was the former foreign drill grounds and polo field around the concession area. In 1951 office buildings of three to four stories for the Ministries of Public Security, Textile Industry, Fuel Industry, Light Industry, and Foreign Trade filled the open grounds along the south side of East Chang'an Avenue proper. In 1953–54, the eight-story West Building was added to the old 1917 Beijing Hotel (now known as the Middle Building) on the north side of East Chang'an Avenue proper. In 1958–59, Beijing Railway Station was built to the south of East Chang'an Avenue proper. Located in a back street, however, it was not exposed to the avenue until the 1990s, when the small alleys and courtyards blocking its north façade were cleared. Building also occurred on the north side of West Chang'an Avenue proper: the Telegraph Service Center was constructed in 1955–57, and the Minority Culture Palace and the Minority Hotel were erected in 1958–59. Around the Tiananmen Square area, the Monument to the People's Heroes was built in the center of the square between 1949 and 1958, and in 1958–59, the Great Hall of the People rose on the west side and the museum complex on the east. On the West Chang'an Avenue extension, the Central Broadcast Building was built in 1957 on the south side, next to Fuxing Gate, and the Military Museum was built in 1958–59 on the north side, some three kilometers west of the Ming-Qing city wall. No large-scale building was constructed on the avenue during the 1960s.

During this period, façade building concentrated on the south side of East Chang'an Avenue proper and on the north side of West Chang'an Avenue proper. The overall façade of the avenue, however, was only sporadically punctuated by multistory buildings. Most areas on either side of the thoroughfare were still occupied by traditional single-story courtyards (fig. 1.11B).

Chinese architecture in the 1950s generally followed the Soviet policy of "socialist content, national form." This was unambiguous when applied to art forms such as painting or opera. In architecture, however, its meaning was never clear, and particularly unclear was the content requirement, which was understood as function by some and as ideology by others.[74] In practice, "socialist content" in the PRC architecture of the 1950s was identified with a style—the neoclassicism promulgated by Joseph Stalin in the 1930s and 1940s. This style combined concrete structure with sixteenth- and seventeenth-century Muscovite architectural elements and revolutionary motifs,[75] characterized by a symmetrical plan with a central body and spreading wings, three

Fig. 1.12. Telegraph Service Center, 1955–57. Lin Leyi, Zhang Zhaoping, and others. *Photograph by author.*

or five horizontally spreading sections in elevation, and a soaring tower in the middle section. Chinese architects later nicknamed it "toad style" (*hamashi*).[76] The "national form" requirement of the Soviet policy was more tangible, but different interpretations resulted in diverse architectural forms, from full-size traditional roofs to decorative motifs noticeable only upon scrutiny. Thus, both "content" and "form" were reduced to style. As Lowell Dittmer has pointed out, the acquisition of identity is an amalgam of "fitting in" and "standing out" that first requires identification with a selected reference group of significant others, then development of characteristics that will impart a sense of distinctiveness and integrity.[77] Architecture in the early years of the People's Republic of China "fit into" the reference group of the socialist bloc by adopting Stalinist neoclassicism,[78] and "stood out" with its distinctive Chinese character through the application of traditional forms and motifs.

Proceeding west from Tiananmen Square, the first façade on the avenue was the Telegraph Service Center, built in 1955–57 (fig. 1.12). Although symmetrical in both plan and façade, with a clock tower in the middle, it looks much lighter than Soviet buildings of the Stalinist era because of the grid patterns of white frames and yellow walls and the rhythmic arrangement of large windows on the elevations. This building was acclaimed as a successful step in the exploration of a "Chinese modern style."[79] Contrasting with the Telegraph Service Center was the Soviet-style Central Broadcast Building (fig. 1.13). Completed in 1957, it was one of the 156 Soviet-aided projects. Although documents from the time stated that Chinese architects were responsible for the design and Soviet engineers were responsible for the technological issues, this building had all the characteristics of the Soviet monumental style, from the pyramidal structure to the European-style lantern on top of the central tower. Acroteria of decorative urns,

Fig. 1.13. Central Broadcast Building (detail), 1957. Yan Xinghua and others. *Photograph by author.*

Fig. 1.14. Military Museum, 1958–59. Ouyang Can, Wu Guozhen, and others. *Photograph by author.*

often seen in seventeenth-century European neoclassical as well as Russian Muscovite architecture, embellished the corners of the roofs. Chinese motifs were completely absent.

If this diversity in architectural style—modernism, Stalinist neoclassicism, and Chinese traditional revivalism[80]—indicated ambiguity of national identity and a shifting of ideology in the earliest transitional years of the People's Republic of China, the Anniversary Projects in the late 1950s set the tone of the architectural style for socialist China. The façades of six of these buildings faced the avenue. Some were predominantly Soviet in appearance and some had more Chinese motifs, but all shared the common feature of combining a Soviet general composition with traditional Chinese details.

The main façade of the Military Museum was predominantly Soviet in style, horizontally divided into five sections, with the central section the tallest (fig. 1.14). Like the Central Broadcast Building, the general outline of the Military Museum was pyramidal, with a central spire raising a gigantic Chinese army emblem. The two sections flanking the central tower were lower, and the two end sections lower still. The central and end sections protruded, and the two sections in between receded, giving the façade some sculptural effect, with shadows playing on the walls. Unlike the Central Broadcast Building façade, that of the Military Museum contained many traditional Chinese motifs. For instance, the protruding eaves atop each section were covered

with yellow glazed tiles, and the three-doorway entrance was a simplified form of the traditional memorial archway (*pailou*), standing seemingly detached from the main structure.

Fig. 1.15. Minority Culture Palace, 1958–59. Zhang Bo, Sun Peiyao, and others. *Photograph by author.*

The façade of the Minority Culture Palace employed more traditional Chinese architectural motifs and materials than did the Military Museum. The central tower was topped by a pavilion with double-eave pointed roofs (*chongyan cuanjian*) covered by blue-green glazed tiles. Four smaller pavilions on a lower level, with roofs in the same style, surrounded the central pavilion at the four corners. The same blue-green tiles covered the sloping roofs of the lower sections flanking the central tower, whose top floor was treated as a traditional veranda (*lang*) with concrete details imitating the columns, beams, and longitudinal brackets (*queti*) in an ancient wooden structure (fig. 1.15). Liang Sicheng had proposed in a 1954 lecture that traditional Chinese architectural "forms" (motifs) and "grammar" (principles) could be employed to fulfill any contemporary needs. He supported his argument with two drawings he had made.[81] To some scholars, this building exemplified Liang's vision of combining a high-rise with national forms.[82] The plan, however, was in the typical Soviet "toad style," and the façade on the avenue had the standard five-section horizontal divisions with a soaring central tower, a composition not very different from that of the Military Museum.

Residing stylistically between the Military Museum and the Minority Culture

Palace, the Great Hall of the People and the Museum of Chinese Revolution and History were neither overtly Soviet nor explicitly Chinese in character (see figs. 2.8, 2.10). Devoid of upturned Chinese roofs and soaring Soviet central towers, they represented a further compromise between "socialist content" and "national form." On one hand, both the Great Hall and the museum complex had overhanging eaves covered with yellow glazed tiles, and national motifs in relief could be observed under the eaves on the exterior walls and in the interior designs. On the other hand, the overall proportion of the façades remained Western. Like the Military Museum, the main façade of both the Great Hall and the museum complex could be horizontally divided into five sections, with the center and corner sections protruding and the two in between receding. The distances between the neighboring gigantic columns of the porch in the main eastern façade of the Great Hall were not identical but decreased from the central bay toward both sides, following the principle of traditional Chinese timber structures. However, the proportion of the façade did not follow traditional Chinese principles. The Song dynasty-building manual *Treatise on Architectural Methods* (Yingzao fashi) specified that the height of a column should not exceed the width of the bay (*zhugao buyu jianguang*), but in the porch of the Great Hall, the column height was two to three times greater than the intercolumniation, a proportion more akin to Western classical architecture. The museum's building had courtyards as spatial organizing elements, but they were not arranged in axial relationships as were traditional courtyards. That this compromise style was used for the two most significant of the Ten Great Buildings was not accidental. The designs were carefully chosen. In 1958 a total of 84 plan and 189 façade proposals were considered for the Great Hall of the People, among which were traditional big roofs, modern glass boxes, and Soviet-style towers.[83] It was this compromise style that best allowed New China both to "fit into" and "stand out" from the socialist bloc in the late 1950s.

The 1970s and 1980s. Three major façades were added to Chang'an Avenue proper during the 1970s: the East Building of the Beijing Hotel in 1973–74, the Long-Distance Telephone Building in 1976, and the Chairman Mao Memorial in 1976–77. In the three years after 1971, "diplomatic projects," including the International Club, the Beijing Friendship Store, and the Diplomatic Apartments, filled a large section of the façade gap on the East Chang'an Avenue extension, and multistory residential blocks were built on both the East and West Chang'an Avenue extensions.

During the 1980s, nine more buildings were added to the façades of Chang'an Avenue proper. Four of them were on West Chang'an Avenue proper: the National Arts and Crafts Gallery of China in 1985, the headquarters of the People's Bank of China in 1987–90, the Ticket Center of Air China in 1985–90 on the north side; and the Beijing Concert Hall in 1981–85 on the south side. Five were on East Chang'an Avenue proper: the Chinese Academy of Social Science in 1980–83, the Dongdan Telephone Exchange Office in 1983–85, and the International Hotel in 1982–87 on the north side; and the Customs Headquarters in 1987–90 and the New Building for the Ministry of Foreign Trade and Economic Cooperation in 1987–92 on the south side. Along the Chang'an Avenue extensions, new construction in the 1980s was concentrated in the east. On the East Chang'an Avenue extension, both the Jianguo Hotel in 1980–82 and the enormous International Trade Center of China in 1989 rose on the north side, while the Changfugong Center was constructed in 1989 on the south side. On the West Chang'an Avenue extension, the China Central Television (CCTV) Center was built in 1988. Projects of smaller scale and lesser significance were also constructed throughout the Chang'an Avenue extensions during the 1980s. By the end of the 1980s, the northern side of West Chang'an Avenue proper already had enough monumental façades to render the former low building areas "gaps," while the southern façade was still dominated by old courtyards (fig. 1.11c).

The concentration of construction on East Chang'an Avenue during the 1970s and 1980s had much to do with the political shift of China's international role from a member of the socialist bloc to a member of the Third World, a term evolved during the Cold War to define countries aligned neither with capitalism nor communism. In the early 1970s, Mao announced his own Three Worlds Theory and redefined "Third World" to include China.[84] Since 1956 Chinese architects had been working in such countries as Mongolia, Vietnam, North Korea, Nepal, Yemen, and Algeria as part of Communist China's foreign aid to "fraternal countries" in "Asia, Africa, and Latin America."[85] During the 1960s, more Chinese-assisted national projects were constructed in many Asian and African countries.[86] Before the 1970s, however, these activities were carried out under the socialist bloc's principle of internationalism, in which China was to export revolution to the rest of the world. During the 1970s, this stance had changed. China began to consider itself a member of the Third World instead of a socialist bloc leader duty-bound to export socialism.[87] The ideological boundary between socialism and capitalism was deliberately blurred.

Because West Chang'an Avenue was mainly associated with punishment, military power, and authority, and East Chang'an Avenue was historically associated with commerce, civil power, and celebration, the development of East Chang'an Avenue was a friendly gesture to show China's desire for more connection with the rest of the world, especially the West. Indeed, the new façades of the 1970s on East Chang'an Avenue were stylistically very different from their counterparts of the 1950s, which were mostly symmetrical, with monumental entrances, resulting in main façades that were grand, serious, and intimidating. The 1970s façades on East Chang'an Avenue, in contrast, were mostly asymmetrical, with entrances and porches that were human in scale and overall images that were more approachable and relaxed (see fig. 4.6).

All of the major buildings on East Chang'an Avenue in the 1970s were linked to new diplomatic developments. The International Club was a service center, with a theatre, reading rooms, an outdoor swimming pool, sport facilities, social rooms, and restaurants, built for the diplomatic communities around the Jianguo Gate area. The Diplomatic Apartments were constructed originally as living quarters for foreigners to rent. The East Building of the Beijing Hotel was added in 1974 to accommodate the rising number of foreign visitors after China was admitted to the United Nations and began opening to the West.[88]

Stylistically, the façades of these new diplomatic buildings were more akin to modernism as represented by the International Style that had prevailed globally since World War II. The key tenets of this style were "regularity rather than axial symmetry, more volume than mass, and no 'arbitrarily' applied decoration."[89] China's ideology had changed. While the lofty goal of the socialist bloc was global Communism, the ultimate aim of a Third World developing China was to become a modern industrialized developed country. Although socialism and revolution still occupied the foreground of ideological discourse in official Chinese propaganda, this shift in national identity could already be observed in the avenue façades in the early 1970s.

Another sign of this shift was the construction on the avenue in the early 1980s of a building designed by an American architect, the first time this had happened since the founding of the People's Republic of China. Like the Fragrant Hills Hotel completed in the same year by I. M. Pei, the Jianguo Hotel was also designed by a Chinese American.[90] Located on Outer Jianguo Gate Street of the East Chang'an Avenue extension, the Jianguo Hotel was similar to an American economy hotel such as the Holiday Inn in both architectural form and hotel management.[91] Run by the state, its moderate standard of hospitality, plain design, and practical use of space were appropriate for a guest house in a Third World country. Its obvious connection with the most powerful developed country in the world indicated the goal of the developing country's arduous development.

After the completion of the Jianguo Hotel, more International Style hotels and high-rise office buildings designed by Western architects appeared on the avenue. The scale became increasingly grandiose, and the international cooperation required became more and more complex. Located on Outer Jianguo Gate Street, on the north side of the East Chang'an Avenue extension, the International Trade Center in 1989 occupied a twelve-acre site, with a total floorage of 420,000 square meters. It had two glass towers of offices, reaching a height of 156 meters (thirty-eight stories; fig. 1.16). Other buildings in the complex included a twenty-one-story hotel, two thirty-story apartments, an 8,000-square-meter exhibition hall, a 13,000-square-meter shopping center, and a parking garage for 1,200 vehicles. The first stage general scheme design was by Robert Sobel/Emery Roth and Sons of the United States. Nikken Sekkei from Japan and Wong and Ouyang from Hong Kong supervised the successive designs of later stages, in cooperation with the local Beijing Steel and Iron Design Institute.[92] Its geometric shapes and enormous curtain walls gave the complex a classic modern character, and its twin glass towers echoed New York's World Trade Center, a timeless symbol of capitalism and modernism.

Buildings along Chang'an Avenue designed by Chinese architects followed this International Style trend reintroduced by Western architects. The International Hotel in the Inner Jianguo Gate Street section on the north side of East Chang'an Avenue proper was a twenty-nine-story (104.5 meter) high-rise with clean white walls creating a neat grid over the dark windows. While the twenty-seven-story (112.7 meter) tower of the CCTV Center on the north side of the West Chang'an Avenue extension on Fuxing Road employed Corbusian ribbon windows,[93] the Changfugong Center on the south side of the East Chang'an Avenue extension on Outer Jianguo Gate Street offered a Miesian-style twenty-five-story (90 meter) block.[94] None of these high-rises was capped with a big roof or decorated by glazed tiles.

Most of the new construction on the avenue during the 1980s was hotels, rental offices, and other commercial buildings. Following the historical convention in the capital, they were built to the east of the north-south axis. Those built on the west side, like the CCTV Center and the Head Office of the People's Bank of China, were mainly government buildings. The latter, built in the late 1980s, though stylistically similar to the New Brutalism in the West, employed traditional and folk motifs in Chinese culture and heralded the rise of nationalism in the coming new decade (fig. 1.17).[95]

A deviation from the modernist style of the 1980s Chang'an Avenue architecture was the National Gallery of Arts and Crafts, built in 1989. As an official national project, it was located on the north side of West Chang'an Avenue. However, its prominent sloping roofs, though considerably simplified, made it stand out among the buildings of the 1980s. Its subsequent history reflected the new directions China would take in the 1990s. Originally designed as a national museum, the National Gallery of Arts and Crafts later became a commercial center with floors dedicated mainly to shopping, entertainment, and rental office space, better known to the people of Beijing as the Baisheng (Parkson) Shopping Center. Almost accidently, a new important commercial center had finally taken root on West Chang'an Avenue. The revived traditional architectural motifs manifested in this building were further explored in the 1990s (fig. 1.18).

Fig. 1.16. International Trade Center of China (detail), 1989. Robert Sobel/Emery Roth and Sons and others. *Photograph by author.*

Fig. 1.17. Headquarters of People's Bank of China, 1987–90. Zhou Ru and others. *Photograph by author.*

Fig. 1.18. National Arts and Crafts Gallery of China, 1985–89. Guo Yichang and others. *Photograph by author.*

The 1990s and after. The façades of Chang'an Avenue have been completely transformed in the decades before and after 2000. A total of twenty-three buildings were added to Chang'an Avenue proper within fifteen years of 1990, twelve on the west side,[96] and eleven on the east side.[97] Buildings housing the Ministries of Fuel Industry and Textile Industry, built in the early 1950s, were also renovated, their façades rebuilt and new floors added on top.

After the intensive construction in the 1990s and early 2000s, the northern side of Chang'an Avenue proper is now filled with monumental façades, leaving only a few small "gaps." The same is true of the southern façade of East Chang'an Avenue proper. Specific projects were planned to fill these minor "gaps." The southern façade of West Chang'an Avenue proper still has a large "gap" of traditional courtyards hidden behind the baroque-style brick wall built in 1912. This is a special section of façades directly facing Zhongnanhai, the former imperial gardens, now a new PRC version of the Forbidden City. Since Zhongnanhai became the residential compound for top leaders of the Communist regime, the construction of tall buildings on the street opposite it has been forbidden, in an effort to keep Zhongnanhai out of public view. The only multistory building from the Republican era, the Capital Municipal Administration Office, which once afforded a view into Zhongnanhai, was demolished shortly after the founding of the People's Republic of China. The recently completed National Grand Theatre was a first step toward breaking this taboo at the dawn of the new millennium (fig. 1.11D).

Monumental façades were also constructed on both avenue extensions. On the West Chang'an Avenue extension, these included the West Railway Station, the China Millennium Monument, the Capital Museum, and the August First Building (the headquarters of the CCP Military Affairs Commission). While these significant state-sponsored government projects were carried out on the West Chang'an Avenue extension, large tracts of land on both sides of the East Chang'an Avenue extension were designated as Beijing's new Central Business District (CBD).

If the most characteristic building type in the 1970s and 1980s was the hotel, the building type that symbolizes 1990s China is the bank office. Nine out of the thirty buildings nominated as candidates for "Beijing's Ten Prominent Buildings of the 1980s" were hotels, and ten out of the thirty candidates for "Beijing's Ten Prominent Buildings of the 1990s" were banks or commercial offices.[98] In response to Deng Xiaoping's call for "constructing socialism with a distinctive Chinese character," China became more and more integrated into the international market. This process of globalization, however, has led to the revival of more traditional Chinese cultural and artistic motifs in architecture.

It seems paradoxical that China's architectural style was international while China

saw itself as a Third World country, and that the
architectural style has turned to nationalism just as
China's national identity has shifted to that of a
competitor in the international market. The use of

traditional motifs is a strategy to stand out, while the abstract manipulation of these
national symbols fits well into contemporary world architectural practice in the 1990s.

Traditional architectural motifs, especially the time-honored "big roof" (*dawuding*),
were widely adopted to represent the national character of China. Some applications
were quite literal. One of the best-known examples was the West Railway Station,
built in 1996 on Fuxing Road, on the south side of the West Chang'an Avenue extension. Its design included a gigantic *ge*-style three-story pavilion atop a grand fifteen-
story modern arched structure, with four smaller *ge* located atop the four corners.[99] A
row of repeating traditional archways decorates the lower section of the main façade.
According to the official explanation, the grand arch symbolized the gate to the Chinese capital (fig. 1.19). However, after former Beijing mayor Chen Xitong, who sponsored big roofs as a design strategy to "take back the image of the old capital" (*duohui
gudu fengmao*), was removed from the CCP Central Committee, no designer was

Fig. 1.20. August First Building (Military Commission Head-quarters), 1999. Zhang Qiming and others. *Photograph by author.*

willing to claim responsibility for the West Station. Nevertheless, the use of the traditional roof as a national architectural symbol did not stop. The 1999 August First Building next door to the 1959 Military Museum on West Chang'an Avenue also has traditional big roofs, a style whose straight eave lines originate in the images in Han dynasty stone carvings (fig. 1.20).

Alongside these more or less literal applications of traditional architectural motifs, other buildings simplified, distorted, manipulated, or deconstructed the time-honored big roof.[100] Since the 1990s, architectural style has diversified along the avenue due to vastly increasing contact between China and the outside world in business, culture, and education. Joint design has become commonplace since China entered the international market, and the era of a dominant official style has ended. The 1996 Henderson (Hengji) Center furnished the façade of East Chang'an Avenue proper with postmodern columns, capitals, pointed roofs, and broken architraves from Western classical and baroque architecture (fig. 1.21). The comments of its chief

architect, Liu Li, exemplify the attitude of the times: "Style doesn't matter. Whether Chinese or Western, modern or classical, architectural forms are good as long as they are beautiful."[101] The 1999 headquarters

of the Beijing Broadcasting and Television Bureau adopted a similar postmodern approach. Another building, a complex of gigantic glass and concrete boxes, the 1996 Oriental Plaza in the prestigious Wangfujing commercial district on East Chang'an Avenue proper has neither Chinese nor Western traditional architectural motifs. While the 1993 CCP Central Committee Propaganda Department headquarters offered a Chinese traditional revivalist structure with big roofs, the International Finance Building of 1996–98 dissolved such traditional rooflines into steel and glass details copied from large international firms such as KPF, HOK, and NBBJ.

The stylistic fragmentation of Chang'an Avenue façades at the threshold of the new millennium was epitomized by two important national projects: the China Millennium Monument of 2000 and the National Grand Theatre of 1998–2007. Both will be discussed in detail in chapter 5. While the former resembles a giant sundial and recalls the forms of altars from China's distant past,[102] the latter was designed by a French architect and is devoid of any traditional Chinese architectural motif. The appropriateness of constructing such a foreign structure in the most revered area of Beijing, and, maybe more seriously, the justification in allowing a Western architect to take charge of a national project of this stature, were widely debated. Further new development soon rendered such controversies obsolete. Almost all of the significant national projects in Beijing in the first decade of the new millennium have been designed by non-Chinese architects, from the Olympic stadium and the new international airport to the National Museum expansion. The new national identity of China as represented by the changing façade of Chang'an Avenue is still in flux.

Chapter Two

National versus Modern: The 1950s

IN TWENTIETH-CENTURY Chinese architecture, nationalism and modernism appeared simultaneously. Traditional Chinese architecture of the timber structure system had been in existence for millennia. By the Tang dynasty, it had reached maturity and produced large-scale halls and towers of pure wooden construction. During the Northern Song dynasty (960–1127), this system was standardized and recorded in the official construction manual, *Treatise on Architectural Methods* (Yingzao fashi), formally published in 1103. The following Yuan, Ming, and Qing dynasties largely followed the *Treatise* tradition in the construction of imperial monuments. Minor structural and stylistic adjustments and terminological variations in these later periods can be found in the Qing dynasty *Construction Principles* (Gongchengzuofa zeli) and the practice in the Suzhou area,[1] as well as occasional combinations or juxtapositions with other architectural traditions (for instance, Tibetan or Islamic architecture) from the peripheral regions of China proper.[2]

European architecture was introduced into China as early as the fourteenth century by early missionaries. Christian churches were constructed in some major Chinese cities, and European-style buildings were sometimes constructed to fulfill the curiosity of the emperors. The most famous examples of these early structures were the Western buildings of the eighteenth century in the Yuanmingyuan.[3] These occasional foreign buildings, however, were not significant enough to trigger the development of a concept of national style to differentiate the two architectural systems. For most Chinese, who called their realm "all under heaven" (*tianxia*) and considered their way of life the only civilized culture in the world, these foreign buildings were nothing but curios from a barbarian culture. It was not until China was repeatedly defeated by foreign powers after the Opium Wars that the Chinese started to regard Western cultures as counterparts of their own. For the first time, Chinese culture became, for the Chinese, one of the many cultures in the world. The time was ripe for Chinese nationalism.

Tellingly, Chinese Classical Revivalism (Zhongguo Chuantong Fuxing) in architecture was invented by Westerners. Around 1920, some European and American architects practicing in Beijing experimented with combining the big roofs they had seen in the Forbidden City and other ancient Chinese monuments with multilayered concrete structures, and initiated the exploration of the Chinese Classical Revival style. Among these pioneers were Henry Killam Murphy, Adelbert Gresnight, and the design company Shattuck and Hussey.[4]

At the same time, the first generation of Chinese architects trained abroad came back to China, opened the earliest architectural businesses run by Chinese, and started their design practices. They brought back a variety of architectural styles then currently practiced in Europe, America, and Japan, including classical revivalism,[5] art nouveau, and functionalist modernism. These young Chinese architects also brought back foreign systems of design and architectural education, such as the American version of Beaux-Arts and the German Bauhaus.[6] Some tried to combine traditional Chinese architectural motifs with multistory concrete structures in order to create a contemporary national style that was different from both ancient Chinese and modern Western architecture.

The value of nationalism in twentieth-century Chinese architecture was soon recognized by the ruling Nationalist Party (Guomindang). In 1927 Nanjing was designated the capital of the Republic of China. During the ten years from 1927 to 1937,[7] a national style of architecture was officially adopted under the new name Original Chinese Forms (Zhongguo Guyou Zhi Xingshi) for use in the construction of the new Nationalist capital. American engineer Ernest Payson Goodrich and architect Henry Murphy were employed by the Chinese government to serve as foreign consultants.[8] Chinese architects also participated in the exploration of national style in the construction of the capital and in their practices in other cities.

It was not accidental that both Chinese Classical Revivalism in the 1920s and Original Chinese Forms in the 1930s resorted to large sloping tiled roofs with upturned eaves as a convenient sign of Chineseness in architecture. Such roofs used to mimic traditional Chinese architecture in modern times are referred to in this book as "big roof," following the habitual Chinese expression *dawuding*. As the most prominent part in the façade of an individual structure, the roof in ancient China was more symbolic than functional. Its shape and color indicated the status of the building and the rank of its owner or sponsor. During the Qing dynasty, the roof form known as *wudian* (pure hip roof) was reserved for imperial palaces and other imperially sponsored projects, including a small number of national temples. Princes with the title *qinwang* could at most use the roof form known as *xieshan* (hip-and-gable roof) in the main structures of their palaces. Common citizens were allowed to top their houses only with simple gable roofs. In terms of color, golden yellow glazed tiles were reserved for imperial structures, green tiles for princely residences, and gray tiles for the roofs of general courtyard dwellings. While designers working in the Chinese-style architecture in the early twentieth century drew their main inspiration from imperial monuments such as the Forbidden City, they treated the roofs formally and largely disregarded their former symbolic associations. *Wudian* and *xieshan* roof styles were the most frequently used, combined with green, blue, or gray tiles instead of golden yellow.

As the main modern form in early twentieth-century Chinese architecture, art deco with ornamentation in Chinese motifs was widely adopted in the construction of buildings associated with modern culture, such as gymnasiums, cinemas, and railway stations, while simple blocks with clean walls and square windows, devoid of extra decoration, were used mainly for factories. In the 1940s, Bauhaus and Bauhaus-inspired architectural educations were introduced at some universities in Shanghai and Beijing. Yet decades of war, first with Japan, and then between Communists and Nationalists, left little time for the seeds of this new modern system to bear fruit.[9]

Theoretical Controversies, 1949–1957

While both nationalism and modernism in Chinese architecture before 1949 had much to do with the exploration of new forms, during the People's Republic of China (PRC) era, discussion of "national" versus "modern" was more theoretical and ideologically oriented. In the 1950s, "national" and "modern" were defined not by explaining what they were or should be but by criticizing what they were not, a methodologically negative approach according to the twentieth-century philosopher Feng Youlan.[10] "National" was defined by criticizing revivalism (*fuguzhuyi*) while "modern" was defined by criticizing formalism (*xingshizhuyi*). Rather than being a dichotomy of opposites, "national" and "modern" complement one another. While both were desirable components of the final satisfying result, that is, Chinese architectural modernization, the supreme aim for twentieth-century Chinese architects was the modernization of the national.

Interwoven with the concepts "national" and "modern" in the architectural controversies of the 1950s was another unity of opposites: form and content. To some extent, without the latter pair, "national" and "modern" would have remained in a formalist discourse. As the theoretical framework for the Soviet art policy "national form, socialist content," the dialectical relationship between form and content gives all forms of art an ideological orientation. In the contradictory relationship within the unity of opposites, content is the principal aspect, and form is secondary. Thus political message should override artistic standard, whether this standard is national or modern.

While the discussion of "form" and "content" was more restricted to the early period of the People's Republic of China, the discourse on "national" and "modern" began long before 1949 and continues to this day. This is why the 1950s remain the most ideologically loaded period in Chinese architecture. Chang'an Avenue, whose buildings are closest to China's political heart and most accessible to public view domestically and internationally, was supremely sensitive to these political and intellectual discourses.

National Form, 1949–1954

During most of the transitional years from 1949 to 1952, officially known as the three years of economic recovery, no specific architectural design policy was implemented. Popular culture from the Nationalist era lingered on, and privately owned industry and commerce coexisted with socialist collective ownership. In Chang'an Avenue architecture, both national and modern styles from the pre-1949 explorations continued. Decorative Chinese motifs were applied to buildings related to cultural activities, while simpler unadorned blocks were used for buildings with more strictly utilitarian functions.

The lack of direct political interference in architectural practice is reflected in the construction that filled the old foreign military drilling fields in the former concession areas south of historic East Chang'an Avenue in 1951–54. There, the headquarters of the Ministry of Foreign Trade belonged stylistically to the national category and the buildings for the Ministry of Fuel Industry and the Ministry of Textile Industry belonged to the modern category. The former bore a Chinese *xieshan* roof with eaves that jutted out and continuous balconies in the form of a traditional *goulan* (balustrade) beginning on the second floor (fig. 2.1). The other two ministries were simple rectangular buildings with virtually no exterior decoration. Their walls were straight and clear-cut. All of the windows were simple square recessions of uniform size arrayed evenly in the walls (fig. 2.2). Both buildings employed the brick-concrete structure introduced into China in the early twentieth century.[11] Compared to pre-1949 Chinese Classical Revivalism and Original Chinese Forms, the roofs of the Ministry of Foreign Trade were considerably simplified. The edges of the eaves as well as the ridge were straight instead of curving up as in ancient monuments. The big roof sat directly atop the straight walls, without the ring of brackets (*dougong*) that served as a transition in traditional architecture. The coexistence of such simplified national and modern forms was due to both the financial stringency and the relaxed ideological restrictions in the early years of the People's Republic of China.

Fig. 2.1. Ministry of Foreign Trade,
1952–54. Xu Zhong and others.
Photograph by author.

Fig. 2.2. Ministry of Fuel Industry,
1951. *Reproduction from* Chang'anjie:
Guoqu, xianzai, weilai, *49. Courtesy of
Zheng Guangzhong.*

At the end of the three years of economic recovery, the first architectural policy was declared at the founding meeting of the Ministry of Architectural Engineering in August 1952. Under this policy, the guiding principles for architectural design were first, utility; second, firmness and safety; third, economy; and fourth (only if the former three principles were not hampered) appropriate consideration of beauty.[12] These principles are strikingly similar to the three Vitruvian requirements of durability (*firmitas*), convenience (*utilitas*), and beauty (*venustas*).[13]

The adoption of a Vitruvian architectural policy is another sign of a lack of ideological orientation in the transitional years. This soon changed. At the beginning of the first Five Year Plan period (1952–57), the Soviet art policy of "national form, socialist content" was formally applied to architecture, along with socialist realism, the official style promoted by the Soviet authorities for art and literature.[14] With categories and concepts such as form, content, socialist, and realism, mostly derived from art and literature, this policy and style invited divergent interpretations and practices when applied to architecture.

For architectural historian Liang Sicheng, "socialist content" meant concern for the welfare of the working people, which he referred to as "Comrade Stalin's love and care for the Soviet people." This Stalinist humanism quickly took a formalist turn. Liang claimed that national form and socialist content could not be separated from one another, and that people's welfare also included beautiful forms that were familiar to and loved by the people. Socialist content was thus by no means in conflict with historical preservation.[15] Moreover, national form should be nothing but the quintessence, or, in Liang's words, the "best principles," of the millennia-long tradition of Chinese architecture. Following Mao's famous formula "future proletarian culture is the national, scientific, and mass-oriented culture,"[16] Liang wrote,

> Future Chinese architecture must be "national, scientific, and mass-oriented" architecture; [and to achieve] "national" [we] must explore and develop the advantages of our millennia-long tradition. . . . For more than twenty years, ever since I joined the Yinzao Xueshe [Institute for Research on Chinese Architecture], I have been doing a comprehensive survey [of ancient buildings] in the countryside with other architects. . . . Our goal was to find a way to make architecture "national, scientific, and mass-oriented."[17]

Liang emphasized two points in his elaboration of the advantages of the Chinese tradition in architecture. One was its universality in serving diverse functions; the other was its formal features and principles, what Liang called its "grammar" (*wenfa*).

The former made it possible for the millennia-long tradition to serve the construction of socialism; the latter offered a "vocabulary" and strategy for the development of new forms. Liang wrote in 1950,

> The structural method of Chinese architecture is, first, to build the framework, then to construct walls and install windows and doors. The curves in the roof are produced by a structure of beams and purlins as well. This structural method affords the designers great freedom. For this reason, under extremely different climatic conditions, from the Sungari River to Hainan Island, from Xinjiang to the East China Sea, different walls, doors, and windows can be built [into the same basic framework] according to localized practical needs. [Such a structural system can] be adjusted for different environments and yet always remain functional. This is the greatest advantage of the Chinese structural method. Europe and America have just started to apply such a frame system since the invention of the reinforced concrete and steel frame structure.[18]

In another article in 1951, Liang argued, "The best feature of Chinese architecture is its universal adaptability. Our architecture has two major characteristics, the bone structure construction method (*gujia jiegoufa*) and courtyard organization in the integration of individual buildings. Both could be adjusted to make a variety of interesting combinations according to changing design requirements."[19] It is noteworthy that Liang seldom used the term "traditional Chinese architecture" (*Zhongguo chuantong jianzhu*), which might suggest separation between the traditional and the modern. He spoke only of Chinese architecture or architectural tradition, which implied a living tradition.

While emphasizing the universality and applicability of the Chinese architectural tradition in his discussion of its structural method, Liang offered his view on national style in more formal and practical terms by proposing a "grammar" for Chinese architecture. In an article published in 1954, Liang listed nine features of Chinese architecture, including the courtyard, the roof, a bracket system, a wooden frame, glazed tiles, and the tripartite division of terrace, body, and roof.[20] In another article, after providing two sketches of buildings that he envisioned representing national architecture, one a vertical high-rise and the other a horizontal multifloored complex, Liang continued, "[With these sketches, I] only want to illustrate two points: first, our traditional forms and 'grammar' are able to handle [the design of] any building regardless of its size and height; second, the number-one issue in achieving a national form is the general outline of a building or complex, then the proportion and rhythm of walls, doors, and windows, and the last is decoration."[21]

If the structural method derived from Chinese tradition fulfilled the scientific requirements of future socialist architecture, the form and "grammar" had more to do with people's feelings. As Liang explained in the same article,

> *Fashi*,[22] the handicraft technique of handling architectural members, created through the direct experiences of generations of laboring people, that is, the "grammar" of architecture, has become the popular form for expression loved by the people for thousands of years. The architectural images created by this grammar have become our proud art that is loved by, familiar to, and understandable to the Chinese nationalities. We must use and develop them to express the thoughts and feelings of our nation.[23]

To avoid the misunderstanding that he was blindly admiring the past, Liang immediately added that "the same thing could be 'cream' [*jinghua*] here but becomes 'dross' [*zaopo*] when applied somewhere else." However, the term *fashi* in Liang's characterization of Chinese architecture would have led people to believe that this "grammar" of Chinese architecture was nothing but a reference to the two official construction manuals published during the imperial era, the Northern Song *Treatise on Architectural Methods* (Yingzao fashi) and the Qing *Construction Principles* (Gongchengzuofa zeli). Liang had done groundbreaking research on both manuals and called them two "grammar textbooks" of Chinese architecture in one of his pre-1949 articles.[24]

For Liang, the opposite of "national form" was not modern but "Western." He wrote, "Architecture of previous periods was for the enjoyment of a very small group of people, while today it is for the people; in the past, it was colonial, while in the future it should be national. We adopt the advantages of Western technology but do not follow their forms."[25] He also called for "selective abandonment [*yangqi*] of the bare glass boxes of the International Style."[26] Liang was careful in his writing to avoid a simplified equation of his promotion of national form with a nonselective copying of historical motifs. His prestige and influence, however, were still partially responsible for the flourish of historical architectural motifs, especially the big roof, throughout the country in the early 1950s.[27] Like the Chinese Classical Revivalism of the 1920s and the Original Chinese Forms of the 1927–37 Nanjing period, roofs as an expression of national form in the early 1950s followed historical models rather faithfully, with decorative bracket sets under the upturned eaves and the appearance of a post-and-lintel frame as suggested by the elimination of walls and the enlargement of windows in the floor directly beneath the roofs. Acroterion sculptural ornaments were simplified, and the traditional roofs were decorative, highlighting selected sections of the buildings (fig. 2.3).

The national form Liang promoted also left marks on Chang'an Avenue, but with more restrained details. The West Building of Beijing Hotel, constructed in 1953, closely followed the 1917 French Renaissance-revivalist Middle Building in proportion and façade division. However, Chinese

Fig. 2.3. Sanlihe Office Buildings for Four Ministries and One Committee, 1952–55. Zhang Kaiji and others. *Photograph by author.*

national forms replaced the older building's neoclassical Western details. Two pairs of roofs of the pointed roof (*cuanjian*) style decorated the two pavilions on the east and west ends of the top floor. The corners of the roofs, which had three layers of eaves covered by yellow glazed tiles, turned slightly upward. The corridor screening the top floor used parallel brackets (*queti*), and the white color delineated the image of a post-and-lintel frame against the general red color of the wall. The windows on the top floor were arched, making reference to the older neighbor to which it was attached. The three-arch entrance in the Middle Building was replaced here with the Chinese archway (*paifang*). Although different in decorative details, the Middle and West Buildings of the prestigious Beijing Hotel, each with two pavilions at the ends of the top floor connected by a corridor, stand side by side like father and son, forming a symmetrical façade along the avenue (fig. 2.4).

Fig. 2.4. Beijing Hotel (from left to right: the 1990 Grand Hotel, the 1953 West Building, the 1917 Middle Building, and the 1974 East Building). Brossard, Mopin, and Cie; Zhang Chengtian; Dai Nianci; Zhang Bo; and others. *Photograph by author.*

Fig. 2.5. Tiananmen Square reconstruction plans, 1954–56. Chen Zhi, Yue Shen, Liu Dunzhen, Dai Nianci, and others. *Reproduction from Chang'anjie: Guoqu, xianzai, weilai, 66–67. Courtesy of Zheng Guangzhong.*

While the exploration of national forms was going on, various proposals for the reconstruction of Tiananmen Square were made to accommodate increased activities there as a result of the rising importance of Tiananmen Tower. Most of the designs proposed in 1954 and 1955 for the government buildings in the square incorporated courtyards to organize building complexes, which Liang considered the most indigenously Chinese form of spatial organization (fig. 2.5).

The Monument to the People's Heroes of 1949–58 in Tiananmen Square was a project Liang participated in directly. The final form of the monument, a design based on the Tsinghua University proposal directed by Liang and Lin Huiyin, Liang's wife

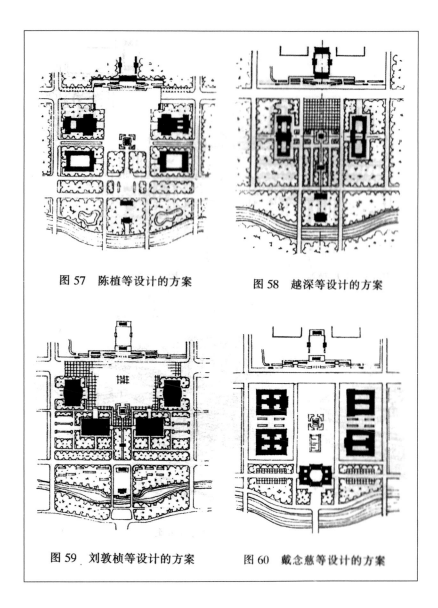

图 57　陈植等设计的方案　　　　图 58　越深等设计的方案

图 59　刘敦桢等设计的方案　　　　图 60　戴念慈等设计的方案

and colleague, was an enlarged stele with a base in the form of a traditional two-layer platform (*xumizuo*) and a roof in the classical *wudian* style.

The Monument to the People's Heroes was the first permanent structure conceived for Tiananmen Square and Chang'an Avenue after the founding of the People's Republic of China, and its design process was not without controversy. Even before Mao proclaimed the founding of the people's republic from the Tiananmen rostrum in 1949, a variety of sites had been proposed for the construction of a memorial structure dedicated to those who had died for the Chinese revolution.[28] It was not until the Chinese People's Political Consultative Conference (CPPCC) meeting on September 30, 1949, that the Tiananmen Square site was finally designated.[29] In the following afternoon, Mao and the other CPPCC members participated in the foundation-laying ceremony, during which a cornerstone was laid halfway between Tiananmen Tower and Zhengyang Gate.

Shortly after, the Capital Planning and Construction Committee called for proposals from all over the country. More than one hundred designs were received.[30] Among these were horizontal terraces similar to ancient altars enclosed by walls, a series of roofed gates enclosing arches, a group of columns rising from a square base, vertical monuments with geometric shapes and art deco details, and a monolithic Soviet-style column supporting a giant statue holding a star (fig. 2.6).[31] According to Liang, schemes were classified into three categories: horizontal plans stretching along the ground, symbolizing that all heroes were from the people; heroic images of gigantic group statues; and vertical monuments in the form of ancient steles or pagodas, symbolizing the revolutionary spirit and lofty character of the people's heroes.[32] By the time the drawings and models were exhibited on the site in Tiananmen Square on National Day in 1951 to solicit public opinion, however, only vertical proposals were left. In May 1952 the Monument to the People's Heroes Construction Committee was founded, with Liang serving as one of the two vice chairs.[33] By October 1953 the design for the lower part of the monument was chosen: a vertical stele with a plinth standing on a terrace in the form of an ancient two-layered platform. The design for the top of the monument, however, was still in debate. Design proposals included the *wudian* roof put forward by Liang's group, a pointed roof, a group statue, a *wudian* roof with a spire raising the Communist symbol of the sickle and the hammer, and many others.[34] Only after another month's discussion was the final decision made to use the *wudian* roof with no spire.

Finalizing an implementation design scheme by processes of categorization and elimination would become typical in PRC architecture. For the Monument to the People's Heroes, Liang masterminded the narrowing down. In a 1951 letter to Peng Zhen, then the mayor of Beijing and the chair of the Monument Construction Committee, Liang criticized the scheme of a roofless stele supported by a three-arched platform. He argued that the arches in the base not only repeated both Tiananmen and Zhengyang Gate but also weakened the stability of the monument, structurally and visually. Liang proposed instead to focus on both the vertical solidarity of the monument (to contrast with nearby imperial structures) and a careful design of its top end (for which he proposed a traditional roof).[35]

The final image of the Monument to the People's Heroes represented the architectural style that Liang promoted as both "Chinese and new" (*Zhong'erxin*), full of national forms but not like any individual Chinese monument from the past. The

▲ 第一次征图中，一些比较矮形的设计方案　The lower planning schemes in the first designs collection

▲ 第一次征图中，一些比较高形的设计方案　The higher planning schemes in the first designs collection

▼ 1951 年国庆，在天安门广场陈列了三个模型　The three models exhibited on Tian'anmen Square on the Grand National Day 1951

Fig. 2.6. Various designs for the Monument to the People's Heroes, 1951. *Reproduction from* Chang'anjie: Guoqu, xianzai, weilai, *57. Courtesy of Zheng Guangzhong.*

Fig. 2.7. Monument to the People's Heroes, 1949–58. Liang Sicheng, Liu Kaiqu, and others. *Reproduction from Chang'anjie: Guoqu, xianzai, weilai, 60. Courtesy of Zheng Guangzhong.*

stele, a modest structure in ancient Chinese architecture, was enlarged, and the *wudian* roof, which traditionally indicated the highest rank and was often endowed with monumental scale, was minimized. These were combined and elevated on a platform evoking an altar for sacrifices. The juncture of the stele and the altar, however, is reminiscent of the plinth in Western classical architecture; the general outline of the stele looked more like an obelisk than a traditional Chinese stele (*bei*). The Chinese word for "monument" (*jinian-bei*) in the Monument to the People's Heroes alludes to both.[36] While numerous later reproductions of the Tiananmen Square monument in provincial, county, and even township settings repeatedly confirmed its Chineseness,[37] the linguistic ambiguity of the word *bei* concealed its Western elements in a hardly noticeable way, which was, after all, what was "new" about the Monument to the People's Heroes (fig. 2.7).

Modernism, 1955–1957

Shortly after Liang published his architectural drawings with Chinese "vocabulary" and "grammar" in 1954, the national forms he supported came under attack. On March 28, 1955, the *People's Daily* published an editorial titled "Combat Extravagance and Waste in the Architectural Field." It called for attention to the economic aspect of architecture and pointed out that "the source of extravagance in architecture is the formalism and revivalism in some architects' minds. . . . They often espouse revivalism and aestheticism in the name of combating structurism[38] and inheriting the classical [Chinese] architectural tradition."

The article in the *People's Daily* did not name Liang, although everyone in the field knew that he was the main target. Many articles directly criticizing Liang's revivalism in architectural practice and education, however, appeared in *Architectural Journal* (Jianzhu xuebao), the leading Chinese publication in the field. Condemnation of buildings with big roofs, and their architects, followed in other journals and newspapers.[39]

Although all of these criticisms focused on economic aspects, especially the costly big roof, the true reason for this sudden shift in theoretical orientation was political. Stalin died in 1954. During the Twentieth Congress of the Communist Party of the Soviet Union (CPSU), Nikita Khrushchev formally criticized Stalin and his policies. The architectural policy of "socialist content, national form" was formally denounced during a conference of Soviet architects, designers, and engineers held in Moscow on November 30, 1954. Chinese representatives also attended this conference and brought this policy change back to Beijing.[40] In China, however, Stalinist art policy and socialist realism as an official style were not openly criticized. They were not seen as wrong but as having been abused by the revivalists. In response, the Vitruvian architectural policy of the three years of economic recovery in 1949–52 was revived in a more succinct format: "utility, economy, and, if the situation allows, attention to beauty." Firmness was now considered part of functional soundness and thus dropped as a guiding principle. The addition of economy to the Vitruvian trinity reflected both a new economic stringency and the Marxist ideology of economic base as the foundation of a society, on which superstructures such as culture and art were built. The conflict between economy and beauty in Chinese policy was deeply rooted in the Marxist unity of the opposites of economic base and superstructure. In a society, the economic base came first, then the superstructure; in architecture, economy had priority, while aesthetics was to be given secondary consideration.

In architectural practice, such connotations led to the equation of beauty with decoration. For modern Western functionalist architects, beauty was the result of functional soundness and economic appropriateness, but for Chinese architects of the 1950s, beauty became the opposite of function and economy. To some extent, Liang's critics were justified. Traditional motifs were mostly used as architectural decorations, disregarding Liang's plea to apply principles rather than copy details. In his 1955 article "Several Criticisms on the Architectural Theory of Formalist Revivalism," Lu Sheng, a professor of architecture at Tianjin University,[41] wrote,

> Architecture has a dual nature: on one hand it is a material of people's life; at the same time, it is an art form to express the ideologies of social classes and has the potential to fulfill the spiritual needs of human beings. Thus architecture serves human beings by both function and beauty, the principle character of architecture. According to Professor Nikolayev, doctor of architecture from the Soviet Union, "The number-one aspect for buildings is to serve the material and economic needs of a society, which is the principle and dominating aspect; its second, the aesthetic aspect, is only derivative."[42]

After expressing this orthodox Marxist view on architecture, Lu proposed a costume analogy of architecture to replace Liang's language analogy. Liang had compared architecture to language and had argued that the new national architecture could be developed by applying time-honored Chinese architectural motifs as vocabularies and structural principles as grammar. Lu claimed that language, which did not belong to living material and had no class nature, was not an appropriate analogy for architecture. Serving people in both life and aesthetics, costume was a better alternative. Parodying Liang's argument for national form in architecture, Lu argued that, in dressing, it was ridiculous to have people wear Han or Tang costume simply because "they were proud clothes loved by, familiar to, and understandable to our Chinese people." To compare architecture with language neglected the material nature of architecture and opened the door to formalism. To equate national form with traditional motifs, especially to equate Chinese grammar in architecture with *fashi* in the Song dynasty manual, led to revivalism. These, Lu concluded, were Liang's mistakes.

Lu defined architectural "form" as the outside image of a building, including its general layout, plan, elevation, and structural method, and architectural "content" as the building's function and technology, and the ideological thought that the building reflected. He claimed that the ideological thought reflected in ancient Chinese architecture lay not in individual structures but in the way they were combined to form a complex. Thus Liang's mistake was that he one-sidedly focused on the details of individual building but neglected the feudal meanings of architectural groupings.[43] According to Lu, Liang paid lip service to "national form, socialist content," and the result of Liang's promotion of national form was only revivalism. However, like everyone else in China at the time, Lu had very little "socialist content" to offer other than saying that "socialist content demands something new and creative and different from the feudal national form." Liang could not have agreed more.

Although Lu's criticism of Liang and his formalist revivalism was more reflective of policy changes in general than of intellectual differences among architects, Lu's criticism had a kernel of truth. He correctly pointed out that what Liang claimed to be an authentic Chinese tradition in architecture was actually just part of that tradition, the official style, or, in Marxist terms, the tradition of the ruling classes. Lu also spotlighted Liang's revivalist historical view of architectural development, in which "architecture of the Qing dynasty was worse than Ming, which was worse than Yuan, which was worse than Song and Tang architecture." Although Lu's purpose in his article was to criticize Liang's ideologically inaccurate historical view, he correctly pointed out that, for Liang, the Tang dynasty represented the zenith of Chinese architecture.[44] Rather than simply discovering, as Liang claimed, he had been actively constructing, intentionally or not, a Chinese architectural tradition based on the ideal of Tang and Song official-style architecture.

If political change in the Soviet Union initiated the criticism of revivalism, Mao's Hundred Flowers Movement in 1956, with its guiding slogan "Let a hundred flowers bloom, let a hundred schools of thought contend,"[45] encouraged new hopes for modernism. The movement was launched as a pro-democratic campaign to invite criticism of the Chinese Communist Party (CCP) and to encourage the voicing of opinions other than those of the party center as a way to strengthen the new socialist regime. *Architectural Journal* ran a special column for "blossoming and contending," in which many leading architects and scholars voiced their views on current problems in the field.

Most of the articles expressed discontent with official dictates and political judgment on architectural style. Significantly, they referred to previously used pejorative terms such as "formalism," "worldism,"[46] "revivalism," and "structurism" as *maozi*. This Chinese word literally means "hat" and can be roughly translated as "label." However, unlike such stylistic labels in Western discourse as postmodernist, high-tech, or machine aesthetics, *maozi* has a strong political connotation, denoting terms used unfairly for personal persecution. For instance, formalism may be wrong; but "formalism" as a *maozi* means that this term has been unjustly applied in a specific political situation to condemn someone. Thus *maozi* is a pejorative description about the incorrect application of a pejorative term. *Kou maozi*, literally "to put a hat on," describes the action of applying a *maozi*. Once the term *kou maozi* itself became a *maozi*, debates were completely lost in the hopeless cycle of discrediting vaguely defined labels. *Maozi* is, in fact, a symbol of the architectural controversies in China for most of the twentieth century. It captures both the theoretical dislocation and the political engagement in the use of terms. The following quote is typical in tone and wording:

> Our view on architecture is too narrow and simple, lacking in analytical research. Some critics apply a "revivalism" *maozi* whenever they see a building with sloping roofs, equating these roofs with palaces and temples; some apply a "structurism" *maozi* whenever they see a building with flat roofs without decoration, calling it a square box; some apply an "eclecticism" *maozi* whenever they see a building with Chinese decorative motifs but without a big roof, deeming it non-Chinese non-Western. This narrow-minded, narrow-sighted critical method has really confused designers, who no longer know where to go. Although there are many roads, none of them is available.[47]

Although the irresponsible behavior of *kou maozi* in theoretical debates was criticized, due to the political rhetoric of the time, the pejorative nature of these labels was not questioned. The source and exact meanings of terms such as "revivalism," "formalism," "structurism," and "eclecticism" remained unclear. Supporters of "national form" criticized "formalism," while supporters of "modernism" criticized "revivalism." New *maozi* were invented. For instance, in support of "national forms," some architects put a "one-sided emphasis on economy" label on those who had once labeled Liang a revivalist and criticized him on the basis of China's economic condition. The Hundred Flowers Movement, however, did bring new voices into the discourse of Chinese architecture in the mid-1950s. One term that came to the fore at that time was the long absent "modern."

For many years after the founding of the People's Republic of China, discourse on architecture had used the term "socialist" instead of "modern" for something new to be created as a demarcation line between China and the capitalist world. A 1956 article by Jiang Weihong and Jin Zhiqiang, then both young architecture students at Tsinghua University, put modernism in the center of the discussion with the bold title "We Want Modern Architecture." In this article, Jiang and Jin enthusiastically praised the simple and clean shapes created by large glass windows, clean walls, and concrete frames. Although the contemporary buildings used to support their argument were all taken from the socialist camp, mainly the Soviet Union and Hungary, historical examples from the West, such as Harrow New City in England, were also cited. The authors claimed that social progress was making national differences in architecture less and less discernable, and that, in the future Communist society, national identity would totally disappear. In this article, however, the opposite of "modern" was not "national" but "classical." Jiang and Jin argued that, although beautiful, classical architecture belonged to the past. China needed modern beauty, and the job of the architect was to create new things. The article took on a Ruskinian tone in claiming that cement was ugly when used to make *xumizuo* platforms and *chuihuamen* (a traditional Chinese architecture gate type, mostly inside a residential courtyard) but beautiful in concrete shells and frames, and ended with a Corbusian expectation of new cars and new buildings for everyone in the Communist society of the future.[48]

Different voices followed. Articles defending national form appeared in the same journal, criticizing the boredom of modernist uniformity and using "formalism," "worldism," and "functionalism"[49] to label Jiang and Jin's equation of "socialist" with "new."[50] However, the majority of those participating in the discussion supported modernism. Zhu Yulin, for instance, justified modern architecture by equating it with realism. He argued,

> "Modern architecture" refers to buildings with roots in modern life, that is, design based on people's current practical needs, new materials, structural features, scientific principles, and modern construction technologies. More light is required in the interior, thus we have big windows; reinforced concrete beams are stronger [than wooden ones], thus they replace parallel brackets; we need to build more quickly, thus standardized members are mass produced; and in frame structure, solid wall gives way to glass curtain wall. Faithful to life and science, [modern architecture] belongs to realism. If functionalism is fidelity to function, and "structurism" is fidelity to structure, they should not be resisted.[51]

Zhu also maintained that architecture, as a living and producing enterprise, should not be classified as superstructure but as material base. Thus the concepts of opposing socialist and capitalist systems should not be applied in this field. He criticized bureaucratic interference in architecture, especially in Beijing, but used "revivalism" and "eclecticism" as labels to condemn "national form."

This was the intellectual milieu when the Telegraph Service Center and the Central Broadcast Building were constructed on Chang'an Avenue. Although the years immediately after the eclipse of Liang and national form cannot be simplified as the rise of "modern architecture," the relatively relaxed political environment, although ephemeral, did leave its mark. Completed in the same year, 1957, both buildings are devoid of the "national forms" of traditional Chinese motifs. There is no sloping roof, and no *goulan* and parallel brackets embellishing the exterior walls. The straight horizontal and vertical elements in bright white and yellow on the elevations of the Telegraph

Service Center form abstract Mondrianesque compositions. The building's rhythmic arrangement of large windows and the exposed reinforced concrete frame in the central section of the main façade would have satisfied supporters of "modern architecture" as being faithful to both structure and materials (see fig. 1.12).

Although the Central Broadcast Building has the standard symmetrical plan and façades of Stalinist Classicism, its forms are drastically simplified. The Soviet-style decorations are confined to the central tower, which has a practical function as the support for the broadcasting antenna. The majority of the façades display a grid of white concrete for the walls and blue glass for the windows (see fig. 1.13). The design of the Central Broadcast Building began in the early 1950s, the same time as the Beijing Exhibition Hall, and thus is understandable for its general Stalinist layout.[52] The latter, completed before 1955, has much more elaborate classical decorations. The reduction of Stalinist embellishment in the Central Broadcast Building captures the transient flirtation with modernism in Chinese architecture during the Hundred Flowers Movement in 1956 and 1957.

Due to their locations on Chang'an Avenue, the Telegraph Service Center and the Central Broadcast Building are not as free in form as some of the examples cited by the supporters of "modern architecture" built somewhere else.[53] Their plans and main façades are highly symmetrical, and they both have a tower rising from the center. However, the practical functions of the towers—one bearing a giant clock, and the other supporting an antenna—provided enough justification for their existence in the eyes of their modernist supporters.

Political Movements and Chang'an Avenue Architecture, 1955–1959

Scholarship on Chinese architecture emphasizes the central role politics played during the PRC era. Mao's casual comments are considered to have had a decisive influence on urban changes and the final schemes of significant buildings. By no means baseless, such a preconception, however, implies that politics was a force outside the architectural discourse, which was passively driven by political pressure. This is far from the truth. Politics was an integral part of architectural discourse during this period, a topic that architects and scholars constantly and self-consciously discussed without derogatory overtones. They tried to define the political dimension in architecture in order to find a guide for architectural practice. Self-conscious inclusion of the political dimension in the discipline also provided a way to go beyond the formal debate on "national" and "modern."

Dichotomies and the Class Nature of Architecture

For Chinese architects and architectural scholars in the first three decades of the PRC era, one of the main theoretical challenges was defining the nature of and finding ways to express a proletarian view in architecture. According to Marxism, architecture, as a form of art and part of the superstructure of society, was not devoid of class nature in a class society. Thus the role of socialist architecture was not to avoid a class stance but to express the class view of the most advanced class in history, namely, the proletariat.

There were two opposing opinions about the class nature of architecture. One held that architecture had class nature in its spiritual rather than its material aspect, and that this could only be reflected in its aesthetics. What was considered beautiful by the ruling class could mean something totally different to the ruled. For instance, the Forbidden City was beautiful and magnificent in emperors' eyes; for the laboring people, it was intimidating. Thus personal feelings based on observation of life and the expression of love and hatred based on class standpoint were integrated into the concept of beauty.[54] In terms of function and technology, however, since the physical structures of buildings could serve anyone, regardless of class status, architecture had no class nature. The opposing opinion argued that architectural function did have class nature, while the standard of beauty was universal. In history, while the ruling classes had luxurious mansions built for enjoyment and building heights were raised for profit making, houses for the laboring classes met only the lowest living standards and were physically restricted by hierarchical rules. The reaction to beauty, however, was mostly intuitive. For instance, since the fall of the Qing dynasty, everyone could enjoy the beauty of the Yiheyuan, the former imperial garden.[55]

If such debates did little to clarify theoretical issues, they provided a discoursal framework for the practical work of reconstructing Chang'an Avenue and the Old City of Beijing. Class nature was a standard, at least in words, to justify the preservation or demolition of historical structures along the avenue. For instance, Tiananmen Tower, as the former central gate to the Imperial City, was feudal in class nature. It was, however, turned into a symbol of New China and acquired a new class identity after Chairman Mao announced the founding of the People's Republic of China on its rostrum. Tiananmen Square experienced a similar transformation during the student demonstrations before and the mass celebrations after 1949. The T-shaped Imperial Tiananmen Square was too small for the functional requirement of mass assembly in the new socialist society, and thus had to be expanded to hold more people and to become a socialist public square. Traditional neighborhoods along Chang'an Avenue needed to be cleared and replaced by socialist monuments. Although inhabited by laboring people during imperial times, they bore the imprint of the dark side of feudal society. The Forbidden City, on the contrary, though once inhabited by the imperial families, had been constructed by laboring people and was thus a symbol of their wisdom and power.

The proletarian view also required architecture for the people. "Art to serve the people" was the guideline for all art workers under the CCP regime, and "art for art's sake" was condemned as bourgeois. The same policy had already been enforced in other forms of art, including painting, music, dance, and drama since Mao's famous Yan'an talk in 1942 (which will be discussed in detail later). When architecture first came to face such an ideological requirement in the 1950s, however, it was too general to provide a practical guideline for architects. During the "Symposium on Residential Architectural Standards and Architectural Art" in June 1959, when the construction of the Anniversary Projects was underway, Liang said,

> The party invited all 600 million of the Chinese people to participate in the design of the Anniversary Projects and, at the same time, asked us to express national form in architecture. In the past,[56] some architects even dared not mention national form. Now they feel a little bolder. But what is national form? Among architects, you are asking me, and I am asking you. Of course, some people immediately think of bracket sets, parallel brackets, big roofs, and so on. Others disagree with such an approach. This issue was clarified only after the party called on our 600 million people to design together. Designing workers followed the mass line, especially young architects and students in universities. They went deep among the people to explore both architectural function and form, to learn what the people need in function and to understand what they like in image. Now we can say that we have just found the way and crossed the threshold. We learned from the people that they always want national form in architecture. However, we also understand that the national style they want is not a copy of old buildings. They have different expectations for different architecture. For instance, they do not want big roofs in front of Tiananmen Tower,[57] but they do want them on the National Gallery. This tells us that people want different forms for different architectural contents.[58]

Liang's talk expressed the disoriented situation some Chinese architects faced in the second half of 1950s when architectural discourse shifted from formal discussion to class analysis. The new theoretical dichotomies of form versus function on the one hand, and form versus content on the other, with an emphasis on class nature, however, brought the previous theoretical controversies under one umbrella. It contextualized the debate about "national" and "modern" in the early 1950s within a larger social and political background, while at the same time carrying forward in more specific terms the general principle from the 1940s of "art serving the people." The formal discussion on "national" and "modern" gave way to a new theoretical framework. While "national" and "modern" were like the yin-yang relationship confined within the unity of formal modernization, the dichotomies of form versus function on one hand, and form versus content on the other, expanded the modernization project to include the entire construction practice. The shift of theoretical orientation from formal to social dimensions prepared the groundwork for the involvement of large-scale political movements in architectural practice.

Dichotomy is an important tool for grasping the features of a given subject in theoretical analysis by dividing its aspects into mutually exclusive categories. Once dichotomy becomes an established way of thinking, however, it forces people to see the world in dichotomies, simplifying it and neglecting the connections between and interchangeability of categories. In the discourse of Chinese architecture during the 1950s, the most frequently used dichotomies were beauty versus function, architectural art versus architectural science, form versus function, architectural form versus architectural content, and theory versus practice. These dichotomies were interrelated and mutually strengthening. Architecture was considered both a science and an art. Architectural science dealt with material, structure, construction, acoustics, light, temperature, and so on, and architectural art was mostly about form. The former was more related to the function of a building, and the latter had more to do with its aesthetics. As the very definition of architectural art implied a natural connection with form and beauty, architectural content, which was a highly debated term, acquired a closer affiliation with function and engineering.

Theoretical discussions on architecture in the 1950s were built on these dichotomies. In an article titled "On Architectural Art, Beauty, and National Form" published in the October 1954 issue of *Architectural Journal*, Zhai Lilin defined the essential nature of architecture as a unity of function and beauty, serving as both a living material and a social ideology to fulfill human beings' spiritual needs. These two aspects of the nature of architecture, however, were not equal. The functional nature was primary, and the aesthetic aspect was secondary.[59]

The dual character of architecture gave birth to two different categories of architectural knowledge: architectural science, which was about functional architecture as living material and a productive tool, and architectural art, which was about aesthetic architecture as social ideology. The unequal relationship in the dichotomy of architecture's essential nature reappeared in the dichotomy of architectural knowledge. Zhai offered six points that supported the primacy of architectural science over architectural art. First, architecture was not pure art, but art combined with practical function; second, building consumed huge amounts of social wealth, thus architecture was directly related to economic issues; third, architecture was first an engineering issue and only secondarily an artistic issue; fourth, architecture enjoyed less freedom compared to other arts due to its functional requirements and its economic and technological constraints; fifth, since architecture was expensive, the best architectural works of a society often belonged to the ruling classes, and there was no proletarian architectural art before the proletariat seized political power; and sixth, since architecture was itself a material tool in economic activity, the development of the productive forces would directly and immediately result in changes in architectural art, while the response of other branches of arts to such development was much slower and more indirect.[60]

Inherited from the Marxist-Maoist theory of the unity of opposites and the dialectical development of contradictions,[61] the dichotomy and its unequal relationship continued in the discussion on architectural content and form. In his article, Zhai defined architectural content as practical function, scientific technology, and ideological thoughts. He wrote,

> In my opinion, architecture is, first of all, a material tool to fulfill the living and producing needs of human beings, and the function appropriate to this utilitarian purpose should be its content. Secondly, architecture requires appropriate material and structure, and thus architectural content should also include the technological requirements of material and structure. Finally, as an art, in terms of its nature and effect, architecture must reflect specific social ideology. For this reason, architectural content should also include ideologies that reflect some kind of real life. Function, technology, and ideology are three types or three different components of architectural content, united in one single architectural form.[62]

Thus, for Zhai, architectural content included almost everything except form. This result was mostly due to the rigid application of the Marxist dichotomy of form and content, which had been working well in the analysis of some art forms, such as literature and painting, but ran into difficulty when applied to other arts, such as architecture and music, because of their nonnarrative nature and openness to diverse interpretations. In order to maintain the consistency in art theory, a counterpart for form had to be defined, and everything that might influence architectural form was grouped under architectural content.

The pitfalls of this indiscriminate application of the dichotomy of form and content were identified by Chen Zhihua and Ying Ruocong. In an article titled "On Zhai Lilin's 'On Architectural Art, Beauty, and National Form,'" they argued that "saying 'function, technology, and ideology are three types or three different components of architectural content, united in one single architectural form' is the equivalent of saying 'pigments, canvas, wooden frame, technique, and ideological thoughts are different types or components of content united in the form of an oil painting.'" They also hinted that, unlike painting, architecture cannot be treated simply as art. Though they did not offer a definition of content or form, Chen and Ying pointed out that Zhai's mistake was the result of oversimplified application of the basic Marxist principle of the dialectic unification of form and content. Dialectical materialism was applied too rigidly and generally in architecture with no specific analysis of the relationship between architecture and society. Form and content were interchangeable in some situations. They called for specific analysis of architectural development in socialist society instead of oversimplified application of Marxist principles.[63]

Other scholars maintained that architectural content should include only ideological thought. They argued that, according to Marxist theory, form was the expression of content; if architectural content included function, technology, and ideology, then architectural form expressed function, technology, and ideology. But this was obviously wrong, since,

> The basic task of architecture is not to express function but rather to serve our practical utilitarian requirements, such as our need for machinery, equipment, food, and clothing; technology is not the objective of expression but a necessary tool for the realization of architecture; form is beautiful only when architectural form perfectly expresses lofty ideological content. . . . Thus it is not appropriate to confuse the basic task of architecture and the tools to realize architecture [with architectural content].[64]

Although there were different views on how to define architectural content and different views on some other details about the nature of architecture, the status of dichotomy as a discoursal framework was never questioned. Every participant acquiesced in the use of pairs of concepts (such as function and beauty, science and art, and content and form) to provide the main platform for meaningful thought and discussion. The nature and function of dichotomy itself remained above discussion. There was also little controversy about the definition of architectural form, which seemed relatively simple and obvious. It referred to the appearance of a building, including the group arrangement of a building complex, plan, and elevation. Consensus disappeared, however, when a formal style was adopted in practice.

The formal characteristics of socialist realism, the official Soviet style for all of the arts, were unambiguous in painting and in sculpture. Implementing socialist realism as a style in architecture, however, was problematic. As its name suggests, socialist realism includes both content, which is socialist, and form, which is realistic. Thus controversies over the style of socialist realism immediately returned to the debate on content and form. There were two different opinions on socialist realism in architecture. One view equated socialist realism with "national form, socialist content."[65] Another view maintained that socialist realism was a creative methodology in literature and art based on the reality of socialist life, while "national form, socialist content" was the directional principle for proletarian cultural construction.[66] The shadow of dichotomy persisted.

The conceptual source of the dichotomy between form and content was the Marxist philosophy of dialectical materialism. Marxism inherited dichotomy from German philosophical tradition as the key concept for understanding social and natural phenomena. These dichotomies were called categories in Marxist philosophy, and included the material and the spiritual, productive forces and productive relationships, and economic base and superstructure. The two parts in a dichotomy were mutually dependent for existence and interchangeable according to changing situations. For instance, when dealing with social production, productive force was content, while productive relationship was form; when dealing with social structure, productive relationship was content, while superstructure (such as the political system, the legal system, and ideology) were forms.[67]

In this sense, content and form in architecture serve as conceptual tools instead of the basis for a policy to guide practice. After defining architectural content as the unification of "function, technology, and ideology" in his 1955 article, Zhai further explained,

> These three types of content are not of equal weight. Function and technology are concerned with the material soundness of architecture and thus belong to architecture's material content, while ideology belongs to the spiritual realm and thus belongs to architecture's spiritual content. Since the primary task for architecture is to serve people's everyday life and productive activities, and since artistic products to enrich people's spiritual life are only secondary, it is obvious that, generally speaking, functional and technological content are primary and basic, while ideological content is secondary and derivative.[68]

Thus, within the dichotomy, form was secondary to content; among different aspects of content, ideological content was secondary to functional and technological content. Such a theoretical framework put more emphasis on engineering and virtually reduced architectural art to superfluous decoration. In theoretical discussion, scholars and architects considered architecture a combination of art and science. In practice and in official propaganda, architecture was treated mainly as engineering work. For the Anniversary Projects in 1958–59, almost all of the official documents and propaganda on the monuments were about the engineering achievements and the speed and quality of construction.

The Anniversary Projects

In 1958 the central government decided to construct about a dozen important national projects in Beijing to celebrate the tenth anniversary of the People's Republic of China in 1959. Some of these projects were intended as meeting and reception halls for use during National Day and after, but most were simply intended to serve as exhibition spaces to showcase a decade of socialist achievement in different fields. Moreover, the projects themselves were among the most significant achievements on display. They were originally called the Anniversary Projects, better known later as the Ten Great Buildings. Most were on Chang'an Avenue.[69] If the Anniversary Projects were primarily exhibition halls to display the achievements of the previous ten years of socialist construction, Chang'an Avenue was the main exhibition space for these halls, a showcase of the showcases.

Efforts were made to make Chang'an Avenue a showcase from the very beginning. When the victorious Communist regime moved into Zhongnanhai in early 1949, historic Chang'an Avenue was a street full of commercial activity. It was not a very prestigious street, and the people living and working there were mostly from the lower levels of society. There were many vendors and temporary shops between West Three-Arch Gate and the intersection with Nanchang Street, the most central section of the avenue.[70] Because Tiananmen Square was designated as the place to announce the birth of New China, and Zhongnanhai was selected as the seat of the central government, the Communist regime was determined to create along the avenue a new appearance befitting a socialist capital. In order to encourage the vendors to leave Chang'an Avenue, and to make it a more elegant urban boulevard, the newly arrived Beijing Municipal Government raised taxes for businesses in the area. On August 5, 1949—before the official founding of the People's Republic of China on October 1— some fifty vendors, including sellers of millet gruel and fried dough sticks, submitted a petition letter to the Beijing government, asking to keep the tax on vendors along Chang'an Avenue the same as in other areas of the city. The Communist government responded harshly. Official comments written in red ink in the original petition letter stated that if the vendors felt that the tax was too high, they should move somewhere else. The man who actually wrote the petition, and probably the initiator of the protest, Xu Jiwu, ultimately made a formal confession and repented, admitting that "we should not have used the same method as dealing with the former Nationalist regime to deal with the people's government" and promising that "something like this will never happen again." He was released on bail.[71]

Chang'an Avenue was designated as a scenic area in 1949,[72] a further step in its development as a national showcase. Throughout the second half of the twentieth century, before a significant national celebration occurred, Chinese authorities would embark on additional work and would claim to "roughly complete" Chang'an Avenue.[73] The construction of the Anniversary Projects for the People's Republic of China's tenth anniversary in 1959 was the first major episode in this series of completions.

Ten Great Buildings was a later designation for the Anniversary Projects. The number ten, a symbolic number of perfection in folk culture, was adopted to indicate both the grandeur of the projects and the comprehensiveness of the endeavor. While some of the ten buildings were added later to make up the number,[74] some of the originally planned projects were never completed. A report dated February 23, 1959, about seven months before the National Day deadline for the Anniversary Projects, indicated that altogether there were sixteen projects planned so far. They fell into three categories: eleven must-be-completed projects, two hope-to-complete projects, and three okay-to-postpone projects. The must-be-completed projects included the Conference Hall for the People's Congress (henceforth the Great Hall of the People),[75] the Museum of Chinese Revolution, the Museum of Chinese History, the Agricultural Exhibition Hall, the People's Liberation Army (PLA) Museum,[76] the Minority Culture Palace, the National Guest House, the Stadium (later known as the Workers' Stadium), the Chang'an Hotel, the Overseas Chinese Union Building, and Beijing Railway Station. Two of these, the Stadium and the Overseas Chinese Union Building, which were not on Chang'an Avenue, were originally planned to be finished in 1958 and were not among the original Anniversary Projects. Not completed as planned, they were added as Anniversary Projects to be completed in 1959. The two hope-to-complete projects, the Science and Technology Hall and the National Gallery, were started, and then postponed due to insufficient supplies of construction materials. The three okay-to-postpone projects were the National Theatre, the Movie Palace, and the Xidan Department Store, none of which had been started yet.[77]

Although not all of the Anniversary Projects were completed in time for the National Day celebration, the speed of construction of some of the key monuments was remarkable, a direct result of the Great Leap Forward movement. The term "Great Leap Forward" formally appeared in late 1957. It later became a nationwide mass movement that emphasized speed in social transformation and economic development. In a departure from the Marxist doctrine of economic base determining superstructure, during the Great Leap Forward, social transformation was believed to be capable of liberating enormous productive forces and leading to rapid industrialization. Within a year, from 1957 to 1958, the basic social structure of China was completely transformed. According to the *People's Daily*, by the end of 1958, 99 percent of the peasant population had been organized into 26,000 people's communes, new basic units for a Communist society. The second session of the Eighth Party Congress in May 1958 adopted the general line of "constructing socialism more, faster, better, and more economically" and set the ambitious goal of surpassing the United Kingdom in major industrial production within fifteen years.[78]

The Great Leap Forward in architecture led to the successful completion of the central monuments of the Anniversary Projects in an astonishingly short period of time, a display of the great achievements of the new socialist regime. Like the movement in general, the construction of the Anniversary Projects emphasized the power of popular will and revolutionary spirit. Rapidity of design and construction were convenient measurable demonstrations of achievement. Both the design and the construction of all of the Ten Great Buildings were completed within ten months, although this was achieved only by cutting some of the other originally planned projects. According to the official report, these cancellations were mainly due to rising costs and shortages of materials. Floor space was increased, and cost overruns occurred. The timely completion of some key projects was a miracle. As late as February 23, 1959, the Great Hall of the People was considered the least likely to be finished in time, especially its central auditorium.[79] Thereafter, the construction of the Great Hall was run as a mass campaign. From February to August 1959, detailed tasks for every single day were planned and daily newsletters printed targeted goals, plans to accomplish them, issues to be addressed, problems to be solved, and slogans calling for more revolutionary spirit.[80]

Construction was carried out simultaneously with design. The construction process highlighted workers instead of designers, while the design process emphasized engineering achievements rather than architectural aesthetics. And at the opening ceremonies, it was government officials and construction workers representatives who presided, not architects. Construction workers were the heroes of the Ten Great Buildings, whose achievement was attributed mainly to the "wisdom of the leadership of the central government" and the "great support of the people."

For the general public and for the political leaders, to whom issues of architectural form and meaning were vague and foreign, the height, size, and speed of construction of the buildings were tangible and easily grasped measures of architectural achievement. The Great Hall of the People, for instance, spanned a dimension of 336 meters north-south and 174 meters east-west. Located on a fifteen-hectare site, its total floorage was 171,800 square meters, and its total volume was 1,600,000 cubic meters.[81]

As many as 433,150 cubic meters of earth were removed for its construction, which consumed a staggering amount of materials. These included 127,700 cubic meters of reinforced concrete, 400,000 square meters of plaster surface, 71,600 square meters of wood flooring, 24,000 square meters of marble, and 27,000 square meters of granite.[82] These construction materials were truly a national effort: twenty-three provinces and municipalities contributed, in addition to Beijing. Organized mass visits to this gigantic monument began immediately after its completion. Most people were impressed by its huge size, especially the interior. The building was acclaimed a victory of Mao's Great Leap Forward and of the party's general line.[83]

Architectural design now had to serve the galloping speed of construction. In keeping up with the Great Leap Forward spirit, "fast design and fast construction" became a fashionable slogan. Methods of mass production were invented. Standardized building units were drawn on separate transparencies so that they could be used repeatedly for different projects, or organized into different compositions to produce blueprints directly. Design was left behind. Almost all of the major Anniversary Projects were built while design and preparation of the materials were still ongoing.[84]

Indeed, the spirit of the Great Leap Forward in architecture was displayed most dramatically in mass movements on the construction site, a perfect stage to enact the slogan "constructing socialism," literally and symbolically. Construction workers were mobilized in a military manner. For the Great Hall of the People, 7,785 excellent workers selected from eighteen provinces and autonomous regions participated in the construction campaign.[85] Construction tasks were treated like military campaigns, and construction teams were organized in military terms.[86] Military strategies, such as "be clear on the target," "concentrate a predominantly superior force," "and charge to the critical spot," became slogans for faster task completion.[87]

For the CCP government, the Ten Great Buildings confirmed the correctness of the Great Leap Forward and the victory of Mao's general line. The buildings provided examples to inspire the Chinese people to embark on more and greater leaps forward in socialist construction and to refute foreign denigrations of the mass movement. Well-planned visits to the Great Hall went on for weeks in 1959. Before October 1, 1959, foreign ambassadors, correspondents, and political and army leaders visited the Great Hall; after the tenth anniversary celebration, the People's Committee of Beijing City organized two concentrated mass visits. The first was in October, when about 50,000 people toured the hall. The second, larger in scale than the first, took place between December 4 and December 26 to accommodate more people. During this time, the Great Hall received a total of 463,588 visitors from Beijing and the provinces.[88]

As stated in the December visiting plan, the purpose of mass visits to the Great Hall of the People was to "arouse socialist working enthusiasm, to further education in the 'general line' and 'Great Leap Forward,' and to make the achievements of the 'Great Leap Forward' widely known."[89] Visitors' responses to the building mainly focused on its scale and technical achievement. Many were amazed that the huge interior space of the Grand Conference Hall for Ten Thousand People did not have even a single column to support the ceiling. The Great Hall proved to the visitors that the new socialist society was superior to earlier Chinese societies. Compared with the Three Great Halls in the Forbidden City, for instance, visitors commented that the new Great Hall was much better because "the wisdom of our laboring people has been fully developed," a result of the socialist society. Others claimed that the Great Hall was "heaven on earth" and that "entering the Great Hall was like entering Communist society."[90]

The Design of the Great Hall

The design of the Great Hall also took a mass line,[91] although it received less media exposure than the construction process. It began with a nationwide call for proposals. In September 1958 design proposals for the Great Hall were gathered from all over the country. A total of thirty-four architectural design units provided eighty-four plans and 189 elevation schemes, among which were Miesian-style glass boxes, Soviet-style central towers, and traditional Chinese big roofs. In September 1958, State Council premier Zhou Enlai chaired a group of leading architects from seventeen provinces that gathered in Beijing to discuss the proposals. The submission by Zhao Dongri and Shen Qi was chosen, and Zhang Bo was assigned as the chief architect for the Great Hall project.[92] This process of collective creation in architecture and urban planning, in which the winner of the design competition does not necessarily serve as the chief architect, was common in the first three decades of the People's Republic of China. The final product was often an eclectic new design that represented a compromise between different views and was meant to combine the advantages of many proposals.

The Great Hall was a stylistic compromise that aimed to produce the correct architectural form. When the policy of "national form, socialist content" was in force in the early 1950s, asymmetrical buildings without extra decorations were labeled "structurism" and "formalism"; when Liang's architectural thinking was criticized as extravagant after 1955, buildings with traditional Chinese roofs were condemned as "revivalism" and yet another form of "formalism." Finally, simplified functionalist boxes were criticized as "one-sided emphasis on economy." Chinese architects of the late 1950s had to avoid all of these negative associations.

Fig. 2.8. The Great Hall of the People, 1958–59. Zhao Dongri, Shen Qi, Zhang Bo, and others. *Photograph by author.*

The Great Hall, as completed in September 1959, was a complex of Soviet neoclassicism without a central tower, Chinese national forms without a big roof, and boxes enclosed by colonnades and surface decorations. Like the neoclassical monuments built in the Soviet Union, the exterior of the Great Hall featured solid walls and monumental colonnades. All four façades were symmetrical. The main façade facing Tiananmen Square was horizontally divided into five sections, with the central and end sections emphasized. The solid masonry façades, however, were carefully designed to display Chinese national character (fig. 2.8). The description of the Great Hall by the Beijing Municipal Architectural Design Institute explained,

Following the conventions of Chinese architecture, the elevation has a tripartite composition: eave section, walls plus colonnade, and base. We did not use big roofs in the eave section, but flat straight eaves were slightly raised [at the corners]. The intercolumniation of the central bay [*mingjian*] is larger than that of the side bays [*cijian*]. The proportion of the column order [*zhushi*][93] was based on both Western and Chinese order systems. The base is inspired by the traditional Chinese platform [*xumizuo*].[94]

The wording of the report was carefully chosen to avoid unfavorable associations with styles previously criticized. Although it emphasized Chinese character, the report especially reminded readers that Chinese architecture was not confined simply to big roofs, which, by the late 1950s, were inextricably associated with Liang and his national forms. Instead, the Chineseness of the Great Hall was embodied in its structural features, proportion, and details. In response to Mao's call for taking essences from "ancient times, the contemporary world, China, and abroad," the word "Western" was used. "Modern," on the other hand, was avoided, since it was still a sensitive word in late 1950s.

Since the terms "national form" and "modern" both had undesirable associations in previous architectural discourse, a new system of terminology had to be invented, and was. Liang's categorization of architectural style in terms of Chinese, Western, new, and old was a product of this new theoretical context. During the conference on the Anniversary Projects in 1959, he proposed that there were four different ways to create buildings in terms of architectural forms: Chinese and old, Chinese and new, Western and old, and Western and new. The best combination, Liang maintained, was Chinese and new. Indeed, this was then the safest way to express a stylistic preference.

A symbol of political power for New China, the Great Hall of the People was designed to represent the national unity and ethnic equality of the nation. A separate room was named for each province and autonomous region, including Tibet, Inner Mongolia, Xinjiang, and Taiwan. The ceiling of the Grand Conference Hall for Ten Thousand People (Wanren Dahuitang), with its multitudes of starlike spotlights centered on a giant red star, represented six hundred million Chinese people united around the Party. The slightly arched ceiling smoothly merged into the walls on all four sides, serving as a metaphor of the starry night sky. It was said that Premier Zhou Enlai personally recommended that the ceiling and walls should be united like "sky and water merged along the distant horizon."[95] Before the 1990s, however, the Great Hall of the People was not accessible to most Chinese people and was rarely used. For the general public, it served mostly as a façade for Tiananmen Square and Chang'an Avenue.

Museums and the Representation of History on Chang'an Avenue

To some extent, all of the Anniversary Projects were exhibitions showcasing the achievements of the first decade of socialist construction. Yet two of the projects are about the past: the Museum of Chinese Revolution and History (now renamed the National Museum of China) and the Military Museum. Both located on Chang'an Avenue, they played a central role in the reconstruction of Chinese history and the incorporation of the past into a meganarrative that legitimized the current regime.

The two museums offered a central platform for an official version of Chinese history. While their physical structures remained mostly the same, the changing exhibition programs within reflected China's social and political changes during the second half of the twentieth century.

History, Museums, and the Rewriting of China's Past

Chinese civilization has the world's longest unbroken tradition of historical record keeping. The historical *Chunqiu*[96] documented the Spring and Autumn Period (770–476 BCE), which took its name from the title of this book. The late-second-century to early first-century (BCE) *Shiji*, by Sima Qian, delineated the history of China from the era of Huangdi (about 3000 BCE) to his own time. Following Sima Qian's model, every major dynasty in China's last two millennia left at least one official history. Altogether, there are twenty-five such official histories today,[97] covering the entire five thousand years of Chinese history, from the legendary Huangdi to the last emperor of the Qing dynasty.

These volumes, called *zhengshi*, or "authentic histories," constituted the official version of China's past. In most cases, the history of a dynasty was completed during the succeeding dynasty, compiled by special officials whose job was to write the history of the previous dynasty. Each dynasty also had officials whose job was to document the current dynasty, providing materials for later generations to use in writing a formal history. Although there were legendary upright officials who refused to flatter those in power and insisted on writing what really happened at the risk of their lives, the twenty-five dynastic histories (*ershiwushi*),[98] as the famous late-Qing to early Republican scholar and political reformer Liang Qichao said, were primarily the genealogies of emperors, dukes, generals, and prime ministers.[99]

According to the Confucian concept of dynasty as heaven's mandate on earth, the emperor, or Son of Heaven, ruled as heaven's agent. However, if an emperor was incompetent or seized power illegally, he might forfeit the mandate of heaven and be replaced by a new emperor or dynasty. In writing a previous dynasty's history, to strengthen the idea of heaven's mandate, early emperors, and especially the dynastic founder, were usually depicted as great heroes and true Sons of Heaven. On the other hand, in order for the succeeding dynasty to legitimize its own legal status as the justified successor, the later period of the previous dynasty was depicted as a time of deterioration and waiting for a new regime to replace it. Records from the previous dynasty fulfilled these needs for historical documentation perfectly. Most documents about the emperors of the previous dynasty compiled by contemporary officials were full of compliments, except for those pertaining to the dynasty's last emperors, who often did not last long enough for the compilation of such positive records.

The practice of writing a continuous history focusing on successions of dynasties gave rise to the Chinese view of history as a series of timeless cycles. All of the twenty-five histories have similar formats, following the model established by Sima Qian, with only minor adjustments. Moreover, these histories highlight the rise, prosperity, and fall of each dynasty, a life cycle that began with a heroic wise emperor but eventually ended in a collapse due to the extravagance or cruelty of an incompetent or evil emperor. History writing under the Communist regime broke away from this dynastic model. Chinese history was no longer depicted as timeless cycles of dynastic rises and falls but as a teleological development toward Communist revolution. The later the history, the more selective it was, as historical events were focused upon in order to justify the current regime and a specific political line. Repeated peasant uprisings that brought down old dynasties and inaugurated new ones were rendered as if they were rehearsals for and premature versions of Communist revolution. While in previous histories peasant uprisings were intermissions in the cycle of dynasties, in the new history writing of the People's Republic of China, dynasties became intermissions in the cycle of constant revolution. As in the façade of Chang'an Avenue, the former "gaps" were filled, and museums played a key role in the procedure of rewriting history.

Museum building in China started right after the end of the long imperial era. In 1912 the Museum of History was founded in Guozijian, the former imperial education center in the capital. In 1918 the displays in the Museum of History were relocated to Meridian Gate, the southern gate tower of the Forbidden City, and Duan Gate in front of Meridian Gate was used as museum storage.[100] In October 1924 the last emperor, Puyi, was expelled from the Forbidden City by warlord Feng Yuxiang's army, thirteen years after the collapse of the Qing Empire. Supported by the Republican government in Beijing, a committee was formed to catalogue the historical and cultural relics in the palace. A year later, on October 10, 1925, the Forbidden City was opened to the public as the Palace Museum, displaying ancient objects from the imperial collection.[101] Not all of the so-called ancient objects on display were, in fact, so ancient. Some were from the late Qing dynasty, which in the 1920s was still part of the life experience of many Chinese. Associated with the imperial past, however, these objects now became part of history, and the museum was used to delineate a boundary between past and present.

No political agenda or ideology guided the exhibition of historical relics before the Communist revolution. Items on display in the Museum of History were organized according to media: metal, stone, jade, bronze, and so on. However, after the Communist takeover in 1949, the museum became an active participant in the rewriting of Chinese history. Items on display were reorganized to construct a new version of Chinese history as a teleological development toward the Communist revolution and the founding of the People's Republic of China. The entire history of China was rewritten to further a party-centered agenda and especially to glorify Mao's political line.

After the founding of the People's Republic of China, various rooms in Meridian Gate and in Duan Gate north of Tiananmen Tower continued to serve as the Museum of History, now renamed the Beijing Museum of Chinese History.[102] At the same time, a new museum, the Central Museum of the Revolution, was founded in 1951 in Wuying Hall, the former imperial publishing house in the courtyard west of the Outer Three Halls in the Forbidden City.[103] The exhibition in the new museum was based on the July First Exhibition in 1951. Named after the official birthday of the Chinese Communist Party, the July First Exhibition, like the exhibitions that followed in the Central Museum of the Revolution, was aimed at propagating knowledge about the new ruling party to Beijing citizens, who had been living under constantly changing regimes with competing ideologies since the fall of the Qing Empire—the Nationalist between 1945 and 1949, the Japanese between 1937 and 1945, and numerous warlords before 1937. In 1955 the July First Exhibition became a permanent Party History display. In 1958 the Party History display was expanded into the New Democratic Revolutionary History exhibition.[104]

In September 1958 the central government decided that new structures would be built to house the Museum of the Revolution and the Museum of Chinese History on the east side of Tiananmen Square for the tenth anniversary of the People's Republic of China. To balance the enormous façade of the Great Hall of the People on the west side of the square, the two museums were later combined into one complex.

The 1959 Museum of the Revolution displayed historical materials from 1840, the year of the Opium War, to 1949, the year when the People's Republic of China was founded. This period was depicted as a time of decline and recovery, leading to the victory of Communist revolution and the birth of New China. The Opium War, which started a long period of decline after the zenith of the Qing Empire, eventually led to the capitalist revolution of Sun Yat-sen, who, though not without class limitations, was a progressive capitalist revolutionary inspired by the 1918 Russian Revolution and sympathetic to the Communists. His successor, Chiang Kai-shek, however, was portrayed as a complete reactionary, whose deeds guaranteed the decline of the Nationalist regime and the rise of Communist China.

Illustrating the Marxist view on social development, the Museum of the Revolution included materials on three different societies: feudal, capitalist, and socialist. In the arrangement of exhibition material, however, the hundred-year-long history was simplified into two periods: the Old Democratic Revolutionary Period and the New Democratic Revolutionary Period. Jindai Shi,[105] or "Recent History," as this period between 1840 and 1949 was known in the Chinese discourse, was characterized by constant revolution. The Old Democratic Revolution, or Nationalist revolution, led to the fall of the Qing Empire and the founding of the Republic of China; the New Democratic Revolution, or socialist revolution, led to the fall of the Nationalist regime and the founding of the People's Republic of China. The former ended in 1912, while the later started in 1919, the year of the May Fourth Movement. With only seven years in between, this periodization of recent history left virtually no room for the Nationalist construction of China.

The thirty years between 1919 and 1949 emphasized a single theme: the growing of Communism in China. The decade of national construction between 1927 and 1937 under Chiang's Nationalist regime was totally neglected. Moreover, the New Democratic Revolution was further simplified as the victory of Mao's line, while the contributions of other early Communist leaders were ignored. The displays highlighted locations critical to the rise of Mao, such as Mount Jinggang, Yan'an, and Xibaipo, all of which became Communist pilgrimage sites after the founding of the People's Republic of China.

China's past as displayed in the Museum of Chinese History was an expansion of this teleological approach to the Communist revolution. Covering the entire history before 1840, the chronological display of objects and pictures was reorganized to follow the Marxist order of social development: from primitive to slave to feudal society.[106] The exhibitions highlighted the struggles between progressive and reactionary forces, between materialism and idealism, between dialecticism and metaphysics, and so on, and the contributions of the revolutionary laboring people. For the new exhibitions in the 1959 building, more material on peasant uprisings was added.[107] Mao's power base was among the Chinese peasants, and his strategy for the Communist revolution in China was "to encircle the bourgeois cities with the Communist countryside." The exhibition presented Mao's Communist revolution as an uprising in accordance with the correct guiding thoughts of Marxism, but also, to some extent, as a continuation of past peasant revolutions.

In January 1959, when the new building for the two museums was still under construction, a decision was made to rename the museums to acknowledge their national status. The Central Museum of the Revolution was renamed the National Museum of the Revolution, and the Beijing Museum of Chinese History was renamed the National Museum of Chinese History.[108] The two museums used to belong to the administrative system of the Beijing Municipal Cultural Bureau. In 1962 the two museums, together with the Palace Museum, were all elevated to the direct control of the Ministry of Culture under the State Council.[109]

Another museum constructed on Chang'an Avenue for the Anniversary Projects in 1959 was the Military Museum of the Chinese People's Revolution (the Military Museum). The historical period covered by the Military Museum was more recent and much shorter than that of the other two museums. Its exhibits started in 1927, the year of the Nanchang Uprising and the birth of the Chinese Red Army, and ended with the Korean War in the early 1950s. While the Museum of Chinese History extended the Chinese Communist Party's political agenda to the entire history of China, the Military Museum encapsulated the Communist victory by focusing on its military aspects.

Museum Architecture and Exhibition Space

There was no prototype of the modern museum in traditional Chinese architecture. In fact, the first museum was made by converting former imperial monuments. During the Nanjing Period (1927–37) of the Republican era, Chiang Kai-shek's Nationalist regime initiated an ambitious project for the construction of the capital that produced a number of government-sponsored buildings. Two museums were built in Nanjing during the ten years of intensive construction, the Central Museum and the Exhibition Hall of Nationalist Party History. The Nationalist regime encouraged the restoration of traditional Chinese culture. The 1929 capital planning[110] required all designs to incorporate Chinese-oriented thoughts. "Original Chinese Forms" were highly recommended, especially for government and public architecture.[111] The Central Museum had a Tang-style *wudian* roof, and the Exhibition Hall of Nationalist Party History had a Qing-style *xieshan* roof. Both followed historical models faithfully. The former was a larger modified version of the Tang dynasty main hall in the Buddhist temple Foguangsi in Shanxi, which had recently been discovered by Liang Sicheng, who participated in the design of the Central Museum. The latter looked very similar to a double-eave city gate tower, of which many remained in 1930s China. The proportion and details of the building reflected Liang's vision of ideal classical Chinese architecture.[112]

Association with a glorious past, however, was no longer a legitimate justification for a current regime during the PRC era. As part of the Anniversary Projects in 1959, the main purpose of the Museum of Chinese Revolution and History in Beijing was to showcase the power of the new socialist system. The first issue was scale. As part of the Tiananmen Square reconstruction project for the tenth anniversary, the scale of the museums had to match the scale of the square, which, according to the 1958 plan, was to be expanded to an east-west dimension of 500 meters. The Museum of the Revolution and the Museum of Chinese History were originally to be two separate buildings, just as the Great Hall for the People's Congress and the Office Building for the Standing Committee of the People's Congress were to be two separate buildings on the opposite side of the square. Since these buildings were to frame Tiananmen Square, proposals for their organization in relation to the square were prepared in 1958. Of the seven proposals chosen for presentation to central leaders, three envisaged four separate buildings, with two on either side of the square, and four combined the two buildings on each side into one structure.[113]

The Museum of the Revolution, the Museum of Chinese History, and the Office Building for the Standing Committee of the People's Congress were similar in scale and relatively small. The Great Hall for the People's Congress, however, was much larger. The central leaders requested that the congress hall be able to hold ten thousand representatives in one room, called at that time the Grand Conference Hall for Ten Thousand People. Given this disparity, it was impossible to achieve a balanced image for Tiananmen Square by framing it with four separate buildings. The combination proposals were better, but the combined structure for the two museums was still much smaller than the single Grand Conference Hall. With the addition of the office building, the combined structure on the west side would have dwarfed its counterpart on the east side of the square. A solution was provided by the Beijing Municipal Planning Bureau, whose proposal achieved a balanced façade by enlarging the museum complex with courtyards while keeping the congress complex a solid block. This was chosen as the plan for implementation (fig. 2.9).[114]

The plan of the museum complex was stretched over a site comparable in scale to that of the Great Hall. The completed building was 313 meters from north to south, and 149 meters from east to west. Even with three large courtyards (76 by 100 meters) and two small ones, only two stories were needed to fulfill the requirements for exhibition floor space. Had the architects used the same wall height as a normal exhibition hall (creating a west façade 15 meters high and over 300 meters long), the building would hardly have been noticeable from the center of the square and the complex would have been out of balance, so the height of the museum complex was artificially stretched as well. The interior height of each of the two exhibition floors was 7 meters. With the addition of a 2.5-meter-high space above the ceiling for structure and utilities, the height of each exhibition floor reached 9.5 meters. A lower floor for storage, valuable collections, workshops, dining rooms, kitchens, and parking lots was added to further elevate the general height to 26.5 meters.[115] Yet this height was still more than 10 meters lower than the 40-meter façade of the Great Hall. As a final effort to make the museum façade more grandiose and continuous, an eleven-bay 32.7-meter-

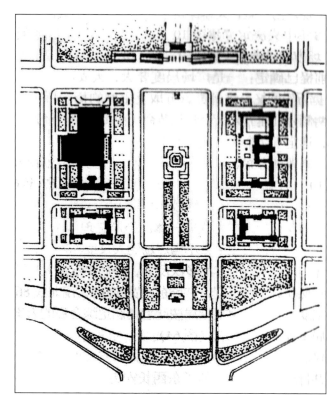

Fig. 2.9. Drawing showing the relationship between the Great Hall and the museum complex proposed by the Beijing Municipal Planning Bureau. *Reproduction from* Chang'anjie: Guoqu, xianzai, weilai, *67. Courtesy of Zheng Guangzhong.*

high colonnade was built on the west façade to connect the Museum of the Revolution with the Museum of Chinese History. The protruding pillars framing the colonnade were 39.88 meters tall, slightly shorter than the average height of the Great Hall (fig. 2.10).[116]

The architectural style of the museum complex was also mainly a result of its role as the counterpart to the Great Hall on the opposite side of Tiananmen Square. The nationwide call for proposals[117] to select a design for the Great Hall generated a wide variety of schemes, from glass boxes to traditional Chinese roofs. Once the form for the Great Hall was decided, however, the stylistic issue for the museum building became relatively simple. Like the Great Hall, the museum complex followed a Soviet neoclassical composition in façade, without either a large area of exterior glass or traditional Chinese roofs. All elevations were symmetrical. The main façade also had a horizontal five-section division and was vertically divided into eave, main body, and base. Both the Great Hall and the museum complex had a structural system with a reinforced concrete frame and using the same materials and color scheme in the main façades: a light red granite base, light yellow concrete that resembled stone for the walls of the main body, and yellow and green glazed tiles decorating the eaves.

Balanced in scale and similar in form, the spatial concept of the museum building has a yin-yang relationship with the Great Hall of the People. While the center of the Great Hall complex is the solid Grand Conference Hall for Ten Thousand People, the center of the museum com-

Fig. 2.10. Museum of Chinese Revolution and History, 1958–59. Zhang Kaiji, Ye Zugui, Huang Qiaohong, and others. *Photograph by author.*

plex is a large void courtyard. While the colonnade at the center of the main east façade of the Great Hall complex is a *shilang*,[118] a solid or actual corridor attached to the main structure, the colonnade at the center of the main west façade of the museum complex is a *xulang*, a void or insubstantial corridor open on both sides. While the columns in the Great Hall *shilang* have a circular cross-section, the cross-section for columns in the museum complex *xulang* is square. According to ancient Chinese beliefs, heaven is circular, and earth is square; heaven is yang, and earth is yin. The yin-yang relationship of the two complexes is confirmed by the cross-section of their columns in the facing façades across Tiananmen Square. The national emblem in red and yellow decorating the top center of the Great Hall's colonnade is also circular, and 4.5 meters in diameter; the museum complex bears a flag-and-star decoration in the same colors, 5.5 meters high and 26.5 meters long, in the top center of its colonnade, and rectangular in shape.

Thus, from general layout to small details, the Great Hall of the People is yang, and the museum complex is yin. But the yin-yang relationship between the Great Hall complex and the museum complex goes beyond the formal level. While acting as a significant complement and accompaniment to yang, yin mainly plays the role of a subordinate follower. The writing of history is subordinate to the will of political power, just as the museum complex follows the lead of the Great Hall.

The spatial organization of the museum complex embodied the subordination of history to politics. Virtually two separate buildings connected by a colonnade and an entrance hall, the museum complex had three main courtyards aligned on a south-north axis, similar to the traditional Beijing courtyard house (*siheyuan*). With its colonnade opening to Tiananmen Square, the central courtyard served as a transitional space for communication within the entire complex. The northern courtyard belonged to the Museum of Chinese Revolution, and the southern courtyard served the Museum of History. According to Chinese tradition, the northern courtyard in a courtyard residence was more important and was often occupied by the head of the family. Since traditionally all windows in a courtyard residence opened to the inside of the courtyards, main rooms in the northern courtyard thus faced south and had more direct sunshine. Farther away from the main gate in the south, the northern courtyard was also more private and occupied a more prestigious location. In the Ming and Qing dynasties, these originally practical considerations in courtyard organization acquired symbolic significance and became conventions in the spatial hierarchy of Chinese architecture. Thus, in the museum complex of 1959, the Museum of the Revolution occupied a more significant position than the Museum of Chinese History.

As the juncture of the two museums, the building in the central courtyard celebrated the sacred lineage of Marxism as perceived in China. Preceded by a portico and a transitional hall, the central hall had the feel of a temple for Communist saints. The largest single interior space in the entire complex—42 by 32 meters—with an interior height of 14.6 meters, the central hall featured marble relief portraits of Marx, Engels, Lenin, and Stalin in the wall facing the entrance, in front of which stood a bust of Mao. While the four foreign Marxist founding fathers provided the international background and theoretical base, Mao applied and developed Marxism in the revolutionary practice of China. Two 10-by-10-meter murals decorated the side walls of the central hall, *The Great Unity of People throughout the World* on the north, and *The Great Unity of People throughout China* on the south.[119] The murals were originally planned to be wooden relief sculptures of groups of people, representing the united nationalities of the world and ethnic groups in China, respectively.[120] Stylized patterns of white doves of peace and Chinese characters for "peace" and "union" decorated the upper part of the entrance wall. Below the central entrance hall, in the basement, was a 700-seat auditorium for lectures and films on revolution and historical topics. No specific function, however, was assigned to the central hall itself. Located at the heart of the whole complex, it set the tone for the entire interior space and all of the exhibitions within.

The color scheme of the interior of the museum complex was mainly red figures against a light-colored background. The transitional hall, from which visitors could turn left into the Museum of the Revolution or right into the Museum of Chinese History, had both a floor and columns of red marble. In the central hall, the walls were covered with light yellow manmade marble, while the floor was made of red and light gray marble. Two rows of octagonal columns covered in light gray marble divided the interior space of the central hall, making it look like a nave and the two sides like aisles. The two rows of columns directed the focus in the central hall to its back wall, where the figures of the four Marxist heroes and Mao were located.

Like the museum complex on Tiananmen Square, the Military Museum was also built to legitimize Mao's political line as the only way to save China. Its exhibitions celebrated Mao's military principles and strategies, whose legendary victories had made such battle sites as Mount Jinggang and the Dadu River new pilgrimage destinations for the People's Republic of China. A marble Mao statue stood at the center of a 14.3-meter-high transitional hall. As in the museum complex on Tiananmen Square, this hall connected two L-shaped side wings and a central hall in the back defining two symmetrical courtyards. Mao's statue was positioned like a standing statue of Guanyin—the Chinese bodhisattva of compassion—in a Buddhist pavilion, with its feet visible from outside the main entrance and a full figure visible only from inside, looming above onlookers in a vertically stretched interior space.

With a floorage of 60,557 square meters, the Military Museum was only slightly smaller than the 65,152.05-square-meter museum complex on Tiananmen Square. Occupying a much smaller site, however, the Military Museum featured a pyramidal composition. While the museum complex horizontally screened the square with its two superscaled floors, the Military Museum rose vertically like a mountain peak, presenting a symmetrical façade on Chang'an Avenue with seven floors plus a tower in the center, four floors for the two side sections, and three floors for the end sections. The 94.7-meter-high central tower supported a giant PLA emblem: a red star containing the two yellow characters for August First (the birthday of the Chinese Communist army) encircled by a wheat sheaf motif, using the same color scheme as the insignias on both the Great Hall and the museum complex.

The Reorganization of Museum Exhibitions on Chang'an Avenue

The museums on Chang'an Avenue experienced significant changes in the 1990s. On July 1, 1990, the Chinese Revolutionary History display in the Museum of the Revolution (with its two permanent exhibitions, the Old Democratic Revolutionary Period and the New Democratic Revolutionary Period) was renamed the China in Recent History display, and the People's Republic of China display was renamed the Contemporary China display.[121] The arrangement of materials according to revolutionary periods was changed to a chronological organization of objects and pictures oriented around successive historical events, including the Opium Wars, the Taiping Heavenly Kingdom, the Xinhai Revolution, the birth of Chinese Communist Party, the Nanchang Uprising, and so on. Since the death of Mao and the end of the Cultural Revolution in 1976, revolutionary spirit had been downplayed in public propaganda. Under Mao, history had been seen as a series of revolutions; after Mao, revolutions were dramatic moments at the verges of social and political changes in history.

Nothing captured this change in museum politics more tellingly than a comparison of two exhibitions on Sun Yat-sen, one before and one after 1976. Born in 1866, Sun was considered the founding father of modern China by both Communists and Nationalists. In 1966, at the dawn of the Cultural Revolution, a temporary exhibit, Memorial Centennial Exhibition on Sun Yat-sen, opened at the Museum of the Revolution. Sun was presented as a transitional figure in the historical progress of China as it evolved from the Old Democratic Revolution into the New Democratic Revolution. The exhibition emphasized Sun's connection with and support of the Communist party, and only leaders of the Left-Wing Nationalists, such as Song Qingling, Liao Zhongkai, and He Xiangning, were mentioned. In fact, the exhibition was more about the Chinese Communist Party than about Sun, whose revolutionary activities before 1924 were full of political mistakes from which historical lessons should be learned. Sun died in 1925. The exhibition program suggested that the critical moment of Sun's political life occurred only at the end of his life and with the help of the Chinese Communist Party, the significance of whose role in the transition of Sun's revolutionary cause from nationalist to socialist was emphasized. The theme of the exhibition was to illustrate that "it was the Chinese people, led by the Chinese Communist Party and Mao, who carried on Sun's unfinished cause of the democratic revolution and marched further on to socialist revolution and construction."[122] This teleological interpretation and narrative of Sun's life largely disappeared thirty years later. In the 1996 Exhibition in Memory of Sun Yat-sen's One Hundred and Thirtieth Anniversary, staged in the same museum, Sun was celebrated mainly as a national hero who overthrew the Manchu Empire and fought for national unification.

The way materials were displayed in the Museum of Chinese History experienced similar changes in the 1990s. By 1997 the permanent exhibition, the General History of China display, no longer followed the Marxist social development scheme but instead reverted to a dynastic ordering. Instead of the Marxist label of "primitive society," the long period before the Xia dynasty was divided into the Paleolithic Period and the Neolithic Period, and the more neutral "Late Qing dynasty" replaced the former ideologically loaded term for the period between 1840 and 1911, "Semi-

Colonial Semi-Feudal Society."[123] Ancient Chinese history was no longer a retrospective extension of post-1840 revolutionary history. As a result, focus on the revolutionary spirit of ancient laboring people gave way to emphasis on cultural, political, and economic development, and on technological improvement.

The most dramatic change in the museum display of Chinese history on Chang'an Avenue occurred at the dawn of the twenty-first century. In 2002 a decision was made to combine the Museum of the Revolution and the Museum of Chinese History into one National Museum of China. After this merger, however, the permanent exhibitions virtually disappeared, and the displays in the History of the Chinese Revolution exhibition vanished entirely. Almost all of the exhibition halls in the 1959 building were used for temporary thematic exhibitions. In 2005 a quick survey of the National Museum revealed that the General History of China display had dwindled to the display Distinguished Items from the Museum Collection, where visitors can now admire famous pieces, from prehistoric ceramics to Ming furniture. Instead of a narrative of Chinese history through material culture, the exhibition is more like a gallery display of fine arts. Items are organized according to material—ceramics, porcelain, bronzes, metalwork, wood, paintings, sculpture, and so on. The scale of the display is now much smaller than the previous general history display and features items frequently cited in books on Chinese art.

Other halls in the National Museum are all used for temporary thematic exhibitions. In November 2005 the first floor of the former Museum of the Revolution held the exhibition Zheng He's Seven Voyages to Western Oceans, and the first floor of the former Museum of Chinese History held the exhibition The Dawn of a Civilization: Treasures from Liangzhu Culture.

While all of the previously mentioned exhibitions were temporary, current visitors to the National Museum will be surprised to discover that the only relatively permanent exhibit is the National Waxen Images display, located on the second floor of the former Museum of Revolution. In dim light, visitors there will find Sun Yat-sen standing opposite the first emperor, Qin Shihuangdi; Mao smiling and gazing at Han dynasty emperors across the passage; Vladimir Lenin speaking to Karl Marx and Friedrich Engels, with Qing emperor Kangxi posing nearby; a sexy Marilyn Monroe exposing her shoulders in front of Chinese Communist heroes and heroines; and Bill Gates smiling ambiguously at the Maoist moral model Lei Feng. All of the celebrities familiar to twenty-first-century Chinese people can be found here, from the third-century BCE Chinese poet Qu Yuan to World War II leader Winston Churchill, from film star Jackie Chan to volleyball player Yao Ming. Surrounded by super-realistic full-size waxen figures standing and sitting on undifferentiated floors, visitors can easily get lost here and find themselves unable to distinguish which figures are live

Fig. 2.11. Interior of the Wax Figure Hall, National Museum, Beijing, 2005. *Photograph by author.*

onlookers. Here the boundary between history and the present, initially set by the first Chinese museum, the Palace Museum, in 1912, disappears. And, ironically, the only permanent display in the National Museum of China is fashioned in the most impermanent material, wax (fig. 2.11).

The change of displays in the museums on Chang'an Avenue was due only partly to the relaxation of ideological control by the party. Economic considerations played a key role as well. Millions of tourists pour into Tiananmen Square every year. After visiting the Palace Museum, the Great Hall of the People, the Monument to the People's Heroes, and Mao's Mausoleum, they usually spend a couple hours at most in the museum. In order to attract more people, the lengthy display on general history in one comprehensive exhibition had to be modified. Tourists are quickly exhausted in the course of an odyssey through five thousand years of Chinese history. What they want is cultural fast-food, a quick taste of China's glorious long past. And, indeed, there are plenty of McDonald's and KFCs around Tiananmen Square and along Chang'an Avenue. These new adjustments reflect changes in public consumption of culture. The waxen figures in the National Museum fulfill these changing needs well. The waxen figure exhibit attracts more visitors than the other halls.

While the center of Chang'an Avenue has become more and more tourist-oriented since the 1990s, the role formerly played by the Museum of Chinese Revolution and History was relocated to Chang'an Avenue's western extension. Originally built in 1959 to showcase the development of the People's Liberation Army, the Military Museum continued to present the Chinese Communist Party's orthodox narrative of Chinese history. Except for the Weapon Halls, the earliest permanent displays from the 1950s are in today's Hall of the Land Reform Revolutionary Wars, Hall of the Anti-Japanese War, and Hall of the War to Liberate the Whole Country. These three exhibitions represent the birth, growth, and glorious triumph of the army led by the Chinese Communist Party. The exhibition on land reform evolution covers the period from 1927 (the year of the Nanchang Uprising and the birth of the Chinese Workers and Peasants' Red Army) to 1937 (the year Japan invaded China). The Anti-Japanese War exhibit covers the eight years of the Sino-Japanese War, from 1937 to 1945. The War to Liberate the Whole Country exhibition covers the civil war period, from the end of World War II to the founding of the People's Republic of China.[124] All of the three original exhibitions focus on party leadership and the central role it played in achieving victory in wars and progress in modern Chinese history.

The first exhibition displays the glorious process of the development of the Chinese Red Army into a heroic and invincible people's army under the leadership of the party. It highlights the early achievements of Chinese Communists, as embodied in Mao: combining Marxism and Leninism with China's reality, leading people's armies to explore the road to Chinese revolution, establishing guiding principles for the armies, and developing a series of best strategies for China. The first exhibition aims to show that the military struggle led by the party was historically necessary to save the country and its people. The second exhibition displays the history of what is known as the national salvation war led by the Chinese Communist Party, under the united front banner of cooperation with the Nationalists. It highlights the central role that the Chinese Communist Party and the Communist armies played in the war against the Japanese. The third exhibition details the role of the people and the People's Liberation Army in the struggle to overthrow the Nationalist regime and the founding of the People's Republic of China under the leadership of the Chinese Communist Party (fig. 2.12).[125]

In 1988, after four years of preparation, two new exhibitions were added to the Military Museum: the Ancient Wars display and the Wars in Recent History display. The former covers the period from prehistory to 1840, and the latter the period

Fig. 2.12. Interior of the Hall of the Land Reform Revolutionary Wars, Military Museum, 2005. *Photograph by author.*

from the Opium War to 1919. After the general history display was closed in the Museum of Chinese History, these two exhibitions in the Military Museum offered the most comprehensive educational material on ancient Chinese political and military history. After Tiananmen Square was taken over by tourism, Chang'an Avenue, its extension and former servant, became the main location for displaying political power and pedagogical propaganda.

Chapter Three

Collective Creation:
The 1964 Chang'an Avenue Planning

CHINESE COMMUNISTS considered artistic creation a special form of social production, one that generated spiritual and intellectual rather than material and physical products. Deeming individualistic expression bourgeois, the socialist approach to artistic production emphasized collective creation (*jiti chuangzuo*). Architecture, comprising both material and spiritual elements, followed the socialist model.

One of the early steps toward collective creation in art was the enunciation of the mass-oriented principle.[1] In 1942 Mao Zedong delivered his famous "Talks at the Yan'an Forum on Literature and Art" in the wartime Communist capital of Yan'an in northern Shaanxi. He called on artists to be familiar with and serve the people. All arts had class nature, and new Chinese art must serve the majority, that is, the workers, peasants, soldiers, and petty bourgeoisie. Artists were exhorted to go deep into the countryside to learn from the laboring people and to feel what they felt in life and struggle. "There are two standards in artistic criticism," Mao argued, "one is political; the other is artistic. . . . However, in any class society and for any class, political standards are primary, and artistic standards are always secondary." Mass-oriented art had to be both artistically competent and politically correct. Or, in Mao's words, "content and form must achieve a unity. . . . We are against both art with wrong political information and political slogans without artistic power."[2]

Mao's talk represented an important milestone in the party's enduring effort to win intellectuals[3] to its cause, an effort that was a main theme in the relationship between art and politics in China for much of the twentieth century. Although they differed greatly in their attitudes toward tradition, revolution, the West, and modernization, the party and the intellectuals did not represent two antagonistic classes. Many of the party cadres were themselves intellectuals, and most of the intellectuals involved in political struggles about cultural policies were party members.

Mao's "Talks at the Yan'an Forum" provided the theoretical basis for artistic creation and practice in socialist China before and after the founding of the People's Republic of China. In the 1940s many artists shifted their attention from self-expression to guiding mass artistic activities, working mostly among farmers and soldiers.[4] In the

1950s mass-oriented movements to encourage artists to serve the party's line continued in the form of artistic campaigns.[5] Meanwhile, new developments in direct mass participation in art creation appeared. During the Great Leap Forward, workers, peasants, and soldiers picked up their brushes and painted their own works. Artworks were produced with incredible speed and in astonishingly large quantity by both professional artists and the masses.[6] In architectural design, the Anniversary Projects of 1958–59 put both collective creation and mass participation into practice. As in the 1949 construction of the Monument to the People's Heroes and the selection of a national flag and insignia, design proposals for the major buildings of the Anniversary Projects were collected from all over the country. The occasion of the People's Republic of China's tenth anniversary, however, was the first time the nation's leading architects were summoned to Beijing to discuss proposals for a national monument.

The collective creation method, which had a profound impact on architectural practice in socialist China, matured in the construction of the Great Hall. The process started with the request for proposals, called the "collection of schemes" (*fang'an zhengji*) in China. Before that, several general design principles were established by the sponsor, usually the party. After schemes were collected, designers were invited to present design concepts and comment on one another's submissions. After this group meeting, individual designers or institutes worked on their schemes separately again, bearing in mind comments from colleagues and officials. A second or third round of group discussion might be organized. Designers presented their revised proposals, pointing out what they had adopted from others' comments or where they had taken advantage of ideas from others' schemes. No jury selected the finalists. Virtually all professional authorities participated in the design of significant national projects. While competition did occur to some degree when each institute tried to persuade others about the value of its ideas, after the meeting everyone was free to use someone else's ideas in the revised proposal. It was not very hard to reach a common comprehensive design in the end, since by that time all designers were more or less working on the same scheme anyway.

The collective creation approach in architectural design resulted in ambiguous authorship for buildings constructed during the early years of the People's Republic of China. The original design for the executive scheme of the Great Hall was provided by Zhao Dongri and Shen Qi, both from the Beijing Municipal Planning Bureau. The chief architect for the final design, however, was Zhang Bo of the Beijing Municipal Architectural Design Institute. According to architecture professor Chen Zhihua, the elevations in Zhang's final scheme were almost the same as a design provided by the Great Hall design group from Tsinghua University. All Zhang did was erase the big Chinese roofs from the top of the façades in the Tsinghua submission.[7]

While later architects and historians debated about who created which early PRC monuments, the ambiguous authorship seemed only natural and caused no problem in the late 1950s. Individualism was condemned, and the individual was viewed as no more than a single small bolt in a giant socialist machine. Unlike design competitions, the collection of schemes in collective creation was more like a pooling of ideas, producing the raw material for a better comprehensive final product. In most cases, project participants knew one another well. Leading architects often visited one another's studios and exchanged ideas during the design process. They met and criticized one another's draft schemes from time to time before the final evaluation and voting, in which they often participated as well. There was no winner during such a procedure. The voting only produced a base plan for the next step in the design. And the project was ultimately assigned to whichever institute was deemed appropriate according to the socialist general plans, and not necessarily to the one that had provided the base plan.

While architectural design followed a procedure in the collective creative process during the Great Leap Forward, later mass movements in art and architecture took more radical forms. Following the three difficult years of 1959–61, in which natural disasters and political disorder together claimed the lives of tens of millions of Chinese peasants, Mao retreated to the "second line" of Chinese political leadership, and Liu Shaoqi became the chairman of the People's Republic. The following period, between 1961 and 1962, was a time of relaxation. Artists returned from the countryside to schools and institutes, art academies opened again, and normal professional training resumed. However, like the previous Hundred Flowers campaign in 1956 and 1957, this temporary relaxation proved to be just an interlude before another even larger political movement—the Great Proletarian Cultural Revolution.

Triggered by a seemingly minor theoretical debate about opera in 1961, the Cultural Revolution at its apex between 1966 and 1969 brought down not only cultural and artistic institutions but also the whole bureaucratic system. Moderate officials at all levels, from work unit leaders to PRC chairman Liu Shaoqi, were replaced by radicals. In the artistic sphere, Mao's wife, Jiang Qing, launched a movement to revolutionize both traditional Chinese (as in the case of "modern revolutionary Beijing opera") and foreign (as in the case of "modern revolutionary ballet") art forms. The former answered Mao's appeal to "use the ancient to serve the present," and the latter responded to his demand to "use the foreign to serve China." While the mass art movement during the Cultural Revolution became ever more concentrated on the personality cult of Mao, the form it took was similar to the mass-oriented principle articulated in Mao's "Talks at the Yan'an Forum" a quarter of a century earlier, only more extreme, on a larger scale, and more violent.

The 1964 Chang'an Avenue Planning

The 1964 Chang'an Avenue planning was sandwiched between the Great Leap Forward and the Cultural Revolution. It occurred just before the collective creative approach dissolved into mass movements. Initiated in the design and construction of the Monument to the People's Heroes between 1949 and 1958, and matured in the Anniversary Projects of 1958–59, the collective approach in the architectural field reached a zenith in the 1964 Chang'an Avenue planning project. During this round of planning, leading figures in the field from all over the country were summoned to meet in Beijing. Specialists from other disciplines, including sculpture, drama, crafts, architectural construction, and municipal civil engineering, as well as government officials, were invited to participate in a week-long symposium in April. Shortly after the meeting, changes in the political environment led to such a reemphasis on the socialist collective spirit that design institutes in China were largely disbanded. In November 1964 the "design revolution" movement was initiated, architects went to the countryside, and mass participation replaced the professional collective creation approach.

Unlike other projects on Chang'an Avenue before and after, which were more or less part of a general plan for the entire city, the 1964 planning was specifically confined to the avenue. The final scheme was meant to be implemented immediately and completed in 1969 for the twentieth anniversary of the People's Republic of China. As a result, the 1964 planning was more detailed than any other round of the avenue design. Virtually every building on Chang'an Avenue proper was specifically designed, with details of plans and elevations—even when their exact functions were unknown. The 1964 project also offered the only images of a uniform avenue. Its stylistic consistency of façades had never been achieved to such a degree before and would not be possible in the future. Later, when China again had the will and wealth to "complete" Chang'an Avenue, the commercialization of the socialist society turned its façades into a collage.

The 1964 round of planning followed the basic work cycle of the collective approach in architectural design, from scheme collection to individual scheme design to group discussion and criticism to comprehensive schemes. The influence of the collective approach was so far-reaching that its strong imprint persisted even in the competition process for the construction of monuments for the twenty-first century—for instance, the National Grand Theatre constructed between 1998 and 2007.

The Procedure

The 1964 Chang'an Avenue planning was initiated to solve the problem of two "gaps." The two empty sites, one at the northeast corner of the Xidan intersection, the other at the east side of Fangjin Alley, were the legacy of the Anniversary Projects of 1958–59. Among the originally planned sixteen Anniversary Projects, two had been abandoned, and three had been postponed. Preparation for the uncompleted projects, however, had begun in 1958.[8] The site for the Xidan Department Store had been prepared, and old buildings at the northeast corner of the Xidan intersection had been cleared away. At the Palace of Science and Technology site on the east side of Fangjin Alley, the foundation had been constructed in 1959.[9] They left two empty sites on Chang'an Avenue.

In response, Li Fuchun, a vice premier of the State Council, submitted a report to the Party Central Committee in 1963, proposing to "roughly complete" Chang'an Avenue by the twentieth anniversary of the People's Republic of China by finishing what the tenth Anniversary Projects had left unfinished.[10] The Central Committee's response, however, was even more ambitious. It asked not just for "rough completion" but instead for "completion" of the avenue by 1969.[11] The municipal government of Beijing started the planning process immediately, with vice mayor Wan Li assigned to be in charge.[12]

In early 1964 six design units in Beijing were invited by the Beijing Municipal Urban Construction Committee to provide separate designs. They were the Beijing Municipal Planning Bureau, the Beijing Institute of Architectural Design and Research, the Design Institute of Industrial Buildings,[13] Tsinghua University, the Research Institute of Architectural Science, and Beijing Industrial University. At the same time, leading architects from the provinces were summoned to Beijing to work on a collective scheme, called the "comprehensive scheme."

The collection of schemes occurred in the absence of a specific design program, with only a few guiding principles laid out: Chang'an Avenue, together with Tiananmen Square at its center, should be the political center of Beijing; it should "serve the party center, serve production, and serve the laboring people"; and it should be "solemn, beautiful, and modernized" (*zhuangyan, meili, xiandaihua*).[14] The total floorage to be completed on the avenue was about 1.5 million square meters.[15] The two empty sites were to be filled by department stores and office buildings,[16] with no specific stipulations as to function. The avenue was to be filled with buildings, but no one knew what exact purpose these buildings were going to serve. It seems the only reason for the completion of Chang'an Avenue was that Chang'an Avenue needed to be completed.

From January to March, the six design units from Beijing worked on their individual schemes, completing them by the beginning of April. Special design groups were founded in all six institutions. Tsinghua University's group was led by Liang Sicheng, Wu Liangyong, and Liu Xiaoshi. The task became the graduation project for students in the Department of Architectural Engineering class of 1964. They provided two successive schemes by April 6. Simultaneously, a comprehensive scheme by designers from all of the six units and five architects from the provinces—Zhao Shen, Yang Tingbao, Lin Keming, Chen Zhi, and Wang Yuanpei—was also completed before the symposium on April 11–15.[17] All of the previously mentioned architects also served on the discussion board to evaluate other institutes' schemes.

Preparation for the symposium to discuss schemes for the 1964 Chang'an Avenue planning started as early as mid-March.[18] By March 28, the Beijing Municipal People's Committee had prepared a list of seventeen architectural specialists from nine provinces to invite to Beijing. The invitation letter indicated that the symposium would begin on April 10 and last for about a week, and asked each invited architect to come with one or two young specialists. The list of invitees from Beijing included a total of thirty people from sixteen different units: twenty-seven specialists from design units and relevant institutions, plus the heads of three government bureaus—the Municipal Construction Bureau under the National Economic Planning Committee, and the Design Bureau and the Information Bureau, both under the Central Ministry of Construction. The majority of the Beijing specialists, nineteen out of twenty-seven, were from the six design units invited to provide planning schemes. And all five architects from the provinces who had participated in the "comprehensive scheme" were included among the seventeen specialists on the other list.[19] The scheme collection, after all, was not a design competition, and the committee of specialists was not a jury. The purpose of the symposium was to share ideas, make comments on one another's schemes, and come up with a common solution, not to select a winning scheme.

Not all of the specialists were from the field of architecture and city planning. For instance, Liu Kaiqu was a sculptor from the National Society of Chinese Artists, and Lei Guiyuan was from the Central Institute of Arts and Crafts.[20] Another document shows that two writers and six representatives from the Drama Institute of People's Art were also present at the meetings, together with reporters from the News Film Factory and the *Beijing Evening Daily*.[21] The 1964 planning also attracted nationwide attention. At least one provincial institute sent architectural specialists to attend the symposium without invitation. By April 10, seventy-six specialists, thirty-one from fifteen Beijing units and forty-five from the provinces, were ready for the discussions, an inclusive group of top figures, much larger than originally planned.[22]

The meetings of the symposium[23] were held in the conference rooms of the International Hotel.[24] The seventy-six discussants were divided into three groups, each chaired by two leading architects: group one by Liang Sicheng and Yuan Jingshen, group two by Yang Tingbao and Wang Yuanpei, and group three by Zhao Shen and Liu Xiaoshi. Meetings continued for five days, from April 11 to 15. April 11 was originally scheduled for site survey, which, due to the rain, was rescheduled in favor of interior activities. On the morning of April 11, six Beijing design units presented their designs for the two individual buildings at Xidan and Fangjin Alley, and the specialists spent the rest of the morning reviewing the general schemes for Chang'an Avenue. The first round of meetings was held in the afternoon. The three groups met simultaneously in different rooms and took notes summarizing each speaker's main points. The following two days were scheduled for site survey. A further four rounds of meetings took place on April 14 and 15.[25]

Discussion was free and spontaneous, and speeches were interrupted sporadically by comments. The five rounds of group meetings were not organized according to particular planning issues. It seems that the prolonged symposium was an effort to give every participant a chance to speak. Meeting notes show that most people formally spoke only once during the five rounds. Only a few made lengthy speeches twice or more.[26] By the end of the symposium, none of the schemes entirely satisfied any of the discussants, including the "comprehensive plan" by all of the six design units from Beijing and the five specialists from the provinces. This might be the reason why Tsinghua University submitted its third scheme in July 1964, three months after the symposium.[27]

The Schemes

Both the comprehensive scheme and the individual proposals by the six Beijing institutions were completed before April 11, including texts, models, and drawings of plans, elevations, and design details (fig. 3.1). Some planning concepts were shared by all schemes. Tiananmen Square would expand southward. Like the northern end, defined by the long façades of the Great Hall of the People and the museum complex, the southern expansion would also be framed by symmetrical structures on the east and west sides. Unlike the paved, empty northern part of the square, with its vertical flagpole and the Monument to the People's Heroes on the central north-south axis, the southern part of the square was envisioned as a public garden.

All schemes proposed keeping both the Zhengyang Gate, including its Archery Tower, and the south moat of the Inner City. Bridges were planned to connect Tiananmen Square with areas south of the moat. Low buildings along the southern

Fig. 3.1. Models of Chang'an Avenue planning, April 1964. *Courtesy of the School of Architecture Archive, Tsinghua University.*

a. Beijing Institute of Architectural Design and Research.

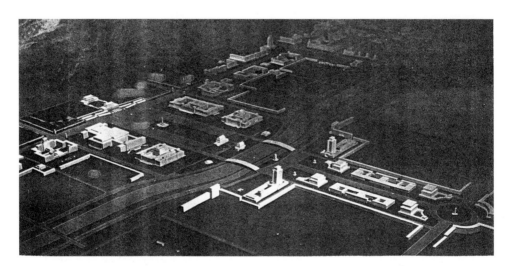

b. Tsinghua University.

c. Beijing Industrial Architectural Design Institute.

d. Beijing Municipal Planning Bureau Design Institute.

e. Beijing Architectural Science Research Institute.

f. Comprehensive Plan.

bank of the moat would be demolished and replaced with multistory slabs punctuated by high-rises, which divided the complex into sections and highlighted the center and ends. Symmetrically arranged, these towers strengthened the north-south axis. Following the shape of the moat and the vanished barbican walls previously connecting the two towers of the Zheng-

yang Gate, the entire complex would form the southern end of Tiananmen Square. Most schemes placed open squares, high-rises, and additional north-south axes symmetrically along Chang'an Avenue, with Tiananmen Square as the center. Open squares were placed at Dongdan and Xidan, the east and west ends of historic Chang'an Avenue. High-rises also highlighted these two historical termini of the avenue, as well as the two ends of Chang'an Avenue proper, Jianguo Gate and Fuxing Gate. All schemes proposed to establish additional north-south axes along the two extant buildings from the tenth Anniversary Projects, the Minority Culture Palace on the north side of West Chang'an Avenue, and the Beijing Railway Station on the south side of East Chang'an Avenue.

One of the major differences between these proposals was the way buildings were organized along the avenue. The Tsinghua University scheme proposed to use the traditional Chinese urban unit of the ward (*lifang*)[28] as the paradigm for government complexes. Buildings were grouped around central courtyards closed in all four directions. In contrast to a traditional walled ward, however, the main façade of the complex faced Chang'an Avenue, while the main entrance to the central courtyard was located in the back (fig. 3.2). Schemes by the Beijing Municipal Planning Bureau and the Beijing Municipal Architectural Design Institute, on the other hand, proposed linear solid blocks lining both sides of the avenue (fig. 3.3).[29] While the former followed a traditional Chinese system in the organization of urban space, the latter avoided the need to demolish a large number of old courtyard houses along the avenue.

The difference had more to do with the spatial concept of the urban streets than a formal approach to individual buildings. While solid blocks turned the urban streets into linear spaces framed by façades, the courtyards extended the street space into a series of side spaces. The former emphasized the unidimensional movement of the street; the latter softened the long linear street with many static spaces among the buildings. All of the schemes proposing solid blocks formed long, continuous façades on both sides of the avenue. The Tsinghua scheme, on the other hand, was more nuanced. In this scheme

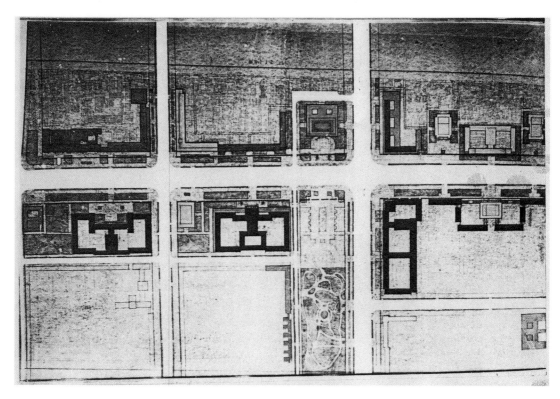

Fig. 3.2

Fig. 3.3

large courtyard complexes (solid buildings encompassing a void space) alternated with small pavilion-like single structures on green fields (void space encompassing a solid building) on the south side of the avenue—a yin façade, since it was mostly in shade.[30] This approach, according to the Tsinghua designers, would allow more sunshine in the space and at street level. During the symposium discussion, the alternation of large building complexes and green fields with small buildings was supported by some for the richness of scene it would create, but opposed by others for its interruption of a unified avenue façade.[31]

When the discussion turned to the reconstruction of Tiananmen Square, three different approaches were proposed. The first was known as the "open" (*fang*) approach. Proposed by Tsinghua University and the Beijing Municipal Planning Bureau, it opened and extended the square to the southern moat of the Inner City by a series of bridges. It called for the construction of buildings to the south of the moat to make Tiananmen Square a huge elongated courtyard, with Tiananmen Tower screening the north, the Great Hall and a new structure to its south screening the west, and the museum complex and a new building to its south screening the east. Both Zhengyang Gate and its Archery Tower would be inside Tiananmen Square.

The second strategy for the reconstruction of the square was described as the "closed" (*shou*) approach. Proposed by the Architectural Science Research Institute, it would stretch the two new structures to the south of the Great Hall and the museum complex into the square to form its southern border. In this approach, the north-south dimension of the square would be much shorter, and the only monument inside would be the Monument to the People's Heroes.

The third option for the square was known as the "half-closed" approach. Proposed by the Beijing Industrial Design Institute and the Beijing Municipal Architectural Design Institute, it was somewhere between the "open" and the "closed" alternatives. This approach proposed that the two structures to the south of the Great Hall and the museum complex only partially screen the south of Tiananmen Square and that Zhengyang Gate serve as the central section of its southern boundary.

Locating the two new structures thus played a key role in the different approaches to the completion of Tiananmen Square. If the façades of the two new buildings were in line with the Great Hall and the museum complex, the square was "open" (fig. 3.4); if they completely blocked Zhengyang Gate on the north-south axis, the square was "closed"; if they protruded into the square but still left Zhengyang Gate unblocked, the square was "half-closed" (fig. 3.5).

In the design of the individual structures, the Bei-

Fig. 3.4. The "open" Tian'anmen Square, drawing of Chang'an Avenue plan, Tsinghua University, April 1964. *Courtesy of the School of Architecture Archive, Tsinghua University.*

Fig. 3.5a. The "half-closed" Tiananmen Square, model of Chang'an Avenue, comprehensive scheme, April 1964. *Courtesy of the School of Architecture Archive, Tsinghua University.*

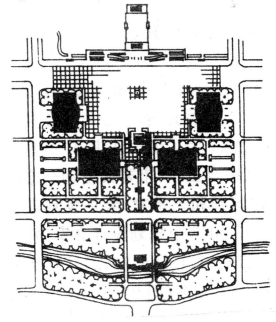

Fig. 3.5b. Mao Ziyao and others, the "closed" Tiananmen Square, drawing for Tiananmen Square reconstruction plan, 1956. *Reproduction from* Chang'anjie: Guoqu, xianzai, weilai, 66. *Courtesy of Zheng Guangzhong.*

jing Municipal Institute submission emphasized horizontality and used mostly flat roofs, while the Tsinghua University scheme emphasized vertical elements on elevations with towers and more complex roofs. By the standards of 1960s China, the Tsinghua schemes were considered more political, due to their "heavy" style in individual building forms, while the Beijing Institute schemes were more "modernized," with their simplified façades and overall lightness of architectural design (fig. 3.6).

Fig. 3.6a. The "light" style,
model by Beijing Institute.
Courtesy of the School of Architecture Archive, Tsinghua University.

Fig. 3.6b. The "heavy" style,
model by Tsinghua University;
April 1964. *Courtesy of the School
of Architecture Archive, Tsinghua
University.*

The Symposium Discussions

The three-day discussion meetings addressed both specific design problems and general theoretical issues. While old categories from the 1950s, such as "national," "modern," "content," and "form," continued into the 1964 discussion, new discourses gave these terms new meanings and theoretical dimensions.

The Modern and the Solemn. As one of the main requirements in the guiding principle "solemn, beautiful, and modernized," the word "modern" was frequently mentioned in the group discussions. The meaning of "modern" in the context of the 1964 planning, however, was different from that of the 1950s. In the 1950s "modern" was defined as a complement to "national," a criticism of formalism. In the 1964 discussion "modern" was treated as the opposite of "political." Politics required solemn and heavy architecture, whereas "modern" created light forms.[32] While "political" had been an integral term in the 1950s discussion on form and content, it was now simplified to mean "formal in appearance." "Modern" was simplified too. Rid of much of its previous ideological baggage, "modern" as a formal quality now proscribed decoration and celebrated the new: new technology, new structure, and new material for a new form.[33]

The taboo on "modern" was over. Liang Sicheng, who had proposed "Chinese, Western, old, and new" in the late 1950s as new terms for stylistic analysis,[34] now argued that the structural principles, construction method, design process, and relationship between form and structure in traditional Chinese architecture were very modern.[35] Liang had been trained in the American version of the Beaux-Arts architectural system, and his writing between the 1930s and early 1950s was characterized by the reconstruction of ancient Chinese architectural history focusing on the rationalist idea of structural integrity.[36] In these articles Liang argued that Chinese architecture was a living tradition whose structural system had matured in the Han dynasty. This system, according to Liang, was both uniquely Chinese and universal. It was uniquely Chinese due to its successful solution of various functional problems through similar and simple architectural means, such as individual units, courtyards, and roofed corridors. It was universal due to its structural integrity: the bracket system was the result of the ancient craftsmen's search for suitable architectural form for the material wood, and the beautiful curves of traditional roofs were attributed not to arbitrary aesthetic taste but to the natural and logical outcome of the inner wooden structure. In other words, form followed function and structure. Chinese architectural tradition was also modern because it was scientific: the principle of the Chinese wooden frame was the same as that of the modern steel frame or frame structure of reinforced concrete; the application of the dimensional unit in both architectural complexes and individual structures by the ancient Chinese was the forerunner of the modular system in modern architecture; and the bracket system and the mortise-and-tenon wooden joint were the responses of the traditional Chinese wooden structure to the antiseismic requirements of architecture.

The term "modern" as used in the 1964 planning discussion carried a positive meaning. While the political aspects of architecture were mainly understood as attaching political meanings to structures, "modern" meant leaving structure as an independent expressive entity. Political character implied arbitrary symmetry, heavy walls, centralized images, and an exaggerated scale of façades, while modern character required asymmetry, open walls, and human scale in façades.

As the formal associations of "solemn" and "modern" seemed incompatible, instead of trying to achieve both, the discussion was shifted to focusing on which sections of the avenue were to be solemn and which were to be lively. Most people agreed that sections closer to Tiananmen Square should be more political and thus solemn and heavy, while sections nearer to Fuxing Gate and Jianguo Gate, the western and eastern ends of Chang'an Avenue proper, should be lighter and provide more street life.[37] Some specialists, however, argued that all of the avenue proper should be solemn because there was only one Chang'an Avenue in China. Zheng Yihou, a young architect recently graduated from Tongji University in Shanghai, argued,

> Chang'an Avenue extends thirty-five kilometers east to west. Chang'an Avenue proper is just the central section of it, seven kilometers out of thirty-five. Is it necessary to further divide this one-fifth into three different sections? The extension east of Jianguo Gate could be light and lively, with more residential buildings. So could the extension west of Fuxing Gate.
>
> Considering the entire city, there are many commercial areas north of Dongdan and Xidan. The Front Gate area has many too. Is it necessary for Chang'an Avenue to be commercial? Urban streets should be differentiated functionally in general plan [like this]. Some are more commercial and lively; some should be political and heavy.[38]

Although not everyone agreed with Zheng, there was little question about maintaining the solemnity of Tiananmen Square and the central sections of Chang'an Avenue. As for the three approaches to complete the square, most speakers favored the closed approach during the first meetings on April 11. They argued that the square was already big enough, with its 500-meter width. If the length was extended to the south of the moat, the empty and elongated space would look more like a wide street than a square. After the field survey conducted during the following two days, however, many specialists changed their minds and voted for the open approach. The east-west dimension of the square was so wide, they concluded, that if it was closed or half-closed, it would lose spatial depth due to the perspective effect and look too squat from the Tiananmen rostrum.[39]

The so-called "open," "closed," and "half-closed" Tiananmen Squares were really about the north-south axis of Beijing. While both the open and half-closed approaches would keep the continuity of the north-south axis, the closed approach would block the axis at the southern boundary of the square. The form of Tiananmen Square was considered mainly from the perspective of the Tiananmen rostrum, from which Communist leaders gazed down during national celebrations. During the discussion, Yin Haiyun, an invited architect from Hubei Province, said,

> Looking from Tiananmen Tower, the north-south axis is more important than the east-west axis. The north-south axis is really there. It conforms to the Chinese tradition and should be more solemn. It should continue to Yongding Gate and should not be closed. Zhengyang Gate and its Archery Tower are on the axis, and [the axis] should not be treated lightly. Front Gate Street will not look solemn and will be powerless if used as a commercial area. The north-south axis should be taken especially seriously.[40]

Although the two new structures to the south of the Great Hall and the Museum of Chinese Revolution and History played a key role in defining Tiananmen Square and the north-south axis, their specific functions were still open for discussion. Most schemes put the National Theatre next to the Great Hall and the Youth Palace next to the museum complex. The arrangement of the Youth Palace met with little objection. Youth represented the future and should have a place in the political center. The placement of the National Theatre in Tiananmen Square, however, was challenged. Some believed that the solemnity of the square might be ruined by the bustling atmosphere and busy traffic of the theatre.[41] Instead they proposed that the Science Palace or a national library would be more in tune with the solemn atmosphere of the square.[42] Others argued that the National Theatre was not merely a place for entertainment but a symbol of the new socialist culture of China. Since national leaders often invited visiting foreign leaders to the theatre after formal meetings, placing the new theatre next to the Great Hall where those meetings were held would be convenient for diplomatic activities. It could be a perfect complement to the National Grand Banquet Hall inside the Great Hall.[43] Yet others supported the National Theatre from a different perspective. They argued that Tiananmen Square was already too serious. The square became virtually lifeless at night, being entirely enclosed by political structures. Architecture to offer more night activities was needed.[44]

The monumental emptiness of Tiananmen Square today is the product of the effort made in 1964 to maintain solemnity. Many believed then that it was impossible to keep vehicles off of such a large empty surface, and the symposium seriously discussed public transportation inside of Tiananmen Square. Even with the closed approach, the north-south dimension of the square would be almost a kilometer across. Dividing Tiananmen Square to create vehicle routes and pedestrian areas, however, was eventually rejected by the majority in order to maintain the solemn character of the political center. Whether or not to save Zhengyang Gate and its Archery Tower was also debated. Although all schemes kept the twin towers in the planning models, alternative possibilities were offered as well.

Like the debate over an open versus a closed Tiananmen Square, the discussion of the redline or required street width of Chang'an Avenue was also about the scale of a symbolic space. The original requirement of 120 meters was too wide for some and too modest for others. While practical designers proposed a redline width of 100 meters, wide enough for a soccer field, more ambitious planners dreamed of the glory of the Tang dynasty, when the capital Chang'an accommodated grand boulevards more than 200 meters wide. They argued that the capital of New China also deserved such a monumental scale. If the street looked empty, then low buildings for exhibitions, commercial services, or rest areas with additional sidewalks could be added between the main traffic lanes and the monumental buildings on the two sides of the sections west of Xidan and east of Dongdan. While the central section between Dongdan and Xidan should remain pure, monumental, and solemn, these peripheral sections could be livelier and fulfill the everyday needs of common citizens.[45]

To highlight the monumentality and solemnity of central Tiananmen Square, the skyline of the avenue's façades would need to be relatively flat, with high-rises only at some key intersections, such as Dongdan, Xidan, and the two ends of the avenue proper, Jianguo Gate and Fuxing Gate. Sections closer to Tiananmen Square would be more solemn, and those farther away from the center could be livelier. There was some debate over the length of the solemn central sections. Some agreed with Zheng Yihou that all seven kilometers of Chang'an Avenue proper should be a solemn street. However, most speakers favored a solemn central section of 3.5 kilometers, with Xidan and Dongdan, located at roughly the midpoints of West and East Chang'an Avenue proper, as the turning points for the change of street atmosphere. A third option proposed to restrict the solemn area to the 1.5-kilometer stretch from Nanchizi to Nanchang Street, only about three times the width of Tiananmen Square.

According to this last proposal, only buildings defining Tiananmen Square would be solemn. The Great Hall of the People and the museum complex were already there in 1964, and the northern façade of the avenue between Nanchizi and Nanchang

Street was the red wall of the Imperial City. Thus this proposal was the equivalent of saying that all future construction on Chang'an Avenue should be lively. In fact, this was what Lei Guiyuan, a professor from the Central Institute of Arts and Crafts, had openly advocated when he said that Chang'an Avenue should become the "socialist Tianqiao."[46] Tianqiao was a commercial street located to the south of the Zhengyang Gate, where artisans, folk musicians, actors, and poor artists gathered and performed during the late Qing and Republican eras. Lei wanted Chang'an Avenue to be the entertainment center for the common people.

Content and Form: The Practical and the Symbolic. In the 1964 symposium discussion, architectural content, a widely debated theoretical term full of ideological associations in the 1950s, was reduced to building function. Most discussions focused on whether or not Chang'an Avenue should be filled with government offices. Supporters argued that streets should be specialized in big cities such as Beijing, and that some streets should be political, quiet, and solemn. Those in search of bustling nightlife could go to other streets.[47] Others argued that, without commercial, service, and entertainment buildings, Chang'an Avenue would be totally lifeless at night. In this view, old urban spaces and structures characteristic of Beijing, such as the Dongdan vegetable market, the circus, and Chang'an Theatre, should be preserved.[48]

The ideological dimension of architectural content resurfaced in the principle of the "three serves": serving the capital, serving the center, and serving production. Among the three, the requirement for Chang'an Avenue to serve production was most specific and problematic. Most specialists opposed putting factories on Chang'an Avenue. Chen Zhi, a senior architect from Shanghai, proposed,

> The "three serves" principle should be followed in all cities, but not necessarily on Chang'an Avenue proper. Otherwise, if we have to put a couple of factories on Chang'an Avenue, they would have to be factories for light equipment [since these do not produce smoke]. Then we have to consider the problem of discordant noise. It's hard to accommodate. We'd better not be so formalist.
>
> Chang'an Avenue should not be filled with office buildings. Nor should it have too many residential buildings. It should serve the needs of the majority of the people. We should think more about how to organize life well on Chang'an Avenue, balancing commercial, cultural entertainment, residential, and office buildings. We also need some teahouses. It's good to keep the Chang'an Theatre.[49]

In terms of architectural form, no one was even slightly pleased with any of the schemes. This was strange, since at least half of the symposium discussants had

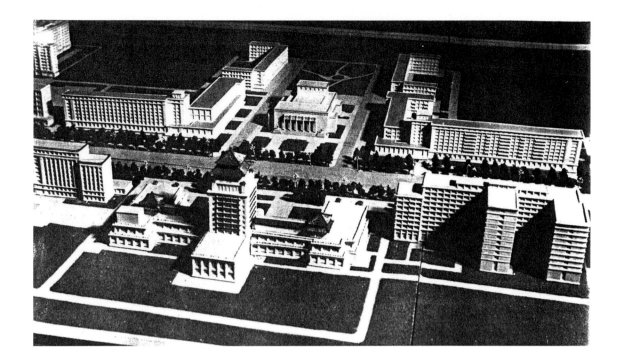

Fig. 3.7. The axes in the model of the comprehensive scheme, April 1964. *Courtesy of the School of Architecture Archive, Tsinghua University.*

directly participated in designing at least one of the schemes.[50] The similarity and axiality of the individual structures came in for the most criticism. All of the buildings shared similar axial, symmetrical, and I-shaped plans. So many buildings on the avenue had their own north-south axes that many discussants worried that the central north-south axis along Tiananmen Square might be weakened (fig. 3.7). In addition to the ground plans, the participants criticized the scale of some of the buildings, finding them unnecessarily large. Chen Zhi maintained that architecture on Chang'an Avenue should be "smaller rather than bigger, shorter rather than longer, and lower rather than higher."[51] Finally, the indiscriminate application of glazed tile in eave decorations was also problematic.[52]

All of the design criticisms in the 1964 planning seemed to refer to the Ten Great Buildings completed five years earlier. In discussing the tripartite principle of "solemn, beautiful, and modernized," Huang Kangyu, an architect from Hubei Province, stated,

> Beijing is China's capital and has now also become the center for world revolution. It needs to be solemn. But "solemn" does not mean "precise symmetry." Symmetry should be considered for the overall perspective of the general plan. Many schemes, however,

emphasize the symmetry of each individual building. Seriousness is excessive, and liveliness is not enough. There is a lack of "revolutionary enthusiastic spirit." Buildings are of different status and should be symmetrical or unsymmetrical accordingly. They should work together to strengthen the central north-south axis. Regarding "beauty," the atmosphere along the seven-kilometer-long avenue should be varied. Having everything serious is not beautiful. It's not welcoming first to fill the avenue with office buildings, then to plant several rows of trees. We'd better have some display windows to make the atmosphere livelier. "Beauty" entails variation in color, shape, and mode. As to "modernization," I believe it is more important because it reflects our new society and the new spirit of the Mao Zedong era. Some buildings have new structures and new plans, but look like stone and brick after artistic treatment. They are not new. "New" means new appearance. National style can only be achieved on the basis of the new.[53]

Toward the end of the symposium, discussions about content became more practical. During the third round of meetings on April 14, Liang finally asked, "Do we really need so much floor area? One and one-half million square meters! Each ministry needs ten to twenty thousand square meters. Even if only one million were for government offices, the floor area would still be enough for at least fifty ministries. Will that many ministries move to Chang'an Avenue?" He also complained, "I think this is really a tough task.[54] We are not clear about what will be on Chang'an Avenue. The character of a street evolves by itself; it is not made up by designers."[55]

Liang was not the only one who was baffled by the request to complete the avenue on such a large scale during such a short time. Cheng Shifu, a city planer and landscape architect from Beijing, said, "I heard it was required that Chang'an Avenue be completed by the twentieth anniversary. That means we need to demolish 600,000 to 700,000 square meters of old buildings and construct 2,000,000 square meters of new ones. It probably won't be accomplished. Why not proceed step by step and be more flexible? Even if money, manpower, and material were not at issue, Chang'an Avenue still needs to be completed section by section."[56]

Money was an issue. The official cost estimate for Chang'an Avenue construction was ¥300 per square meter. In the 1960s the cost for most architectural projects in China was less than ¥100 per square meter. China was still poor. Some asked why the avenue should set a bad example as a luxury in open disregard of the poor average living standard? The answer was symbolic significance. There was only one Chang'an Avenue in the whole country, and the Chinese people wanted a great thoroughfare to embody the glorious achievements of the motherland.[57]

Whether to complete Chang'an Avenue section by section or once and for all was also debated. Some maintained that it could be "roughly completed," saving old buildings in good condition, fixing those still usable, and filling in gaps with some new monuments. Some proposed that the standard of Chang'an Avenue construction could be lowered and the scale reduced. In the future, the buildings could be replaced by higher and grander ones, or new layers could be added, as the economy permitted.[58] Others argued that, since Chang'an Avenue was so important, every building on it should be top quality. It was better to leave the site empty than to fill it with second-rate buildings.

The Chang'an Avenue of 1964 was serving the city well. Most of the buildings were in good condition, and the street was already full of life. After the site survey on April 13, Tang Pu, a senior architect from Chongqing, observed that the current avenue was flourishing, and that it was sad to demolish all of the old buildings—most of which were good— and erase the prosperous traditional way of living. He proposed moving the National Theatre to Dongdan and making Xidan a "People's Entertainment Park" to preserve the thriving atmosphere on the avenue.[59]

The rationale for reconstructing Chang'an Avenue was purely symbolic, driven by its political significance. The avenue, together with Tiananmen Square, was the center of Beijing and China. It was the route and service corridor connecting Tiananmen Square with the rest of the capital. If Tiananmen Square was the political heart, then Chang'an Avenue was the main artery. Most important diplomatic activities and events took place in or around the square. When significant visitors (especially political leaders from other countries) traveled from the international airport northeast of Beijing to the National Guest House, located just north of the West Chang'an Avenue extension, Chang'an Avenue was on their route, a must-see. From the avenue, foreign visitors received their first impressions of the city and its urban space. For this reason, the east end of Chang'an Avenue proper, Jianguo Gate, was considered the "start," and Fuxing Gate on the west side, the "end." Several schemes therefore designed structures at these two points as gates, following the concept of the traditional *que*-style gate tower. Especially popular during the powerful Han dynasty, these symbolic gates, with two symmetrical and often freestanding towers, framed passageways and marked transitions to sacred sites. Such structures would emphasize the ritual nature of passage along the avenue.

Chang'an Avenue was meant to display the superiority of socialism to the world. Even the functional and stylistic considerations of its different sections were symbolic. Some suggested that West Chang'an Avenue should be national, while its eastern counterpart should be "international," meaning that, as Huang Kangyu had said, "Chang'an Avenue should serve not only the Chinese but also the proletarian and laboring people of the whole world."[60]

While most of those at the symposium emphasized the necessity of not weakening the north-south axis of Beijing, Dai Nianci, future head of the Ministry of Construction, argued for a more significant status for Chang'an Avenue:

> I heard that the main railway station for Beijing will be at Yongding Gate [the former southern gate of the Outer City]. It seems that this is to strengthen the central north-south axis. In the past, emperors lived in the Forbidden City. Other people traversed this north-south axis when they came to see the emperors. It was really superlative and full of imperial atmosphere. However, today things are the opposite. We have already established Chang'an Avenue as the main axis, where the large-scale, significant buildings are all located. This is the reality. Only on paper does Front Gate Street form the north-south axis. If we really want it to be an axis, then the main buildings should be on Front Gate Street instead of on Chang'an Avenue. Then the East and West Chang'an Avenues we are discussing today would be totally different.[61]

Dai's point was clear. Chang'an Avenue was already the de facto main axis of the socialist capital, not a continuation of the imperial axis, and therefore should be more important.

The Tsinghua Design: An Expansion of Imperial Tiananmen Square

The three schemes provided by the Department of Architectural Engineering at Tsinghua University exemplified the progression of the planning design. While the two earlier schemes had only sketchy drawings and models and a brief textual introduction, the third proposal, created after the symposium discussion, was very detailed and responded specifically to the comments and criticisms raised during the meetings.

The Tsinghua designers emphasized the Chinese tradition and political significance of the avenue from the very beginning. The introduction of their first scheme maintained that, as the center of the Chinese capital and the locus of national administration and cultural concentration, Chang'an Avenue and Tiananmen Square should represent the wisdom and legacy of all Chinese nationalities. The planning, it read, should "be commensurate with our cultural tradition of five thousand years, our great nation of 600 million people, our great party, and the significant status of our country in the international Communist movement. In a word, it should match the great Mao Zedong era. . . . Chang'an Avenue architecture should express the spirit of our time and national style, and be mostly solemn and grand in form, with some lively buildings only as accompanying elements." The first draft also proposed to break

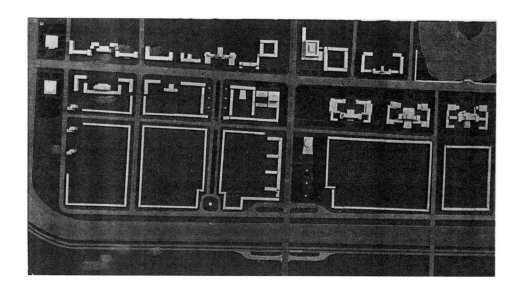

the common spatial image of the street with large green fields separating monumental buildings.[62]

The first draft laid down most of the major principles found in later Tsinghua schemes. First, Tiananmen Square was the focal point of the planning. The sections of the avenue closest to Tiananmen Square enjoyed significant political status and had a

Fig. 3.8. Model of Chang'an Avenue for the first planning scheme by Tsinghua University, February 1964. *Courtesy of the School of Architecture Archive, Tsinghua University.*

more solemn architectural style. The most significant sections were a T-shaped region that encompassed the section of Chang'an Avenue between Dongdan and Xidan, and a north-south section of Front Gate Street (then also known as Zhengyang Gate Street) from Tiananmen Square in the north to Zhushikou in the south. Street width, building forms, and planting embellishments were to be reduced in other sections of the thoroughfare. Secondly, Tiananmen Square would extend across the moat. Buildings around the square would be politically significant, such as a memorial hall for international Communist leaders, a museum of the history of the workers' movement, a workers' cultural palace, or a national theatre. Thirdly, the convention of lining both sides of the street with façades would be abandoned. Instead, buildings would be organized in groups and interspersed with large green fields, in a more traditional Chinese style. Buildings on the north side of the street could be taller and larger, while buildings on the south side would be spaced farther apart to allow more sunshine into the avenue (fig. 3.8). More green fields were needed for mass gatherings. The moat would be expanded to create a scenic view onto Tiananmen Square.[63]

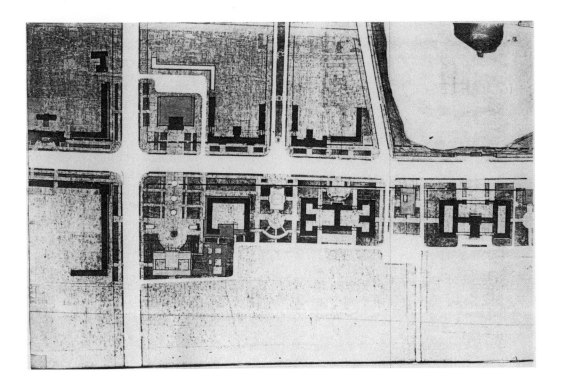

Fig. 3.9. Drawing of Chang'an Avenue for the second planning scheme by Tsinghua University, April 1964. *Courtesy of the School of Architecture Archive, Tsinghua University.*

The introduction to the second draft proposal mostly repeated that of the first, with two major differences: Chang'an Avenue's status as the east-west axis of Beijing was acknowledged (fig. 3.9), with Front Gate Street as its north-south counter-part;[64] and the reference to planning difficulty due to the lack of specific requirements was deleted. The cautious notes in the first draft, which suggested that some responsible units do further research and come up with a planning program to provide a more scientific base for planning,[65] disappeared in the second draft, although the underlying problem was left unsettled. The uncertainty of architectural content, that is, the specific functions of the avenue's buildings, was partly resolved in the third scheme, in which architectural content became the first topic of discussion for each planning area.

Completed after the symposium, the textual explanation of the third Tsinghua scheme was much longer than the previous two. The preface upheld the main design intentions criticized during the symposium meetings and expressed these more clearly in detail, including the stylistic strategies needed to achieve the hierarchical spatial organization demarcated by the T-shaped central area; the alternation of grouped complexes of government buildings and small service structures on green fields; the completion of Tiananmen Square and the strengthening of the north-south axis, with high-rise buildings screening the south bank of the moat; and the specific locations of the green urban areas. The total floorage to be constructed would be two million square meters on an area of 120 hectares. An estimated six hundred thousand square meters of extant buildings would have to be demolished.[66]

The three chapters of the textual explanation incorporated some of the suggestions made during the symposium discussions but mostly responded to criticisms raised by specialists in defense of their main design concepts. Defense of the open approach occupied about half of the "Tiananmen Square" chapter. The Tsinghua designers argued that the first thing to consider in the design of the square was its political significance. Although the square proposed by the closed approach would have been the largest in the world, able to hold 550,000 people, it was still not large enough for a country of 600 million people with a potential need for mass gatherings of one million participants. The political function, the Tsinghua text maintained, was the prerequisite, and the artistic composition was the tool. When a new situation raised an unprecedented question about new architectural content, the tool was to serve the aim. The designers believed that such an open square space best met the spirit of the new era and the taste of the masses.[67]

The "Chang'an Avenue" chapter provided a detailed list of the ten extant and seventy-five new buildings to be constructed on Chang'an Avenue and Tiananmen Square. Five of them, the Tiananmen Tower, the Monument to the People's Heroes, the Zhengyang Gate, the Archery Tower, and an unnamed future monument, were in the square on the north-south axis. Eighteen were around Tiananmen Square and along Front Gate Street, including the Great Hall, the museum complex, the Youth Palace south of the Great Hall, an unnamed building south of the museum complex, two service buildings, two residential buildings, two hotels, two commercial buildings, and six office buildings. Sixty-two out of the eighty-five buildings were on Chang'an Avenue, with thirty-one on each side of the square. Among the thirty-one buildings on West Chang'an Avenue, only thirteen were office buildings; among the thirty-one buildings on East Chang'an Avenue, only ten were identified for government use. Apparently, the symposium's criticism that there were too many office buildings on the avenue had been taken to heart to some degree in the revised scheme.[68] The numbers were misleading. Because the Tsinghua scheme alternated large office buildings with small service buildings on the south side of the avenue, the number of buildings did not reflect the real proportion of construction allocated to different uses. In fact, in terms of actual floor area, office buildings occupied 536,900 square meters of the total listed construction area of 830,200 square meters on East Chang'an Avenue; on West Chang'an Avenue, the new construction allocated to office buildings was 465,700 square meters out of a total of 795,700.[69] Chang'an Avenue, especially the section between Xidan and Dongdan, was still predominantly occupied by government office buildings as conceived in 1964.

The organization of buildings in groups around central courtyards was also defended. The primary purpose of courtyard organization, wrote the Tsinghua designers, was to "strengthen the prevailing power of the central area [by enlarging its individual building complexes]." Central courtyards offered enough space for exterior activities. In addition, courtyard organization allowed flexibility for the area division of a building complex. Each office building complex had a total floorage of about 60,000 to 80,000 square meters, which could house two to three government ministries. Larger ministries could occupy a complete complex, while smaller ones could share a complex with others. The disadvantage of using courtyard organization for building complexes, the Tsinghua designers admitted, was that they occupied larger site areas, so more old structures would have to be demolished.[70]

In response to criticism that there was too much axial symmetry in the plan and in individual architectural designs, the third Tsinghua scheme argued that, historically, symmetry had produced great architecture and cities. Although considered rigid and mechanical by many, symmetry was the major traditional feature of Beijing's layout. Historical Chang'an Avenue had many symmetrically arranged pair structures, including Dongdan and Xidan, the East and West Chang'an archways, East and West Three-Arch Gates, and Chang'an Left and Right Gates. However, no one felt they were rigid. On the contrary, the Tsinghua designers argued, without the general symmetry, Beijing would lose its power of order.[71]

As the focus of the textual introduction, the "Chang'an Avenue" chapter explained the design of some key junctures in detail—for instance, the squares at Xidan, Dongdan, Jianguo Gate, and Fuxing Gate. The last two sections were designed as the new "gates" marking the two ends of Chang'an Avenue proper (fig. 3.10). Structures framing the avenue at these junctures evoked the traditional gate towers (*que*), which had impressed so many "barbarians" during the Han and Tang dynasties. Chang'an Avenue was conceived of as a showcase mainly for foreign visitors. The text explained,

In order to highlight the central thoroughfare and make Chang'an Avenue more complete and exact, this scheme treats the Jianguo Gate and Fuxing Gate areas as "gates." However, since their statuses are different, the designs are varied too. Jianguo Gate is the real "gate" that welcomes foreign visitors from the airport in the east and has a large open area of green field on its east side, while Fuxing Gate is actually an "exit" followed by buildings. For this reason, the design emphasizes Jianguo Gate and makes it grander, while Fuxing Gate is plain in comparison.[72]

If the progressiveness of Chang'an Avenue, that is, the modernity in Chinese architecture, was conceived under a Western gaze, a conception common to both designers and politicians, the specific planning forms carried on Chinese conventions in political urban experiences. The epilogue of the textual explanation for the third Tsinghua scheme

Fig. 3.10. Design of Jianguo Gate area in the model of the third Tsinghua scheme, June 1964. *Courtesy of the School of Architecture Archive, Tsinghua University.*

criticized the version of modern architecture unduly based on technological advancement and promoted the requirements of ideology and the life experiences of the people as the defining aspects of socialist design. The Tsinghua designers wrote,

We believe that the meaning of "modernization" is broad, including both the embodiment of the spirit of the times and the application of advanced technology. There is no question that the construction of Chang'an Avenue should widely involve new technologies; however, the application of new technologies is not the aim but the tool to achieve "more, faster, better, and more economically.". . . To equate the spirit of the times with new technologies represents an insufficient understanding. The decisive factors for the artistic image of Chang'an Avenue are specific ideological content and the requirements of everyday life—for instance, Chang'an Avenue's significant status as the political center of the capital, the experience of the people, the spirit of the times and conventional habits, the embodiment of national culture, and so on.[73]

Although the text emphasized the spirit of the times, the spatial experience indicated by the plans and models of the third Tsinghua scheme more resembled imperial urban space. To some extent, the proposed avenue in the Tsinghua design was an expansion of the T-shaped Imperial Tiananmen Square. Walled and gated during the Ming and Qing dynasties, the square was defined by the Tiananmen Tower in the north, the Great Qing Gate (renamed Gate of China after 1911) in the south, Left Chang'an Gate in the east, and Right Chang'an Gate in the west.[74] With the destruction of its defining structures, including the Thousand-Pace Corridor and all surrounding gates except for Tiananmen, and the expansion of the square into an open public space, the T-shaped Imperial Tiananmen Square disappeared during the 1950s. The ghost of this imperial space, however, persisted in the schemes for the 1964 Chang'an Avenue planning.

The textual explanation of the third Tsinghua scheme has a special part dedicated to Front Gate Street, which was not originally included in the 1964 planning. The ill-proportioned T-shape composed of historic Chang'an Avenue and the expanded Tiananmen Square can easily be noticed from the site drawings. The horizontal (east-west) arm was too long, and the vertical (north-south) arm was too short, a proportion very different from the vanished Imperial Tiananmen Square, which had a long vertical arm defined by the Thousand-Pace Corridor. By adding Front Gate Street to the central T-shaped area, however, the proportions of the new central area were very similar to Imperial Tiananmen Square. In the extended T-shape of the plan, Dongdan and Xidan were comparable to the Left and Right Chang'an Gates, Jianguo Gate and Fuxing Gate were similar in status to the East and West Three-Arch Gates, and Zhushikou was comparable to the Great Qing Gate in the vanished T-shaped Imperial Tiananmen Square. Together, they formed a new administrative center, just as the tripartite Tiananmen Square group had functioned during the Ming and Qing dynasties.

The Tsinghua scheme was not the only one that proposed a T-shaped central administrative area. The Tsinghua designers, however, stated it most clearly and adhered to it most steadfastly. In fact, as long as Tiananmen Square was retained as the center of the plan and historic Chang'an Avenue as its extensions, a T-shaped central area was formed. The Tsinghua scheme, however, strengthened this T-shaped political space by emphasizing its architectural hierarchy and defining its ends in a more recogniz-

Fig. 3.11. The T-shaped
Chang'an Avenue, model for
the third scheme, Tsinghua
University, June 1964. *Courtesy
of the School of Architecture
Archive, Tsinghua University.*

able form. From this viewpoint, the open approach
to the development of Tiananmen Square can be
understood as the effect of a "T-shape complex." A
Tiananmen Square of four equal sides, as proposed
by the closed or half-closed plans, would not have
been in harmony with a prolonged vertical arm in
the T-shape (fig. 3.11).

Similarities between the vanished T-shaped Imperial Tiananmen Square and the
new T-shaped central area in the 1964 Chang'an Avenue planning existed not only on
a formal level but also in terms of ceremonial functions. The time-honored symbolic
difference between left (east) and right (west) was still alive. Some specialists, for

instance, suggested that the architecture of West Chang'an Avenue should be mainly national (political), while buildings on East Chang'an Avenue should be international (commercial).

The Collective Approach, the Avant-Garde, and Architectural Modernization

The collective approach in architectural design, as exemplified in the 1964 Chang'an Avenue planning, was an artistic policy meant to combat individualism. As enunciated by Mao in his 1942 Yan'an speech, art was to serve the people, and not to remain merely a form of personal expression or a means of pursuing individual artistic ideals. If this social and political policy applied to "pure" art forms such as painting, sculpture, and literature, then it applied even more emphatically to the more practical art forms of architecture and urban planning. The collective approach also offered China a way to reach fast, comprehensive solutions to significant national architectural projects.

The significance of the 1964 planning was dramatized by events following the symposium. Three months after the symposium, architects and urban planners were called upon to leave their institutes and join the people in the construction of the socialist motherland. Professional architectural and city planning practices were abandoned. These revolutionary actions are reminiscent of Western avant-garde movements in the early twentieth century. If the earlier Western movements were sporadic expressions of individual artistic ideals, the mass movement in Chinese architecture during the Cultural Revolution put these ideals into large-scale social practice.

In between the Avant-Garde and the Kitsch

The ideology underlying the collective approach and the mass movement in Chinese architecture was very close to the original meaning of avant-garde art when it first appeared in the nineteenth century. A military term for the advance guard of an army in the Middle Ages, "avant-garde" was first used in connection with art as early as the 1820s in the writings of the French socialist Henri de Saint-Simon. In Saint-Simon's time, the avant-garde in art denoted paintings and sculptures that could play an emancipating role in society. Therefore, the revolutionary aspects of art resided not in form but in content, that is, in the social information conveyed by the artworks. In the mid-nineteenth century, the opposite of the avant-garde ideal was "art for art's sake," which emphasized the independence of art and its inherent separation from ethics and politics.[75]

Toward the end of the nineteenth century, however, these two opposites merged. Instead of addressing social concerns, avant-garde movements mostly explored new forms.[76] After World War I, the isolation of art from society was criticized by such movements as Dadaism, the Bauhaus, constructivism, surrealism, and de Stijl. In spite of their remarkable differences in approach, these postwar avant-garde movements shared the common view that art should be integrated into life. What they were pursuing was not simply art for art's sake but something more fundamentally significant, and intellectuals who abdicated all responsibilities and avoided social reality were criticized as "real philistine."[77]

These interwar art movements were categorized by German critic Peter Bürger as "the historical avant-garde." Bürger defined the avant-garde as the rebellion against the institutionalization of art and argued that, as a result of two hundred years of the development of aestheticism since Kant, art had divorced itself from society and became an autonomous social subsystem, the institution known as "art." Aesthetics favored form and treated social, political, and economic content as external to art. Challenging the autonomy of art, the historical avant-garde of the 1920s aimed to reintegrate art into the praxis of life.[78] Ironically, these antiartistic arts were ultimately accepted by the very institutions they were fighting against, and found themselves collected by and exhibited in museums. The historical avant-garde failed in its original aims. When the neo-avant-garde of the 1950s and 1960s applied the same strategy to challenge the autonomy of art, the effort was pointless because their very protests were already accepted as art. By reenacting the character of the avant-garde, the neo-avant-garde did not eradicate the idea of individual creativity but rather affirmed it.

In every aspect, the collective approach in Chinese architecture during the early decades of the People's Republic of China seems to have practiced the ideal of the historical avant-garde without being institutionalized. Both the collective approach and the historical avant-garde viewed art as a critical way to construct a new society instead of as a venue for pure artistic creation. Never truly achieved by the historical avant-garde, the undermining of institutional art was fully realized in China during the late 1960s. Artists and architects were called upon to learn from the people and then were sent to the countryside to form workshop-style design units, in which they worked both as tutors and as students of the masses. An officially promoted model-working process called *gandalei*,[79] the application of simple local material and vernacular structure in building construction, took shape under the instruction of professional architects.

While the historical avant-garde in the West was mainly motivated by individual reflections on the ideal relationship between art and society, the collective approach in Chinese architecture was part of a general sociopolitical movement that individual architects had little power to resist. Although vehemently voicing hostility to institutional art, the historical avant-garde took full advantage of art institutions and was a form of individualism. It was not accidental that all Western avant-garde arts were castigated as "decadent bourgeois formalism" in China during the early decades of the People's Republic of China. The collective approach in Chinese architecture, in its antiformal stance and emphasis on content, was closer to the Western avant-garde in Saint-Simon's time than to the historical avant-garde of the 1920s. If the Western neo-avant-garde of the 1950s and 1960s was a copy of the gesture of the historical avant-garde's revolutionary restoration of art's pre-nineteenth-century situation, the collective approach in China during the same period was the very "origin" at which such a restoration was aiming.

In the 1964 avenue planning, Chinese architects were focused not on innovations in architectural forms but on how to create a solemn socialist capital and on how to convey, on a modern boulevard, the superiority of the new political system. Yet, according to American critic Clement Greenberg's definition, this orientation could produce nothing but kitsch, the opposite of avant-garde. Greenberg argued that the essence of modern art resided in its avant-gardism, while art polluted by ethical or political concerns was kitsch.[80] Following such a formalist definition of avant-garde, Greenberg developed the concept of value judgment in art, along with formal standards.[81] For him, the value of art was objective, and form determined quality. Content was irrelevant. Emphasizing content in art was propaganda—in other words, kitsch.

Playing with content, kitsch was form without originality. For some scholars, the challenge of institutional art by the historical avant-garde was the origin, while the reenactment by the neo-avant-garde in the 1950s and 1960s was kitsch.[82] Chinese architecture of the same period followed the Soviet model in both style and policy. Most of the Anniversary Projects in 1958–59 adopted Stalinist neoclassicism in plan and façade. The 1964 planning, together with the designs of individual buildings along Chang'an Avenue in different schemes, followed the models established by the Great Hall and the museum complex. The Soviet principle of "national form, socialist content" and the socialist realism style dominated architectural discourse in China for decades. If Stalinist architecture was kitsch, a totalitarian copy of western neoclassical architecture, Chinese architecture in the 1950s and 1960s was a copy of it, the kitsch of kitsch.

In fact, the collective approach went against originality by definition. The final product of collective creation was often a compromised solution that took from a variety of schemes and balanced different opinions. It had no "origin," and was also deliberately authorless. While the participation of the masses blurred the boundary between artistic creation and popular fashion, the involvement of political leaders in the designing process colored the final design with state ideology and blurred the boundary between art and propaganda. The collective approach was double kitsch. The literal meaning of the German word *kitsch* is "trash." While Dadaism became avant-garde by turning trash into art, Stalinist neoclassicism was considered kitsch because it turned art into trash. The Chinese collective creation could be trash too.

Historical Models and the Collective Approach

The dilemma of the collective approach, at once avant-garde (the "origin of origin") and kitsch (the "copy of copy"), was mostly the result of a linear model of history. Bürger's notion of historical avant-garde and neo-avant-garde was itself the very product of the avant-garde as a symbol of the progressive nature of modernism through its explorative and adventurous connotation. "Avant-garde" often means being ahead of one's time, pursuing artistic activity not for the present but for the future. The present sets the example that the future will follow, just as the past set the example followed by the present; the present founds the origin and the future will copy, just as the past founded the origin that the present copies. Underlying such a notion of avant-garde is a linear model of history.

The linear model of history is based on the genealogy of continuous successions and causal links between events. By focusing on the totality of a centralized narrative, this historical model constructs progressive developments characterized by constant alternations of evolution and revolution: from gradual accumulation to drastic change, from originality to multiple copies, and from authenticity to manifold variations. Hegelian dialecticism is often portrayed as the opposite of the linear model of history. Except for the substitution of linear development with a spiral ascendant pattern, however, the Hegelian dialectical model of history is as causal and progressive as the linear model. The hidden program of the "world spirit" in the Hegelian model makes the evolution of history highly teleological.

Foucault called both linear and dialectical models "history in the traditional form," in which discontinuity was deemed as both the given condition and an abnormal situation. It is the historian's job to restore the normal, continuous, and coherent form. For Foucault, such a master narrative is arbitrary. It is constructed by a certain group of people or by institutions representing their interests and exercising their power. The new historical model Foucault proposed is discoursal, in which discontinuity and rupture are the normal conditions of history.[83] The discoursal model highlights differences instead of constructing a total history with highly selective material; emphasizes different levels of succession characterized by the interaction between past, present, and future instead of a linear chronological succession; and defines terms within specific discourse and self-consciously selects and constitutes a series of terms and concepts proper to the discourse instead of using them as if they were universal and natural and could be applied to any situation.

Treating the collective approach in Chinese architecture as either avant-garde or kitsch makes a linear connection between China and the West. As American art critic and theorist Rosalind Krauss has pointed out, the categories and terms in the discussion of art are meaningful only within a specific discoursal structure.[84] "Avant-garde" was specifically defined in Chinese discourse. An avant-garde "style" or approach might mean completely different things under specific social historical contexts in the West and in China, illustrating Foucault's argument that identical enunciations in different discourses are not in fact identical.

When in the 1920s Chinese students went abroad to study art, the realistic quality of Western neoclassical art attracted their attention most; none of them was interested in dada or other historical avant-garde movements. The art they developed was considered avant-garde in twentieth-century China.[85] Similarly, what interested the first Chinese architecture students studying overseas was the formal grandeur of Beaux-Arts and the scientific aspects of structural rationalism.[86] None of them was attracted to the avant-garde de Stijl or Bauhaus movements. What was considered conservative in the West might be revolutionary in China, and what was avant-garde in Western art might be commonplace in traditional Chinese art. Because traditional Chinese society had long neglected the value of individual personality, it would have been pointless to introduce into China the Western avant-garde arts of the 1920s and 1930s, which emphasized the integration of life and art, an idea inspired by medieval European society, whose attitude to art was more or less similar to that of early twentieth-century China. In such a social context, a more traditional Western art, with its emphasis on personal expression, would have had a more powerful social and cultural effect.

From such a perspective, the collective approach and mass movements were closer to premodern architectural practice than to the avant-garde. However, the equation of the collective approach with kitsch is also problematic. American art critic and historian Hal Foster argued that, like many other categories, the historical avant-garde was a retroactive effect of countless artistic responses and critical readings. Without later reenactments, originality is meaningless. The historical avant-garde is as much a conceptual construction of the neo-avant-garde as the origin that inspires it.[87] On the other hand, the copy and repetition that divest art of its originality and make it kitsch are simply impossible in the discoursal model of history. Foucault argued, "The fact that two enunciations are exactly identical, that they are made up of the same words used with the same meaning, does not, as we know, mean that they are absolutely identical."[88] Artistic movements should not be understood as simply revolutionary change on one hand and a redundant return to the original on the other.

The collective approach followed during the early PRC era was neither an effect caused by the historical avant-garde movement nor a copy of the Soviet policy. It played a special role in the discourse of Chinese architecture. Opposing the individualism developed by early Chinese avant-garde movements during the Republican era, the collective approach of the 1950s and 1960s destabilized institutional art practice. Just as the repetition of the neo-avant-garde in Western discourse increased the visibility of the historical avant-garde, the collective approach of the early PRC era made visible the avant-garde quality of the individualism and Westernization of early twentieth-century Chinese art. However, on the other hand, while Soviet policies such as "socialist content, national form" and socialist realism served as ideological supports for a monumental style preferred by the Soviet regime, in China they led to an emphasis on the social dimension of architecture. Style, with its professional associations, was finally abandoned at the height of the collective upsurge when architectural practice merged with mass movements.

In the 1960s the collective approach and mass movements drew scholars' and architects' attention to vernacular architecture. Architectural discourse in China had been focused on the dichotomy of national (as represented by the imperial tradition) and modern (as represented by Westernization). The vernacular voice called into question a single unified national style. During the 1960s architects began to carry out surveys on regional traditions in Chinese architecture. Thus, on one hand, the collective approach challenged the formal approach in the construction of a Chinese national style by bringing in both foreign and vernacular traditions; on the other hand, it restored the conventional role architecture had played in traditional Chinese society and politics.

To some extent, the collective approach highlighted the way architectural meaning was generated. In the linear model of history, the author as the source of creation and originality was the main creator of meanings. Art history, as Krauss had criticized, was reduced to the lineage of master artists and a "history of proper names." From a discoursal point of view, Foucault and Roland Barthes questioned the possibility of a consistent meaning in an original text and the communication of "original" meanings. Readers were the givers of meaning, and every act of reading would produce new meanings. Authorless as most products of collective creation in architecture were, the PRC practice left the role of giving meaning to the public experience in political and daily life.

In the discourses of Western art, while the meaning of "avant-garde" is constantly changing, "Modernism" with a capital "M" is deliberately and specifically defined. "Modern" used to simply mean "present," and the original sense of Modernism in Western art is chronological, connoting art produced in the "modern era." "Modern era," however, can be defined differently depending on what is considered characteristically modern. The term refers to the time span that extends from the present back to the time when such characteristics first came into being. Thus the designation of a modern era is actually about origin, and Modernism in art is associated with specific styles, values, and ideologies. From the point of view of humanism, for instance, the modern era could refer to the period of history from the end of the Middle Ages to the present; from the point of view of the productive forces in Marxism, the modern era starts with the Industrial Revolution in the mid-eighteenth century.

Origin, however, is more an effect of later construction and a product of linear history. The Renaissance was thought of at the time as the revival of a classical past, not as the origin of modern humanism. Thus the transformation of "modern," a chronological term denoting "present," into "Modern," an ideological term connoting specific values, was possible only after the linear model of history came under scrutiny. Postmodernism, as it was called, turned present-tense modernism into past-tense Modernism, together with its enthusiasm for progressive history, machines, technology, individuality, and other sociopolitical beliefs. Thus Modernism in Western art has become a specific term denoting a specific historical period that ended in the mid-twentieth century, and connoting specific values in art—for instance, abstraction and the media-specific quality.

While pinned down as a historical term in the West, in Chinese discourse the "modern" in Modernism retained its chronologically open nature. The Chinese word for "modern," *xiandai,* literally means "the present time" and denotes a more recent time period than does the current English "modern." For this reason, when referring to the modern era in the Western sense, the Chinese use another word, *jindai,* which literally means "the recent past." The Chinese word for the contemporary era is *dangdai,* which literally also means "the present age." But, as we already have the word *jindai* to refer to the general modern era, some scholars also use *xiandai* to denote the contemporary era.

The terminological difference between the Chinese and Western discourses is more than the division of history into periods; it is deeply embedded in the Communist ideology in the reconstruction of Chinese history. According to the official divisions of political history used during the early years of the People's Republic of China, "ancient history" (*gudai*) referred to the period before the 1840 Opium War; "modern history" (*jindai*) referred to the period between 1840 and the May Fourth New Culture Movement in 1919; and contemporary history, or *xiandai*, referred to the period after 1919.[89] In recent years, as the early decades of the People's Republic of China have receded into the past, contemporary history *xiandai* is used more to refer to the period after 1949, while modern history *jindai* has grown to cover the period between 1840 and 1949. In Chinese, however, the English word "modern" is translated more often (and in common usage) as *xiandai*, which actually means "contemporary." This discrepancy between the Chinese and Western terms for "modern" is neither the outcome of a translation mistake nor an accident due to lax scholarship, but rather the result of a linear model of history maintained by the Chinese discourse on art, as well as a deliberate choice made by the Chinese discourse of art to form a historical continuity.

China has systematically recorded its history for almost three thousand years. Each dynasty set up a bureau solely to compile the history of previous dynasties. In this tradition of historical record keeping, there was a single, clear main lineage of succession and a passing on of tradition even during the most chaotic periods of Chinese history. In fact, the *dai* in the Chinese words *xiandai* ("contemporary," "modern") and *jindai* ("modern," "the recent past") also means "dynasty." The linear model of history was already well established before contact with the West, and when Western theories about history came to China, the linear model and the Hegelian model were well received by Chinese intellectuals.

Historically, the avant-garde was also the product of a linear model of history. If "avant-garde" is understood to mean being ahead of one's time, then this sense of avant-gardism still occupies the very center of the Chinese modernization project. In the West, "avant-garde" and "Modernism" were two different terms that shared significant historical overlap. For early Modernist art critics such as Clement Greenberg, the avant-garde was the essence of and embodied the most important characteristics of Modernist art: originality, challenging the conventions in ideology, and a self-critical and self-defining tendency to achieve each medium's pure form in methodology. For American art historian Donald Kuspit, the historical avant-garde was synonymous with Modernism, and the neo-avant-garde was synonymous with postmodernism. Both Peter Bürger and Hal Foster clearly differentiated Modernism from the avant-garde. Using a Marxist model, Bürger defined avant-garde as a critical attitude toward the very art institution in which it was operating. Foster, on the other hand, proposed the Freudian model of repression and repetition to understand the relationship between the avant-garde and the neo-avant-garde. For American art historian Paul Wood, both Modernism and the avant-garde are historically changing ideas. Avant-garde as defined by Bürger and medium-specific formalism as defined by Greenberg were just two of the many manifestations of Modernism. By the 1980s Rosalind Krauss had already announced that "the historical period that the Avant-garde shared with modernism is over."[90] Such a split, however, has never occurred in the Chinese discourse.

In China, avant-garde Modernism continued when "modern" (*xiandai*) was replaced by "modernization" (*xiandaihua*). After 1957, when a 1956 article titled "We Want Modern Architecture" was officially criticized and its authors classified as rightists, the term "modern architecture" virtually disappeared from public discussions. In the 1964 Chang'an Avenue planning, it was replaced by another term, "modernization." Compared to the term "modern architecture," which had so many connotations of Western formalism, "modernization" was a relatively neutral term. Its meaning was closer to the original meaning of "modern," a temporal term simply connoting "up-to-date." The frequently used statement in the 1964 planning "to express the greatness of our time" was just an alternative expression for "modernization." The Chinese term, however, was much fussier than the Western "modern," since the spirit of the time could mean very different things to different sociopolitical agendas.

In 1991 Lü Peng and Yi Dan, coauthors of an influential book on modern Chinese art during the decade of 1979 to 1989, defined "avant-garde" not only as "original form" but also as "revolutionary" and "critical spirit." They further expanded these qualities of avant-garde to define Modernism and claimed that as long as an artwork was functioning to resist the aesthetic conventions formed over a long period of time, it could be counted as modern, even if its style was familiar to most people. Thus it was precisely the linear progressive aspect, antitraditionalism, and avant-gardism that were emphasized in the Chinese term *xiandai*. However, for Lü and Yi, Modernism and avant-garde were not the opposites of tradition but the very methods by which tradition was created. Lü and Yi claimed that nothing was closer to "the real spirit of tradition" than "the aesthetic attitude of searching for survival and resisting destiny in the avant-garde."[91] Avant-gardism thus is framed by the Chinese modernization project as the driving force in creating a continuous historical narrative.

By replacing "modern" with "modernization," the modernization process in Chinese architecture, as represented by Chang'an Avenue, was doomed to never be fully achieved. "Modernization" connotes always being up-to-date, and thus an ongoing process. Chang'an Avenue was always "to be completed" but never actually completed. This was the same dilemma faced by the historical avant-garde in Western art, which had developed a love-hate relationship with the future. On one hand, the avant-garde in a culture needed to legitimate its status by claiming that what was being done would be the mainstream in the future. However, once this "future" arrived and the avant-garde became the mainstream, it lost its status as avant-garde. Like the avant-garde, the Chinese modernization project, deliberately positioned at the verge of the present and the future, constantly marginalizes itself, never to be fully accomplished.

Chapter Four

Modernization in a Postmodern World: The 1970s and 1980s

THE 1964 CHANG'AN AVENUE planning was the last nationwide collective creative project in Chinese architecture before the Cultural Revolution. After that, the political climate, with its stress on the collective spirit, eventually led to the total abandonment of institutionalized design. All that remain of the months of hard work by the six leading institutes in Beijing and of the heated discussions during the five-day-long symposium by leading professionals from all over the country are some photographs of the giant models made by different design units, piles of drawings, and about two hundred pages of discussion notes. The overall plan was never realized. The most controversial issue of the 1964 planning, namely, how to complete Tiananmen Square, the central section of Chang'an Avenue, was solved only after Mao died in 1976. Moreover, the issue was resolved in a way that none of the participants in 1964 could have anticipated.

The Chairman Mao Memorial and the Completion of Tiananmen Square

Built in 1976–77, the Chairman Mao Memorial occupies a prominent position in Tiananmen Square. To its north is the Monument to the People's Heroes, the first structure built in the square after 1949; to its south is the historic Zhengyang Gate, the most important entryway into the Inner City of imperial Beijing. Tall but narrow, the Monument to the People's Heroes is basically a stele without any interior space. Thus the memorial remains the only true architecture within the square and directly faces Tiananmen Tower on the opposite side of Chang'an Avenue.

The Chairman Mao Memorial is also the structure that redefined Tiananmen Square. Before its construction in 1977, the square encompassed only what is now its northern area, between the Great Hall and the museum complex, while what is now the southern area of the square was occupied by the Gate of China surrounded by woods. Within a year of Mao's passing, the Gate of China was demolished and the memorial was built on its site. The woods were cleared, and the area surrounding the memorial became part of the expanded Tiananmen Square.

The Chairman Mao Memorial's orientation is unusual in Chinese architecture, especially for a significant national monument. In traditional Chinese architecture, buildings and their main entrances usually face south, as this is believed to be the source of auspicious energy. The main façade of the memorial, however, faces north. With Tiananmen Tower in the north, the Great Hall in the west, and the museum complex in the east, the memorial completes the enclosure of Tiananmen Square and surrounds its empty space to lend monumental façades to public ceremonies. Tiananmen Tower is the place where Mao announced the founding of the People's Republic of China, and the memorial is his mausoleum. Thus the two structures marking the northern and southern boundaries of Tiananmen Square also represent the beginning and the end of the Mao era.

The Chairman Mao Memorial, however, was built not just for Mao but also to fulfill the political needs of his successor, Hua Guofeng. It was a structure built to consolidate Hua's power and his position as the true successor to Mao. The memorial was designed not as a tomb but as a hall of worship to promote Mao's revolutionary legacy, which was the only rationale to legitimate Hua's position in the party at the time.

The Location

Mao died on September 9, 1976. On October 8, Hua announced the decision to build a memorial hall for the former "great leader and guide." Although the late leader had mentioned on a few occasions that his body should be cremated after he died, the official announcement in the October 9 *People's Daily* not only revealed the decision that the Chairman Mao Memorial would be constructed in Beijing but also that a crystal coffin containing Mao's body would be kept in the memorial for public homage. The location of the memorial was not specified in this announcement.

As early as mid-September 1976, architects, artists, and workers from eight provinces—Beijing, Tianjin, Shanghai, Guangdong, Jiangsu, Shaanxi, Liaoning, and Heilongjiang—were summoned to Beijing to study prospective sites and initiate preliminary design work.[1] After paying their respects to Mao's remains, they worked day and night, according to an article in *Architectural Journal*, with tears in their eyes. Several possible sites were selected and studied during field surveys in Beijing, including Fragrant Hills in the western suburbs, Coal Hill (Jingshan), Tiananmen Square, and the area inside the former Imperial City between Tiananmen Tower and the Meridian Gate. Tiananmen Square was finally chosen.

The official explanation for choosing that site emphasized the political significance of Tiananmen Square and claimed that the decision represented the will of the people.[2] Closer observation reveals that many of the other sites failed because of their resemblance to conventional prerevolutionary sites for tombs. Imperial mausoleums in China were usually built along a hillside, following a north-south axis, with a screen of mountain ranges to the north and a relatively flat area opening to the south whenever possible. Such an imperial scheme was followed not only by the emperors of the Ming and Qing dynasties but also by the Sun Yat-sen Mausoleum built in Nanjing in the Republican era.[3] The proposed sites along the hillsides at Fragrant Hills and Coal Hill followed this imperial model; they were eliminated during the first round of the selection process. The site within the Imperial City between Tiananmen Tower and the Meridian Gate might have been a more dramatic revolutionary gesture in terms of the disruption it would have caused to the imperial order. Inserted immediately in front of the south gate of the Forbidden City, the construction of the memorial would have required the demolition of the Duan Gate, a ritual entryway leading to the former imperial palace. The site, however, was squeezed behind Tiananmen Tower, and the space in front of the Meridian Gate was too narrow to provide the public visibility the future memorial required (fig. 4.1). Tiananmen Square, on the other hand, would provide the memorial with high visibility from all directions, including Chang'an Avenue.

Fig. 4.1. Proposals for the Chairman Mao Memorial: a. Fragrant Hills site; b. the site between Tiananmen and Meridian Gate, 1976. *Reproduction from* Architectural Journal *(April 1977): 34, 31. Courtesy of* JZXB.

Two options were available for the memorial's location in Tiananmen Square. One followed the 1964 Chang'an Avenue planning by locating the memorial on either the east or the west side of the square;[4] the other put the memorial in the center. It did not take long before a decision was made in favor of the latter. The Chairman Mao Memorial was to be located on the north-south axis of Beijing in line with Tiananmen Tower and the Monument to the People's Heroes. On an ideological level, the central location would highlight the great heroic image of Mao and express the political significance of the memorial. On a formal level, the central location would prevent the memorial from being dwarfed by the two extant relatively larger buildings, the Great Hall and the museum complex, and make it the dominant structure in the architectural ensemble of Tiananmen Square.[5]

The exact site still had to be narrowed down. Since the area north of the Monument to the People's Heroes had to be reserved for public assembly, it was unanimously agreed that the memorial should be located to the south of the monument. However, there were still four different proposals for the location along the north-

a.

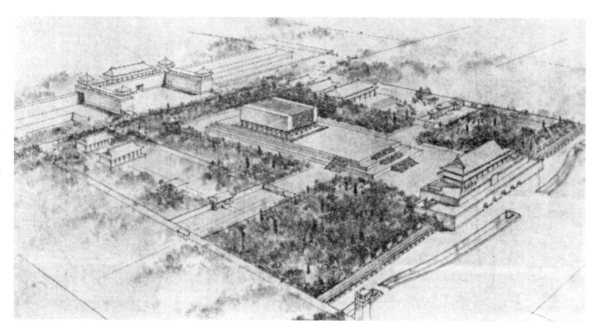

b.

south axis between the monument and Zhengyang Gate. The first was to put the memorial close to the monument and make the two a memorial group, an idea rejected on the basis that both would lose individuality and that the larger scale of the memorial would overwhelm the monument. The second was to demolish Zhengyang Gate and its Archery Tower and use its site for the memorial; this proposal was also abandoned, because the memorial would be exposed to the busy traffic and bustling commercial life of Front Gate Street, ruining the solemn atmosphere. The third was to put the memorial close to Zhengyang Gate, a plan that was also rejected, since the height of the towers might dwarf the memorial. The fourth proposal was to locate the memorial at the midpoint on the north-south axis between the Monument to the People's Heroes and Zhengyang Gate, 200 meters from each, which became the final site where the foundation stone was laid. The rest of the southern area of Tiananmen Square joined its northern part to be paved as assembly ground, expanding the capacity of the square from 400,000 to 600,000 people. Such a site plan, according to the official explanation, embodied the theme "Chairman Mao is among the people and lives forever in our hearts," since the memorial would be surrounded by the masses during significant political assemblies.[6] The site was finally anchored, both physically and ideologically.

The decision was also made to have the main façade and the entrance of the memorial face north. Framed by the two opposite architectural orientations of Tiananmen Tower and the memorial, Chang'an Avenue became the boundary and juncture of past and present, feudal and socialist, and history and modernity.

The Selection of Schemes

While the selection of the site for the Chairman Mao Memorial did not follow the 1964 Chang'an Avenue planning, the collective approach used in the design procedure did. The new version of collective architectural creation in the 1970s was known as the "three combinations" (*sanjiehe*) of "leaders, the masses, and specialists."[7] Hua Guofeng and the Chinese Communist Party (CCP) Central Committee made the final site decision and also reviewed and narrowed down the design schemes. Design schemes were provided by a mixture of "old, middle-aged, and young" architects from eight provinces. The final design group consisted of "workers, cadres, and professionals" from different design institutes in Beijing. During the design process, more people and design units proposed ideas and schemes and made comments and suggestions. Every detail in the design, from the construction drawings to the selection of materials, was decided only after going through this newly updated collective procedure of the "three combinations."[8]

The construction of the Chairman Mao Memorial reenacted the standard "miracle" of early People's Republic of China (PRC) architecture, when the whole country was mobilized for one project. Within half a year, the building was standing in Tiananmen Square. Workers, cadres, designers, and People's Liberation Army soldiers worked on the site day and night. All thirty provinces contributed construction materials and equipment. Before shipping materials or equipment to Beijing, some places held special ceremonies to express the people's great respect for Mao.[9] While political leaders such as Hua gave general instructions, calling for a memorial that was at once practical, firm, solemn, beautiful, and in the national style,[10] and the masses provided the materials and labor, the professionals made the connections and offered design schemes for the former to choose from and for the latter to carry out.

The Scale. The scale of the Chairman Mao Memorial was designed taking into account the vista before the leaders on the rostrum of Tiananmen.[11] The height was chosen so that from the rostrum, the view of Zhengyang Gate would be blocked by the memorial, thus avoiding the intrusion of the former imperial gate's sloping roofs into the view beyond the memorial. At the same time, the height of the memorial had to be lower than the Monument to the People's Heroes since the monument was vertical and much smaller in size. The appropriate height was finally decided as 33.6 meters. The memorial had to be wide enough to block the Zhengyang Gate and narrow enough to maintain Tiananmen Square's openness. The appropriate width, therefore, was set at 75 meters. This height and width also guaranteed that, looking from any point in Tiananmen Square and on Chang'an Avenue, the memorial was higher than the Zhengyang Gate and its Archery Towers but lower than the Monument to the People's Heroes (fig. 4.2).

The Style. All of the schemes proposed in September 1976 looked like tombs, with solid walls, small windows, and a long passageway leading to the main entrance. Some of them resembled the stone stele frequently found at Chinese tomb sites (fig. 4.3a). The most important model that Chinese architects may have been following, however, was Lenin's tomb in Moscow's Red Square, constructed more than half a century earlier and with which they were very familiar. The official explanation for the many heavy and solemn designs was that Chinese architects were overwhelmed by great grief at the time. The instructions from the party leaders indicated that what Hua wanted was not a tomb but something more forward-looking. Architects were organized to study Mao's writing and to seek inspiration from his revolutionary romanticism and from the proletarian attitude to life and death. Revolutionary soldiers had died for the people, but remained alive in people's hearts and would encourage

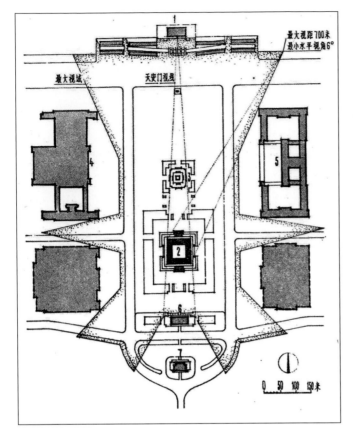

Fig. 4.2. Analytical drawings for a proper scale of the Chairman Mao Memorial in Tiananmen Square: a. plan drawing; b. section drawings, 1976. *Reproduction from* Architectural Journal *(April 1977): 7–8. Courtesy of* JZXB.

a.

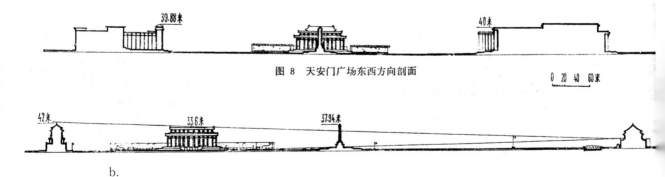

图 8　天安门广场东西方向剖面

b.

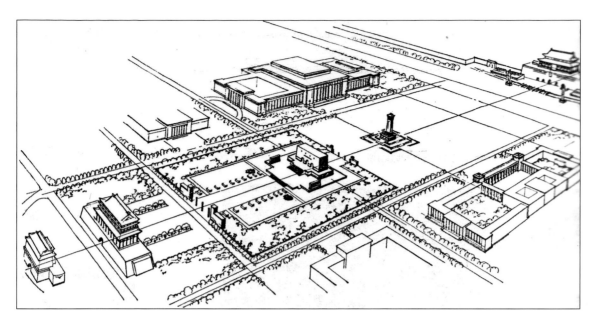

Fig. 4.3a

them to march forward.[12] What the memorial should emphasize, therefore, was not the end of the Mao era as embodied in a tomb but rather the continuation of Mao's cause and a smooth transition into a new era, with Hua as the center.

Fig. 4.3. Different schemes for the Chairman Mao Memorial: a. Design in the form of a stele. *Reproduction from* Architectural Journal *(April 1977): 31, 34, 36. Courtesy of* JZXB.

This critical change in the direction of the design was made in early October 1976, when the Gang of Four, including Mao's wife, were arrested by Hua in collaboration with other first-generation CCP leaders. Designers quickly reached an agreement that the memorial should be both solemn and open. Most schemes proposed during the second round of design applied a surrounding colonnade to make the building lighter and more open. Some schemes combined colonnades with solid walls. Others featured traditional-style courtyards (fig. 4.3b). At least one proposed a dome to represent a rising, or setting, red sun, surrounded by a ring of sunflowers at its base, on top of a colonnaded hall. Yet another scheme proposed a giant column piercing the sky from a horizontal base of solid walls and colonnades, also with a sun and sunflowers decorating the base and top of the column (fig. 4.3c). Although these last two schemes were in the minority, a sun and sunflowers, representing Mao and the people, respectively, were popular decorative motifs common to all of the schemes.[13] The colonnade style was chosen as the direction for further development.

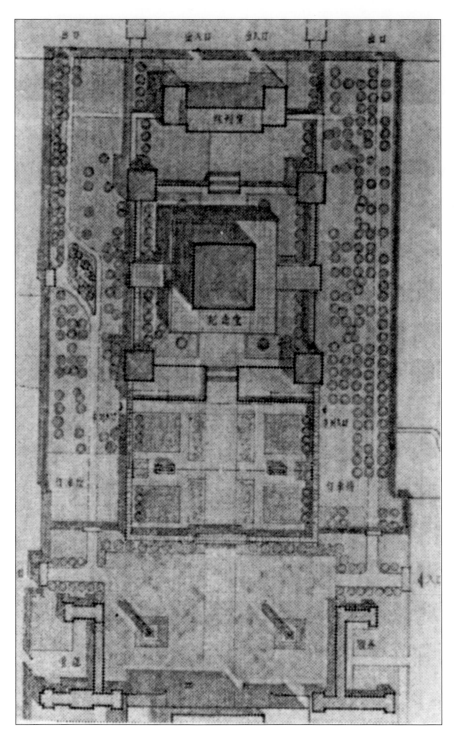

Fig. 4.3b(1). Design in the form of
a courtyard, plan drawing.

Fig. 4.3b(2). Design in the form
of a courtyard, perspective
drawing.

Fig. 4.3c. Design in the forms of
revolutionary symbols of column,
sun, and sunflowers, 1976.

图 20

The official explanation for the selection of the colonnade style was that it was in harmony with both traditional Chinese architectural form and the extant new buildings on Tiananmen Square, the Great Hall and the museum complex. As in traditional Chinese architecture, the façade was divided into the base, the body with colonnades, and the eaves. Designers unanimously agreed that the base should be a double-layer terrace of red granite, symbolizing that the socialist China founded by Mao would never change color.[14] After the selection of a colonnade style, the scheme variations once again focused on the roof.

Many colonnade schemes were produced that varied only in the style of the roof. Since the decision had already been made to place the memorial in the center of southern Tiananmen Square and to use four identical colonnaded façades, indeed, there was little design work left to do in terms of architectural form.[15] The final decision paid lip service to the political slogans of the time, including the "three combinations of the masses, leaders, and professionals," and national form, socialist content, and modernization. However, when President Hua and the party finally chose a scheme to implement, there was little rationale to justify the elimination of the rest. The options proposed were so similar that the leaders must have been very confused (fig. 4.4).

The Interior. The interior of the Chairman Mao Memorial was designed mainly as a place of worship. Located at the very center is the Hall of Reverence, with the crystal sarcophagus containing Mao's body. To its north is a large hall with a seated statue of Mao made of white marble; to its south is a smaller hall focusing on a wall inscribed with one of Mao's poems in his own calligraphy. Thus, along the central north-south axis of Beijing within the memorial, three halls of worship pay homage to Mao's image as a great leader, his corpse as a revolutionary holy relic, and his writing as a representation of the revolutionary spirit. The rest of the interior is made up of entrance halls, lounges, and auxiliary rooms.

Details of the interior, including the materials and decorative motifs, were imbued with symbolic meanings. Construction and decorative materials were collected from all thirty provinces of China, including Taiwan. Behind the marble statue in the north hall is an embroidered Chinese panoramic landscape, forming a background twenty-four meters long and seven meters high for Mao's sculptural portraiture, symbolizing his great contribution to the creation of a unified "New China." The electric ceiling lights were designed in the form of sunflowers, representing the Chinese people, who

图 7

图 8　　　　　　　　　　　　图 9

would benefit from Mao's revolutionary thoughts for generations to come, like sunflowers receiving sunshine. The hall with the crystal sarcophagus was designed like a bedroom. The black Mount Tai granite that forms the base of the sarcophagus was an allusion to Mao's famous saying "A sacrifice of dying for the people is greater in significance than the weight of Mount Tai." The red Manchurian marble on the floor of the south hall symbolized red China, the everlasting heritage of Mao.

The interior decoration, according to the designers, was a combination of traditional Chinese architectural style with modern scientific principles and revolutionary motifs. The ceiling decoration was inspired by a traditional cupola *zaojing* (caisson ceiling). Traditional glazed tiles were used throughout the building.

The Dilemma. In spite of great efforts to make the monument distinctively Chinese in character, the Chairman Mao Memorial is, ironically, closest in style to the Lincoln Memorial in Washington, DC. Both are square structures surrounded on all sides by a colonnade. Even the numbers of bays on each side are the same. Both have eleven bays, with the central bays being slightly wider than the rest (fig. 4.5). Statues and words are used in both monuments to emphasize and propagandize the values they represented. The environs of these two structures are also similar. Chairman Mao Memorial faces Tiananmen Tower in the distance, with the Monument to the People's Heroes in between, just as the Lincoln Memorial faces Capitol Hill, with the obelisk in the middle.

Chinese designers in 1976 were quite conscious of and uneasy about the resemblance of their schemes to the Lincoln Memorial, and tried hard to minimize it by adding traditional Chinese motifs and new revolutionary symbols. Their efforts were not successful. For China, as for other Asian and African nations, the imperial powers of the West have been both the definer of "modernity"—the mark of progress—and the target to struggle against for their place in the world. This is the dilemma for Chinese architectural modernization, and the irony in the design of the Chairman Mao Memorial is a perfect symbol of such a dilemma.

Although Hua became Mao's heir apparent before Mao's death in September, his power was far from consolidated. At Mao's death, Hua's authority was challenged from two opposite directions: the younger-generation political radicals, including Mao's widow Jiang Qing, who had been the main force supporting Mao's Cultural Revolution; and Mao's old comrades, who had survived numerous political movements and remained sympathetic to Liu Shaoqi, Deng Xiaoping, and others who had been suppressed during the Cultural Revolution. Compared to both groups, Hua was a latecomer to the political stage in Beijing, having been promoted from provincial party secretary to vice premier only after Premier Zhou Enlai became seriously ill and

Fig. 4.5. Chairman Mao Memorial, 1976–77. Xu Mengpei and others. *Photograph by author.*

was hospitalized in 1975. It was clear that the younger-generation radicals had a better chance of claiming themselves the true successors of Mao's revolutionary spirit. Leaders of this group, later designated the Gang of Four, appeared prominently with Hua during Mao's funeral ceremony in Tiananmen Square on September 18. On October 6, however, they were all arrested. Two days later, Hua officially announced the decision to build the memorial. Less revolutionary than the radicals and less practical than Deng, Hua's only justification for his supreme position was as the chosen heir by Mao,[16] a position that he tried to highlight by building the memorial.

Hua lasted only two years as the supreme leader of China. After Deng Xiaoping came to power in 1978, the interior of the Chairman Mao Memorial was redesigned to legitimate Deng's claim as the center of the second generation of CCP leadership. The lounges in the memorial were opened and dedicated to Mao's three former revolutionary colleagues, Liu Shaoqi, Zhu De, and Zhou Enlai, thus turning the memorial originally designed solely for Mao into a collective memorial to the first generation of PRC leaders. Deng is now acclaimed as the "chief architect of Chinese reform and opening up," a turning point in modern Chinese history marking the end of the Cultural Revolution and the initiation of the market economy. Viewed from this historical perspective, the contradiction in the design of the Chairman Mao Memorial, rather than representing a dilemma in Chinese architectural modernization, appears to be a perfect symbol of Hua's brief rule, a transitional bridge linking the revolutionary era of Mao and the reform era of Deng.

Hotels

The political and social life of China experienced dramatic change after Mao's death in 1976. The Chairman Mao Memorial stands at the threshold of this historical transformation. Before 1976, the socialist way of building continued to emphasize the collective spirit; after that, economic reform started to introduce contemporary Western practice and individualism to Chinese architecture. After more than a decade of hibernation after the Anniversary Projects, construction revived on Chang'an Avenue as early as 1972, in the form of hotels and other accommodations for foreign visitors. More hotels were added throughout the 1980s, with growing foreign involvement in both design and investment.

From Gandalei to the "Three Combinations"

The radical design revolution initiated in 1964, immediately after the Chang'an Avenue planning, asked designers to leave their institutes and work with the masses on the scene at construction sites, implementing a new method known as *gandalei*. First invented by workers in Heilongjian at Daqing, the petroleum site that became Mao's model industrial city, *gandalei* applied local materials and vernacular techniques in design and construction and emphasized separate, small structures built in a short period of time.[17] Design drawings were also supposed to be understandable to workers and peasants who were not trained in architecture.

This new method was a product of the specific political situation of the late 1960s, when both Soviet Russia and the United States were hostile to China. In July 1960 Khrushchev recalled all Soviet experts working in China, thus revealing the hostility that now existed between the former "comrades plus brothers." China criticized the Soviet Union as "revisionist" and "socialist imperialist." In 1969 the relationship degenerated into armed hostilities when Chinese and Soviet troops fought over the sovereignty of Zhenbao (Damansky) Island in the Wusuli (Ussuri) River. A strong sense pervaded China that a real war could break out at any time. As a precautionary measure, construction in large cities ceased, and major industrial plants were dispersed across China's underdeveloped hinterlands, a historical phenomenon generally referred to as "three-lines construction." *Gandalei* was mainly influential in the countryside, and predominantly in the construction of dwellings and factories. No monument was built on Chang'an Avenue during this period.

Neither design revolution nor *gandalei* lasted very long. When the Sino-Soviet relationship was damaged beyond repair, China revived its interest in developing new relationships with the West. In July 1971, US secretary of state Henry Kissinger made a secret trip to China, followed by president Richard Nixon's visit in February 1972 and the normalization of diplomatic relations between the two countries. In October 1971 the People's Republic of China replaced the Republic of China in Taiwan as a permanent member on the Security Council of the United Nations. With these changes in international relations, a growing diplomatic population in China led to the revival of construction in large cities.

Design policy also swung back to the more moderate collective approach known as the "three combinations," referring to the combination of leaders, the masses, and specialists, or, in a more specific formulation, cadres, workers, and designers.[18] In the 1970s virtually all achievements in architecture and urban planning were attributed to the miraculous power of the "three combinations." It became such a popular slogan in the media that no details about its exact meaning were offered when it was evoked to justify a design. Gradually, its original designation was forgotten and the term acquired ideological significance in its own right. Numerous versions of the "three combinations" were implied or specified in written records, including combinations of older, middle, and younger generations; construction, design, and theory; teaching, production, and research; and workers, technicians, and teachers.[19]

Although the exact meaning of the "three combinations" was not specifically pinned down and seemed somehow irrelevant in the discourse, its emphasis in the new policy was apparent. It abandoned the radical approach of relying totally on the masses that was associated with the design revolution movement of the late 1960s, yet continued to downplay the role of professionals in the design process. In practice, the "three combinations" reduced the contribution of architects to mere technical support. Such a policy indicated the party's continued distrust of intellectuals, as first expressed in Mao's "Talks at the Yan'an Forum" in the 1940s. Architects were to be guided by their leaders and reeducated by the masses through on-site design and shared participation in both design and construction.

The Diplomatic Projects

In keeping with the retention of Western developed countries as models for emulation, the decades of the 1970s and 1980s saw an unprecedentedly large number of Western-inspired movements in architecture, art, and politics in the People's Republic of China.[20] Although the development of the relationship with the United States in the early 1970s was acclaimed as the "victory of Chairman Mao's revolutionary diplomatic line," it resulted in an increase in diplomatic personnel and foreign visitors from the capitalist West. In order to house the growing foreign population, facilities that met current Western living standards were planned on East Chang'an Avenue near the former concession area.[21]

The design of new facilities started as early as 1971.[22] In 1972 three major projects—the Number Nine Apartment Building, the International Club, and the Beijing Friendship Store—were completed on the East Chang'an Avenue extension specifically to serve the foreign population in Beijing.[23] In 1973 the Diplomatic Apartments, with a floorage of 34,000 square meters, were completed just next to the Beijing Friendship Store, extending the so-called diplomatic projects (*waishi gongcheng*) area farther eastward along the avenue.[24] In 1974, before the twenty-fifth anniversary of the People's Republic of China, the new East Building of the prestigious Beijing Hotel was added east of the old 1917–19 Middle Building.[25] All of this construction was completed within two years.

The International Club provided foreign visitors and diplomatic personnel with space for recreation and social activities (fig. 4.6). With a floorage of 13,831 square meters, it had an outdoor swimming pool; a movie theatre; rooms specifically dedicated to fitness, billiards, ping-pong, chess, and card games; a bowling alley; a barbershop; a banquet hall; a hall for cocktail parties; and various dining rooms. Most of these entertainments were unheard of by the majority of the Chinese in the 1970s. All of the rooms had air-conditioning and heating. The outdoor swimming pool had a filtered circulation system and could be used for diving and racing. Although only five stories tall, the Beijing Friendship Store was equipped with two elevators (one for customers, and one for goods), an unusual arrangement, since, according to construction codes of the time, only buildings of more than six stories could have elevators.

These buildings contrasted starkly with the living standards of the average Beijing citizen. In China of the 1970s, air-conditioning and family bathrooms were still luxuries. Most of the city used public toilets in narrow residential alleys, facilities that usually lacked baths and were shared by the whole neighborhood. In the early 1980s,

when the famous Chinese writer Xiao Jun was interviewed by reporters in San Francisco, he was asked, "Mr. Xiao Jun, what is your deepest impression about the United States?" Xiao had answered, "The toilets

Fig. 4.6. International Club, 1971–74. Ma Guoxin and others. *Photograph by author.*

here are really good!"[26] Even at the end of the 1980s, Liu Xinwu, another renowned Beijing writer, was still complaining of the poor quality and filthy smell of the shared toilets in China's capital. He announced,

> On the toilet issue, I admit that I am a supporter of "wholesale Westernization." . . . Since we Chinese want to join modern civilization, there is no reason for us to reject such cultural wealth. Today, although we already have Western-style toilets for the minority of foreign guests and leaders, there is still little or no attention given to public toilets. Filthy latrine pits fill China, and there is no sign of improvement. I hope my idle comments will not be considered redundant or disobedient.[27]

Liu's "idle comments" illustrated a contradictory condition in China in the 1970s and 1980s. On one hand, the Western lifestyle, including its toilets, was still deemed bourgeois decadence, from which the socialist China should keep away; on the other hand, it was a symbol of modernization, which a modernizing China should strive for.

Stylistically, the new diplomatic buildings were deliberately designed as modern, following the principles of the International Style, as codified by Henry-Russell Hitchcock and Philip Johnson in 1932.[28] Asymmetrical, with L-shaped buildings defining courtyards, they were characterized by the interchange and inter-infiltration of interior and exterior spaces. On the main façade of the International Club, facing Chang'an Avenue, the open porch in the middle and the void corner of the circular balcony made the building have more to do with "volume than mass," matching the first of Hitchcock and Johnson's principles. The rhythm of the slender rectangular columns of the porch, with its sun-shading boards, met the second principle of "regularity rather than axial symmetry as the chief means of ordering design." Finally, there was no big roof, no pretentious central tower, no glazed tiles, and no sculptural embellishment, in a word, no "arbitrary applied decoration." Compared to other monuments built in previous periods on the avenue, which were mostly symmetrical, with immense colonnades and solid walls, these new buildings were less solemn and much lighter in general appearance.

The asymmetrical plans and elevations were made after careful selection. In the design of the Diplomatic Apartments, three different schemes had originally proposed a symmetrical block with a strong axis in plan, a Y-shaped plan, and an overlapped double-rectangular plan.[29] The first was abandoned due to its lack of "flexibility in composition" (basically meaning "asymmetry"), and the second because it was not in harmony with the surrounding buildings. Its complex shapes were also a challenge for the prefabricated assembly method of construction, the key to architectural industrialization at the time and a synonym for architectural modernization. Although the third option was also criticized for requiring more types of prefabricated members because of the "plan variation [from normal symmetrical forms]," it was preferred because of its "richness and liveliness in shapes and façades, which was required by general planning."[30] The overlapping double-rectangular plan was chosen for its lack of solemnity. Since solemnity in architecture was often interpreted as political, the adoption of an asymmetrical plan for the Diplomatic Apartments was deliberately apolitical (fig. 4.7).

The East Building of the Beijing Hotel

The construction of the prestigious Beijing Hotel on East Chang'an Avenue spans almost the entire twentieth century. It started with a small restaurant in 1900 and was developed into a hotel run by the Sino-French Industrial and Commercial Bank in 1907. The earliest extant building is today's Middle Building, designed by the French company Brossard, Mopin, and Cie and completed in 1917.[31] In 1953 the West Building, designed by the Ministry of Architectural Industry Design Institute,[32] led by architect Dai Nianci, was added to the west side of the Middle Building along Chang'an Avenue. The 1973–74 addition, known as the East Building, was the second expansion during the PRC era. In 1989–90 the Beijing Hotel underwent a total renovation,[33] in which all three buildings were connected and a new fourth building on Chang'an Avenue, known as the Grand Hotel Beijing (Guibinlou), was added to the west of the 1953 West Building.[34] The façades from four different periods spread along the north side of East Chang'an Avenue like a screen, displaying the stylistic changes of Chinese architecture during the twentieth century (see fig. 2.4).

The styles of the four Beijing Hotel buildings bear clear imprints of their time periods. The 1917 Middle Building is a colonial-style Renaissance Revival structure, characterized by horizontal divisions on the façade and such Western architectural motifs as arches and cornice brackets. The 1953 West Building explores combining national form with socialist content in its simplified traditional Chinese motifs, such as double-eave roofed pavilions and the memorial archway, applied to a solid masonry façade. The 1990 Grand Hotel Beijing juxtaposes a direct copy of a traditional archway and a section of the red wall from the former Imperial City with the modern structure. The 1974 East Building, in contrast to all of the buildings before and after it, distinguishes itself from the ensemble of façades by its lack of historical references. Compared to the other buildings in the Beijing Hotel complex, it also appears less solid and more open. The grids of vertical columns and horizontal balcony bands on the façades make the entire structure seem much lighter.

The East Building also stands out from the group because of its height. It is eighty meters high, with eighteen stories. While the other three buildings all have seven stories and façades unified by cornice-like horizontal motifs, the main tower of the East Building is set back from Chang'an Avenue and rises twice as high as the rest of the group. Beijing Hotel is the first modern building on the north side of the avenue east of the Forbidden City, which is only about half a kilometer away. While the East Building certainly dwarfed all of the imperial monuments around the Forbidden City, new height-control laws guaranteed that the East Building itself would not suffer thus. The urban planning codes of Beijing issued in the 1980s required that buildings in this area should not exceed a forty-five-meter height limit to preserve the traditional spatial character of the Forbidden City. Built in the early 1970s, the eighty-meter East Building is an exception. Such height on Chang'an Avenue proper could have been possible only at a time when the yearning for modernization loomed high and the revolutionary spirit, with its antitraditional stance, had not completely died out. The Beijing Hotel East Building captured such a transitional moment.

Architectural Modernization: From Industrialization to Style

Both the diplomatic projects and the Beijing Hotel East Building were constructed using the assembly method. Major parts, such as the reinforced concrete beams and floor slabs, were prefabricated in factories and assembled on the construction sites. In the 1970s this assembly method in architectural design and construction was considered the key step in architectural industrialization, a synonym for architectural modernization.

The modernization project of China had reached a new threshold by the late 1970s. Before Mao's death in 1976, the focus had been on political and social revolution, including revolution in architectural design. Mass movements were the main force for professional development. In the architectural field, mass movements had gone through three main stages: institutional collective creation in the 1950s, design revolution in the 1960s, and the "three combinations" in the 1970s. Chinese modernization shifted gradually toward socioeconomic improvement after 1976. During the Third Plenum of the Eleventh Central Committee of the Chinese Communist Party in December 1978, with unambiguous clarity the modernization project acquired its official framework, known as the "Four Modernizations." The "Four Modernizations" referred to modernization in the areas of industry, agriculture, science and technology, and national defense—all intended to be achieved by the end of the twentieth century.[35]

At the time, architecture was mainly considered a type of industry. In order to be modernized, architecture first needed to be industrialized. Architectural industrialization replaced the "three combinations" as the central issue of discussion in *Architectural Journal* in 1978. Although there were disagreements and debates about the specific meaning of "architectural industrialization," the general consensus was that to industrialize architecture, design must first be standardized so that parts could be manufactured systematically in factories.[36] Some articles also called for changes in construction organization to cope with the industrialized building procedures.[37] Although designers were assured that architectural industrialization would not sacrifice architectural art and that architects would still have plenty of scope to exercise their talents,[38] there was a shared concern among many architects that industrialization and standardization would lead to monotony in Chinese cities.[39]

The discussion of "architectural industrialization" was the first organized discussion in the field of architecture published in a major Chinese professional journal. The editor's note in the first 1978 issue of *Architectural Journal* stated,

> In order to achieve the magnificent aim of the Four Modernizations by the end of this century, all trades and professions are engaged in excited discussions and are making their own specific development plans. How can we achieve technological revolution in the architectural fields? This is a significant issue that concerns every aspect of the architectural profession, design and planning, scientific research, construction, production, and so on, as well as the relevant government departments. We hope that comrades in the architectural field will all pay attention to this issue, and engage in dynamic discussions on questions about the way to achieve technological revolution in architecture, the contents, approaches, methods, and technical policies of architectural industrialization, and especially the way architectural design and planning is adapting to the requirements of architectural industrialization. [We] hope everyone will carefully explore the positive and negative experiences of both Chinese and foreign architecture, combine them with the specific situation of our country, and air views freely according to the policy of "let a hundred flowers bloom, let a hundred schools of thought contend."[40]

Such an appeal in an official professional journal signaled a shift in architecture from a revolution-oriented collective approach to technology-oriented professional study.

The enthusiasm for industrialization as a key step toward architectural modernization waned toward the end of the 1970s. As more and more identical concrete slabs appeared in cities all over the country, it seemed that the previous fears about monotony as a result of design standardization had come true. Although the design process was far from standardized, and the assembly method in construction was far from popularized—in fact, on-site assembly was used only for the most prestigious situations, such as the diplomatic projects on Chang'an Avenue—the push for industrialization and standardization encouraged direct copying of existing buildings. Many construction drawings, especially those for residential architecture, were used repeatedly in different cities.

In reaction to this stylistic monotony, more voices called for exploration in architectural form. At a symposium in Beijing, "Architectural Modernization and Architectural Style," organized by the Chinese Architectural Society in October 1978, speakers expressed dissatisfaction with the lack of variety in architectural form, and the issue of "national form" was raised again. An article titled "The Importance of

Exploration in Architectural Forms" appeared in the first issue of the 1979 *Architectural Journal*.[41] These appeals would have been condemned as formalism in the early 1970s. At the same time, the use of symbols such as torches, red flags, beacons, red suns, sunflowers, and stars to emphasize socialist or revolutionary content was criticized. Such blatant application of political concepts in architectural design, one writer argued, was against the nature of architectural art, which was based on function and could only evoke qualities such as solemnity or liveliness, richness or simplicity, and delicacy or boldness, but not political ideologies.[42]

After almost two decades of emphasis on the revolutionary social function of architecture (from the early 1960s to 1979), the discussion about form and style revived. Yet the discussion that began in 1979 and continued throughout the 1980s was significantly different from that of the 1950s. Conveying ideological content was generally considered to be beyond the ability of architectural design and relatively trivial compared to innovations in form and function. While the exploration of national form in the 1950s had been more philosophical, analyzing the relationship between form and content that aimed to be both Chinese and socialist, the discussion of architectural form that began in 1979 and lasted into the 1980s was more methodological, analyzing specific ways of achieving forms and styles that were both national and modern. The former period asked "what," while the latter asked "how."

This shift was triggered partly by accessibility to new theoretical work in architecture coming out of the West. For the first time since the Cultural Revolution, articles introducing contemporary Western architecture appeared in early 1979.[43] In an article on the application of visual analysis in architectural creation, Bai Zuomin cites Hans Blumenfeld's *Scale in Civic Design* and Paul Zucker's *Town and Square*, and borrows G. W. Elderkin's model of the visual analysis of the Acropolis in Athens to analyze buildings in Tiananmen Square.[44] Sigfried Giedion's concept of space as the key element in the analysis of architecture similarly inspired Chinese architects to look at architectural form in a different way. As Giedion had done in his influential book *Space, Time, and Architecture: The Growth of a New Tradition*, some architects applied the concepts of space versus volume and interior versus exterior to reevaluate traditional Chinese architecture.[45] Dynamic space was appreciated and studied.[46] Some authors equated the previous architectural dichotomy of form versus content with space versus function.[47] As a result, in the exploration of national form, the traditional Chinese garden, with its complex spaces, asymmetrical plans, permeation of interior and exterior, and rich scenery views, became the main inspiration for achieving new Chinese modern architecture.[48] The spirit of Chinese architecture now resided in its space; big roofs, memorial archways, and glazed tiles celebrating national form became outmoded.

As the requirements for political correctness in architectural design suddenly disappeared at the end of the 1970s, the yearning for originality—"new creation" in fashionable Chinese terms—built up in the 1980s, as is evident in the pages of *Architectural Journal*. Architectural form was considered an inseparable part of function and structure. It was accorded such high esteem in architectural creation that some authors acclaimed "Long live form!"[49] To legitimate the pursuit of form, its proponents argued that it had objective existence that could not be evaded; that it should not be equated with beauty, let alone decoration; that it should not be considered the opposite of function; and that it was not incompatible with economy.[50] Various sources were mobilized to inspire new creations, from traditional gardens to modern sculpture,[51] from aesthetic concepts to information theory, systems theory, and cybernetics.[52] "Liberation of individuality" and "self-expression" were encouraged. As in other cultural fields in the early 1980s, numerous articles called for "breaking spiritual shackles" and the cultivation of personality in architecture. Targets for criticism included not only the collective approach in architectural creation from the 1950s to the 1970s but also the recent "standardization and industrialization."[53]

All of the articles calling for architectural creation widely cite famous buildings in contemporary Western and Japanese architecture as examples to support their claims. With their sudden access to the outside world in the 1980s, Chinese architects were eagerly learning from the West.

From National Construction to the International Hotel

Chinese architects in the 1980s studied foreign architecture not only from books and journals but also by direct observation of buildings designed by Western architects on Chinese soil. In 1980–82, the first building in the PRC era designed by Westerners and operated on Western lines appeared on Chang'an Avenue. This was the Jianguo (National Construction) Hotel on East Chang'an Avenue near Jianguo Gate, at the east end of Chang'an Avenue proper.

The Jianguo Hotel was designed by a Hong Kong firm headed by Chinese American architect Chen Xuanyuan. Construction started in July 1980 and was completed in April 1982. Located on a site of 10,970 square meters, the hotel has 528 guest rooms and a total floorage of 29,506 square meters. With an initial investment of US$20 million, the Jianguo Hotel was meant to be not a luxurious but a middle-rank hotel, comparable to a Holiday Inn in the United States.

Most other buildings on Chang'an Avenue at the time had large-scale façades, often symmetrical and monolithic, facing the avenue. The Jianguo Hotel, however, has its

Fig. 4.8. Jianguo Hotel, 1980–82. Chen Xuanyuan and others.

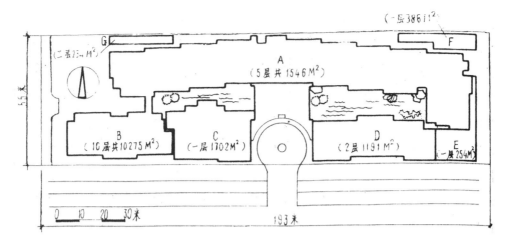

a. Site plan. *Reproduction from Architectural Journal (September 1982): 38, courtesy of* JZXB.

b. Jianguo Hotel entrance off of Chang'an Avenue. *Photograph by author.*

volumes broken down into several smaller-scale buildings, which are asymmetrically arranged around a water courtyard (fig. 4.8). Along the avenue, the façades of five individual buildings of different heights and widths form a continuous diversified front. The tallest building, a ten-story guestroom block, is at the west end. The main atrium, an individual building, connects with other parts of the complex by corridors. Other monuments on the avenue often have immense central entrances located on high platforms approached by wide stairs that are authoritative and intimidating. The main entrance of the Jianguo Hotel, however, is unpretentious and welcoming. Hidden in a concave semicircular wall and recessed from the busy avenue, it creates a private, street-level environment on a human scale. Behind the divided, long façade of the hotel on Chang'an Avenue is the zigzag screen of a five-story guestroom building, visible from street level but modest in character. In general, the Jianguo Hotel lacks the grandeur of other earlier avenue buildings that place everything under one roof in order to achieve a giant façade. It breaks the convention of combining a high main structure with low apron buildings, an architectural composition seen so often in Chinese cities at the time.

With a design not unusual in the West, the Jianguo Hotel drew great attention from Chinese architects in the 1980s. To some extent, inviting a foreign company to design a hotel on Chang'an Avenue was meant to enable Chinese architects to learn from the outside world at home. On June 15, 1982, only two months after the completion of the Jianguo Hotel, a symposium was organized by the *Architectural Journal* editorial committee and the Beijing Architectural Design Institute to discuss the designs of two hotels recently completed in Beijing: the Jianguo Hotel and the Huadu Hotel, a hotel of similar size and grade designed by Chinese architects. Although participants in the symposium praised and criticized different aspects of both hotels, the predominant theme was what was lacking in the Chinese design as compared to the buildings designed by the foreign architects. Among other things, the Chinese design for the Huadu Hotel was criticized for lack of spatial variation, too much attention to decoration, lack of liberation in "design thought" (lack of freedom in thinking about design), and conservativeness in design approach and motifs.[54] The Jianguo Hotel, on the other hand, was praised for its variety in spatial experience, its natural and welcoming environment, and its emphasis on the convenience of guests instead of extra decoration. The spatial organization was acknowledged to possess characteristics of ancient Chinese architecture.[55] The amount of effort foreign architects put into the design of the guestrooms, especially the bathrooms, impressed their Chinese colleagues, and was contrasted with the Chinese habit of making central atriums and banquet halls the focal areas in design. Criticism of the Jianguo Hotel design focused primarily on its lack of familiarity with the Chinese lifestyle and with the special conditions of a developing country.[56]

Similar symposia were organized for Chinese architects to exchange comments on the first building during the PRC era designed by a world-renowned architect—I. M. Pei's Fragrant Hills Hotel, completed in 1983 in the western suburbs of Beijing. The Fragrant Hills Hotel provoked large-scale discussions on the future direction of modern Chinese architecture. Admirers of the building acclaimed its Chinese soul within a physical structure of modern materials and forms, while others complained that it was too expensive and that the scale of the hotel complex ruined the beautiful scenery of Fragrant Hills.[57] Despite this difference of opinion, this project was extremely influential on Chinese architecture in the late 1980s. In fact, some decorative motifs first used in the Fragrant Hills Hotel were widely copied and have become symbols of Chineseness in later buildings.

In 1987 the International Hotel (Guoji Fandian) on East Chang'an Avenue proper, designed by Chinese architects, concluded the learning process. To some extent, this project was intended to showcase what Chinese architects could achieve in the pursuit of modern Chinese architecture. In the first sentence of an introductory article, the designers proudly announced that the International Hotel was "a large-scale hotel with both modern and Chinese characteristics that we financed by ourselves, designed by ourselves, constructed by ourselves, and equipped with our own equipment and materials."[58] Located on the north side of East Chang'an Avenue, like the Jianguo Hotel, the International Hotel is much larger in scale and closer to Tiananmen Square. It has 1,049 guestrooms and suites, with a floorage of 105,000 square meters. In contrast to the Jianguo Hotel, which has no clear division between major structure and apron buildings and which spreads along Chang'an Avenue horizontally, the International Hotel has a hotel tower of twenty-nine floors and a two-story apron building housing the main atrium, banquet halls, and other business facilities (fig. 4.9). While the Jianguo Hotel has many small-scale buildings arranged freely around a central water courtyard, the International Hotel is a single structure with a strong north-south axis linking different parts inside, which, according to the designers, embodies the traditional method of spatial organization.[59]

The International Hotel aimed to achieve "both Chinese and new, both national style and the character of the current age." While the Chineseness in earlier monuments was largely expressed through the national forms of exterior decorations, including traditional roofs, brackets, and *pailou* (memorial archways), the national style in the International Hotel resides mainly in its interior, a result of the space-oriented search for national form. The main building is a clean, white concrete tower with regularly spaced rectangular windows. The entrance and main atrium, however, incorporate traditional architectural motifs (such as memorial columns like those in front of the Tiananmen Tower, a caisson ceiling *zaojing,* and red and golden yellow coloring) and traditional interior decorations (painted screen panels, semipermanent wooden space dividers [*luodizhao*], wood carvings, and bamboo weavings). The formal motifs of the circle and the octagon, which, according to the designers, were the most popular shapes in folk designs, are applied everywhere to unify the design.[60] Using a formal motif to give a building recognizable character might have been inspired by I. M. Pei's Fragrant Hills Hotel, whose diamond motif was admired by many Chinese architects because it was both Chinese and modern.

Fig. 4.9. International Hotel, 1984–87. Lin Leyi, Jiang Zhongjun, and others. *Photograph by author.*

Modernism, Postmodernism, and National Form

In the 1980s, just as Chinese architects had broken the shackles of political require-ments in architectural design and gathered the momentum to modernize Chinese architecture, they suddenly discovered that the world facing them was no longer modern but postmodern. Modernism, as represented by functionalism, industrial-ization, and International Style, was under criticism in the West. Embarking on a modernization project guided by the new Four Modernizations slogan, Chinese architects' first response to postmodernism was that it was a new development of modernism. The first article in *Architectural Journal* introducing postmodernism called it "neomodernism" (*xin xiandaizhuyi*).[61] Architectural theories in the West since the 1950s were relatively unknown to the Chinese because of the political isola-tion of the People's Republic of China before the 1970s. As Chinese architects in the early 1980s familiarized themselves with more new developments in Western architecture during the last three decades, they developed different attitudes toward postmodernism.

Postmodernism as a New Theoretical Framework

There were in general three different responses to postmodern architecture among Chinese architects during the 1980s. Wholehearted modernists responded with total rejection; a second response argued that postmodernism was for Western developed countries but would not do any good in a developing country such as China; the third attitude welcomed postmodern architecture as a way to break the modernist monopoly and achieve regional diversity.

The first attitude rejected postmodernism on the basis that modernism was not "dead" but still the driving force in contemporary architecture. Modern architecture, proponents of this approach argued, was never as rigid and inhuman as the postmod-ernists had contended. For modernists, the modern movement in architecture, like the Communist revolution, began with the struggle for a better life for the common people. Proponents claimed that "monotonous boxes" were not the unavoidable out-come of modernism, and "International Style" was not the only modern architecture. Diversity could be achieved without postmodernism.[62] There were, however, mod-ernist extremists among this group, who claimed that International Style was the inevitable result of historical development. As cultural exchanges among the peoples of the world were increasing, national differences were decreasing, undermining the basis for architectural differences among different regions and nations. "People from all nations wear suits," they argued, and so, "instead of arguing whether we should support or oppose 'International Style,' it is more important to study why 'International Style' has appeared everywhere in the world."[63] Others suggested that regional or national character should not be the concern of architecture. As long as architects were solving specific functional problems and being creative, regional or national character would emerge automatically.[64]

Supporters of the second attitude recognized the discrepancy in contemporary architectural development between China and the West. They argued that, while contemporary architecture in the United States was "postmodern," contemporary Chinese architecture was "late-coming modern" (*chixiandai*). In the 1970s, when the United States tired of the monotonous modernism of the 1950s and geared toward a new eclecticism, China was just shaking off the eclecticism of the 1950s and marching on to modernism, as characterized by industrialization and standardization. While contemporary eclecticism in the United States came after modernism, the eclecticism of China in the 1950s was premodern.[65] Although based on the assumption that architecture had only one possible path to follow, the Western model, such an assessment expressed an opinion popular even today. China had missed the lesson on modern architecture and needed to make it up.

The third attitude, like the postmodernism it was supporting, blamed the current monotony in architectural form on modernism. Western theoretical works on semiotics and Charles Jencks's books on postmodernism were translated and introduced to China, as well as designs by such postmodern architects as Robert Venturi, Philip Johnson, and Michael Graves. Many people used postmodern theory to justify exploration into traditional architecture in the process of creating new Chinese architecture. They argued,

> Some may think that orthodox Western modernist architecture reflects the characteristics of new materials and new technologies and represents the style of the 1970s. They do not understand that architectural forms always reflect specific aesthetic viewpoints, and that the aesthetic source of modern architecture is cubist art. The architectural form of "International Style" boxes cannot represent the style of the 1970s. Today, however, monotonous "square boxes" are still popular throughout the country, and are used [indiscriminately], both north and south, regardless of regional differences. . . . On the other hand, research into and inheritance of the national and cultural traditions of our country are indiscriminately condemned as "revivalism," with no "spirit of the times," and are totally rejected. After acquainting ourselves with the developing trend of Western modern architecture, shouldn't we think it over again?[66]

The different attitudes toward postmodernism were not only responses to the new theoretical impact of the West but also a way for Chinese architecture to continue its own discourse. Throughout the controversies on postmodernism, the focal points are always national form and modernization. To some extent, postmodernism provided 1980s China with a new framework to continue the ongoing debate. During this process, such concepts as "tradition," "modern," "national form," and "socialist content" all acquired new meanings.

It was postmodernism's emphasis on specific cultural meanings that attracted most Chinese architects' attention. They found that regardless of the diversity, inconsistency, and confusion of different postmodern architects and theories, they all emphasized national and local cultural characteristics in architectural design.[67] Compared with such practical interests, other aspects of postmodern theories were less popular. Most Chinese architects took the new postmodernist terms and imbued them with new meanings by applying them to the discourse of Chinese architecture.

In the beginning of the 1980s, postmodernism was first understood in China as a reaction and rebellion against the monotony of modernism. Few architects paid attention to its theoretical sources or Western background. On one hand, they found in postmodernism a new way to fight against the monotony in architectural form that had appeared in contemporary Chinese architecture since the late 1970s. On the other hand, the postmodern emphasis on meaning and the spirit of a specific place equipped Chinese architects with a new terminology and methodology in dealing with national form.

In the Chinese context, the arbitrary nature of the meaning of "sign" in Western semiotics disappeared, as well as the differentiation of sign into index, icon, and symbol. "Sign," or *fuhao*, as framed in the Chinese architectural discourse of the 1980s, was equated with cultural motif or any conventional concept that might have something to do with architecture. The semiotic "reading" was understood as exploration in meaning rather than form. Reading as a way to generate meaning, instead of look for meaning, was foreign. For Chinese architects, meanings were firmly embedded in history and function.[68]

"Context," or *wenben*, was another postmodern term newly adopted by Chinese architects in the 1980s. For Chinese architects, context was the cultural and physical environment into which new forms should fit rather than a structuralist framework that gave rise to meanings. Such a linguistic transformation of "context" allowed Chinese architects to use contextualism to argue for either modernism or national form, depending on their different standpoints. The former believed that postmodernism was not a total rejection but a continuation and new form of modernism.[69] The latter argued that "context" referred to both physical and abstract environments, and that revivalism based on appropriate architectural context was at least one of the many venues for creation.[70]

The Semiotic Dimension of National Form on Chang'an Avenue

Although its transplantation was not without misinterpretation, the new postmodern framework allowed Chinese architects in the 1980s to go beyond formal or spatial exploration of national form and to make a semiotic transformation of cultural symbols in architecture. Architectural vocabularies were drawn from a broader cultural sphere, not just limited to traditional architectural motifs. Unlike the previous adoptions of national, political, or cultural motifs, new symbolism was applied not simply on the decorative level but throughout the entire design concept in general.

One architectural sign was the gate. Many buildings on Chang'an Avenue constructed in the late 1980s and early 1990s employed the image of a gigantic gate. Instead of using the traditional gate simply as a decorative motif, the gate as a symbol became the key design concept. The Customs Headquarters of 1987–90 on East Chang'an Avenue uses the gate to symbolize the building complex as the gate through which goods are imported into and exported out of China. Its two towers—one for the National Customs Bureau, the other for the Beijing Customs Department—are connected on the top, making the center of the complex a gigantic void doorway. The West Railway Station, completed in 1996 on the West Chang'an Avenue extension, is also an enormous gateway framed by symmetrical solid concrete walls, symbolizing the entrance and exit of the capital. Built in the 1990s, the entire complex is topped with time-honored double-eave pavilions and decorated with other architectural motifs from China's imperial past (see fig. 1.19).

Not only architectural symbols but also cultural symbols from both imperial and folk traditions became common vocabulary in new architectural creation after the postmodernist semiotic transformation. The Head Office of the People's Bank of China, a 1987–90 construction at the western end of West Chang'an Avenue proper, employs symbols from China's folk traditions. The plan and the general image of the building mimic *yuanbao* (a gold or silver ingot used as money in dynastic China) and *jubaopen* (a treasure bowl in folklore that will generate jewels). Previously denounced as feudal and superstitious during Mao's time, these signs were now considered acceptable as traditional Chinese cultural symbols of prosperity. As the headquarters of China's central bank, this building merited such traditional motifs as appropriate symbols for a new national identity.[71] Stylistically, the juxtaposition of solid walls of raw concrete and uninterrupted shiny glass surface is more in tune with the New Brutalism popular in the 1960s in the West than with any Chinese traditions (see fig. 1.17).

Buildings constructed in the 1970s and 1980s on Chang'an Avenue reflect the cultural political changes in China during these two decades, as well as the theoretical and ideological repercussions they caused in architectural design. The general trend was a rising quest for freedom in architectural creation and a moral distrust of a direct application of national form. However, a profound sense of history and tradition loomed so large in the minds of Chinese architects that, as soon as a new theoretical framework allowed, they quickly applied it to inaugurate a new phase of exploration in national form. Neither International Style nor Chinese architectural motifs would be sufficient to achieve a new Chinese architecture that was both national and modern. It is among the buildings of the 1970s and 1980s that we find the least amount of time-honored Chinese roofs with sloping and upturned eaves on Chang'an Avenue. Modernization in a postmodern world prepared new ground for the future development of Chinese architecture.

Chapter Five

Collage without Planning:
Toward the New Millennium

WHILE DETAILED PLANS were prepared for Chang'an Avenue with few structures actually built before the 1990s, in the last decade of the twentieth century the thoroughfare became crowded with monumental façades without any comprehensive planning. Buildings of different historical styles stood side by side with new experiments for the coming millennium, turning Chang'an Avenue into a collage.

Behind this architectural collage of façades were struggles among different forces: commercial, social, political, intellectual, and popular. The rise of commerce and the socialist market challenged the longstanding monopoly of political control over Chang'an Avenue's image. The restoration of the social status of intellectuals added new voices to the discourse on Chang'an Avenue architecture. Not only writers and artists but also the general Chinese citizenry no longer hesitated to express their personal feelings about the image of the "Number One Street of China."

Commercial Patches and Political Patches

By the 1990s Deng Xiaoping's policy of promoting a socialist market economy had been in force for over a decade, and China had become fully integrated into the global market. Under the slogan of constructing socialism with Chinese character, Chinese society was reinvigorated in its struggle for economic success. The Chinese Communist Party (CCP), whose legitimacy had previously rested on its status as a revolutionary party fighting against capitalist imperialism, lost this ideological claim to rule. Official party documents continued paying lip service to Marxism-Leninism and Mao Zedong Thought. In reality, few people still subscribed to the Maoist ideology focused on revolutionary spirit and class struggle. The relaxed intellectual environment and the conflict between the old political system and the new economic reality gave rise to the democracy movements of the late 1980s that ended with the tragic military suppression of June 4, 1989, known as the "Tiananmen Massacre" in the West and as "political turmoil" by the party.

During the spring of 1989, while Tiananmen Square was occupied by protesting

students and their supporters, Chang'an Avenue was where the real conflict took place.[1] To some extent, the term "Tiananmen Massacre" is a deliberate misnomer that takes advantage of the symbolic eminence of the square. Documentation from both the party and the protesters indicate that no one died in the square and that most of the deaths actually occurred along the avenue. According to CCP sources, "counterrevolutionary mobs" killed People's Liberation Army (PLA) soldiers near the Minority Culture Palace and on Jianguo Gate Bridge—both on Chang'an Avenue—and blocked communication on the avenue by burning buses;[2] according to some witnesses, by the time troops finally reached Tiananmen Square shortly after midnight, West and East Chang'an Avenues had become bloody trails of death and destruction.[3]

After the June Fourth Democratic Movement,[4] on one hand, the political trauma was diluted by a continued effort to highlight economic development and encourage the pursuit of private wealth; on the other hand, the party redirected its political ideology to focus on patriotism and nationalism. Chang'an Avenue architecture during the 1990s reflects these two tendencies in post–June Fourth China. Architectural projects on the avenue after 1989 can be categorized into two groups: one glorifies the Chinese nation—for instance, the China Millennium Monument, the Military Commission Headquarters (August First Building), the headquarters of various central government ministries, and the reorganization of museum displays; the other is primarily the product of profit pursuit, such as the Oriental Plaza, the Guanghua Chang'an Building, and the Henderson Center. The former group purposefully aimed at certain political goals; the latter is the natural outcome of a commercial market. While the former group has been firmly controlled by the party, the latter has been mostly manipulated by overseas capital, especially investment from Hong Kong.

Both cooperation and conflict between political ideology and commercial profit occurred on Chang'an Avenue, creating political and commercial patches. Inserted along the avenue's hundred *li* façades, these patches gradually filled in the gaps between earlier monumental structures. On the whole, the political patches are concentrated in the western sections of Chang'an Avenue, and the commercial patches are concentrated more in its eastern parts. The traditional symbolic associations with East and West Chang'an Avenues continued.

The Commercial Patches

The greatest victory of the free market on Chang'an Avenue in the 1990s was Oriental Plaza, a gigantic complex guarding the southern end of Wangfujing, the most famous commercial street in China. Located on East Chang'an Avenue about one kilometer east of Tiananmen Square, it was the largest civil property development project in

and Wangfujing District. They could either
the entire 10,000-square-meter area or do
. Encouraged by Beijing officials and sup-
by the enormous wealth of the Hong Kong
Zhou accepted the offer without hesitation
de an even more ambitious proposal. She
nd redevelop the entire area between Wang-
tion. The redevelopment area was 100,000
ed by the Beijing officials. As the saying in
gfujing equals one inch of gold." Given the
square meters was an astronomical figure.
Forbidden City. Beijing officials accepted

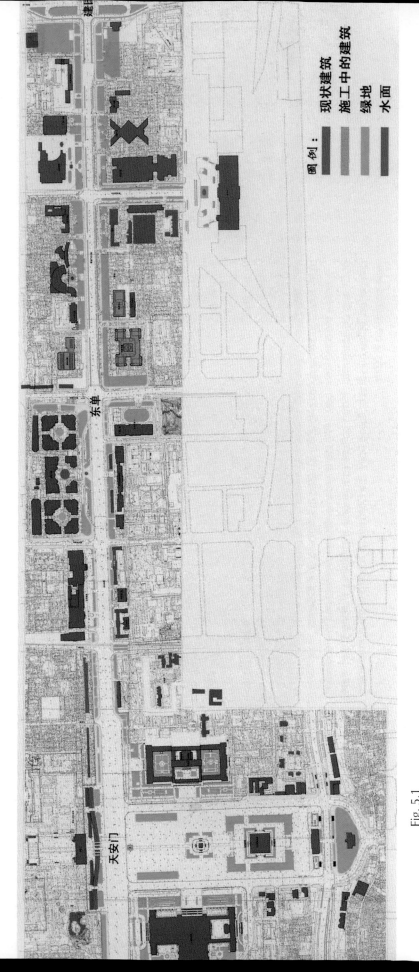

图例：

现状建筑
施工中的建筑
绿地
水面

东单

天安门

Fig. 5.1

Fig. 5.2. Oriental Plaza, 1997–99. Palmer and Turner Group and Beijing Institute of Architectural Design and Research. *Photograph by author.*

Avenue
rebuild
nothing
ported
tycoon,
and ma

offered to take all of the adjacent blocks a
fujing Street and the Dongdan interse
square meters, ten times what was offe
Beijing goes, "One inch of earth at War
unrivaled land prices in this area, 100,0
It was one-seventh the size of the entir
her plan.[8]

students and their supporters, Chang'an Avenue was where the real conflict took place.[1] To some extent, the term "Tiananmen Massacre" is a deliberate misnomer that takes advantage of the symbolic eminence of the square. Documentation from both the party and the protesters indicate that no one died in the square and that most of the deaths actually occurred along the avenue. According to CCP sources, "counterrevolutionary mobs" killed People's Liberation Army (PLA) soldiers near the Minority Culture Palace and on Jianguo Gate Bridge—both on Chang'an Avenue—and blocked communication on the avenue by burning buses;[2] according to some witnesses, by the time troops finally reached Tiananmen Square shortly after midnight, West and East Chang'an Avenues had become bloody trails of death and destruction.[3]

After the June Fourth Democratic Movement,[4] on one hand, the political trauma was diluted by a continued effort to highlight economic development and encourage the pursuit of private wealth; on the other hand, the party redirected its political ideology to focus on patriotism and nationalism. Chang'an Avenue architecture during the 1990s reflects these two tendencies in post–June Fourth China. Architectural projects on the avenue after 1989 can be categorized into two groups: one glorifies the Chinese nation—for instance, the China Millennium Monument, the Military Commission Headquarters (August First Building), the headquarters of various central government ministries, and the reorganization of museum displays; the other is primarily the product of profit pursuit, such as the Oriental Plaza, the Guanghua Chang'an Building, and the Henderson Center. The former group purposefully aimed at certain political goals; the latter is the natural outcome of a commercial market. While the former group has been firmly controlled by the party, the latter has been mostly manipulated by overseas capital, especially investment from Hong Kong.

Both cooperation and conflict between political ideology and commercial profit occurred on Chang'an Avenue, creating political and commercial patches. Inserted along the avenue's hundred *li* façades, these patches gradually filled in the gaps between earlier monumental structures. On the whole, the political patches are concentrated in the western sections of Chang'an Avenue, and the commercial patches are concentrated more in its eastern parts. The traditional symbolic associations with East and West Chang'an Avenues continued.

The Commercial Patches

The greatest victory of the free market on Chang'an Avenue in the 1990s was Oriental Plaza, a gigantic complex guarding the southern end of Wangfujing, the most famous commercial street in China. Located on East Chang'an Avenue about one kilometer east of Tiananmen Square, it was the largest civil property development project in

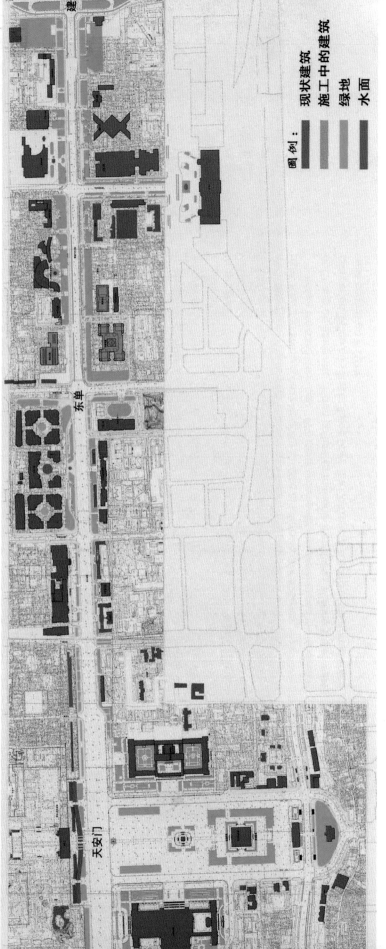

图 例：
现状建筑
施工中的建筑
绿地
水面

建

东单

天安门

Fig. 5.1

Asia at the time of its completion in 1999. The US$2 billion project was financed by Hong Kong capital. In its final form, the complex comprises eleven buildings, including one "super-five-star" hotel and ten commercial office buildings, all connected at the basement and ground levels. The project also includes two separate residential buildings at the rear of the complex for the relocation of the site's former courtyard dwellers (fig. 5.1).

The architecture of Oriental Plaza defies all city planning rules of Beijing, illustrating the victory of commercial power over political control of urban space. According to official regulations issued in 1987, the building height on the Oriental Plaza site was not to exceed forty-five meters.[5] The Great Hall was forty meters high, and the museum complex about thirty. In the original 1994 design, however, the tallest building in Oriental Plaza reached eighty-five meters, twice as high as the limit set by the city planning codes. Only after protests by Chinese architects and the intervention of the central government were the heights lowered to sixty-eight, fifty-nine, and forty-nine meters, diminishing as the complex approaches Tiananmen Square.[6]

The architectural volume of Oriental Plaza also totally disregards the city planning principles for the Old City of Beijing—the area within the former walls of the Inner City and Outer City. All of the successive versions of master plans for the capital emphasized the maintenance of a historical urban texture characterized by small-volume individual courtyard structures linked by alleys (*hutong*). Both architectural professionals and municipal officials generally agreed that new buildings in Beijing's Old City should merge with the old checkerboard street system instead of spanning several blocks in one gigantic structure.[7] Oriental Plaza, however, extends 500 meters along the avenue, and the original plan was for one comprehensive structure. Although the final completed complex is divided into three sections, the visual continuity of the façades still dwarfs all of its neighbors (fig. 5.2).

The insertion of such a gigantic structure into the historical center of Beijing, however, did not occur without the encouragement and cooperation of government officials. According to Zhou Kaixuan, the initiator and manager of the Oriental Plaza project and a close friend of the project sponsor, Hong Kong billionaire Li Ka-shing, the original plan in 1992 had been to simply purchase a small six-story building on Chang'an Avenue, the Children's Cinema, and replace it with a store. During negotiations with the municipal officials of the Dongcheng District, however, they were told that the entire 10,000-square-meter site on which the building was located needed to be developed comprehensively according to the master plan of East Chang'an

Fig. 5.2. Oriental Plaza, 1997–99. Palmer and Turner Group and Beijing Institute of Architectural Design and Research. *Photograph by author.*

Avenue and Wangfujing District. They could either rebuild the entire 10,000-square-meter area or do nothing. Encouraged by Beijing officials and supported by the enormous wealth of the Hong Kong tycoon, Zhou accepted the offer without hesitation and made an even more ambitious proposal. She offered to take all of the adjacent blocks and redevelop the entire area between Wangfujing Street and the Dongdan intersection. The redevelopment area was 100,000 square meters, ten times what was offered by the Beijing officials. As the saying in Beijing goes, "One inch of earth at Wangfujing equals one inch of gold." Given the unrivaled land prices in this area, 100,000 square meters was an astronomical figure. It was one-seventh the size of the entire Forbidden City. Beijing officials accepted her plan.[8]

The tallest buildings on the Oriental Plaza site were previously six stories, and most of the structures directly on Chang'an Avenue were only two stories high. They had all been built within the twenty years since China opened its doors in 1979, to fill in the former "gaps" between the one-story *siheyuan* courtyards. In the 1990s these multistory buildings themselves became "gaps." Behind them remained old one-story courtyard houses that the earlier Beijing city plans had marked for preservation. The Oriental Plaza project erased them all. In order to expedite the demolition of these buildings, the Hong Kong investors paid more to those who left their homes quickly. Those who vacated their houses within ten days were eligible for the first-grade relocation fee, within twenty days, the second-grade, and so on. This policy proved to be very efficient. Within a month, all of the courtyard houses at the back of the site were ready for demolition. According to Zhou, the smooth and rapid relocation of the courtyard dwellers speeded up the excavation of the multistory buildings at the front of the site, directly on the avenue.[9] Site preparation for the construction of Oriental Plaza was not as easy as Zhou's personal account might suggest. For instance, negotiations to relocate the largest McDonald's restaurant in the world, built in the 1980s, lasted for two years, from 1994 to 1996.[10] The site was fully emptied for the commencement of construction work at the end of 1996.

The power of commercial expansion also overshadowed cultural preservationists' protests. Harsh criticism from prominent scholars and scientists of the scale of Oriental Plaza led only to minor adjustments in its height and volume. During construction in December 1996, a Paleolithic archeological site some twenty thousand years old was discovered. Even such a significant cultural discovery caused no revision to the plan of the commercial complex. Accommodating the ancient site carved out only 400 square meters of the complex's total floorage of 880,000 square meters, and the museum was tucked away inside the third floor, underground, next to a subway entrance.[11]

It seems that even the political image of the capital could be sacrificed in pursuit of commercial development. In August 1995 the Chinese People's Political Consultative Conference (CPPCC) issued a long statement condemning the design of Oriental Plaza. In addition to transgressing the city's height control regulations, the statement specifically pointed out that the colossal building complex would divert attention from Tiananmen Square, the symbol of New China. Although the revised design had broken the original volume into three sections, the visual continuity of the façades still made it one gigantic, integrated structure that dwarfed both the Great Hall—the symbol of the political power of Communist China—and the museum complex—the central site for displaying the party's version of Chinese history that legitimized the current regime.[12] The statement also pointed out that the Oriental Plaza design was fueled by blatant profit-seeking greed at the expense of the political image of the people's capital. Even such a harsh appeal from inside the Communist regime could not stop the march of the international market on Chang'an Avenue, which scholar Anne-Marie Broudehoux refers to as "Hong Kong's takeover of China" in 1997.[13]

While Oriental Plaza obviously represented a financial victory in the political heart of the Chinese capital, there are different stories about how the relationship between politics and the market led to the realization of this Hong Kong project. The most popular version associates the project with the former Beijing mayor, Chen Xitong, who was ousted from office and imprisoned in 1995 due to a corruption scandal within the Beijing municipal government. A major charge that led to Chen's fall after twelve years as one of the most prominent and powerful Communist leaders was the allegation that he and his associates accepted more than US$37 million in bribes from Li Ka-shing. Another version alleges that in July 1997, when president Jiang Zemin attended ceremonies celebrating Hong Kong's return to the motherland, Li and Jiang reached an informal agreement that eventually led to the continuation of the project even after Chen fell from power. The Hong Kong investor in the project tells quite a different story. According to Zhou, former Beijing mayor Chen had nothing to do with Oriental Plaza. Zhou's business was mainly with the government of the Dongcheng District, and Li Ka-shing was hardly involved in the early stages of development. "The project just went through the proper real estate procedures, from lower official levels to higher ones, and that is all," she told a journalist.[14]

While Zhou's account might be too simple given the open secret of bribe taking in China's socialist market economy since the 1980s, the direct association of the project with a political leader who had recently lost power is equally questionable. It is too easy to connect disgraced projects with disgraced persons. Chen was famous for his enthusiasm for "retrieving the character of the ancient capital," and he became notorious after his removal for having imposed his personal taste on Beijing's new architecture. He was given the nickname Chen Xiting, a caricature that replaces the last character of his real name, Chen Xitong, with the character for "pavilion," alluding to his inclination to top every new building with traditional pavilions. Neither the original design nor the completed Oriental Plaza, however, contains the features typically associated with Chen-style projects.

Named "Oriental Plaza," the building complex has no plaza at all. Interchanging solid and glazed blocks fill the entire site, set back from the street just on the redline,[15] as required by city planning regulations. The basement floors fill the entire 100,000 square meters of the site area. The predominant design consideration was to maximize the floorage. The solid walls are flat and straight, interspersed with curved glass surfaces. Except for the regular square patterns composed of windows of different sizes, the exterior walls are devoid of decoration. And the only patterns on the glass curtain walls are formed by the mullion lines. The main entrance, in the center of the middle section of the building complex on Chang'an Avenue, is in an enormous concave circular glass curtain wall preceded by a long, wide flight of steps leading pedestrians from the sidewalk of the avenue directly into the main atrium of the hotel. This is the largest open-air area in the entire complex and was originally the only open-air area before the Chinese scholars' protest forced the breakup of the monolithic volume of the original design. Even the inclusion of this original open area might have been motivated more by a desire for better profit-generating feng shui than for any aesthetic, cultural, or social considerations. Popular among Hong Kong real estate investors, the feng shui theory requires the main entrance of a building to open into a sizable half-enclosed area to contain benevolent energy (*qi*), which will bring wealth and luck to the businesses inside.

Standard explanation[16] of the Oriental Plaza design in China, however, does emphasize the cultural character of the building complex. The association with traditional Chinese architecture is stretched. Although the three open areas around which the three groups of buildings are organized were claimed to be in the form of the traditional courtyard, the physical character of the spaces have very little in common with that traditional space. While the Beijing courtyard house is rectangular in shape, all three of the Oriental Plaza courtyards are circular; while the traditional courtyard's horizontal dimension is much larger than its vertical dimension due to the fact that all of the buildings around the courtyard are virtually one story, the Oriental Plaza courtyards are more like sky wells, whose defining walls are much higher than the diameter of the open space. Moreover, while the main buildings surrounding traditional courtyards are located on the main north-south and east-west axes of the complex, the towers defining the courtyards of Oriental Plaza are all located at the corners, leaving the axes of the complex open. Finally, the overhanging decorative members protruding from the tops of the towers are meant to mimic the far-reaching eaves in traditional roofs, but at street level they are only visible as long, narrow shadows floating above the shining surfaces of the concrete slabs.

During the 1990s commercial expansion replaced more than courtyard houses on East Chang'an Avenue. The historical landmark Grand Chang'an Theatre was relocated inside a seventeen-story commercial office building named the Guanghua Chang'an Building. The former renowned theatre for Beijing Opera occupies a small part of the first floor. Above it, more floorage was added for more profitable businesses. On the exterior façade facing Chang'an Avenue, a simplified archway decorates the main entrance in a flat and shinning blue glass curtain wall with yellow glazed sloping roofs raised on cylindrical columns (fig. 5.3).

Fig. 5.3. Guanghua Chang'an
Building, 1994–96. Wei
Dazhong and others. *Photo-
graph by author.*

The Political Patches

While market forces advanced on East Chang'an Avenue by replacing small-scale neighborhoods with gigantic commercial complexes supported by overseas[17] investment, new monuments indicative of political development in the 1990s appeared on West Chang'an Avenue under government sponsorship. Unlike the national projects in the 1950s, which were meant to glorify the Communist revolution and render past history as an oppressive, dark night before the dawn of the new socialist age, the new monuments glorified the past and yearned for a new golden age for the Chinese nation.

The best example with the strongest nationalist tone is the China Millennium Monument, completed in 1999 on the West Chang'an Avenue extension. The monument was dedicated to the commencement of the new century and millennium. The name of the monument, China Millennium Monument (Zhonghua Shijitan), can be understood as either an altar within China dedicated to the new century or an altar

dedicated to a new Chinese century. The latter suggests that the coming century will be a Chinese renaissance, or, to use the official terminology, the "great renaissance of the Chinese nationality."

Fig. 5.4. Plaza of Holy Fire, Bronze Causeway, and the "Main Altar," China Millennium Monument, 1999. *Photograph by author.*

The main structure of the China Millennium Monument houses various spaces for conferences and exhibitions. The main interest in the monument, however, lies not in the main structure's specific functions but in the symbolism of the architectural imagery. The entire monument is comprised of three parts: the Plaza of Holy Fire at the south end, the circular building in the form of a giant sundial located in a park at the north end, and the Bronze Causeway connecting the two (fig. 5.4).

The Plaza of Holy Fire is a microcosm of China the motherland. The plaque at the site explains that the circular floor of the plaza, one meter below ground level, is paved with 960 square granite slabs, representing China's vast territory of 9,600,000 square kilometers. At the south wall of the sunken plaza, a cascade of 300 electronic lights with light-guide fibers represents the beauty of the shining seas of the motherland. Along both the eastern and western sides of the plaza, a steady current of water cascades down the steps, symbolizing the two major "mother rivers" of Chinese civilization, the Yellow and the Yangtze. The floor of the plaza rises slightly toward the center, representing the rise of Chinese nationality. At the very center of the plaza is an ever-burning flame, the Chinese Holy Fire, kindled at the Paleolithic Beijing Man site, Zhoukoudian,[18] representing the "eternal creative force of Chinese civilization."[19] At the north end of the plaza is a map of China on a circular plate with gilded dragons decorating its fringe. At the south end, raised above the sea of lights, rests a marble horizontal stele incised with Han dynasty *fu*-style prose celebrating China's long history and recent rebirth. On the other side of the stele facing Chang'an Avenue is the engraved name of the monument, written in calligraphy by president Jiang Zemin.

To the north of the Plaza of Holy Fire is the Bronze Causeway. The central bronze part is 3 meters wide and 270 meters long; inscribed on its sides is the entire chronology of human history, from three million years ago to 2000 CE, and on its center, China's major cultural and political events (fig. 5.5). The historical information becomes more and more detailed as the end of the second millennium approaches, with the last century illustrated not only by the traditional calendar of Ten Heavenly Stems (Tiangan) and Twelve Earthly Branches (Dizhi) but also by their corresponding symbolic animals. Like the exhibitions in the Museum of Chinese Revolution and History and the Military Museum, the recording of historical events in the Bronze Causeway has a teleological agenda that legitimizes the socialist revolution. The political aspect of the monument, however, is deliberately played down in the official explanation, which only mentions that the text inscribed in the bronze "succinctly recounts important events of Chinese history in science and technology, culture, education, and other fields."[20]

In the original design, however, the so-called Bronze Causeway was not meant to be walked on. Instead, a clear stream of water was to run along its surface, a movement "harmonizing and contrasting with the stillness of the pavement to indicate the continuity and renewal of the nation's history."[21] However, the water in the Bronze Causeway, and in the fountains elsewhere in the monument, actually runs only during special days of celebration. Most of the time the Bronze Causeway remains dry and is a de facto passageway, leading visitors from the Plaza of Holy Fire to the altar. Without the water, the inscriptions in the bronze panels are hard to read, and pilgrims are often found crouching over the central passageway, slowly moving through the carefully designed history toward the giant altar ahead.

The main structure at the north end of the Bronze Causeway is the largest repository of Chinese cultural symbolism of the three parts of the monument. It consists of two parts: a dynamic upper rotunda in the form of a giant sundial, representing *qian* (heaven, male, yang, etc.) and a static peripheral base in the form of a stepped terrace,

representing *kun* (earth, female, yin, etc.). The *qian*-body is forty-seven meters in diameter and twenty-eight meters high, with a roof slope of 19.4 degrees. Its central rotunda revolves once every 2.6 to 55 hours, depending on the control of the rotating speed. A 27.6-meter-long bronze needle stretches up into the

Fig. 5.5. The Bronze Causeway and the "Main Altar" with the *qian* and *kun* bodies, China Millennium Monument, 1999. *Photograph by author.*

sky from the top of the *qian*-body, symbolizing the infinity of time and space. The *kun*-body is eighty-five meters in diameter, with seventeen circular tiers of steps paved with light yellow granite slabs. The outer wall of the *qian*-body is carved with fifty-six relief panels, representing the fifty-six ethnic groups of the Chinese nation in their unity and solidarity. The top parts of the *kun*-body, where *qian* joins with and rotates in *kun*, are two semicircular corridors, six meters wide, four meters high, and seventy meters long (140 meters in total length), inside of which bronze statues of

Fig. 5.6. The joint of the *qian* and *kun* bodies, China Millennium Monument, 1999. *Photograph by author.*

forty of the most outstanding figures in Chinese cultural history will be housed.[22] Passing through the corridors, visitors can pay homage to these cultural heroes in the *kun*-body while observing the fifty-six ethnic designs inscribed on the outer wall of the *qian*-body. Ethnic diversity is unified into the single linear cultural history of the Chinese nation, just as *qian* is united with *kun*, and male is united with female (fig. 5.6).

Qian and *kun* are two of the most time-honored Chinese philosophical, cosmological, and ideological symbols. Dating back to legendary early Chinese kings five thousand years ago, they first appear in the Confucian classic *Book of Changes* (Yijing). While their literal meanings are "heaven" and "earth," they represent the most basic opposite forces in nature and society—for instance, yang and yin, male and female, husband and wife, father and son, and ruler and subject. *Qian* and *kun* are also replete with the Confucian moral values of the prerevolutionary Chinese literati. As the *Book of Changes* puts it, "As heaven moves constantly, so should the superior man rely on himself and work ceaselessly; as earth extends infinitely, so should the superior

man embrace all with magnanimous virtue."[3] The inscriptions on the site also explain, "'*Qian*' refers to the eternal, ceaseless movement of celestial bodies, embodying an idea of eternal edification, endeavor,

Fig. 5.7. Interior, Century Hall, China Millennium Monument, 1999. *Photograph by author.*

and progress, while '*kun*' stands for the all-embracing earth, displaying a spirit of tolerance, magnanimity, and harmony. The main structure as a whole, combining a harmony of movement and stillness with a grandeur of conception, manifests the Chinese nation's great spirit of ceaseless endeavor, as well as its broadminded emphasis on virtue and tolerance." Nationalist ideals imbedded in China's long imperial history are here revealed as the predominant ideology behind the construction of the China Millennium Monument.

While the passage from the Plaza of Holy Fire to the altar enshrines a strong nationalist ideology, the functions housed inside the main altar structure reinforce it using a different format. The roofs of the revolving giant sundial *qian*-body can serve as a raised amphitheatre during celebrations. Inside the sundial is the Century Hall (fig. 5.7), whose interior circular wall is a five-meter-high, 117-meter-long relief sculpture with an area of 588 square meters, the largest stone relief sculpture in China. The entire relief, called *Ode to the Chinese Millennia* (Zhonghua Qianqiu Song), is divided into four sections. The first displays the "rational spirit in Chinese civilization of the pre-Qin period," with an emphasis on the sources of Chinese thought; the second displays the "magnanimous spirit in Chinese civilization from the Han to the Tang dynasties," with an emphasis on the magnificent quality of the Chinese nation; the third displays the "loyal integrity during the period from the Song to the Qing dynasties," with an emphasis on the power of personality of the Chinese people; and the fourth displays the "historical duet of enlightenment and national salvation in recent and modern Chinese history," with an emphasis on the independent and self-strengthening spirit of the Chinese nation. According to the official explanation, this relief sculpture encapsulates the spirit and developmental framework of the five-thousand-year-old civilization of the Chinese nation.[24]

The imagery in the relief consists of both historical figures (from the legendary ruler Huangdi to the first emperor Qin Shihuangdi to Deng Xiaoping) and cultural symbols (from a Shang dynasty bronze tripod to a Tang dynasty palace to the Monument to the People's Heroes in Tiananmen Square). It ends with an inscription in president Jiang Zemin's calligraphy: "The Chinese nation will achieve a great renaissance based on the final attainment of the unification of the motherland and the construction of a rich, powerful, democratic, and civilized socialist modern country." The relief was created by the best craftsmen, with fifteen types of stone of different colors from all over the country. While the Bronze Causeway outside provides a textual narrative of the rise of the Chinese nation, the relief sculpture inside visualizes this narrative in tangible form and is a succinct illustration of the Bronze Causeway.

On the same second floor as the Century Hall in the *qian*-body, the *kun*-body houses a Western Art Exhibition Hall to the west and an Eastern Art Exhibition Hall to the east, bisected by the rotating *qian*-body. A Modern Art Exhibition Hall is located in the northern part of the first floor in the *kun*-body, whose southern part is the main communication space leading to various staircases, elevators, and escalators. Directly below the rotating *qian*-body on this floor is a souvenir shop. The basement houses a Multimedia Art Exhibition Hall and a wide-screen cinema called the Millennium Theatre.

Other government-sponsored monuments added on West Chang'an Avenue during 1990s include the Military Commission Headquarters and the Capital Museum. The former used archaic style roofs with straight eave lines and the imagery of the Great Wall, symbolizing the military forces of the People's Liberation Army as the new "iron Great Walls" of the People's Republic of China (PRC; see fig. 1.20). The Capital Museum employs the highly abstract imageries of the overreaching big roof and the ancient bronze tripod (*ding*), juxtaposed with glass curtain walls and steel

plates (fig. 5.8). Like the China Millennium Monument, national symbolism plays a central role in the design of both buildings.

Fig. 5.8. Capital Museum (detail showing the motifs of ancient bronze vessel *ding* and abstract "big roof"), 2005. AREP (France) and China Architecture Design and Research Group. *Photograph by author.*

Contrasts and Complements

The contrast is sharp between commercial buildings, as represented by Oriental Plaza, and political monuments, as represented by the China Millennium Monument. While to maximize commercial profit Oriental Plaza occupies every inch of its site and forces itself to vertical reaches well beyond the height limit set by the city planning code, the China Millennium Monument leaves most of its site open as a passageway, spreading horizontally along the ground. The former building is devoid of decoration, while the latter is full of symbolism. Oriental Plaza houses complex functions inside a relatively simple box of imposing concrete and glass façades. The China Millennium Monument, in contrast, houses relatively simple interior functions but elaborates on exterior design that emphasizes visitors' outdoor experience while moving through the architectural space.

The commercial patches and the political patches added to Chang'an Avenue during the 1990s, however, also complement each other. While the construction of Oriental Plaza involved various political episodes and might have been impossible without strong political support from top leaders, the China Millennium Monument was commercialized after its completion. Most of the exhibition spaces are rented out for temporary shows. The Millennium Theatre screens patriotic history documentaries as well as imported Hollywood hits. Entry to the entire monument can be purchased for ¥30.[25] If visitors want to ring the huge bronze Chinese Century Bell in the park where the altar is located, they are charged ¥5 for three strikes. Although the words inscribed on the bell are as solemn as those on the Monument to the People's Heroes in Tiananmen Square, and the gilded inscriptions on the surface are as magnificent as those on a Zhou dynasty bronze vessel, they are little more than a curio display. Chang'an Avenue's 1990s political monuments are mostly an accumulation of public spectacles for tourist consumption. To some extent, they are not much different from the public space represented by Disneyland in the West.[26]

The Chinese Patches and the Foreign Patches

During the 1990s more and more buildings financed by overseas capital and designed by foreign architects appeared on Chang'an Avenue. While buildings designed by Chinese architects continued the struggle to balance the national with the modern, overseas architects found an opportunity to continue postmodernist exploration in non-Western cultural contexts. The two approaches converged on Chang'an Avenue, mutually misunderstanding each other while constructing a dialogue to promote understanding. The avenue became a collage of multilingual communication, in which statements may or may not have been interpreted as intended by the speaker.

The Chinese Patches

The architectural theory of postmodernism introduced into China in the 1980s provided Chinese architects with a new framework for continuing the debates on national versus international and traditional versus modern. While Aldo Rossi's typology inspired some Chinese architects to reevaluate their architectural traditions, Robert

Venturi's preference for hybridity over purity and Michael Graves's play with historical motifs offered specific strategies to incorporate time-honored architectural details in new design.

To some extent, postmodernism justified in theory the development of a new national style based on historical architectural motifs. In specific design practice, however, instead of being comprehensively applied to an entire building, these historical motifs were often superficially attached to main structures, juxtaposing glass surfaces and tiled concrete walls. Historical motifs were reduced to cultural signs and became fragmented and decorative.

The most frequently adopted historical motifs were traditional pavilions, roofs with overreaching and upturning eaves, the memorial archway, and the *xumizuo* masonry terrace. In the Chang'an Club, completed in 1993 on East Chang'an Avenue, two pavilions with yellow tiled roofs and red columns protrude from the white wall atop the corners of the main façades facing Chang'an Avenue. A corridor in the same style and colors connects the pavilions, and, above them, a flattened gable mimics the form of a *juanpeng* roof in a traditional Beijing dwelling. The main entrances on the ground level are also framed in similar but larger pavilions, located on a *xumizuo* terrace of white marble (fig. 5.9). However, compared with earlier buildings in national forms (for instance, the Minority Culture Palace of 1959 and the National Gallery of 1962), the historical motifs in the Chang'an Club are confined to narrow bands across the main façade; the areas directly below or surrounding them do not continue the historical references. In the Minority Culture Palace, *xumizuo*-style rostrums and sloping roofs with green glazed tiles appear on every floor, and yellow glazed roofs dominate the façades of the National Gallery. Historical motifs also continue in the interior of these buildings in the form of simplified *caihua* (paintings on the wooden frames and ceilings) decorations. While the use of national forms in the buildings of the 1950s and 1960s achieved an integrated traditional flavor, historical motifs in the Chang'an Club are like fragments of memory floating in a neutral background of glass and concrete that is otherwise indistinguishable from any other commercial building on Chang'an Avenue.

The juxtaposition of historical fragments with modern glass and concrete structures can be observed in many other Chang'an Avenue buildings designed by Chinese architects in the 1990s. These include the renovation project for the Ministry of Textile Industry office building in 1991, the new building added to the Beijing Hotel in 1990, the All China Women's Federation Building of 1995, the Ministry of Communication office building of 1992–94, the Guanghua Chang'an Building of 1994–96, the Huanan Mansion of 1991, and the Huacheng Plaza of 1997. The office building for the propaganda department of the CCP Central Committee of 1992–93 is an exception

Fig. 5.9. Chang'an Club, 1991–93. Wang Huide, Zhao Shuying, and others. *Photograph by author.*

whose structure is more comprehensively covered by overreaching roofs and large pavilions. This closer affiliation with architectural styles from China's imperial past is a result of its specific location on Chang'an Avenue, immediately to the west of the former Ming-Qing imperial garden, Zhongnanhai.

Another strategy to combine national with modern in the 1990s was to follow the proportion and composition, both in plan and façade, of "traditional" Chinese architecture, but to use contemporary construction materials such as concrete, steel frames, and glass. According to this approach, what characterized Chinese architecture in plan was the courtyard organization of space, and what made a façade Chinese were the three vertical sections of overreaching roof, the post-and-lintel frame, and the solid base. Such a characterization of Chinese architecture was strongly promoted by Liang Sicheng from the 1930s through the 1950s. In the National Electricity Distribution Center on West Chang'an Avenue, completed in 1998, two giant pillars hold an enormous upturned steel-framed roof above a steel-and-glass box. The proportion of eave to the steel frames under it recalls that of rafters to brackets in Chinese timber structures. The main body below is divided into two sections: the upper part contains more transparent glass areas than solid wall, mimicking the traditional post-and-lintel framework; the lower part contains more solid wall than open space, like

the masonry base in a traditional hall. The details of the building, however, demonstrate a substantial influence from steel-frame structures designed by overseas architectural firms. The gothic-inspired spires on the tops of the buttresses in the upper part of the façades are directly copied from buildings by the American firm KPF, and the giant roof

Fig. 5.10. Chang'an Avenue in the early 2000s with abstract "big roofs" in modern materials (the 1998 National Electricity Distribution Center is the second from right). *Photograph by author.*

in the form of an upturned truncated pyramid recalls works by the Taiwanese architect Li Zuyuan (C. Y. Lee; fig. 5.10). While the first approach inserts historical details into new structures, this one, the second approach, sacrifices specific details to general composition. Other buildings that reflect an approach similar to the Power Distribution Center include Zhongliang Plaza of 1992–96 on East Chang'an Avenue and the 1999–2003 Commercial Building of the Armed Police Department on West Chang'an Avenue.

A third approach adopted by Chinese architects to deal with national forms was to dissect historical motifs in Chinese architecture, predominantly the roof, and reconstruct the fragments to form an incomplete image evoking China's architectural past. An example of this approach is the 1994–98 Beijing Book Mansion. Instead of showing a complete roof, the four slopes on top of the building are disconnected by solid walls, which, according to the design explanation, protrude into the sky like the stone pillars

Fig. 5.11. Beijing Book Mansion, 1994–98. Liu Li, Zhou Wenyao, Shao Weiping, and others. *Photograph by author.*

of a traditional archway. The angle of the east and west slopes is sharper than that of the north and south slopes. Viewers are meant to imagine the extensions of the east and west slopes meeting at a line—the ridge—above the center of the main façade and thus forming a gable whose invisible vertical walls could meet the extensions of the north and south slopes. The complex roof slopes could thus be a fragment of a traditional *xieshan* (hip-and-gable) style roof. According to the design explanation, the Beijing Book Mansion also adopts such traditional motifs as the gate in vernacular dwellings and achieves the "organic integration of modern life, cultural tradition, and local characteristics" (fig. 5.11).[27]

The Foreign Patches

In the 1990s three buildings designed by foreign architects, in collaboration with local architectural design institutes, as required by law, were completed on Chang'an Avenue proper. They were the China Industrial and Commercial Bank of 1994–98, by SOM, with the Beijing Institute; the Bank of China of 1996–99, by Pei Cobb Freed and Partners, with the Chinese Architectural Science Research Institute; and the COSCO Building (Yuanyang Mansion) of 1996–99, by APEC/NBBJ, with the Mechanical Engineering Design Institute. All of the three foreign architectural firms were American.

Both SOM and NBBJ are famous for their commercial design of steel-frame structures with extensive use of glass. Aiming mainly for commercial success instead of experimental design innovation, they have produced large numbers of elegantly designed buildings all over the world since World War II. In the 1950s SOM helped to popularize the

Fig. 5.12. China Industrial and Commercial Bank, 1994–98. SOM and Beijing Institute of Architectural Design and Research, Li Zhaohui, Zhang Xiuguo, and others. *Photograph by author.*

Miesian-style glass box in the West. In the 1980s and 1990s this firm's work was highly influenced by the high-tech trend of the 1970s for open transparent structures and exposed frameworks.

The China Industrial and Commercial Bank on West Chang'an Avenue is not much different from other SOM buildings in other parts of the world. The main façade on Chang'an Avenue, however, does adopt a tripartite division of base, main frame, and overreaching eave (fig. 5.12). Overreaching eaves, however, are by no means unusual in SOM buildings. In projects such as the 1987 Arlington International Racecourse in Illinois and the 2002 Dallas Convention Center, the protruding eaves are even more dramatic than those of the bank in Beijing. They are either a response to the functional requirement to shelter the tiers of seats below, as in the former, or integrated into the main structural framework, as in the latter. The upturned eave in the China Industrial and Commercial Bank, however, is arbitrarily attached to the façade, neither functionally necessary nor part of the structural framework. The steel frame

Fig. 5.13. Headquarters of
Bank of China, 1996–99.
I. M. Pei, C. C. Pei, and others.
Photograph by author.

of round columns standing on a stone base was acclaimed by some Chinese architects as embodying both the spirit of high technology specific to the 1990s as well as the lingering charm of traditional Chinese architecture.[28] The general composition of a circle within a square in the plan represents the traditional Chinese concept of round sky and square earth (*tianyuan difang*); the main façade has a traditional Chinese architectural proportion; the base embodies the imagery of the Great Wall; the steel frame resembles a traditional Chinese timber structure, and so on.[29] Although the apparently superfluous eave might be part of SOM's purposeful design to fit the specific architectural context of the site, such interpretations are misleading.

The Bank of China on West Chang'an Avenue is officially attributed to I. M. Pei. Designed by his son, C. C. Pei, the building has some of the main features of most I. M. Pei buildings. The interlocking of glass bodies with concrete volumes characterizes many I. M. Pei buildings.[30] In the Bank of China on Chang'an Avenue, a glass body containing the central atrium inserts into solid walls containing modularized windows (fig. 5.13). The glass body is a miniature of the 1989 Bank of China Tower in Hong Kong designed by I. M. Pei, with its characteristic diagonal steel frames and gradual setbacks toward the top. The interior garden in the atrium was interpreted as having much Chinese flavor. I. M. Pei was born in Canton and raised in Suzhou, the famous garden city of Southeast China. Many I. M. Pei buildings have gardens or plantations in a central interior public space—for instance, the Guggenheim Pavilion in New York, completed in 1992, and the Warner Building in Washington, DC, completed in 1993.

C. C. Pei's Bank of China building is one of the very few asymmetrical structures on Chang'an Avenue. It also lacks the painstaking struggle to demonstrate national character so common in other buildings along the central section of the avenue. I. M. Pei was, at that time, so famous in China for his Bank of China in Hong Kong that, it could be argued, a signature building by a world-famous architect overrules a preoccupation with Chineseness. Such a trend of collecting signature buildings by internationally famous architects became commonplace for Chang'an Avenue at the turn of the millennium, rendering the previous struggle over national versus modern style outmoded. The competition for the National Grand Theatre tells such a story.

The National Grand Theatre

Although the Chinese word for theatre, *juyuan,* can refer to many different types of performance space, the "theatre" in National Grand Theatre was originally conceived of as primarily for Western-style opera, then considered the highest form of all performing arts. Western-style operas were once believed to best be able to represent the new socialist culture of China, although most of them are of European origin, and most Chinese will normally not go to these operas. Thus there was much debate at the turn of the century about the justification for the National Grand Theatre project. It shares the same contradictions as Chinese modernization itself. Although the Chinese Communists promised to take whatever was good from "ancient, contemporary, Chinese, and foreign" in the creation of a new socialist culture, the Western model was the predominant paradigm for the modernization project.

Historically, there were three approaches to the relationships between traditional Chinese culture and modern culture. The first was provided by May-Fourth-generation intellectuals, such as Chen Duxiu and Hu Shi, who saw no compatibility between traditional Chinese culture and modernity, and proposed a total rejection of Chinese tradition and a wholehearted embrace of wholesale Westernization.[31] The second approach was represented by such figures as Lu Xun and Mao Zedong, who believed that Chinese modernization could be achieved only by combining national tradition with Western modern culture. In the Model Operas (Yangbanxi) performed during the Cultural Revolution, traditional Chinese opera (*xiqu*) was modernized by the adoption of a Westernized orchestra and stage settings, and Western ballet was nationalized by using Chinese folk dances to tell revolutionary stories. A third approach argued that traditional Chinese culture was already very modern, so Chinese modernization needed only to self-consciously develop the advantages of Chinese tradition. While the third approach seemed to be against Westernization, as it indeed claimed to be, its true result was not. The very "advantages" of Chinese tradition were often selected according to Western standards. For this reason, the Westernization agenda of the third approach became even more powerful by turning itself into an invisible prerequisite.

National Theatre as the Anniversary Project and Its Site

By the time of its completion in 2007, planning for the National Grand Theatre of China had lasted almost half a century. As one of the Anniversary Projects for the tenth anniversary in 1959, it was then simply referred to as the "National Theatre."[32] Located on the south side of Chang'an Avenue, the National Theatre was planned for the site next to the Great Hall (fig. 5.14).

The scheme collection for the National Theatre was organized in 1958. The scheme by the Department of Construction, predecessor of the future prestigious School of Architecture, at Tsinghua University was chosen as the design to implement. A Tsinghua professor, Li Daozeng, then in his twenties and the main designer for the winning scheme, would play an important role in the future development of the National Grand Theatre design. Almost all of the models and drawings made in the late 1950s were destroyed during the Cultural Revolution. A single watercolor rendering by Li has been preserved in the School of Architecture Archive at Tsinghua University, which shows that the 1958 Tsinghua design was similar to the adjacent Great Hall in style (fig. 5.15a). The building is sitting on a platform, with wide steps leading to its major entrances. The symmetrical façades are vertically divided into two sections. The eaves of both sections are decorated with yellow and green glazed tiles, the same as the eave treatments in the Great Hall and the museum complex. It was said that the convention of using glazed tiles for the eaves of flat roofs, founded by the Ten Great Buildings, originated in Tsinghua's design for the National Theatre.[33] The corners of the glazed-tile eaves rise up slightly, mimicking the raised overreaching eaves of traditional roofs. As in the

Fig. 5.14. Drawing in "The Document of the Design Scheme Competition of the National Grand Theatre," showing the site for the National Grand Theatre within the larger urban context of Chang'an Avenue and Tiananmen Square. *Reproduction from Zhongguo Guojia Dajüyuan Jianzhu Sheji Guoji Jingsai fang'anji, 20. Courtesy of Zhou Qinglin.*

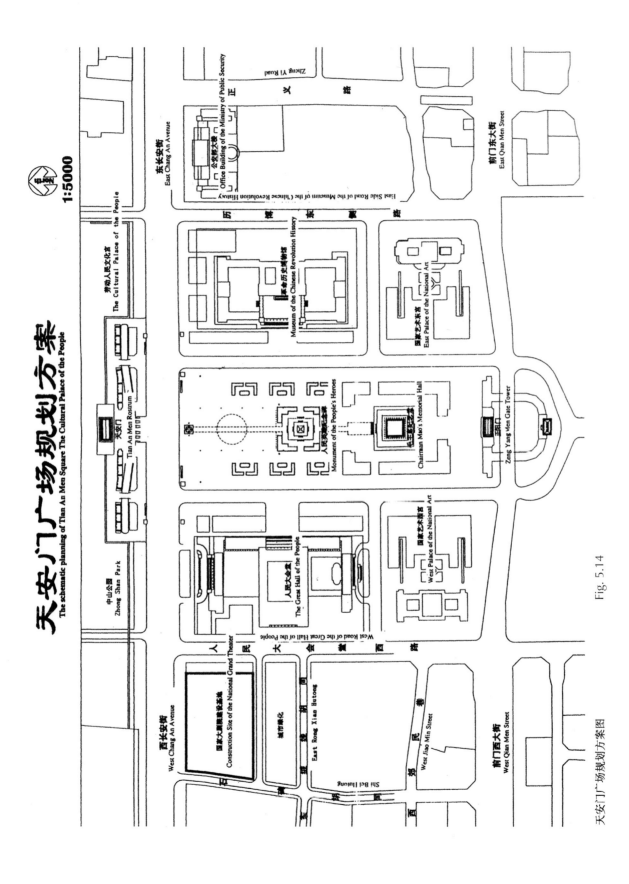

天安门广场规划方案
The schematic planning of Tian An Men Square The Cultural Palace of the People

1:5000

中山公园　Zhong Shan Park

劳动人民文化宫
The Cultural Palace of the People

天安门　Tian An Men Rostrum

西长安街　West Chang An Avenue

东长安街　East Chang An Avenue

公安部大楼
Office Building of the Ministry of Public Security

正义路　Zheng Yi Road

历史博物馆东侧路
East Side Road of the Museum of the Chinese Revolution History

中国历史博物馆
Museum of the Chinese Revolution History

国家艺术宫
East Palace of the National Art

前门东大街　East Qian Men Street

人民英雄纪念碑
Monument of the People's Heroes

毛主席纪念堂
Chairman Mao's Memorial Hall

正阳门
Zeng Yang Men Gate Tower

人民大会堂
The Great Hall of the People

国家艺术宫
West Palace of the National Art

人民大会堂西侧路
West Road of the Great Hall of the People

国家大剧院建设基地
Construction Site of the National Grand Theater

城府胡同
East Rong Xian Butong

西交民巷
West Jiao Min Street

石碑胡同
Shi Bei Hutong

前门西大街　West Qian Men Street

Fig. 5.14

天安门广场规划方案图

Fig. 5.15a. 1958 National Grand Theatre scheme by Tsinghua University. *Courtesy of Li Daozeng.*

Great Hall, colonnades screen the main entrances at the ends of grand exterior stairways.

The National Theatre project was abandoned in early 1959, allegedly due to a shortage of funds and time.[34] It was not the only project for the tenth anniversary that went unrealized. The National Science and Technology Hall, for instance, was also abandoned, and the National Art Gallery was not built until 1962. The National Theatre, however, was the only project since that time to leave a huge empty site on Chang'an Avenue. Each of the PRC leaders since Premier Zhou Enlai believed that the National Theatre would be built in the near future, during his tenure of office. The site, however, experienced various controversies before design resumed in the 1990s.

In the 1964 Chang'an Avenue planning, some schemes placed the National Theatre directly on Tiananmen Square, to the south of the Great Hall. Occupying such a critical site, the National Theatre would have become one of the key factors in defining Tiananmen Square's "openness."[35] As part of Tiananmen Square, the National Theatre was conceived of as the embodiment of a new socialist culture. Its function as a performance venue would have become secondary. Yet such a location was opposed by many specialists during the April symposium, precisely because of the nonpolitical function of the theatre as a performance space.[36]

After the 1964 planning, the location of the National Theatre became uncertain. At the end of the 1970s, the Ministry of Culture again proposed building the theatre, but the proposal was turned down. Some sources attributed the failure to economic constraints after the Cultural Revolution.[37] The same economic conditions, however, did not stop the completion of the Chairman Mao Memorial just one year after Mao's death. With the construction of the memorial, the question of an open or closed Tiananmen Square no longer existed. The site selection was simplified. In the early 1990s, when colonial-style buildings with Western classical domes[38] south of the Great Hall and the museum complex were declared historical heritages and their domes restored (the 1964 planning had unanimously proposed their demolition), the only possible site for a politically significant National Theatre was narrowed down to the original 1958 site west of the Great Hall.

The original site, however, had been in jeopardy for decades. Proposals for other uses of the site appeared as soon as the National Theatre was dropped from the list of Anniversary Projects. In September 1959 the site west of the Great Hall was proposed for the construction of residences for members of the Standing Committee of the National People's Congress (SCNPC). The proposal was more a result of the fear of a vacancy on Chang'an Avenue than a response to a practical need for housing. It was made in accordance with "Comrade Peng Zhen's [then the mayor of Beijing] intention to quickly improve the appearance on the two sides of Chang'an Avenue."[39] The avenue had to be completed, and the empty site had to be filled.

The site was not used for the residences. In early 1980s the standing committee, which was housed in the southern courtyard of the Great Hall, decided to build a new office building on the site. In 1983 the old buildings west of the Great Hall were cleared and the base pit was dug. The project for the new office building, however, was abandoned due to strong opposition from the general representatives of the NPC, who argued that such a costly project was untimely for China due to the current economic situation. The ¥90 million already spent on the NPC project had left only a large pit that would lie quietly in the heart of the Chinese capital for another two decades.[40]

Between 1959 and the late 1990s, although nothing was physically done on the National Theatre project, a large number of smaller local theatres were built throughout the country. They resembled the 1958 Tsinghua scheme for the National Theatre in proportion and façade division, with simplified decorations and at smaller scales. Designers were likely not looking at the Tsinghua drawings when designing these local theatres but following the example of the Great Hall and the museum complex. Li Daozeng, who became China's leading specialist in theatre design for his work in 1958, continued his research for the National Theatre, hoping to have it built one day.

The battle over the site continued until 1997, when the final decision was made to construct the theatre, and not the NPC office building, next to the Great Hall. Documents indicate that the battle was mainly between the Ministry of Culture and the Standing Committee of the National People's Congress.[41] The design for the theatre, however, was already underway as the debate continued. In 1990 the Ministry of Culture set up a preparatory office for the project, whose job was to organize the research on its feasibility and collect new design schemes in the following year. The new project, now officially called the National Grand Theatre, was much larger in scale and more expensive than the original 1958 project. The floorage had been expanded from 38,098 to 100,000 square meters,[42] with an estimated cost of ¥1 billion. Instead of the one Western-style opera house, as in the 1958 program, the new schemes had to combine an opera house, a concert hall, and a Chinese *xiju* theatre in one building.

The schemes prepared in the early 1990s were called feasibility research schemes. Li Daozeng, who had built several theatres elsewhere, was one of the major scheme providers. Like his 1958 scheme, Li's 1991 scheme also had a symmetrical plan, with the opera house in the center, and the concert hall and Chinese *xiju* theatre on either side. The three theatres were separated by two courtyards and connected by offices and service rooms. Classical motifs were applied in the postmodern fashion newly introduced into China. Instead of the glazed tiles of the 1958 project, the upper parts of the façades were topped by arches and arched beams. Floating fragmented arches directly attached to glass decorated the two side entrances of the main façade. Motifs from I. M. Pei's recently completed Fragrant Hills Hotel, such as dark diamond-shaped windows on white walls, also appeared in Li's 1991 scheme. Here, however, the figure-ground color relationship was reversed: small pieces of diamond-shaped white wall relieved the dark glass backgrounds above the entrances. The protruding walls above the central stage of the opera house were encircled by a colonnade with pointed arches reminiscent of gothic architecture, like Minoru Yamasaki's colonnades at Seattle's Pacific Science Center. The façades of Li's 1991 National Grand Theatre scheme were full of symbols from Western classical architecture (fig. 5.15b).

At this point, the standing committee renewed its claim on the site for its new office building. Supporters argued that, in terms of the architectural environment, the NPC project would balance both sides of Tiananmen Square better and would conform to its political atmosphere. Others, however, believed that the theatre would make Tiananmen Square livelier and a true people's square. Moreover, the

site had already been chosen by the much "respected and beloved Premier Zhou Enlai" for the construction of the National Theatre. These arguments led to further postponement of both projects.[43]

Fig. 5.15b. 1991 National Grand Theatre scheme by Tsinghua University. Li Daozeng and others. *Courtesy of Li Daozeng.*

The Six Plenum of the Fourteenth CCP Congress in 1997 finally broke the stalemate. During this top-level meeting, the party decided that, before 2010, two significant national cultural projects would be completed: the National Grand Theatre and the National Art Museum. The projects were listed in the conference report. In October 1997 the central committee proclaimed that the National Grand Theatre was to be constructed over the existing pit to the west of the Great Hall as soon as possible. A Proprietor Committee (Yezhu Weiyuanhui) and a Technical Committee (Jishu Weiyuanhui) were founded under the Leadership Small Group (Lingdao Xiaozu) for the National Grand Theatre Project.[44] The Leadership Small Group, led by the party secretary of Beijing Jia Qinglin, included high officials from the Central Committee and the Standing Committee of the National People's Congress, heads of various relevant State Council ministries, and Beijing mayor Liu Qi. The Proprietor Committee was also comprised largely of officials from the party, the state, and the Chinese People's Political Consultative Conference. However, it included two professionals from the government, chief engineer of the Ministry of Construction, Yao Bing, and chief architect of the Ministry of Construction Architectural Design Institute, Zhou Qinglin. The Technical Committee was comprised of architectural and engineering professionals only, addressing the artistic and technical aspects of the collected schemes.[45]

The estimated cost was raised again to ¥3 billion. Only two months were allocated for completion of the initial scheme, and construction was slated to start the following spring. The schedule called for the rough completion of the project by 2001, and for

putting the building into use before the Sixteenth CCP Congress in 2002.[46] Obviously, in 1997 the party anticipated a smooth and rapid design process and a more lengthy construction period.

The design process for the National Grand Theatre would have been quite simple if Chinese architects had competed for the project only among themselves. Within a month, eight schemes had been collected and three design finalists chosen: Tsinghua University, the Beijing Municipal Architectural Design and Research Institute (hereafter the Beijing Institute), and the Ministry of Construction Architectural Design Institute (hereafter the Ministry Institute).

Li Daozeng's Tsinghua scheme was not very different from his initial scheme six years earlier. The plan remained the same. Postmodern decorative motifs were simplified, and four golden equestrian statues were added on the four corners of the central opera house. The color scheme had changed from white and brown to light yellow, golden, and blue, colors more in tune with those of the Great Hall next door. The columns, however, instead of the simple white cylinders of 1991, now had more decorations, in keeping with the column style of the Great Hall. Stylistically, Li's 1997 scheme was somewhere between his 1958 and 1991 schemes (fig. 5.15c).

● 1997 年国家大剧院初选方案之一模型
南向（李道增设计）

● 1997 年国家大剧院初选方案之一
局部（李道增设计）

Fig. 5.15c (facing page and this page). 1997 National Grand Theatre scheme by Tsinghua University. Li Daozeng and others. *Courtesy of Li Daozeng.*

While Li's schemes showed no interest in traditional Chinese motifs, schemes by the Beijing Institute and the Ministry Institute both had sloping overhanging roofs. They were simplified and called for modern materials, metal and glass. While the roofs of the Ministry Institute scheme emphasized the continuous slopes in traditional Chinese architecture, the roofs of the Beijing Institute scheme mimicked the upturned eaves in an exaggerated form. The scheme by the Beijing Institute also followed the colonnade design of the Great Hall, in which the distance between the columns of the central bay was greater than that of the side bays, adhering to what was believed to be a characteristic of traditional Chinese architecture. The Ministry Institute scheme was the only one of the three without a colonnade. Its general proportions, however, were closest to those of a traditional Chinese timber structure.

None of the designs of the three Chinese finalists satisfied the central leaders. In order to make the National Grand Theatre a first-class "artistic temple" of the world, the Chinese government then decided to choose a scheme by hosting an international architectural competition.

The international architectural competition organized for the National Grand Theatre lasted for almost sixteen months, from April 13, 1998, when competition invitations were sent out, to July 22, 1999, when the design by the French company Aeroports de Paris (hereafter ADP), with the assistance of the Chinese design unit from Tsinghua University, was declared the scheme for implementation. The competition process was later officially divided into two rounds of competition with three scheme modifications.

The competition was open to anyone. However, in order to guarantee the participation of the best architects in the world, on April 13, 1998, the Proprietor Committee invited seventeen architectural design units to provide schemes, including eleven Chinese institutes and six foreign companies. This group would be paid. In addition, nineteen units, including five from China and fourteen from abroad, volunteered. The thirty-six participators submitted forty-four schemes on July 13, 1998, including twenty-four Chinese and twenty overseas schemes. The Technical Committee assessed the entries from July 14 to 23, and then a jury evaluated them from July 27 to 31.[47]

There were two consultant teams to address the two major issues, architectural design and theatre design. China's top architects formed the First Consultative Team, led by Wu Liangyong, professor of urban planning from Tsinghua University and member of both the Chinese Academy of Science and the Chinese Academy of Engineering. Theatre specialists made up the Second Consultative Team. For the first round of competition, Wu also chaired the jury of eleven members, which included eight Chinese architects and three foreign architects—Arthur Erickson from Canada, Ricardo Bofill from England, and Yoshinobu Ashihara from Japan.[48]

The function of the consultative teams in the 1998 National Grand Theatre competition was ambiguous. There was already a Technical Committee to provide professional service to the patron, which was the Chinese government, as well as an outside jury. According to Western conventions of architectural competition, the jury is solely responsible for the final selection of schemes. However, the Chinese had already developed a well-established scheme-selection procedure—the collective approach—during Mao's time. To some extent, the idea of consultative teams was a legacy of the previous practice of collective creation. Bridging the patron and the jury, it blurred the boundary between an architectural competition and a scheme collection. As the National Grand Theatre competition continued, most of the controversies were generated between the consultative teams and the jury.

Originally, the jury was to submit three entries to the Leadership Small Group for consideration as schemes to implement. After voting by secret ballot, however, the jury decided that none of these schemes were fully qualified and chose as the recommended schemes five entries that had received more than half of the votes. The authors of the five recommended schemes would go on to participate in a second round of competition. The five selected schemes (fig. 5.16) were:

No. 101 by ADP of France
No. 106 by Terry Farrell and Partners of the United Kingdom
No. 201 by Arata Isozaki and Associates of Japan
No. 205 by the Ministry Institute of China
No. 507 by HPP International Planungsgesellschaft mbH of Germany

The Leadership Small Group approved the jury's suggestion, and the Proprietor Committee held the second round competition from August 24 to November 10.

The authors of these five selected entries, however, were allowed little sense of victory, because not only were their schemes considered merely relatively better, but the second round of competition was soon expanded to allow almost all of the original invited participants to submit entries again. In addition to the five "victorious" units, another four Chinese institutes and five foreign companies that had participated in the first round were allowed to provide new entries. In the end, the total submission for the second round reached fourteen entries.[49]

The expanded participation must have been the result of considerable lobbying and backstage maneuvering. An unusual result according to standard design competition practice in the West, it may have been a solution to the problem created by the fact that some of the Chinese jury members' home institutes were not chosen in the secret balloting. In order to give their home institutes a second chance, jurors manipulated the process until their home institutes were chosen. Tsinghua University is likely to have been the most significant lobbyist. None of its three designs was among the final five, yet Tsinghua had the longest history of involvement with the National Theatre project. The Tsinghua scheme by Li Daozeng had been chosen by Premier Zhou Enlai as the scheme to implement in 1958. Tsinghua had also won the preliminary scheme selection process in 1997. Before the 1998 competition, Tsinghua University had been considered by both the media and the public as one of the strongest competitors; Li was described by the media as having a "National Theatre complex."[50] And, finally and most importantly, Wu Liangyong, a Tsinghua professor, served as both the chair of the jury and the head of the First Consultative Team.

The inference that the source of the problem was the lack of Chinese representation among winning designs is also supported by the fact that, of the nine participants added in the second round, only the four Chinese institutes were invited by the Pro-

a. Scheme No. 101 by ADP (Paul Andreu).

b. Scheme No. 106 by Terry Farrell and Partners.

c. Scheme No. 201 by Arata Isozaki and Associates.

Fig. 5.16. The five selected schemes from the first round of the international competition for the National Grand Theatre, April to July 1998. *Reproduction from* Zhongguo Guojia Dajüyuan Jianzhu Sheji Guoji Jingsai fang'anji, *98, 110, 216, 126, 78. Courtesy of Zhou Qinglin.*

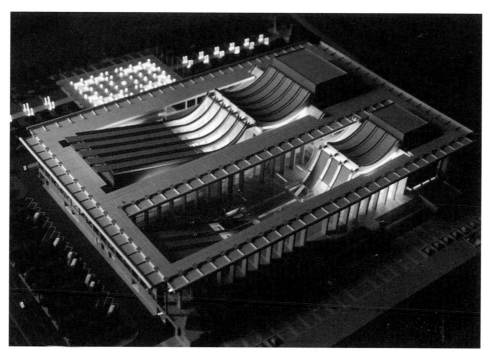

d. Scheme No. 205 by the Ministry of Construction Architectural Design Institute of China.

e. Scheme No. 507 by HPP International Planungsgesellschaft mbH.

prietor Committee, while the five foreign companies were volunteers. The only possible explanation is that, in order to increase Chinese involvement in the project, more Chinese institutes were invited for the second round of the competition; but after accepting the Chinese participants, there was no reason to reject foreign companies when they volunteered. In addition, after the first round of competition, Yoshinobu Ashihara of Japan resigned from the jury, and for the second round his position was filled by a Chinese architect. It is possible that Ashihara's resignation was due to his indignation over the manipulation of the competition process by some Chinese members, which was especially unfair to Japanese architect Arata Isozaki, whose entry was considered the best by many Chinese and foreign professionals.[51]

During the evaluation process of the second round from November 14 to 17, the Proprietor Committee proposed a new scheme selection method. Instead of simply voting for one or more winning schemes, the jury was instructed to choose two entries from the five revised recommended schemes from the first round (first group), one from the four invited Chinese institutes (second group), and one from the five foreign volunteers (third group). Thus the final number of schemes submitted to the Leadership Small Group would be four.[52] Disregarding the result of the first round of the competition, this new selection method would secure the survival of at least one Chinese scheme after the second round of competition.

The result of the second round of voting, however, again defied expectations. Instead of four participants, five were chosen to continue in the competition. The two winners from the first group were ADP of France (fig. 5.17a) and Arata Isozaki and Associates of Japan; the single winner from the third group was Hans Hollein and Heinz Neumann Design Group of Austria (fig. 5.17b). However, the second, or Chinese, group, produced two winners instead of one—the Beijing Institute and Tsinghua University (fig. 5.17c)—because, according to the official explanation, they received the same number of votes. The true reason for the selection of two Chinese schemes instead of one as originally planned is unclear. It is certain that the jury could achieve no consensus on which schemes were the best. Every scheme favored by some jury members was strongly opposed by others, which made the final decision making difficult. The only conclusion acceptable to all jury members was that none of the selected schemes was good enough. The jury even reminded the Leadership Small

a.

b.

c.

Group and the highest decision makers to consider the situation carefully and to avoid making any final choice.

Consequently, all the Leadership Small Group could do was to continue the competition, which was now said to have entered the stage of scheme modifications. The first modification required each foreign company to cooperate with one Chinese institute and offer one scheme. Three such pairs were designated to provide three schemes. At this point, Arata Isozaki and Hans Hollein both dropped out of the competition. The prolonged and unpredictable process they had already endured had apparently convinced them that they were not going to get the project anyway and the wisest thing to do was to quit. Their positions were filled by Terry Farrell and Partners of the United Kingdom, and Carlos Ott and Associates of Canada. A third Chinese participant, the Ministry Institute, was also added to make three pairs: France's ADP and Tsinghua University, the United Kingdom's Terry Farrell and the Beijing Institute (fig. 5.18a), and Canada's Carlos Ott and the Ministry Institute (fig. 5.18b). The first modification phase lasted from December 15, 1998, to January 31, 1999.[53]

The outcome of the first modification, again, was different from what was originally planned. The pair consisting of France's ADP and Tsinghua University, instead of providing one scheme, submitted two: one mainly by ADP with the assistance of Tsinghua (fig. 5.17a), and the other primarily by Tsinghua with the assistance of ADP (fig. 5.18c), making a total of four entries. At this point the foreign jury members quit en masse. Maybe they finally realized that their opinions made no difference. They had learned that the Chinese would pay lip service to the significance of their opinions but would always find a way to bypass their decisions, a method of working Arthur Erickson diplomatically called "uniquely Chinese."[54]

With no foreign personnel on board, the jury was disbanded. A new Specialists Committee, chaired by Wu Liangyong, was formed by combining members from the two former consultative groups and the remaining Chinese jury members. The Leadership Small Group now invited the Specialists Committee to evaluate the four schemes from the first modification. According to the official explanation, most experts agreed that the schemes were impressively improved but still not satisfying. A second modification was made between March 2 and May 4, 1999. Meanwhile, on the suggestion of some experts and with the approval of the Leadership Small Group as well as the Municipal Planning Department, the construction site was moved seventy meters

a.

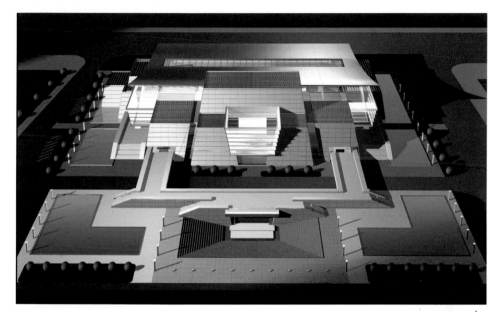

b.

c.

a.

Fig. 5.19. Schemes selected from the second and third modifications of the international competition for the National Grand Theatre, March to July 1999: a. ADP and Tsinghua University; b. Terry Farrell and Beijing Institute; c. Tsinghua University and ADP. *Reproduction from Zhongguo Guojia Dajüyuan Jianzhu Sheji Guoji Jingsai fang'anji, 55, 65, 73. Courtesy of Zhou Qinglin.*

south, and the patches of greenery were relocated from south of the main building, as required in the original program, to the north side on Chang'an Avenue.[55]

The same four schemes in revised versions were submitted for evaluation after the second modification. The scheme submitted by the Carlos Ott–Ministry Institute pairing was eliminated at this stage. According to a statement from the Leadership Small Group, the scheme designed by ADP with the assistance of Tsinghua University was then favored by most experts for its unique idea, novel form, and original concept. Later events, however, threw this interpretation into question, as in the following years hundreds of Chinese intellectuals and experts, including Wu Liangyong, who was the chair of not only the former jury and First Consultative Group but also the later Specialists Committee, submitted to the party protests against the ADP scheme.

The ADP scheme presented in the second modification, however, changed the site again in order to fit its concept. The building was moved farther south to align with the Great Hall, and the southern boundary of the site was expanded to West Front Gate Street. The Leadership Small Group appreciated ADP's changes to the site, calling them an "environmental improvement of the Tiananmen Square area," and asked all three remaining units to provide a third modified scheme according to ADP's new vision of the site. These three units were ADP, assisted by Tsinghua University

b.

c.

(fig. 5.19a); Terry Farrell, assisted by the Beijing Institute (fig. 5.19b); and Tsinghua University, assisted by ADP (fig. 5.19c). Eliminated in the first round of competition, Tsinghua University miraculously appeared in the last modification, not only as an assistant but also as the only Chinese institution in charge of an individual entry.

In early July, the Proprietor Committee invited some of the deputies of the

National People's Congress and the Chinese People's Political Consultative Conference to discuss and comment on the three schemes after the third modification. News leaks revealed that most of the deputies supported the design by ADP of France. The Leadership Small Group finally recommended the submission of all three designs to the central government for examination and final decision.[56] The central government finally chose the ADP scheme, and Tsinghua University was designated the Chinese cooperative unit.

Throughout the 1998–99 National Grand Theatre competition, Tsinghua University made persistent and eventually successful efforts to remain involved in the project. As Freud said, a personal feeling, once repressed, will surely resurface in the future. The National Grand Theatre complex belongs not only to Professor Li but also to the School of Architecture at Tsinghua University.

If the result of the competition seemed ridiculous to foreign architects and scholars, it was not so for the Chinese. The 1998–99 competition process had much in common with the collective creation approach in architecture during the first three decades of the People's Republic of China, which was within living memory for most of the Chinese leaders, jury members, and participants in the competition. The scheme selection process started as something similar to a standard design competition, but as the process evolved, it became increasingly similar to the collective creation approach, with its pooling of ideas. After the first round of competition, participants already knew one another and were familiar with one another's schemes. The five winning schemes from the first round became models for other participating units to learn from, and the second round had little sense of real competition. Starting with the first modification, all entries were collectively created by two cooperating units. The entries for the third modification all looked similar in spite of the vehement debate among designers. During the three modifications, there was collaboration not only between cooperating units in the same pair but also among scheme designers, experts from the evaluation teams, officials in the Leadership Small Group, and other higher decision makers. Specific comments and instructions were given to the designers before every modification, and designers could even suggest changes to the construction site to better suit their schemes. This would never have happened in a design competition in the West.

The Schemes: Expecting the Unexpected

The main focus of the competition was architectural style. In terms of architectural plan, there was very little room for manipulation. Four theatres, three large and one small, had to be fitted into a relatively small site. A total floorage of 120,000 square

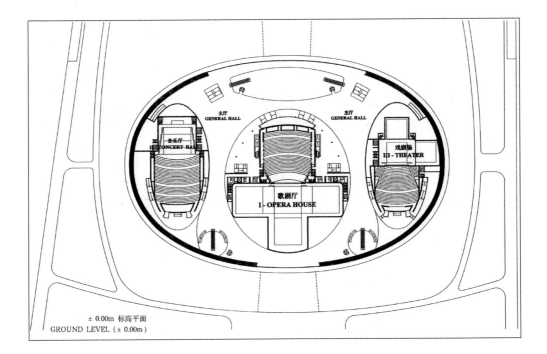

± 0.00m 标高平面
GROUND LEVEL (± 0.00m)

meters was designated for a site of 38,900 square meters. The four theatres—a 2,500-seat opera house (22,529 square meters), a 2,000-seat concert hall (11,987 square meters), a 1,200-seat *xiju* theatre (12,006 square meters), and a 300-to-500-seat mini theatre (7,427 square meters)—occupied more than half of the nonparking

Fig. 5.20. National Grand Theatre, plan drawing, 1998–99. ADP (Paul Andreu). *Reproduction from* Zhongguo Guojia Dajüyuan Jianzhu Sheji Guoji Jingsai fang'anji, *59. Courtesy of Zhou Qinglin.*

floorage. After filling in the three large theatres, only a corner of the site remained unused. Because the height of the entire building was capped at forty-five meters, and because the theatre's function required the above-stage area to be high, it was impossible to stack the large theatres.

Actually, there were only two possible ways to arrange the three large theatres in the plan. The first was to line them up one after another, from east to west, which would leave some space for other functions on the north and/or south sides, as in the ADP scheme (fig. 5.20). The second option was to line two of the theatres on the same side, from north to south, and then put the third one on the opposite side, which would leave some space in a corner. This was the approach Arata Isozaki took (fig. 5.21). There were some possible variations of these two basic types, but most schemes followed one or the other.

Since the plans of the different entries were similar, the real competition focused

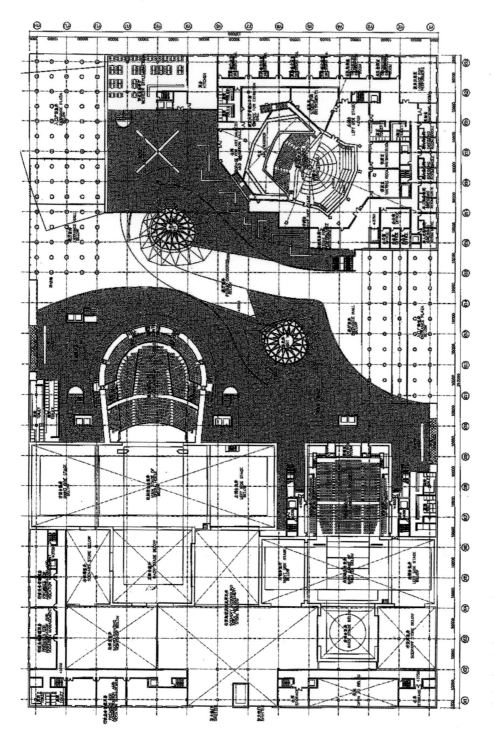

一层平面 (3.75m)　2nd FLOOR LEVEL (+3.75m)

Fig. 5.21

on architectural form. The design program called for the form to be in harmony with its environment due to the significance of its proximity to Tiananmen Square and for it to serve as an organic component of the architectural group there. The design was required to artistically express power with solemnity and grace, and, at the same time, to show a distinctive affinity for the people and the trends of the time.[57] The program for the competition also stipulated that the future theatre had to "be a monumental work to carry the Chinese cultural [*sic*] forward, to reflect the spirit of the time, to collect modern architectural arts and high technologies in the world, and to contribute to the development of human performing arts."[58] The requirements to capture both Chinese culture and the spirit of the time, with an emphasis on modern arts and technologies, led most competition participants to take the same action without prior consultation—manipulating, simplifying, dissecting, and recomposing traditional architectural motifs and cultural symbols using new materials, predominantly glass and metal.

For both Chinese and foreign architects in the first round of competition, the time-honored curved roof was the paramount symbol of Chinese architecture. Many entries crowned the theatre complex with gigantic roofs of various formats. Some were manipulated or simplified beyond recognition but still referred superficially to the traditional Chinese roof. Scheme 104 by the Beijing Institute, for instance, returned to the upturned overhanging eaves with brackets that had first appeared in its 1997 scheme (fig. 5.22). Scheme 201 by Arata Isozaki transformed the three elements of Tiananmen Square architecture—the roof, the colonnade, and the base—into abstract figures using 3-D computer-manipulated programs. Scheme 507 by HPP offered a Miesian-style box of steel and glass, but with a big roof and a high platform, following traditional Chinese architectural proportions (fig. 5.16e). Scheme 302 by French architect Jean Nouvel provided three deconstructionist roofs with fragmented pieces of disconnected and overlapping slopes, ridges, and eaves. Others simplified,[59] dissected, and recomposed the traditional Chinese roof in a more rational way.[60] Traditional Chinese architectural motifs other than the sloping roof (for instance, courtyards,[61] bridges in front of Tiananmen Tower,[62] and the traditional archway[63]) were also used in some entries.

In addition to architectural motifs, traditional cultural symbols were also associated with architectural forms in the first round. Both scheme 105 by the Beijing Institute and scheme 205 by the Ministry Institute (fig. 5.16d) incorporated the image of the *guqin*—an ancient seven-stringed Chinese zither—in their designs. While scheme

Fig. 5.22

Fig. 5.22. National Grand Theatre design, 1998–99. Beijing Institute. *Reproduction from Zhongguo Guojia Dajüyuan Jianzhu Sheji Guoji Jingsai fang'anji, 90. Courtesy of Zhou Qinglin.*

105 only shaped an opening in the cement floor in the image of a *guqin*, in scheme 205 the entire outline of the building is inspired by the ancient instrument. Nouvel's scheme 302 incorporated color symbolism.[64] Other cultural symbols used in various schemes included painted Beijing Opera masks,[65] the red lantern,[66] the phoenix,[67] and motifs alluding to the famous *guqin* music "High Mountains and Flowing Waters."[68]

The Chinese and foreign entries in the first round can easily be distinguished. In general, Chinese schemes were characterized by painstaking efforts to make attractive façades that divided the elevations into smaller parts according to classical or traditional proportions. In contrast, instead of creating subdivided compositions, schemes by overseas architects treated the building complex as one comprehensive body and proposed a monolithic geometric superstructure whose main interest resided in the texture of materials.

The stylistic difference between the Chinese and the foreign entries parallels the difference between postmodernism and supermodernism in Western architecture. The rise of postmodernism in the 1960s challenged the modernist values founded by previous masters such as Le Corbusier, Ludvig Mies van der Rohe, and Walter Gropius. The functional rationalism and formal abstraction in modern architecture was criticized by Robert Venturi as expressionless and dull due to its lack of complexity and contradiction.[69] Instead of the "less is more" cherished by Mies and his followers, Venturi declared that "less is a bore." Postmodernism as codified in Charles Jencks's *The Language of Post-Modern Architecture* was mainly a classically inspired style. The historical motifs and figurative and symbolic ornamentation rejected by modernism once again became a popular approach in architectural design. Instead of the functionally universal space of the International Style, postmodernism emphasized the creation of meaning in architecture and the specific character of the place based on urban context and collective memories.[70] This postmodernism, introduced to China in the 1980s, had a tremendous influence on Chinese architecture of the 1980s and 1990s. Books by Venturi, Jencks, Christian Norberg-Schulz, and Aldo Rossi were translated into Chinese and widely read by architects and architecture students.

In Western architecture, however, postmodernism was already receding in influence by the 1990s. The movement's professional and academic visibility was blurred by a new architectural movement known as deconstructivism that appeared in the 1980s and was promoted by an exhibition in 1990 at the Museum of Modern Art in New York. As the twentieth century drew to a close, there was a sudden increase in glassy, transparent, and translucent monolithic buildings, which, according to Dutch architectural critic Hans Ibelings, demonstrated little concern for formal consider-ations.[71] Rodolfo Machado and Rodolphe el-Khoury describe these solid, massive structures—occasionally mitigated by light and transparency—as looking as if they have been made in one piece with the capacity "to deliver tremendous eloquence with very limited formal means."[72] With the revival of simplified forms devoid of decora-tion, the modernist maxim "less is more" was also back in the form of minimalism.[73] This was what Ibelings termed "super-modernism," characterized as a new "sensitivity to the neutral, the undefined, the implicit, qualities that are not confined to architec-tural substance but also find powerful expression in a new spatial sensibility."[74]

While a concern with the division of elevation and the expression of symbolic meaning was a common characteristic of the Chinese entries for the National Grand Theatre, almost all of the foreign schemes were characterized by monolithic super-structures and large-span constructions that played with the texture and color of trans-parent or translucent surfaces. In the 1990s the Chinese were still exploring Western postmodernism; but by then, the West had moved on to supermodernism, and the Chinese were again "left behind." While Chinese architectural professionals were still enjoying postmodern grammar and vocabulary, China's political leaders had already started looking for the newest the world had to offer.

Chinese architects soon recognized the gap between their practice and this latest development in the wider architectural world. By the second round of the National Grand Theatre design competition, many Chinese entries had adopted the mono-lithic superstructure. The Beijing Institute abandoned its earlier compilation of smaller glass and solid bodies and now covered everything inside a relatively flat sur-face. The new entry by Tsinghua University also adopted a megastructure supported by twelve gigantic pillars, serving as transportation cores with elevators and stairs inside (fig. 5.17c). The entry by the Ministry Institute, which made only minor revi-sions and insisted on retaining its old approach, was not chosen for the next round.

The copying of appreciated forms and concepts from others' first-round schemes was not uncommon in the entries for the second round. The rich and complex inte-rior design in Arata Isozaki's first-round scheme, characterized by frequent changes of floor elevation and the use of bridges to connect different floors, was copied by the Beijing Institute scheme (figs. 5.21, 5.23). The new scheme by HPP borrowed both the exposed wavy ribs in the roofs from the Ministry Institute's first-round scheme and the glass sky wells from Isozaki's design.

A common awareness of rivals' schemes and patrons' attitudes toward them informed the

Fig. 5.23. National Grand Theatre, plan drawing, 1998–99. Beijing Institute. *Reproduction from* Zhong-guo Guojia Dajüyuan Jianzhu Sheji Guoji Jingsai fang'anji, *258. Courtesy of Zhou Qinglin.*

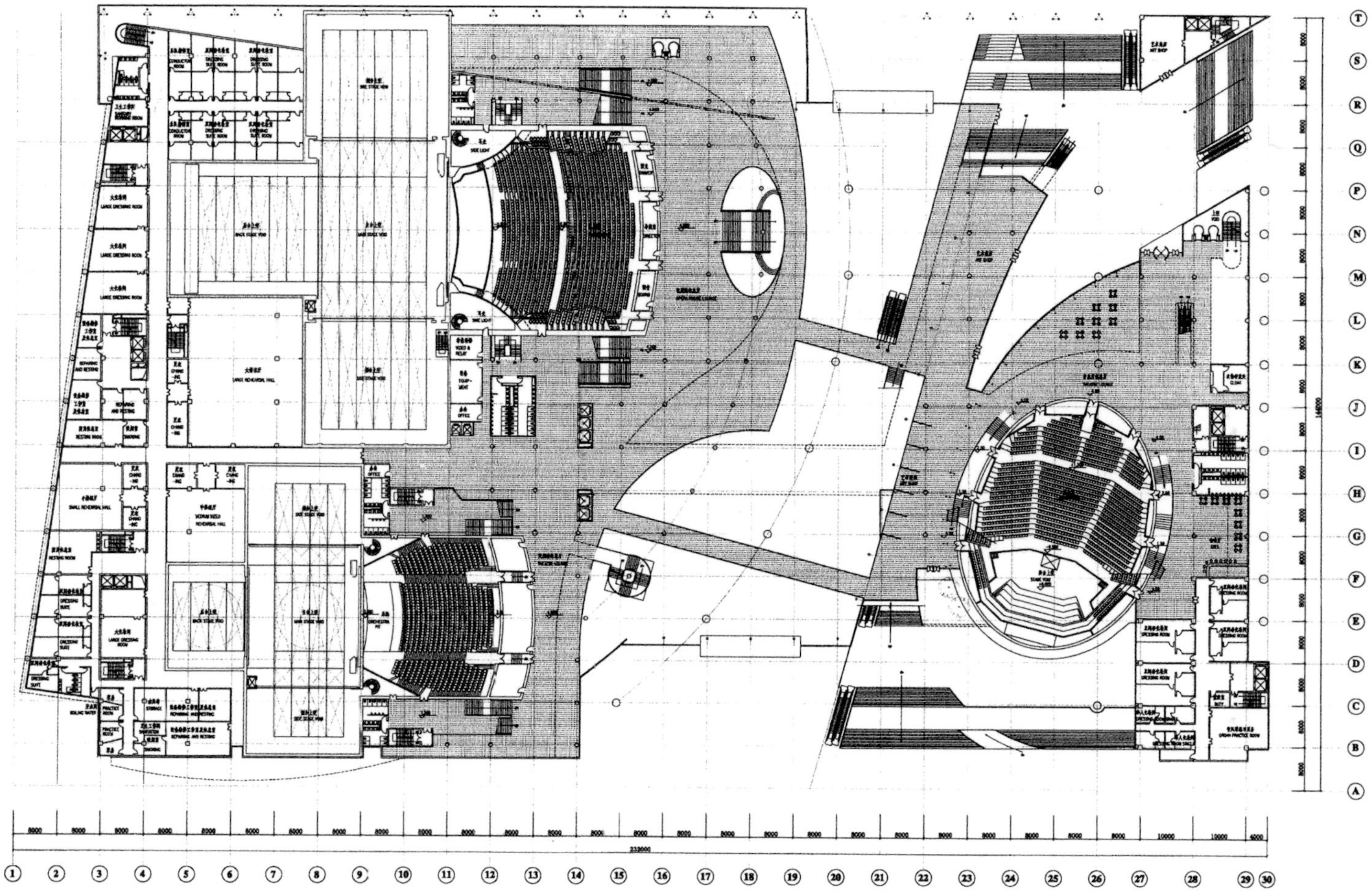

二层平面

2nd FLOOR PLAN

Fig. 5.23

three levels of modification.[75] ADP had proposed a halved oval shape in a pool in the second modification scheme. All three remaining finalists immediately understood the Proprietor Committee's preference for this scheme. During the third modification, the other two schemes, by Terry Farrell and Tsinghua University, also become round and curving, with its main structures located in a pool (fig. 5.19).

Toward the end of the modification process, final schemes became increasingly similar: all were neutral monolithic transparent megastructures. Schemes with façade-construction and roof-symbolism were eliminated one by one. Finally, a form that could hardly be more neutral (in that it was devoid of cultural reference to a specific nation) and minimalist was selected. It was partly translucent and partly transparent. It was an "egg."

The huge egg, the brainchild of Paul Andreu, the chief architect of ADP, was located in a square pool. Andreu covered everything with a monolithic shell of titanium, split in the center by a curvy, symmetrical glass opening. Seen together with its reflection in the water, the egg shape was completed, glimmering, and ephemeral. The form was so simple and devoid of symbolism, Chinese or otherwise, that people could find little to describe or criticize about it. It was like the primordial egg, neutral and universal, ephemeral and at the same time eternal. This was hardly what the Chinese had anticipated at the beginning of the competition.

By the tacit consent among Chinese officials and architects before the competition, the National Grand Theatre was to be recognized at first sight as "a theatre, a theatre that belongs to China, and a theatre close to Tiananmen Square."[76] The egg, however, had little association with either Tiananmen Square or Beijing. It was so universal, timeless, and characterless a shape that no nation, including China, could claim a specific cultural affinity to it. Ironically, Andreu, the main designer of the egg, claimed that it was specifically for China and that nothing could be more appropriate. He said in the scheme introduction, "There is no other building like it in the world. It is a unique building, born in unique circumstances for a singular place, inconceivable anywhere else. Its design expresses the serenity and simplicity of the most ancient harmony between opposites."[77]

This is the same irony inherent in Chinese modernization itself. Maybe what China expected at the time was nothing but uniqueness. Whatever was unique could be claimed as national, as long as it conformed to the latest developments in the West.

Paul Andreu and the Final Scheme: Victory of a "Universal Space"

No matter how much Andreu asserted the Chineseness and site-specificity of his scheme for the National Grand Theatre, his design bore a strong similarity to his previous designs, many of them airports.[78] Constructed outside cities on empty sites, due to their gigantic size and attendant environmental problems, such as noise, the airport is architecture without context. As one architectural critic pointed out, the task Andreu deals with in airports is "to create a piece of city where the city does not exist."[79] However, once an airport is constructed, as a result of the airport's mass needs, its formerly empty site becomes a new city center for future development and "starts to compete with the very city it was originally intended to serve."[80] Without context, the airport form is often neutral, with little reference to regional style, an "architectural airport aesthetic" summarized by Hans Ibelings as "exposed steel construction (a space-frame or gigantic trusses), a marked preference for vaulted roofs, a color palette of grey, white, pale blue and light green and, above all, acres and acres of glass."[81] This is an almost exact description of Paul Andreu's National Grand Theatre.

Almost all previous projects by Andreu—airports, railway terminals, and later, stadiums—were megastructures. Even his 2000 Osaka Maritime Museum is covered by a huge glass dome. Andreu's architecture is characterized by its enormous public interior space beneath a monolithic shell that is often separate from the inner structures that are unified by it, so that the complex and scattered spaces are disguised with a single identity. In the Abu Dhabi airport, "the terminal's huge interior space, held up by a ventral core, is flooded with light and transparency. This creates the overall effect of a night sky sheltering passengers from the bright sunshine, although natural light does gradually creep in on the horizon to create a deceptive sense of a newly dawning day."[82] Like the sky, Andreu's shell is not part of the structure proper, but added to form a spatial illusion. In the Osaka Maritime Museum, the interior floors are separate from the hemispherical shell. The scattered subspaces of rooms, staircases, bathrooms, and elevator make the plan of the exhibition space resemble a diagram of cell structure. Andreu used exactly the same technique to unify the four theatres in the National Grand Theatre. They are all covered by a titanium and glass shell that is separate from the individual structures of the four theatres beneath it.

Airport design provides Andreu with technological solutions for spatial construction and also an architectural philosophy. For Andreu, the airport is not just a new type of architecture but also the very symbol of the contemporary human condition. He writes,

> Aeroplanes have changed the nature of political boundaries. Put in mathematical terms, one might say that because of aircraft, national borders have ceased being continuous lines on the earth's surface and became nonrelated sets of lines and points situated within each country. Any surviving illusions about "natural" borders were duly "snuffed out" by the possibilities of flight.[83]

The airport has destroyed political boundaries and unified the world. In other words, the airport is the producer as well as the product of globalization. Old-fashioned traveling on the ground and crossing political borders, which Andreu calls "a rite of passage," has changed, and the present airport type illustrates a new way of life. "No doubt one day soon a way will be found for machines to check passengers, who will move through with no further need to pause. This will put a final term to any surviving trace of a rite of passage."[84]

The neutral monolithic architecture represented by airports, characterized by Filippo Beltrami Gadola as "universal space,"[85] left a strong mark on Andreu's schemes for the National Grand Theatre. At first Andreu tried to create a dialogue between the new theatre and the old buildings around it. Although his scheme in the first-round competition was a geometric megastructure of glazed steel, the rooflines were straight and similar in height to the neighboring Great Hall. Grand tiers of steps leading to the main entrance opening to Chang'an Avenue were reminiscent of the grand façades of the Ten Great Buildings from the 1950s. His next two schemes, the second-round scheme and its first modification, were not very different from his original design, with only minor changes in exterior materials. The building remained a square box of transparent glass and solid walls.

In the second modification, almost at the close of the competition, however, Andreu's scheme returned to what had been so prevalent throughout his career—a huge shell. All of the theatres and other facilities were now covered by a monolithic shell. The grand stairs had disappeared, and the main entrance had been moved below the water, similar to the entrance to Andreu's Osaka Maritime Museum. The curving shape of the glass opening in the titanium shell also closely resembled the entrances of his 1998 Charles de Gaulle Airport extension.

Maybe, finally, Andreu realized that what the Chinese leaders were expecting was exactly what he was so good at. Maybe no one knew what was expected anyway. There was no need to flatter with attempts at Chineseness. The later Chinese criticism of Andreu's design for its lack of Chineseness was mainly a mixture of sour grapes about Chinese competitors who had been passed over, loss of national self-esteem, and loss of face.[86] Although everyone claimed that the National Grand Theatre should be a perfect combination of modern and Chinese, when the final decision had to be made, the Chinese were still looking for what was considered the most advanced in the world, the Western "original." During the competition process, foreign architects first tried listening to what the Chinese officials wanted, but they found that the Chinese were actually looking to them. They were finally assured that they should just do what they wanted to and what they were good at, and the Chinese would follow. The

National Grand Theatre competition ended with both the victory of a "universal space" and a confirmation of Western hegemony.

The story of the Chinese architects in the 1998–99 National Grand Theater competition was quite different. Behind Tsinghua's manipulation of the selection process was an insistence on Chineseness, represented by the Tiananmen Square architecture of the tenth anniversary of the People's Republic of China. In the 1990s, Tiananmen Square, with its surrounding monuments, the Great Hall and the museum complex, was already the prime symbol of national spirit. Maintaining the square's architectural harmony was the driving force behind designs by Tsinghua's architects over the years; from the beginning to the end, Li Daozeng's schemes for the National Theatre followed the style of the Great Hall. Simultaneously resisting Western dominance, cultural surrender, and public psychology, Li's final design was doomed to fail. He was a tragic hero.

However, what was behind the architectural harmony of Tiananmen Square? Tiananmen Tower and Zhengyang Gate, with its Archery Tower, were imperial monuments from the Ming and Qing dynasties. The Great Hall and the museum complex were combinations of Stalinist classicism and motifs from ancient Chinese buildings. The Chineseness Tsinghua had insisted on in the 1998 competition could be traced back, after all, to Western neoclassical architecture, which had now become fully national for the Chinese after the Ten Great Buildings in 1958–59.

No wonder Li finally set four groups of golden statues, in the manner of Paris's Palais Garnier, on top of the roofs in his last scheme for the National Grand Theatre. No wonder it failed. His was a design of the nineteenth-century West competing with the twenty-first-century West.

After the Competition: The Battle over the "Egg"

Immediately after its announcement in July 1999, Andreu's chosen scheme for the National Grand Theatre was widely debated, primarily in China and France. In China, discussions took place not only among architectural professionals and historians, and not only in cultural circles, but also throughout the entire society. People from all walks of life and all social strata were eager to express their opinions and concerns. Views were shared through many different channels. Critical articles appeared in professional journals as well as in newspapers and popular magazines; architects and scholars involved in the project were interviewed on television and radio; column discussions were opened on several major Chinese websites. Of all of these different media, the Internet emerged as the most powerful in the fight for popular support,

Fig. 5.24. National Grand Theatre, 1998–2007. ADP (Paul Andreu) and Tsinghua University. *Photograph by author.*

sharing of opinions, disclosing of scandals, spreading of rumors, and release of emotions. It was the popularization of that most global medium—the Internet—that made possible, and at the same time promoted, a nationwide, global, instantaneous discussion of an architectural project—the first such discussion in China.

People either liked or hated Andreu's final scheme. Opponents called the huge titanium-glass shell "a broken egg with egg white flowing on the ground," "a big stupid egg" (*dabendan*), "a gigantic tomb," or "a donkey's turd." Supporters praised the minimalist dome as "an egg giving birth to a new era," "a pearl," or "a drop of clear water," and welcomed its great contrast with the environment as an architectural revolution in Tiananmen Square. The relatively neutral nickname "the duck's egg" was favored by Andreu himself for its structural soundness, mathematical accuracy, and symbolism of the beginning of life (fig. 5.24).[87]

Criticisms of Andreu's scheme emerged primarily on three fronts: legitimacy, practicality, and style. The criticism about legitimacy focused mainly on the selection procedure. The argument was that Andreu had not won the competition. There was, in fact, critics pointed out, no winner of the two rounds of formal competition, since none of the entries qualified. Andreu's scheme, it was argued, had been chosen not by the jury but by the manipulation of the Proprietor Committee. The jury had been disbanded after two rounds of formal competition, and those who were against Andreu's scheme had been deliberately removed from the Specialists Committee formed later to evaluate schemes during the three rounds of modification. The two rounds of competition were impartial, and produced no winner; but the three rounds of modification were unjust and led to Andreu's scheme. The other argument about legitimacy was that underhanded dealing had taken place between Andreu and certain Chinese officials. Directly or indirectly, the charge goes, Andreu bribed Chinese officials in order to win the project. In other words, it was the profit of some corrupt individual that led to Andreu's success, not the quality of his design. The scandalous stories that spread online sometimes provided quite specific details, including names, dates, and exact amounts of money; the anonymous authors of these "news" items narrated them as facts. However, these charges have been impossible to either verify or prove false.

Three major arguments against Andreu's scheme are based on practicality: safety, economy, and maintenance. First, Andreu's building, at least in design, was considered unsafe. The long underground entrance and indirect approach to the theatres would make evacuation difficult during a fire. Moreover, since all of the theatres would be buried seven to eight meters underground, with a pool overhead, it would be a disaster if the pool ever collapsed or the water broke through. Secondly, Andreu's scheme would be very costly. It was said that Andreu had increased the original cost estimate of ¥2 billion to almost ¥5 billion.[88] The useless gigantic shell alone would cost ¥700 million. Third, maintenance of the building after its completion would be difficult. The windy, sandy weather of Beijing would make the shining surface of the "giant pearl" dirty—the reason some people called it "a donkey's turd"—and hard to clean. The monolithic interior space and the metal and glass surface would also waste energy and make maintenance extremely costly.

Criticisms of style focused on the lack of contextual consideration and respect for Chinese culture. Opponents argued that the scheme was not in harmony with the architectural environment around Tiananmen Square because, somehow, the shining surface would spoil the red walls and glazed-tile roofs of the Forbidden City, the minimalist form would ruin the political atmosphere of Tiananmen Square, and the building's scale was so large that it would dwarf the neighboring Great Hall. The scheme was also considered disrespectful to Chinese culture since the design embodied no Chinese architectural spirit whatsoever. Critics claimed that Andreu's design was totally formalistic, reflecting neither the function it served nor the architectural context. Protesting commentators in particular invoked the original requirements of the "old three looks" (*laosankan*)—that the design should at first glance look like "a theatre, a theatre that belongs to China, and a theatre close to Tiananmen Square"—

to prove the unqualified nature of the scheme. The requirements of the "old three looks," however, had disappeared from the documents from the later parts of the scheme selection procedure. This is one of the main reasons people thought there might be some backstage deal that cleared the way for Andreu's success.

The supporters of Andreu's scheme argued against the three criticisms. In response to the criticism about legitimacy, supporters argued that the procedure was completely transparent and legal. The three rounds of modifications were evaluated by the Specialists Committee, who voted on the finalist's schemes. The story of a backstage deal, supporters say, was entirely made up by those with ulterior motives.

In response to the criticism of practicality, supporters argued that all of the problems could be solved and had already been carefully considered by the designers from the very beginning. They were confident that Andreu and the ADP had enough experience to deal with the technological issues of constructing and maintaining a large project like this. Moreover, cool air from the pool and the fountains would mitigate the notoriously hot, dry air of Beijing summers.

In response to the criticisms about style, supporters argued that there are many different ways to harmonize with surrounding buildings, contrast sometimes being quite an effective one. They pointed out that there was by no means just one approach to carrying on the traditional Chinese spirit. Traditional Chinese architectural character, they claimed, does not mean big roofs, red walls, traditional decorative motifs, or rectangular yards. Supporters asked, "Do we want just another Tiananmen Tower or Great Hall of the People for the new millennia?" The building was designed for Chinese people and on Chinese earth and would therefore surely be a Chinese building in Chinese history. They argued that instead of simply following history, Andreu's design showed that it was possible to create a new heritage. Besides, they explained, the Great Hall was dramatically different from the Forbidden City in style yet was considered very Chinese now. And, although the scale of Andreu's design was huge, the transparent and reflecting surface would make the structure appear much lighter than the solid walls of its neighbors, and the reflections of the surroundings by the metal, glass, and water would form a unique dialogue with its context. Besides, the dome of the new theatre was slightly lower than the Great Hall, so it would not overshadow it.

Although the debates involved a large population drawn from a variety of social sectors, including journalists, architects, students, and ordinary people, it seems that there were major promoters for both sides. The protesters were mainly older-generation intellectuals, while the defenders of Andreu's scheme were mostly younger-generation architects and members of the Proprietor Committee. It is interesting, and maybe not accidental, that key figures on both sides had connections with Tsinghua University.

Two people were most active in working to overturn Andreu's scheme: Peng Peigen, professor of architecture at Tsinghua University, and Xiao Mo, a 1950s Tsinghua graduate who later became an architectural historian working at the Chinese Art Research Institute. On March 8, 2000, Xiao Mo published the first journal article vehemently chastising Andreu's scheme in *China Reading Weekly* (Zhonghua dushu bao),[89] and he continued to write and distribute articles critical of Andreu and his scheme in various media. Xiao Mo finally compiled the relevant articles into a book, *The Egg of the Century: Debates on the National Grand Theatre of China* (Shiji zhi dan: Guojia dajuyuan zhi bian), which was published in 2004 in Taiwan. Peng Peigen, meanwhile, was an activist who gave frequent public talks criticizing Andreu. He also tried to overturn Andreu's scheme by organizing petitions to convince top leaders that the chosen scheme had serious disadvantages.

The two most active supporters of Andreu's scheme, Zhou Qinglin and Wu Yaodong, were also linked to Tsinghua University. Zhou Qinglin was a Tsinghua graduate who became the chief architect of the Ministry of Construction Architectural Design Institute in 1986 and was the only practicing architect in the Proprietor Committee. Wu Yaodong was a young scholar who graduated from Tsinghua in the 1980s and later became a faculty member in the architecture department. He was one of the main architects on the Chinese side to collaborate with Andreu on the National Grand Theatre project. Among other media appearances, these four were the main participants in two major television debates, in July 2000 on Phoenix TV in Hong Kong, and in May 2004 on CCTV in Beijing.[90]

It seems that the first person to question the legitimacy of Andreu's scheme was a Frenchman. On September 16, 1999, Frederic Adman claimed in the French newspaper *Le Monde* that Andreu's scheme had been chosen through questionable procedures.[91] Chinese protesters' criticism, however, had first focused on economic issues. On March 14, 2000, at the Fourth Meeting of the Ninth National People's Congress, Guangxi representatives complained that Andreu's design was formalistic and too expensive, saying that it was not practical for a developing country to spend so much money on a theatre.[92] At the same time, however, the media revealed the construction schedule for the theatre: work would start on April 1, 2000; the structure would be finished by the end of 2002; and the entire project would be completed by March 2003.[93] On March 30, 2000, the head of the Ministry of Construction told reporters that a newly founded National Grand Theatre Art Committee was already working on plans for future performances and that new works to be performed at the theatre were being created. His speech also indicated that Jiang Zemin, the highest leader of China at the time, was directly involved in the National Grand Theatre project.[94] On April 1, 2000, however, when reporters went to the site for the groundbreaking ceremony, they found only a few guards and workers there, who told them the ceremony had been cancelled. According to an online article, reporters saw Beijing mayor Jia Qinglin arrive and hold a meeting with the Proprietor Committee, the Leadership Small Group, and representatives from the construction companies. Reporters were told by their editors that official orders forbade the publication of the stories they had written about the cancellation of the ceremony.[95] Construction did start, but without an opening ceremony.

Two serious events threatened Andreu's scheme after construction began. The first occurred on June 10, 2000, when forty-nine members of the Chinese Academy of Science and the Chinese Academy of Engineering submitted a written statement to the central government criticizing Andreu's design and calling for the suspension of the project; 114 architects signed a similar appeal on June 19.[96] While the architects' appeal mainly took issue with the project's architectural style, the Chinese Academy members' letter criticized the project's practicality. In fact, the June 10 letter criticized not only Andreu's design but also the Proprietor Committee's whole design program. It claimed that what led to such a bad design was the irrationality of the original design program, which called for four theatres in one building.[97] Wu Liangyong, chair not only of the selection jury but also of the First Consultative Team and the Specialists Committee during the 1998–99 competition, was among those who signed the letter.

The second serious threat to Andreu's scheme came on May 23, 2004, when Terminal 2E of the Charles de Gaulle Airport in Paris, also designed by Andreu, collapsed after only ten months in service. Further exacerbating the issue for the National Grand Theatre was the fact that two Chinese citizens were among the four persons killed.[98] The news spread quickly in China, and, once again, the National Grand Theatre became the focus of heated public controversy. Criticism of Andreu's scheme revived, now with a clear focus on the legitimacy of the competition procedure and the safety of the design.

The June 2000 letters of appeal from the two groups of respected members of Chinese society led to the suspension of the project for almost a year, from July 2000 to June 2001. There are, however, different explanations for this pause in construction. Some media reported that the suspension was to allow time to hear more opinions. Other reports, quoting unnamed officials, stated that the temporary pause was only to perfect the design details. During the suspension period, members from the Proprietor Committee traveled to major Chinese cities, such as Guangzhou and

Shanghai, to solicit feedback from leading architectural specialists.[99] The project resumed quietly at midnight on June 1, 2001, without advance announcement.[100]

The 2004 Paris airport accident gave new hope to opponents of Andreu's scheme, who resumed their criticism not only of safety issues but also of the integrity of the selection procedure. French articles criticizing Andreu were translated and circulated in the Chinese media. According to an article on the Chinese government website People's Net (Renmin wang), the French media disclosed that Andreu had bribed Chinese officials in the National Grand Theatre competition.[101] Such accusations, as well as many others in both the French and Chinese media, were denied by the Proprietor Committee, who called them worthless rumors.[102] The Chinese government also defended both the legitimacy of the selection process for Andreu's scheme and the safety of its design, although the airport accident in Paris did prompt further investigation to ensure the safety of the theatre project. The Chinese government insisted that the project would proceed as originally planned.[103] At that point, however, the project was already at least a year behind schedule. It was not completed until 2007, four years later than originally planned.

Behind the Debates

Behind the debates on the National Grand Theatre was Chinese intellectuals' concern about the Chineseness of Tiananmen Square and Chang'an Avenue. After decades of socialist construction, the site had become a sacred embodiment of the national spirit of China and the hope for a revival of China's past greatness in the new millennium. In such a cultural historical context, the design of a national monument by a foreign architect near Tiananmen Square was considered an invasion, equal to any of the past military humiliations inflicted on China by the West.

Gu Zhengkun, a professor of English at the Peking University and a scholar of Chinese-Western comparative cultural studies, criticized Andreu's scheme as a postcolonial cultural invasion. He invented the term "artist tort" (*yishu qinquan*), by which he meant artists' imposition of their values on the public in total disregard and violation of people's feeling. He explained,

> "Artist tort" is a term I made up. . . . It refers to the phenomena of some artists imposing their own aesthetic taste on the people with their authority through the promotion of the media. This causes people to unconsciously abandon their own taste and accept the artists' aesthetic values. In other words, when artists no longer consider people's taste as traditional artists did, but impose their taste on the people at will in the

name of "originality," they are committing "artist tort." They violate people's aesthetic rights. . . . This incident [Andreu's winning of the National Grand Theatre project] worries me because it shows how easily a foreign culture can so brutally violate the aesthetic rights of the Chinese people, without any consideration for traditional Chinese aesthetic conventions. This is absolutely an "artist tort."[104]

Gu's concept of "artist tort" oversimplifies the situation and virtually precludes any serious artistic creation. For Gu, the aesthetic taste of a nation is unanimous, unchangeable, innate, and innocent of any outside influence. He does not consider that his aesthetic tastes, as well as those of the people whom he claims to represent, are also the result of education and are susceptible to change. The blind antiforeignism and xenophobia in his argument, however, illustrate vividly how strongly and how devoid of hope the Chinese intellectuals felt about counteracting Western cultural dominance. Gu continued,

Postcolonialism is a new form of colonialism in the contemporary world, that is, militarily dominant, imperialism monopolizes capital and infiltrates the cultures of underdeveloped countries. It exports the Western lifestyle, culture, customs, artistic forms, and values to third-world countries. The people of these underdeveloped countries will unconsciously absorb them, generally lose their national consciousness, and eventually be assimilated by Western culture. This is the general framework of postcolonialism. A better translation for the term would be "neocolonialism," which is easier to understand and clearly differentiates it from old-fashioned colonialism. Andreu's blob-shaped National Grand Theatre scheme is a typical representation of this new cultural invasion by a small group of Westerners who are obstinately imposing their aesthetic tastes on the Chinese people.[105]

Gu's criticism is valid only when seen against a larger cultural political background. The final choice of Andreu's scheme does reflect a postcolonial situation in global culture; however, it is misleading simply to repudiate Andreu's scheme for the National Grand Theatre as an action of cultural invasion. No cultural invasion can occur without the consensus of the culture being invaded. After all, Western media and architects criticized Andreu's scheme as well, and toward the end of the competition, Chinese architects tried to catch up with Andreu in the production of a monolithic universal form. Why did criticism of the competition procedure arise only after Andreu's scheme was chosen and not earlier in the process? The answer may be that the Chinese architects were also willing to do whatever it took to win. To some extent, Andreu's refutation of this criticism as "architects' jealousy" is justifiable.

Two points made by Andreu in various public talks defending his scheme generated vehement counterattacks from Chinese scholars. First, in response to the criticism that his scheme did not reflect Chinese culture, Andreu once argued that his aim
was deliberately to "cut the history" instead of simply following it. Secondly, Andreu
argued that most advanced architecture is at some point attacked by the general
public, who do eventually accept it as part of a nation's cultural heritage. Here, he
cited, for instance, the Sydney Opera House, the Eiffel Tower, the Pompidou Center,
and the Louvre expansion project, which was designed by an ethnic Chinese architect
and whose glass pyramid was originally criticized as a foreign insult to the French
nation's history.

The Chinese response to Andreu's first argument was largely based on taking it out
of context. By "cut the history," Andreu meant that he was trying to get rid of historical burden, not to totally disregard Chinese culture. He expressed such views very
clearly in various contexts.[106] The Chinese critics' refutation of Andreu's second argument about the general unpopularity of new architecture was more convincing. They
argued that none of the first three buildings Andreu mentioned was located in such a
central, historical, and politically sensitive spot as the National Grand Theatre; that
the cultural legitimacy of those buildings was by no means eventually unanimously
accepted; and that I. M. Pei's glass pyramid is just an entrance, not a whole building,
and has a much smaller visual impact than Andreu's giant egg. They further argued
that Andreu's scheme would be acceptable if it were located somewhere else in
Beijing.

The central unasked question for most Chinese intellectuals was, why not have a
Chinese architect design such a significant project on such a significant site? All of the
emotional debates about the legitimacy, practicality, and style of Andreu's scheme,
were really about the politics of the site.

Top Chinese politicians, however, kept silent from beginning to end, and made no
public statement about the project. The selection procedure was authorized by specific committees independent of political power, at least in name. Some sources indicated that Andreu hinted at top-level support for his scheme, while Chinese critics
claimed that Andreu was misleading the Chinese leaders. Perhaps these claims by
Andreu's opponents were simply a strategy to gain more popular support.

Both sides, however, understood the importance of gaining support from top
leaders. Those protesting Andreu's scheme only targeted midlevel leaders, whom they
believed to have misled the top leaders. Opponents proposed that among the courses
offered to political leaders in charge of cultural affairs, architecture, urban planning,
and historical preservation should be included. According to some protesters, Andreu
once claimed that by protecting his scheme, he was in fact protecting the "party

center." Protesters countered by saying that it was Andreu who alienated Chinese leaders from the people, and that they, the critics, were really protecting the political leaders through their efforts to eliminate Andreu's scheme.[107]

The reliability of the factual information taken from these adversarial debates is questionable. However, it is clear that if top leaders expressed disapproval of Andreu's scheme, neither the Proprietor Committee nor the Leadership Small Group would have been able to defend it. The top leadership either supported Andreu's scheme or was totally disengaged from the selection procedure. History tells us that the latter was almost impossible. There are two possible answers to the question of why Communist leaders chose Andreu's scheme: they actually liked it, or they wanted to show the world that contemporary China was open and forward-looking. The second possibility seems more plausible. The construction of Andreu's scheme for the National Grand Theatre of China on Chang'an Avenue was a political gesture made in awareness of world opinion.

For decades, Chinese intellectuals have been taught that the decline of China in modern history was mainly due to Western imperialist oppression, and that its recent rise was the result of the Communist revolution. Tiananmen Square and Chang'an Avenue, as witnesses to this official version of Chinese history, have thus become sacred sites. With the National Grand Theatre project, however, the very party that had imbued Chinese intellectuals with such an ideology appeared to have abandoned them in supporting a foreign architect and his very un-Chinese ideas. Yet, ironically, at the professional level, these intellectuals were themselves not essentially different from their political leaders in following the game of stylistic development whose lineage was constructed by Western practice and whose principles were founded according to Western standards.

Chapter Six

Chang'an Avenue and the Axes of Beijing

FOR MORE THAN five centuries the city of Beijing had been dominated by an imperial north-south axis, when Chang'an Avenue started to be constructed as the east-west thoroughfare of the socialist capital in the mid-twentieth century. As it grew during the early decades of the People's Republic of China (PRC), the avenue soon overshadowed the north-south axis. While the issue of developing an east-west axis to compete with the imperial north-south axis was raised in the controversies over the reconstruction of Beijing as early as 1950, it was not certain then that such an axis had to be Chang'an Avenue. Occupying the critical location between the imperial Forbidden City and Communist Tiananmen Square, however, Chang'an Avenue gradually became the de facto east-west axis of the city. Although academic debate continued, at the dawn of the twenty-first century the status of Chang'an Avenue as the main east-west axis was officially codified in the "Beijing city master plan (2004–2020)" (fig. 6.1).

The north-south axis of Beijing had long been emphasized as a symbolic axis representing a centralized imperial power, while the east-west axis of Chang'an Avenue was originally conceived of mainly as a functional urban thoroughfare. However, the construction of monumental façades and the concentration of national projects and celebrations along Chang'an Avenue transformed the utilitarian street into a new symbolic urban space, a showcase of the new Communist regime's power. As a result, when nationalist fervor increased at the end of the twentieth century, both the north-south axis along the imperial monuments and the east-west axis along the avenue became symbols of the "Great Renaissance of the Chinese Nation." While the north-south axis represented China's glorious past, the east-west axis embodied the rise of modern China. The two axes of Beijing, however, were unbalanced once again: the north-south axis was much shorter and less unified than Chang'an Avenue. New projects to expand the north-south axis were initiated at the beginning of the new millennium.

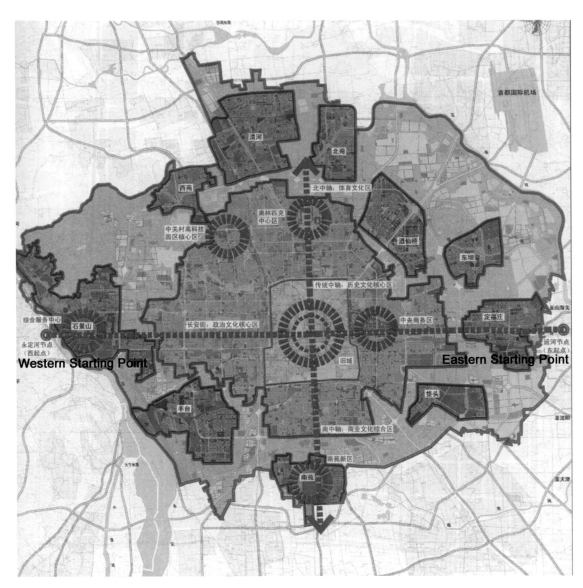

Fig. 6.1. Beijing city master
plan (2004–20), 2005.
Reproduction from Beijing guihua
jianshe, *49. Courtesy of Chen
Shaojun.*

The Ancient Capital and Its Imperial North-South Axis

Beijing has served as the imperial capital of China for centuries, and its status as the capital of local regimes when China was politically fragmented goes back millennia. During the Eastern Zhou period (771–221 BCE), Beijing, then called Ji, was the capital of the State of Yan. Later it served first as the Southern Capital (Nanjing) of the Liao dynasty (947–1125) founded by the nomadic Khitans, a regime contemporary with the Han Northern Song dynasty (960–1127), then as the Middle Capital (Zhongdu) of the Jin dynasty (1115–234) founded by the Jurchens, a regime contemporary to the Southern Song dynasty (1127–279). During the Yuan dynasty, under Mongol rule, Beijing for the first time became the national capital of a unified China. The strategic position of Beijing was clearly understood by the Mongols. It was an ideal place from which they could control China proper and at the same time maintain easy access to their original homeland, the endless Mongolian prairie and the Gobi Desert, to which they could retreat when the political situation was not promising, as they did in 1368 when Ming armies captured Beijing and overthrew the Yuan dynasty.

The Yuan capital was then called Dadu, the Great Capital. The Mongols abandoned the Jin Middle Capital and built their new capital to its north, oriented according to the cardinal directions (fig. 6.2). The placement of Dadu's city walls was among the most regular of all ancient Chinese capitals. They formed an almost-perfect square,

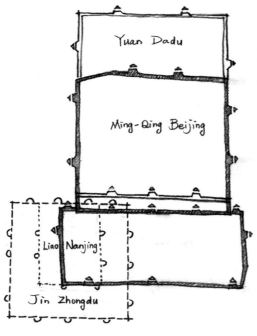

Fig. 6.2. Locations of Liao, Jin, and Yuan capitals in relation to Ming-Qing Beijing. *Drawing by author.*

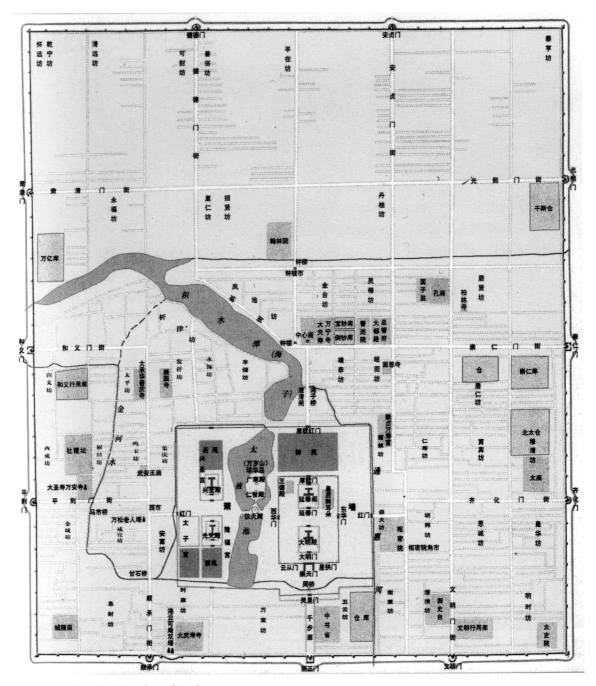

Fig. 6.3. City plan of Dadu,
capital of the Yuan dynasty
(1271–368). *Reproduction from
Chang'anjie: Guoqu, xianzai,
weilai, 27. Courtesy of Zheng
Guangzhong.*

with an area of fifty square kilometers and a perimeter of 28,600 meters. The north-south dimension of 7,600 meters was only slightly larger than the east-west 6,700 meters. Three layers of city walls created three concentric areas: the Palace City inside the Imperial City inside the general city proper. Eleven gates protected openings in the outermost walls: three each on the south, east, and west sides, and two on the north. The walls of both the Imperial City and the Palace City had four gates, one at each of the four cardinal directions. Straight major avenues and broad streets connected these gates and divided the city into rectangular wards and blocks (fig. 6.3).[1]

The entire Yuan Dadu could be divided into two parts, along a line between the two central gates on the east and west city walls: a northern part, and a southern part, each with its own north-south axis, parallel but not joining each other. The southern axis was slightly to the east of the axis in the north. According to architectural historian Fu Xinian, such a dislocation in the north-south axis was the result of the large bodies of water located in the south central area of the city. The axis started at the geometric center in the north part of the city, dividing the northern city into two perfectly equal halves at the east-west midpoint, but had to shift 129 meters eastward in the southern part of the city to avoid the lakes.[2]

Along the northern axis, the Drum Tower marked the city's geometric central point, in line with the Bell Tower to its north. The north-south axis of the southern part ran through both the Imperial City and the Palace City. Starting with the Central Pavilion near the center of the city, this imperial axis extended southward, linking all of the main gates of the three layers of city walls, as well as other significant imperial monuments.

Throughout the Yuan dynasty, the southern part of Dadu was populous and prosperous, while the northern part, especially the areas north of the Bell Tower, remained desolate and only sparsely inhabited. When the Ming rulers took over Yuan Dadu and renamed it first Beiping then Beijing,[3] the northern city walls were moved about 3,000 meters south to facilitate the defense of the city. The entire area north of the Yuan dynasty Bell Tower was left outside the Ming city walls. When the third Ming emperor Yongle decided to move the national capital to Beijing and started its reconstruction in 1416, the imperial north-south axis of the former Yuan Dadu was maintained. Although the former Yuan palaces were all destroyed by Ming armies after the Mongol rulers retreated from their Great Capital, the new Ming Palace City and Imperial City were constructed on roughly the same sites. In order to completely annul the imperial energy (*wangqi*) of the former dynasty and thus prevent its restoration, the new dynasty had to demolish all of the major imperial monuments of the Mongol regime and construct completely new palaces. Debris from the former Yuan palaces and the new construction was piled into an artificial hill, located on the site of the Yanchun Pavilion, the former sleeping chambers of the Yuan emperors and empresses. Although known today as Coal Hill (Jingshan, literally "Scenery Hill"), during the Ming dynasty it was called Zhenshan, which means the Hill to Vanquish Evil Spirits. The imperial energy of the Yuan dynasty along the north-south axis was not only destroyed but also buried and controlled by Coal Hill.

Because the central position of the former Yuan palaces on the imperial north-south axis was now occupied by Coal Hill, the new Ming palaces had to be constructed to its south. As a result, the southern walls of all three concentric layers of the city—Beijing city proper (the future Inner City), Imperial City, and Palace City—also moved about 800 meters farther south. The Bell Tower and the Drum Tower in the northern part of the city, previously 129 meters west of the imperial axis in Yuan Dadu, were now relocated to be in alignment with the imperial north-south axis. Since much of the northern part of Yuan Dadu was abandoned, most of its north-south axis disappeared; its remainder, with the Bell Tower and Drum Tower, now joined the imperial Ming axis. Thus the two north-south axes of Yuan Dadu were united into one dominant imperial axis in Ming Beijing. When the Outer City was added in 1553, the imperial north-south axis extended farther south (see fig. 1.1).[4] The Manchu rulers of the following Qing dynasty did not make any major physical changes to the Ming capital. They were among the few rulers who did not burn the palaces of the previous dynasty. Thus from 1553 to the mid-twentieth century the city of Beijing was dominated by a 7,500-meter-long north-south axis, referred to by many Chinese as the dragon vein (longmai).[5]

According to feng shui (geomancy) theory, longmai, the "dragon vein," is the north-south mountain range due north of a good dwelling site that helps to keep auspicious energy (juqi) in the site. In a city, the dragon vein refers to the auspicious continuity of geographic or man-made elements running from north to south. Beijing had both. As a dwelling site, the plain where Beijing is located is screened by the Yan Mountains in the north and west; as a city, it has the imperial north-south axis as the dragon vein (fig. 6.4). In Chinese feng shui, the natural and constructed environ-

Fig. 6.4. The ideal *longmai* (dragon vein) for a city in feng shui geomancy. *Drawing by author.*

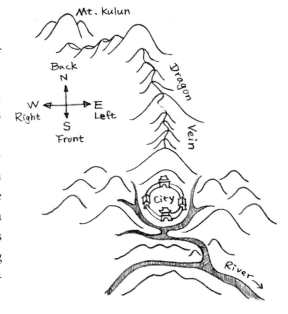

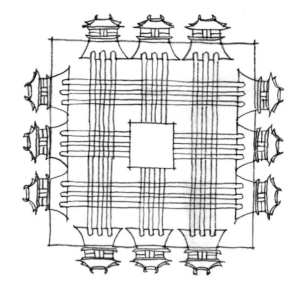

Fig. 6.5. The plan of Wangcheng, the capital for the Son of Heaven, according to the description in the *Rituals of Zhou. Drawing by author, modified from Liu Dun-zhen, Zhongguo gudai jianzhushi, 36.*

ment is a macrocosm of the human body. Originally a medical term, *mai* refers to not only physical arteries and veins but also to invisible channels through which energies travel in the body. Because in traditional Chinese culture the dragon is the symbol for the emperor, or Son of Heaven, the dragon vein in the imperial capital also suggests that the north-south axis of Beijing was the channel where the imperial energies traveled.

The north-south orientation of the Chinese city also had close associations with the human body. In the traditional Chinese view of orientation, south is referred to as "front," north as "back," east as "left," and west as "right." This concept was codified as early as the first millennium BCE in the Zhou dynasty document "The Record of Craftsmanship" (Kaogongji) from the Confucian classic the *Rituals of Zhou* (Zhouli):

> When the master craftsman constructs the state capital, he makes a square nine *li* on each side. Each side has three gates. Within the capital are nine north-south and nine east-west streets. The north-south streets are nine carriage tracks in width. The court is located in the front (south) and the markets in the back (north). On the left (east) is the Ancestral Temple, and to the right (west) are the Altars of Soil and Grain.[6] (fig. 6.5)

A similar perception of north-south orientation can also be observed in individual buildings. In China, whenever possible, the main façades of the major buildings in a complex always face south. Since China is located in the northern hemisphere, facing south allows maximum interior sunshine in winter and minimum interior sunshine in summer. This originally functional consideration acquired symbolic significance in political space, as emperors "faced south to rule" (*miannan er zhi*). While the status of east and west represented by left and right are equal, starting from the center and extending outward, the status of north and south are not. The north-south orientation has a direction, beginning in the north and extending southward, like the gaze of the emperor.

The history of a north-south axis running through the center of the imperial capital and lining up major national monuments can be traced back to the *Rituals of Zhou*. In the famous section cited above, a north-south axis is implied though not explicitly mentioned. Three gates on each side of the city walls and nine streets in each orientation suggest the existence of a central north-south passageway as well as an east-west one. The north-south passageway is an axis, while the east-west one is not, because the east-west elements (the left Ancestral Temple and the right Altar of Soil and Grain) are arranged in symmetry while the asymmetrical elements (the back markets and the front courts) are lined up from north to south.

Although no ancient city discovered so far has fully complied with this Zhou orthodoxy, the *Rituals of Zhou* had tremendous influence in capital building during China's two-thousand-year imperial history. During the Age of Disunion (220–589), both the Northern Wei capital Louyang (493–534) and the capital of the southern dynasties, Jiankang (modern-day Nanjing, capital of the Eastern Jin, Song, Qi, Liang, and Chen, 317–589), had a long imperial way stretching southward from the imperial palace in the northern part of the city. Government ministries were organized mainly along this imperial way, with the Ancestral Temple to its east and the Altar of Soil and Grain to its west, as required by the *Rituals of Zhou*. Such a strong imperial axis also characterized the Sui-Tang dynasty capital Chang'an (589–907) and the Northern Song dynasty capital Bianliang.[7] This specially defined axis, however, is not found in Chang'an and Louyang of the Han dynasty (202 BCE–220 CE), when there had been no dispute about which regime was to carry on the orthodox Chinese imperial line. The first clear and explicit formulation of the imperial north-south axis after the Zhou dynasty was made during the Age of Disunion, when China was split into many competing local regimes, which suggests that the ancient orthodoxy in urban planning was revived to justify the regimes as the legitimate bearers of Chinese tradition.

The imperial axis in Ming-Qing Beijing was primarily an axis of monuments. In total there were more than ten gate towers and seven major imperial halls directly located on this north-south axis, as well as the Drum Tower and the Bell Tower at its north end. Framing it on both sides were such significant centers of ritual and government activities as the Temple of Heaven, the Temple of Agriculture, the Six Ministries (Liubu), the Five Departments (Wufu), the Imperial Ancestral Temple, and the Altar of Soil and Grain. The large-scale monuments, with their brilliant golden yellows, reds, and blue-greens, along the long, straight north-south axis contrasted strongly with the rest of the city, which was mostly crowded with humble courtyard dwellings of gray bricks and roof tiles. The imperial north-south axis in Beijing formally emphasized the supreme status, paramount authority, and absolute power of the Son of Heaven.

The formal dominance of such an imperial north-south axis in Beijing survived the Republican era. When Mao Zedong proclaimed the founding of the People's Republic of China on the rostrum of Tiananmen on October 1, 1949, he stood on one of the many ceremonial gates along the north-south axis, a gate that was soon to be singled out and transformed into a façade for Chang'an Avenue.

Reconstruction: Two Approaches and Three Proposals

After the fall of the Qing Empire in 1911, the imperial monuments and centers of ritualistic sacrifice along the north-south axis of Beijing were opened to the public one after another. In 1912 the outer reaches of the vast area set aside for the Temple of Heaven became a forestry research institute, and the following year, its central area became a public park. The same year, the doors in the gate towers around Imperial Tiananmen Square were removed and the walls connecting these gate towers were demolished. In 1914 the Altar of Soil and Grain became Central Park. The protective walls (*wengcheng*) of the Zhengyang Gate and the Thousand-Pace Corridor were demolished in 1915, and in 1924 the imperial Ancestral Temple was opened to the public as the Peace Park. Part of the Temple of Agriculture became a sports school, and its main sacrificial hall was used for memorial services for seventy-two heroes who died in one of the uprisings against the Qing regime. In 1928 the imperial Coal Hill garden also became a public park.

With the founding of the People's Republic of China in 1949 and the designation of Beijing as the national capital, the threat to the imperial axis became more than a functional change. The potential for a dramatic physical transformation aroused keen emotions among certain Chinese scholars and architects. As part of the controversy around the location of the new administrative center, debates were initiated regarding whether the historic Old City[8] should be preserved. There were two different approaches: one approach was to insert government offices into the Old City; the other was to construct a new center in the western suburbs.

In December 1949, Soviet advisors presented their "Report on the Issue of Beijing City's Future Developmental Plan" and "Proposal on the Improvement of the Municipal Works of Beijing" (hereafter "the Soviet proposals") during the urban planning meeting organized by the municipal government of Beijing.[9] They proposed to locate the administrative center in the Old City and opposed the idea of developing a new area for the central government, a plan they considered too costly. They also pointed out that the best strategy would be to rebuild a major avenue or a major square and

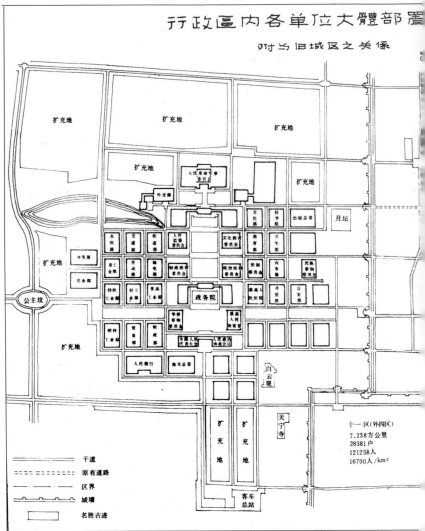

Fig. 6.6. Liang Sicheng and Chen Zhanxiang, drawing in the Liang-Chen Scheme showing the relationship between the new government center and the Forbidden City, 1950. *Courtesy of Lin Zhu.*

develop a new government center around it. Their drawings indicate that the avenue was Chang'an Avenue and the square was Tiananmen Square.[10] Reportedly, this Soviet proposal had already generally been agreed to by the municipal government of Beijing (see fig. 1.4).[11]

Most leading Chinese scholars and practitioners in the field of architecture and urban planning attended the December meeting. Two months later, in February 1950, Liang Sicheng,[12] the most renowned Chinese architectural historian of the twentieth century, and Chen Zhanxiang, a British-trained urban planner invited to Beijing by Liang,[13] proposed a different plan for the capital of the nascent People's Republic of China in their "Proposal for the Location of the Central Administrative Area of the

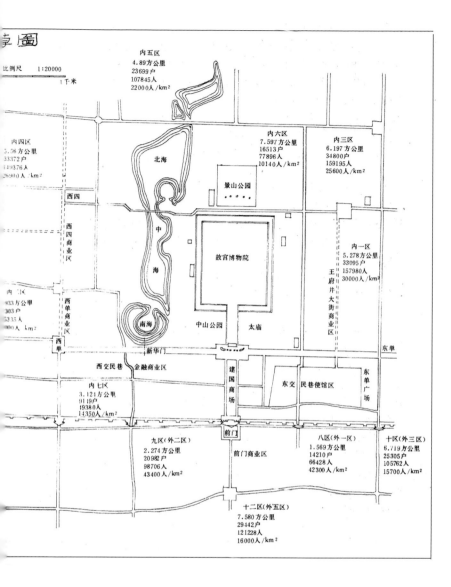

People's Central Government." This plan, better known as the Liang-Chen Scheme, proposed a new administrative center located in the western suburbs of Beijing, with a new north-south axis parallel to the imperial north-south axis along the Forbidden City (fig. 6.6).[14]

With text extolling the Old City and drawings resembling imperial Beijing on both formal and symbolic levels, the Liang-Chen Scheme had a profound sense of nostalgia. This nostalgia was more than a mechanism to "enjoy the sadness of loss"[15] during a time of fast modernization; it was an active effort to preserve it for the future, a "recycling process" that "kept the past alive in the present in a concrete material way and thus created a tangible basis for nostalgia."[16] Such a tangible basis for nostalgia was precisely what the Chinese Communists wanted to destroy. The Liang-Chen Scheme was rejected by the Communist authorities.[17]

While the Liang-Chen Scheme treasured and tried to preserve the Old City of Beijing by leaving it alone, the Soviet advisors considered such a strategy an abandonment of the historic city. They argued that "one should give up reconstructing and reorganizing the Old City only when Beijing was deemed valueless in history and architecture."[18] In April, two Beijing-based architects, Zhu Zhaoxue and Zhao Dongri, proposed another general plan for the capital, in which the new administrative center would remain in the Old City and face the Imperial City of the Ming-Qing dynasties across Chang'an Avenue (fig. 6.7). If the implementation of the Liang-Chen Scheme was doomed by the opinions of the "socialist big brother," it was the Zhu-Zhao Scheme that offered a visually concrete alternative to it.

While the Liang-Chen Scheme followed in the footsteps of the past by preserving, mimicking, and strengthening the imperial axis, the Zhu-Zhao Scheme constituted a formal and symbolic challenge to the past by transgressing and weakening the time-honored north-south axis. The new north-south axis for the new administrative center proposed by Liang and Chen, parallel to and 5.2 kilometers west of the imperial axis, could never have compared favorably to the old axis either in scale or in status. It was much shorter and less symmetrically framed than the axis along the Forbidden City. The plans made it look like a descendant of the old imperial axis, or a younger brother at most. Zhu Zhaoxue and Zhao Dongri, on the other hand, clearly stated that their new scheme was meant to create a new east-west axis to compete with, if not to dominate, the north-south one.

The east-west axis in the 1950 Zhu-Zhao Scheme, however, was not Chang'an Avenue but the entire strip of land containing new socialist monuments between Chang'an Avenue and the southern wall of the Inner City of Beijing.[19] Zhao also explained in 1993 that what they had proposed as the east-west axis was an axis of monuments south of Chang'an Avenue instead of the empty avenue itself (fig. 6.8).[20] Chang'an Avenue was envisioned as a border dividing the Imperial City to the north and the new administrative center to the south. The entire area between the avenue proper and the south wall of the Inner City was reserved for the central government along an east-west axis: in the middle, directly facing the Imperial City, were the central administrative organs; on the west side were the cultural, educational, and political-legal branches; and on the east side were the departments of finance and economics. The confrontation between old and new on the two sides of the avenue

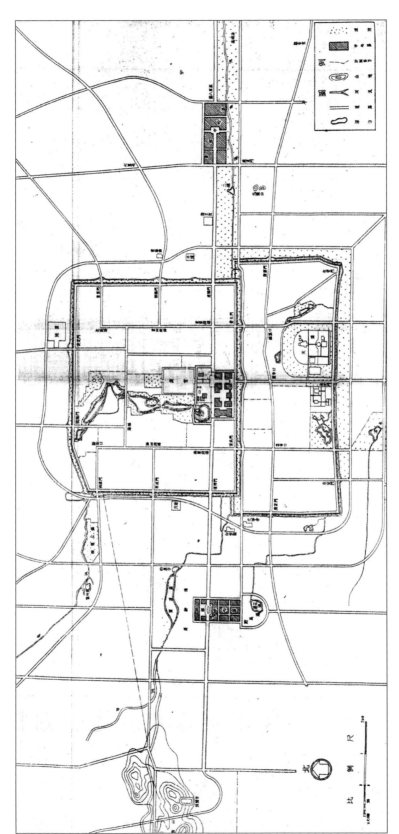

Fig. 6.7

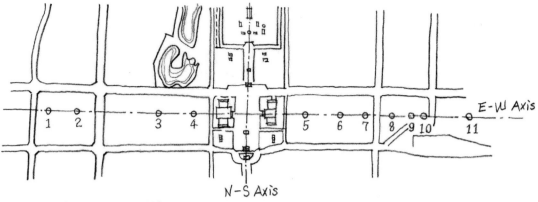

1~11 Government Buildings.

Fig. 6.8. Zhao Dongri's east-west axis of monuments, 1993. *Drawing by author, modified from* Wang Jun, Chengji, *235.*

disconnected the imperial north-south axis. The future development of Beijing was also envisioned to follow the avenue. An Eastern Center and a Western Center formed an asymmetrical balance, which would join the central government center through Chang'an Avenue. Bisected by such a long avenue running from the eastern border of Beijing all the way to Babaoshan in the western suburbs, the imperial north-south axis would be completely overshadowed.[21]

A closer observation of the drawings in the Zhu-Zhao Scheme shows that Chang'an Avenue was not exactly the border between the old imperial center and the new government center. The middle part of the long strip reserved for the central government just to the south of the Forbidden City was specifically defined, almost like a new Forbidden City, with a new secondary north-south axis (fig. 6.9). This middle section, however, was not along Tiananmen Square, where it would have merged into the imperial axis and thus strengthened it, but slightly off the old north-south axis to the west. This new north-south axis was secondary because it was much shorter than both the traditional imperial north-south axis and the east-west axis Zhu and Zhao proposed. However, it posed a great potential threat to the traditional north-south axis. While the Liang-Chen Scheme located the new north-south axis outside Beijing's city walls and left the entire Old City and its imperial axis untouched, the new north-south axis in the Zhu-Zhao Scheme was so close to the imperial axis that the development of the new axis would certainly conflict with and require the alteration of the ancient monuments along the imperial axis.

The secondary north-south axis in the Zhu-Zhao Scheme was aligned with the former Altar of Soil and Grain, the sacrificial complex on the west side of the imperial

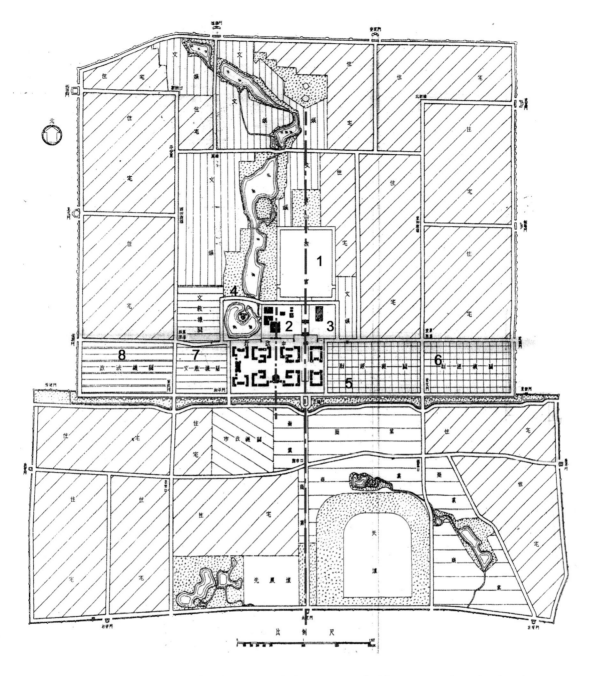

Fig. 6.9. Zhu Zhaoxue and Zhao Dongri, drawing in the Zhu-Zhao Scheme showing the central area near Forbidden City with new government functions: 1. Forbidden City; 2. Altar of Soil and Grain; 3. Imperial Ancestral Temple; 4. Zhongnanhai; 5. and 6. finance and economics agencies; 7. culture and education agencies; 8. political legal agencies. *Courtesy of the School of Architecture Archive, Tsinghua University.*

north-south axis. On the west side of the Altar, Zhongnanhai was already designated as a residential compound for Communist leaders; on its east side, the former Imperial Ancestral Temple (Taimiao) was renamed the Cultural Palace for the Laboring People. The site of the former Altar of Soil and Grain thus became the center of the new spatial-power framework. When the living quarters of those in power moved westward from the Forbidden City to Zhongnanhai, the north-south axis followed. In the Zhu-Zhao Scheme, Tiananmen Square on the traditional north-south axis was not the political center of the New China. There was barely a square in front of Tiananmen Tower. The square on the new north-south axis was much larger. The drawings in the Zhu-Zhao Scheme also show that the physical environment of the Ming-Qing Altar and Temple would have been changed drastically in order to accommodate new functions, although some historical structures would have remained.[22]

The Socialist Beijing and Its New East-West Axis

In the Zhu-Zhao Scheme, Chang'an Avenue was not yet the east-west axis. Moreover, it was not even a unified thoroughfare running through the central administrative center. Most traffic had to go around the new center. Like its traditional counterpart and northern neighbor, the Forbidden City, the new government center also blocked east-west communication in the heart of Beijing.

The Merging of Chang'an Avenue and the East-West Axis

The visual power of a long, wide Chang'an Avenue in the drawings for the Zhu-Zhao Scheme had a fundamental impact on the future planning of Beijing.[23] In the 1953 city master plan, Chang'an Avenue was already unified and ran through the center of the city, although it did not extend much farther eastward and was not completely straight. At that time, the city walls were still in existence, and the avenue shifted slightly northward at the western city wall. In the 1954 master plan, the avenue extended farther eastward, seemingly endless in the drawings, and became a thoroughfare traversing the entire east-west span of the city. The turns in the plan from the previous year had disappeared. The width of the avenue, however, was still not completely uniform. Some sections of the West Chang'an Avenue extension were wider than their eastern counterparts. In the 1957 master plan, the inconsistency in width also disappeared, making Chang'an Avenue a long, straight, wide, and open thoroughfare.

The development of a major avenue running through the urban center of Beijing might have been inspired by Moscow. Beijing in the early 1950s faced problems similar to those of postrevolution Moscow in the 1920s. Like Beijing, Moscow had also served as the imperial capital of Russia for centuries. It had layers of city walls, with the tsarist palace, the Kremlin, at the center. After the October Revolution in 1917, Moscow was designated the capital of the Soviet Union and its city walls were gradually demolished. A new government center for the Communist regime was constructed next to the Kremlin Palace around Red Square. Tverskaya Avenue, the main avenue for parades during public ceremonies in the Soviet Union, became the most significant thoroughfare of Moscow, running between the Kremlin and Red Square. Given the close involvement of Soviet specialists in Beijing's master plan and the extent of Soviet influence in every field in the early years of the People's Republic of China, such a connection seems tenable.

While the Zhu-Zhao Scheme would certainly have won the support of Soviet advisors, the Liang-Chen Scheme was disadvantaged by its foreign associations. The Zhu-Zhao Scheme shared many concepts with the previous Soviet proposals. Both wanted to insert the new administrative center into the Old City and to develop government buildings along a major avenue. Zhu and Zhao cited the reconstruction of Moscow's historical center, the Kremlin, in support of the proposal to rebuild the historical center of Beijing.[24] Although Liang and Chen also used the Soviet Union's experience as moral and professional legitimization of their proposal—citing the historical preservation of Novgorod, Kaliningrad, and Smolensk to support their argument for leaving the Old City alone—they strongly opposed the idea of developing a new government center along major urban streets. Their proposal specifically recommended avoiding lining the streets with monumental façades. They declared that the façade-lined streets of nineteenth-century Europe were both backward and the opposite of Chinese tradition, and proposed an alternative approach that they called the "Oriental tradition of courtyard organization."[25]

In many respects, the Liang-Chen Scheme resembled the urban planning of the puppet Beijing government at the time of the Japanese occupation.[26] During the Sino-Japanese War from 1937 to 1945, Beijing was occupied by Japanese troops and became the capital of a puppet government. In the 1941 "Beiping Urban Plan," the Japanese planned two new districts in the eastern and western suburbs of the Old City. The new western district was mainly residential, and the new eastern district was mostly industrial. In the center of the new western district, however, was a new administrative center organized around a north-south axis, with a public square on its south end.[27] After the Japanese surrendered in 1945, the Nationalist government hired Japanese technical personnel to prepare a new general plan for Beijing in 1946; the result was very similar to the 1941 Japanese plan (fig. 6.10).[28] The 1941 Japanese plan had previously been criticized by the Nationalist government as an "invasion plan," since its

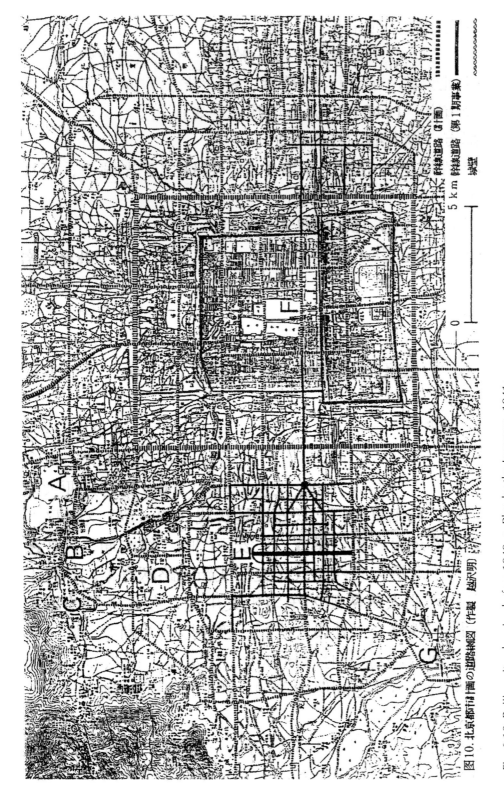

Fig. 6.10. Beijing city planning before 1949: a. Plan by the Japanese, 1941;
b. Plan by the Nationalist government, 1946. *Reproduction from Dong Guangqi,*
Beijing guihua zhanlue sikao, 300, 307. Courtesy of CABP.

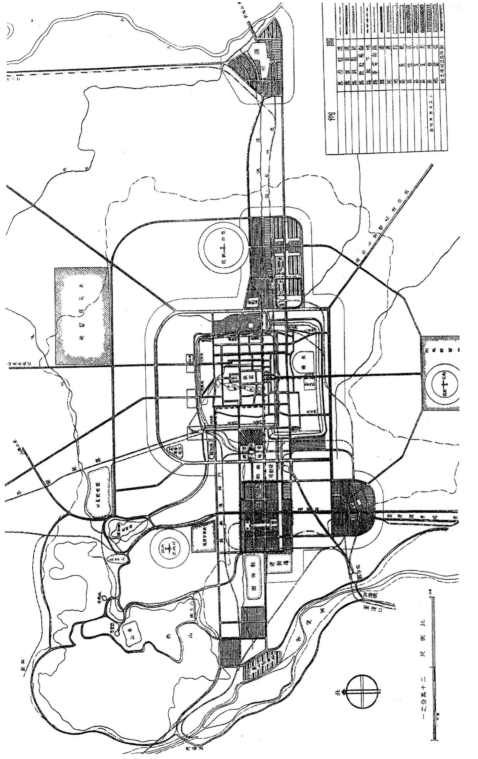

b.

new western district was far from the Old City and run completely by the Japanese occupiers, leaving the Chinese Old City to deteriorate.[29] However, both the 1941 Japanese plan and the Nationalist records from 1946 praised the Old City of Beijing as an invaluable historical area and proposed to keep it mainly as a tourist attraction and cultural center. The Liang-Chen Scheme was in complete agreement with this. Moreover, Liang's original plan might have been even closer to the 1941 Japanese plan. According to Chen, it was he who suggested to Liang in 1949 to move the new administrative center closer to the Old City of Beijing. Chen told Liang that his new government district was too far away from and thus not good for the development of the Old City, and Liang agreed.[30] This was the same as the previous Nationalist regime's criticism of the 1941 Japanese plan.

The Liang-Chen Scheme's close resemblance to the plans of the previous regimes was a fatal disadvantage. In the early years of the People's Republic of China, the new district in the western suburbs of Beijing was tarred by its association with the Japanese. The new western district planned by the Japanese in the early 1940s was a product of colonization and racial segregation. While the Chinese remained in the filthy, dilapidated Old City, the Japanese occupiers lived in a new, modern colony in the western suburbs. This segregation occurred in many Japanese-run cities in Manchuria, and so, in the minds of the Communist leaders, the new western district of Beijing was saddled with negative associations. If the nostalgic sentiment of the Liang-Chen Scheme was at odds with the revolutionary spirit of the Chinese Communists, following in the footsteps of the previous Japanese and Nationalist regimes was unacceptable.

While the Soviet Union might have influenced the unification and extension of Chang'an Avenue, the avenue's designation as an urban axis was deeply imbedded in Chinese tradition. The city of Moscow was not oriented according to cardinal directions, as Beijing was. Moscow had a circular shape, with ring roads and avenues radiating from the center. In contrast, most ancient Chinese cities were rectangular, with a grid of perpendicular streets and avenues following the cardinal directions. Most regional Chinese cities during the imperial era were divided into four major sectors by a cross of north-south and east-west avenues. Unlike imperial capitals such as Beijing, with its Palace City and Imperial City at the very center, the center of regional cities was usually an open space where two principal roads met. Thus, apart from Beijing, the urban axis in the early twentieth century was often associated with the main north-south and east-west thoroughfares of a city (fig. 6.11).

For many architects and city planners in the 1950s, the axis of Beijing also meant the main urban thoroughfare running through the geometric center of the rectangular city. The 1954 Beijing city master plan stated in the section "Road and Square

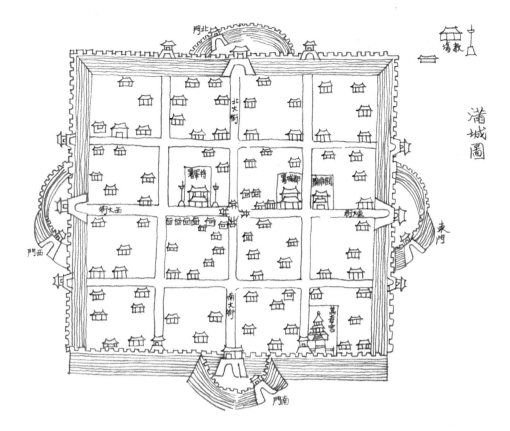

Fig. 6.11. The capital city of Ningxia Prefecture in Qing dynasty, with its urban axes of streets, originally a woodblock print in the *Gazetteer of Ningxia Prefecture*, 1780. *Drawing by author.*

System" that "in order to facilitate communication in the city center and improve connections between the center and other parts of the city, the north-south and east-west axes should be greatly extended in length and expanded in width, to a dimension of no less than 100 meters."[31] Not only the east-west but also the north-south axis was conceived of mainly as a thoroughfare. From this perspective, the destruction of the walls and gates along the north-south axis in the 1950s can be understood as an attempt to transform the axis of imperial monuments into an axis of open thoroughfare.[32]

Although the history of axial planning in Chinese architecture and cities can be traced as far back as the Zhou dynasty, the use of the term "axis" in the discussion and analysis of architecture and city planning is a recent phenomenon. In *History of Chinese Architecture* (Zhongguo jianzhu shi),[33] the first book on traditional Chinese architecture by a Chinese author and originally published in 1933, Yue Jiazao claimed that the uniqueness of Chinese architecture was its "precisely located central stem and left-right symmetry" (*zhonggan zhi yanli yu zuoyou zhi duichen*).[34] The word "axis" was

never used. Liang Sicheng first used the term "cen- Fig. 6.12. Axes of buildings in traditional Chinese architecture. *Drawing by author.*
tral axis" (*zhongzhouxian*) in a 1932 article to char-
acterize the courtyard organization in Chinese
architecture, and emphasized that it was usually

north-south oriented, with secondary structures built symmetrically on the left and
right sides.[35] While Yue was a revolutionary-turned-literati scholar, Liang was trained
in the United States in the Beaux-Arts tradition, whose eclectic architectural design
emphasized symmetry and axiality.[36] It is possible that Liang used the term "axis" in
his early writings to analyze Chinese architecture because of his exposure to this term
during his training abroad in the 1920s. Both Yue's "central stem" and Liang's "central axis" referred to the principal structures along the central north-south route in
a traditional Chinese courtyard complex, such as gates, halls, pavilions, and towers
(fig. 6.12).

Thus in the 1950s there were at least two different meanings for "axis." One referred
to the axis of monuments common in large-scale architectural complexes in ancient
China; the other referred to the axis of an open thoroughfare as seen in many regional
Chinese cities. In terms of the east-west axis of Beijing, some architects (for instance,
Zhu and Zhao) insisted that it should be an axis of monuments, like the traditional
north-south axis along the Forbidden City; others (for instance Chen Gan, a well-
known city planner in Beijing who participated in the preparation of Tiananmen
Square for the founding ceremony in 1949[37]) argued that it was the east-west thoroughfare Chang'an Avenue. Chen summarized the city plan of Beijing as being "one
center, two axes, three rings, four-sided orderliness." He further proposed that the
two axes in Beijing city planning represented tradition and innovation, respectively.
In an early 1959 article, after discussing both the outstanding heritage status and the
backward conditions of old Beijing, he argued,

> We have used the framework of the Old City and developed a horizontal axis
> running all the way through the city, perpendicular to the north-south central axis.
> Thus a general coordinate axis system for city planning in Beijing was formed. The
> entire layout of the city was stabilized in a solemn composition that is both traditional
> and innovative.
>
> Tradition is manifested in:
>
> (1) Keeping the original central axis as the guiding principle of the general city layout.
>
> (2) Keeping the original checkerboard street system as the framework of the urban
> texture.
>
> (3) Keeping the solemn composition with the symbol of national political power at
> the center.

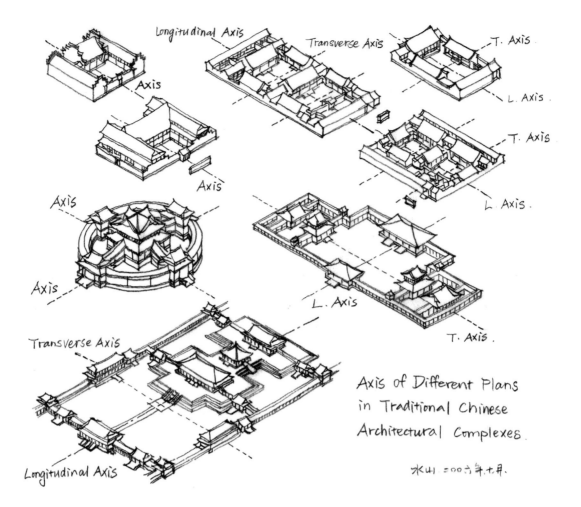

Longitudinal Axis

Transverse Axis

T. Axis

Axis

L. Axis

Axis

T. Axis

Axis

L. Axis

Axis

L. Axis

Transverse Axis

T. Axis

Axis of Different Plans in Traditional Chinese Architectural Complexes.

水山 二〇〇六年十月.

Longitudinal Axis

Innovation is manifested in:

(1) Unifying, widening, and extending East and West Chang'an Avenues into a horizontal axis of twenty kilometers spanning the entire east-west dimension of the city. Running from Tong County in the east to the Shijingshan District in the west, this east-west axis matched the north-south central axis and further integrated the city and stabilized the composition. This is a significant, bold breakthrough for the Old City of Beijing. Such [an approach to] the reconstruction and expansion [of old cities] is rare not only in the history of Chinese urban construction but also in the world as a whole. This is really an unprecedented masterstroke.

(2) Moving the key point symbolizing the urban center from the Forbidden City and the Hall of Supreme Harmony to Tiananmen Square and the position of the national flagpole. Although this was a relocation of only a few hundred meters, it unmistakably made a distinction between two entirely different historical periods.[38]

Chen also later explained that the expanded sixteen-kilometer-long north-south axis and the forty-kilometer-long east-west axis formed two "coordinate axes" for Beijing city planning.[39]

Although Chen Gan and Zhao Dongri disagreed about whether the east-west axis should be Chang'an Avenue or an axis of new monuments to its south, they both designated Tiananmen Square as the coordinate origin. Future development largely followed Chen's prediction. Chang'an Avenue was developed into the east-west axis of Beijing. Even today, many sectors to the south of Chang'an Avenue remain one-story courtyards and have yet to become an axis of monuments (see figs. 1.7, 6.8).

The rise in Chang'an Avenue's status led to the construction of its monumental façades. In order to make at least one relatively complete façade for the avenue in a short period of time, it was decided in 1954 that construction would concentrate on the northern side.[40] This might have resulted from the strong Chinese convention in architectural orientation that facing south was most comfortable, auspicious, formal, and authoritative. Thus, although the Zhu-Zhao Scheme located the central administrative center to the south of Chang'an Avenue, more monumental projects along the avenue were constructed on its north side in order to take advantage of the best orientation, which made the avenue the de facto east-west axis.

Redefining the "Nature of Beijing" and the Status Change of Chang'an Avenue

While Chang'an Avenue became the thoroughfare and de facto east-west axis of Beijing as early as the late 1950s, its status as a symbolic axis came much later. For decades, Chang'an Avenue served mainly as the communication channel linking the symbolic center of Tiananmen Square with the rest of the city. Since the 1980s, however, the role the avenue has played in the city has become more and more symbolic. This transformation of Chang'an Avenue's status from a functional thoroughfare to a symbolic axis coincides with the redefinition of the urban nature (*chengshi xingzhi*) of Beijing after the Mao era (1949–78).[41]

The designation of the capital city's nature was a major issue for every master plan of Beijing. When the seat of the Communist regime moved to Beijing in 1949, it was designated a "consumer city," which was considered backward, rather than a "producer city," which was considered progressive. According to Soviet advisors, a socialist capital should be not only a city of culture, science, and art but also a major industrial center. The percentage of the working class in a city's population was of both symbolic and political importance. In a late 1949 report, Soviet advisors informed their Chinese colleagues and fellow Communist officials that 25 percent of the population of Moscow was working-class, while in Beijing, only 4 percent was. Thus Beijing was still a consumer city and needed large-scale industrial construction. The central government accepted the Soviet advisors' suggestions and made it a principle in urban reconstruction to "transform the consumer city into a producer city." The percentage of the working class in Beijing's population had to be increased, as this was the "indispensable prerequisite for a capital of a people's democratic country."[42]

In the 1954 city master plan, Beijing was designated the "political, economic, and cultural center, which was to be constructed especially as the strong industrial base and the technological and scientific center of our country." The report by the Beijing Municipal Committee addressed to the central government condensed the definition of Beijing's nature to "political, cultural, scientific and artistic center, and at the same time a large industrial city."[43] There were four major industrial areas in the 1954 plan: light industry and small- to medium-scale heavy industry in the east; unsanitary and combustible industries in the south; metallurgical and heavy industries in the west; and precision instrument and precision optical machinery industries in the northeast. The industrial areas as planned in 1954 concentrated in the eastern and western suburbs. Moreover, the mountainous area farther west and the eastern plain areas close to Tong County were reserved for future industrial development.[44]

As future industrial development was planned mainly along the east-west dimension of the city, Chang'an Avenue became the most important functional thoroughfare linking these industrial areas with the political center at Tiananmen Square. In the 1950 Zhu-Zhao Scheme, Chang'an Avenue was one of three thoroughfares linking the eastern and western suburbs of Beijing.[45] In the 1954 plan, however, the avenue became the longest and widest (about 100 meters) east-west thoroughfare.[46]

The 1958 plan made only minor revisions to the 1954 plan's definition of the nature of Beijing. It was now designated the "political center and cultural educational center, which will be soon constructed as a modern industrial base and scientific technological center."[47] While the industrial areas in the 1958 plan were more dispersed throughout the capital and its mountainous satellite cities, a safety precaution in case of war, the status of Chang'an Avenue was slightly raised compared to the 1954 plan. Ministries of the central government and significant national buildings such as museums and a national theatre were now planned for construction along the avenue, whose rough completion was now scheduled to occur before the tenth anniversary of the People's Republic of China.[48]

The turning point in the definition of the nature of Beijing came in 1980. In its April "Instructions about Capital Construction Principles," the secretariat of the party Central Committee simplified the characteristics of the Chinese capital into two points: "First, the capital is the national political center, the nerve center, and the [source of] morale for the party and the people, not necessarily the economic center;

secondly, it is China's showcase to the world, and the whole world looks at China through Beijing." The instruction from the party center emphasized the significance of culture, scenery, hygiene, historical heritage, science, education, and public order in the capital. Economic aspects were played down, and the development of industry, which was so ambitiously pursued during the Mao era, was carefully deemphasized. The April 1980 instructions specifically pointed out that "the focus in economic development of Beijing is tourism, service trades, food industry, high-technology, light industries, and the electronics industry. Heavy industry is not to be developed in Beijing directly but rather through exporting capital, equipment, and technical specialists from the capital to the provinces, which will help to alleviate the population pressure in the capital as well."[49]

The instructions from the party center about the redefinition of the Chinese capital's nature were codified in the 1982 Beijing city master plan, in which the nature of Beijing was defined as "the capital of our great socialist country, the national political center and cultural center." The construction and development of all enterprises were to be readjusted to serve such an urban nature. Beijing was deemed to have had a sufficient industrial base and need only to develop light industries and traditional handicrafts in the future.[50]

It was also the 1982 Beijing city master plan that first formally codified the status of Chang'an Avenue as the east-west axis of the Chinese capital. The section "Old City Reconstruction" stated,

> In planning layout, we kept and developed the original north-south central axis, and unified and extended East and West Chang'an Avenues to form a new east-west axis. The two axes meet at Tiananmen Square. After various reconstructions, Tiananmen Square has become the central square for people's mass activities in the capital. The layout of the Old City, with the Forbidden City at the center symbolizing the overweening feudal emperors, has been changed.
>
> . . .
>
> We should continue completing the reconstruction of Tiananmen Square and Chang'an Avenue. Leading organs of the party center and the nation, as well as some significant large-scale cultural institutions and other public buildings, should be arranged here to form a solemn, beautiful, and modernized central square and main thoroughfare.[51]

Instead of a functional road to connect Tiananmen Square with the capital's eastern and western suburbs, Chang'an Avenue became one of the definers of the center. In the official narrative, origin and effect were reversed, giving the false impression that Tiananmen Square was significant because it was the place where Chang'an Avenue met the central axis. With the deletion of "main industrial base" from the definition of the nature of the capital, the plan was now for Chang'an Avenue to be filled with political and cultural institutions. The "continue completing" wording suggests the ongoing nature of the construction of Chang'an Avenue, parallel to the constantly updating process of the Chinese modernization project.

The nature of Beijing as defined in the 1982 plan was further modified in 1992. The phrase "world-famous ancient capital and modern international city" was added to "great socialist Chinese capital and national political and cultural center." Chang'an Avenue's status as the east-west axis of Beijing was confirmed. However, in order to achieve the goal of global metropolitan status, the construction of commercial and service facilities, in addition to political and cultural institutions, was now allowed on the avenue.[52] In another major change from 1982, the 1992 Beijing city master plan revived emphasis on the north-south central axis and on historic preservation for the future development of the capital,[53] trends that would be further strengthened in the master plan of 2005.

From the very beginning of the PRC era to the early 1990s, the city planning of Beijing was characterized by the gradual elimination of the industrial aspects from successive definitions of Beijing's nature and by the gradual increase of Chang'an Avenue's symbolic significance as an east-west axis.[54] These two developments were not random. As the Chinese architectural modernization project placed decreasing emphasis on utilitarian function, the practical drive behind the avenue's development was downplayed, and the thoroughfare's role in the city accordingly grew more and more symbolic.

The "Solid" Axis and the "Void" Axis

The imperial north-south axis is referred to as the "solid" axis because of the monuments located directly on it; the new east-west axis of Chang'an Avenue is referred to as the "void" axis because it is an empty thoroughfare framed by but not consisting of monumental façades. The north-south axis of Beijing, with its numerous ceremonial gates and imperial monuments, was a symbol of imperial China; the avenue was developed after 1949 in opposition to it. The continuous addition of government buildings and national cultural projects of the highest political significance made Chang'an Avenue the primary showcase of socialist achievement in China.

The character of Chang'an Avenue contrasts with that of the north-south axis in many different ways. Although both the north-south axis and the avenue are passageways, the latter is a real one, while the former is mainly symbolic. Before 1912 most of the central gateways on the north-south axis were reserved for emperors and kept closed most of the time. For example, the central south gate of the Inner City, Zheng-yang Gate, was reserved for the emperor to pass through during his lifetime; after he died, his body had to leave the city through other gates.[55] The Great Ming Gate (Qing dynasty Great Qing Gate; Republican era Gate of China) on the south end of the Tiananmen Square was only opened for national ceremonies; daily access to the Imperial City was through the Left and Right Chang'an Gates.[56] In fact, all of the important gates on the north-south axis had specific ceremonial functions: Tiananmen Tower was for issuing imperial edicts, Duan Gate was just a ritual or ceremonial gate (*yimen*) without any practical function as a doorway, Meridian Gate was for departing on expeditions and for receiving captives, and Taihe Gate was for imperial banquets and receptions (*chaohe*).[57]

The primary function of the north-south axis was to demonstrate the hierarchy of imperial power. That function excluded the everyday life of the average citizen. The use of the five arched entrances in the base of Tiananmen Tower, for instance, was governed by strict rules. The central one was restricted to emperors; the two imme-diate side archways were reserved for princes, dukes, and officials with ranks higher than the third *pin*;[58] the two further side archways were for officials ranking fourth *pin* and lower; other servants were allowed to use only the simple entrances in the walls on either side of Tiananmen Tower.[59] The design of the monuments on the solid north-south axis was also governed by hierarchical rules. The most significant imperial monument, Taihe Hall, has a double-eave *wudian* roof, the highest grade of traditional Chinese roof types, while Taihe Gate in front of it is topped with a double-eave *xieshan* roof, the roof style of secondary significance. Qianqing Gate behind the Taihe Hall Complex (Outer Three Halls) has only a single-eave *xieshan* roof, which is even lower in grade. Taihe Hall has nine bays plus an all-around corridor, while Taihe Gate has seven bays and an all-around corridor, and Qianqing Gate is a five-bay structure without a corridor. Taihe Hall is located on a three-layer *xumizuo* (masonry base with decorated moldings), while Taihe Gate is on a one-layer *xumizuo*, and Qianqing Gate has no *xumizuo*. In terms of details and decorations, Taihe Hall has the most elaborate bracket sets, while Taihe Gate and Qianqing Gate have simpler versions of the same structural detail. All of the structures on the imperial north-south axis, however, are covered with glazed tile of imperial yellow, which contrast with the rest of the city's gray-tiled roofs that are sporadically dotted by princely com-pounds with glazed-tile roofs of blue and green.

The ways that space is revealed along the north-south axis and along the avenue are also different. The space along the north-south axis is closed, divided, and opaque. It is concealed by layer after layer of walls and gates. During the Ming and Qing dynasties, the only place to see this imperial axis was from the top of Coal Hill, which was the backyard of the imperial palace, inaccessible to the public. Common Beijing citizens had no opportunity to experience this axis except as an inconvenience to their daily lives when they had to detour around the imperial enclosures in order to get to another part of the city. The Imperial City contributed the longest segment of the traditional north-south axis, blocking more than two-thirds of east-west communications in the Inner City of Beijing. Common people associated access to the inner parts of the north-south axis with extremes of officialdom—either supreme honor (for instance, passing the highest level of imperial examination) or lowest humiliation (such as the annual trials and proclamations of decapitation).[60] The paramount presence along the north-south axis was imperial dignity and authority.[61]

The space along Chang'an Avenue, on the contrary, is open, egalitarian, and transparent. Any point on the avenue reveals a road leading into the infinite distance. As a thoroughfare, the avenue is clear and definite. A bright, straight, and wide road had symbolic significance in modern China. In 1954 Mao Zedong wrote, "Let there be a visible path for all of the people of our country, let all of the people of our country feel that there is a clear and definite and correct road for them to follow."[62] Chang'an Avenue thus leads into not only a spatial but also a temporal distance, an arduous but promising future.

Both Chang'an Avenue and the imperial north-south axis are now ceremonial. However, the ceremonial and political processions along the avenue challenge the authority of the north-south axis. Many significant political events in Beijing since 1913 took the form of dramatic protest marches or mass parades along the avenue.[63] All of these pre-1949 mass parades were protests against the authorities behind the red wall on the north side of the avenue; however, after the founding of the People's Republic of China, the avenue was developed by the Communist authorities as an avenue to display power, especially during the annual PRC anniversary celebrations. In this respect, the Communist regime not only continued the pre-1949 transgression of the north-south axis but also sanctioned it. This was a forceful declaration of the People's Republic of China's new national identity as a revolutionary regime, in direct opposition to the traditional identity of the regimes before it. The revolutionary ceremonies along the east-west axis contrast dramatically with the ritual processions along the imperial axis. Periodic performances of government-sponsored national ceremonies, with mass parades along the avenue, strengthen the visibility of the new, broad, long thoroughfare, and the symbolic role of the east-west axis.

Ceremonial activity along Chang'an Avenue after 1949 was much more in keeping with Chinese custom than such activity on Tiananmen Square. The post-1913 mass assembly (*jihui*) in Tiananmen Square differed from traditional Chinese ceremonies,

trict; the eastern part will be constructed as the Central Business District (CBD); the western part will be constructed as a comprehensive cultural amusement district. The cultural function of the Chang'an Avenue axis will be improved.[73]

If the words "political" and "industrial" represent the spirit of China during the 1950s and 1960s, "culture" has become the most fashionable word since the 1980s. In the 2005 Beijing city master plan, everything is termed "cultural," from politics to art to commerce to entertainment, rendering the word "culture" virtually meaningless in the context of city planning. The indiscriminate use of this term, however, signals a significant ideological shift. Tired of the endless political movements of the Mao era, Chinese society became focused on a craving for culture in the 1980s, when material from both China's long past and abroad became newly available to Chinese intellectuals. "Cultural fever" and various new movements in art and literature during the 1980s created a yearning for both the traditional, as in the "searching roots" literature, and the modern, as in a variety of new Chinese avant-garde movements. This cultural ferment prepared the ground for the rise of neonationalism in the 1990s, which combined political power with historical glory, commercial success, and cultural nostalgia.

To some extent, the designation of different functional districts along the north-south and east-west axes of Beijing embodies the ideology of neonationalism as a combination of history, politics, and commerce. The drawings in the 2005 Beijing city master plan provide a clearer and more concise representation of the two axes than do the texts (fig. 6.1). In the drawing "Central City Functional Structure Plan," the north-south axis is divided into three parts: the middle part is named "traditional central axis: historical cultural nucleus district"; the northern part is called "northern central axis: physical culture district"; and the southern part is named "southern central axis: comprehensive commercial cultural district." The western part of the east-west axis is titled "Chang'an Avenue: political cultural nucleus district"; and the east part includes the CBD.[74]

In previous Beijing master plans, the north-south axis was confined within two ends while two arrows pointing east and west presaged the growth of Chang'an Avenue. In the 2005 master plan, the relationship is reversed. The east-west axis of the avenue is planned with a western starting point—the Yongding River—and an eastern starting point—the Grand Canal, while the north-south central axis extends from Tiananmen Square endlessly in both directions, indicated by arrows.

The rise of nationalism has truly resurrected the north-south axis. While the 1964

Chang'an Avenue planning featured a nationwide effort, urban design for the Central Axis in 2002 was carried out by means of an international scheme-collection process. The scheme provided by the Beijing Municipal Institute of City Planning and Design named the northern part of the central axis the Time Axis (Shidai Zhouxian), the middle part the Tradition Axis (Chuantong Zhouxian), and the southern part the Future Axis (Weilai Zhouxian). The central Tradition Axis represents history and commemoration, the northern Time Axis represents the present and celebration, and the southern Future Axis represents the years to come and the rise of China.[75]

A concrete step for the construction of the north-south axis of Beijing at the dawn of the twenty-first century was the Olympic Park. On July 13, 2001, Beijing was declared the host city for the 2008 Olympics. In preparation for this long-waited event, an international design competition titled "Conceptual Planning and Design of Beijing Olympic Green" was organized. The scale of the 2002 competition for the Olympic Park was much larger than the 1998–99 competition for the National Grand Theatre. More than one hundred institutes from twenty-one countries participated, and more than ninety schemes were initially selected. The competition was as much about the design of the Olympic Park as the planning of the central north-south axis, which was the most important issue addressed in the competition program.[76] The extension of the imperial central axis had begun, bearing the new historic task of achieving a "great renaissance of the Chinese nation (fig. 6.14)." The Chinese modernization project, a task once shouldered by Chang'an Avenue, has now been passed on to the north-south axis.

Conclusion:
Chang'an Avenue in a Global Context

THE 2008 OLYMPICS drew the world's attention to Beijing. Many people were impressed by the Olympic Park and the opening ceremony held in its main stadium, popularly known as the "Bird's Nest." Some praised it as a masterpiece of modern art and engineering; others pointed to the enormous quantity of high-quality steel that went into its construction and criticized its high cost; still others saw it as a sign that China had been completely integrated into the global market, since both the park and the main stadium were designed by foreign companies. However, few recognized the critical location that the Olympic Park occupied in Beijing's system of axes and the connection between the 2008 Olympics and China's imperial past.

The Olympic Park is the new starting point of Beijing's north-south axis. The artificial landscape of hills and streams at the north end of the park represents the beginning of Chinese civilization in about 3000 BCE. From there, the five thousand meters of the park's north-south length are divided into five sections, each representing one thousand years of Chinese history. The Bird's Nest is located at the chronological position of the Tang dynasty, the widely acknowledged golden age of China's cultural and political power. Such an official glorification of the imperial past would have been unthinkable twenty years ago, when socialism served as the guiding ideology and antitraditionalism fueled the modernization project, as represented by Chang'an Avenue. The dragon vein has truly returned, and with it, a revival of Chinese nationalism and a yearning for China's glorious past.

While the newly revived north-south axis of Beijing has become the symbol of Chinese national tradition, Chang'an Avenue continues to be viewed as the axis of modernization. Like other famous boulevards in other national capitals (for instance, Avenue des Champs-Élysées in Paris, Tverskaya-Lyusinovskaya in Moscow, and Via dell'Impero in Rome), Chang'an Avenue defines the urban fabric of Beijing. No other boulevard, however, runs through the entire urban area of a city with such a consistent and visually powerful form. Its scale and geometric regularity are unique among the great avenues of the world. The development of Chang'an Avenue, like that of other famous boulevards, is also closely intertwined with national history, modernity, and identity. For instance, Athinas Street in Athens and Unter den Linden in Berlin were both meant to convey a new national identity by a selective inclusion of the nation's past.

When the two Chang'an Avenues were joined to form a unified thoroughfare, it was not intended to be a symbolic center. Chang'an Avenue was originally built to modernize an ancient capital through the reorganization of the road system for more efficient communication. As a major element in the architectural modernization of Beijing, the avenue was planned and replanned to meet the changing modernization ideals of different periods of the People's Republic of China (PRC) era. Each period claimed to "roughly complete" the avenue according to then-current modernization ideals, filling in monumental buildings and creating new "gaps" along its ever-changing façades. The "gaps" were not so much physical gaps as symbolic ones left by discrepancies in the Chinese modernization project. When Chang'an Avenue finally became a symbolic axis in the urban framework of Beijing, it was designated as the new axis representing modernity. As a counterpart to the north-south central axis representing tradition, the symbolic nature of the avenue is imbedded not in a static physical or spatial existence but in the dynamic process of its evolution.

Modern Communication and Avenue des Champs-Élysées in Paris

Unlike Chang'an Avenue, whose status as an axis of the capital was a modern creation, the Avenue des Champs-Élysées in Paris functioned as the main axis of the French capital in both imperial and modern eras. The royal sections merged seamlessly into the modern and commercial sections in a continuous display of French history.[1]

While imperial Chinese ceremonial processions during the Ming and Qing dynasties took place along the north-south axis of Beijing, penetrating layer after layer of walls and gates, ceremonies in Paris proceeded along great boulevards, especially the Champs-Élysées. During the Franco-Prussian War, in March 1871, occupying Prussian troops marched back and forth along the Avenue de la Grande Armée and then down the Champs-Élysées in celebration of their victory. Seventy years later, Hitler's Nazi troops repeated this parade along the same avenues.

Grand boulevards lined with trees and monumental façades are a product of the modern West. In 1646, Louis XIV of France authorized the destruction of the defensive walls and fortifications of Paris and their replacement with tree-lined avenues. These avenues eventually became the most animated thoroughfares in Paris, known as interior boulevards or *les grands boulevards*. Ringing the interior boulevards were the exterior boulevards, connected in the midnineteenth century when Baron Georges-Eugène Haussmann added a series of diagonal avenues. Haussmann's new street system created two new axes for Paris, the east-west axis, with the Champs-Élysées as its central section, and the north-south axis connecting Porte d'Orléans with Gare de l'Est. The two thoroughfares intersect at the center of the city.[2]

The axes of Paris are different from the axes of Beijing in many ways. While the two axes of Paris were created simultaneously in the nineteenth century, the east-west axis of Beijing was created more than five hundred years after its north-south axis. Oriented exactly according to the cardinal directions, the axes of Beijing are much straighter and more regular than Paris's axes, whose orientation followed not a cosmic model but earlier street patterns. Zigzagging in the city and visually tying the city together, Paris's axes are weaker as formal axes than Beijing's Chang'an Avenue, which bisects the entire city into two halves and intersects the north-south axis at the very center of the city. Paris's axes are created by connecting preexisting streets to improve traffic flow, while Beijing's Chang'an Avenue cuts into the historical fabric of the Old City and has destroyed imperial monuments that once stood in its path.

The boulevard on the urban axis of Paris comparable to Beijing's Chang'an Avenue is the Champs-Élysées. Straight, wide, and lined with trees and monumental buildings, the physical appearance of the Champs-Élysées and its prestigious status are similar to those of Chang'an Avenue. The cultural and functional contexts of these two avenues, however, are very different. While the Champs-Élysées was initially created in 1667 as an ornamental promenade rather than a utilitarian thoroughfare for traffic, like other boulevards in Paris,[3] Beijing's two Chang'an Avenues remained two humble minor streets separated by the central imperial axis for five hundred years until they were recently joined and transformed into a prominent modern avenue. The Champs-Élysées has a clear beginning, the Louvre, and extends in one direction, west. Chang'an Avenue also has a starting point, Tiananmen Square, but extends both westward and eastward, making it visually and virtually infinite in extension for future urban planning. Most importantly, the Champs-Élysées starts with traditional historical monuments and smoothly merges into modern sites. Its starting point was historically created and existed long before the creation of the axis itself. The starting point of Chang'an Avenue, the Communist Tiananmen Square, however, was a modern creation. Instead of embodying a continuous transition between past and present, as does the Champs-Élysées, Chang'an Avenue represents an abrupt change, with a clear-cut boundary between past and present, old urban fabric and new development, historical memory and utopian future.

As the inefficient flow of traffic through Beijing was the initial impetus for joining the two Chang'an Avenues, transportation problems were the driving force behind the development of the Parisian street system. The horse-drawn omnibus that had served Paris since 1661 survived as late as 1913. However, by the 1870s tramways had become an important part of the transportation system, rendering the horse-drawn omnibus outmoded. In 1929 the trams were completely replaced with buses. In the 1960s and 1970s, buses started losing passengers to private cars and the Metro system, both of which were faster, more convenient, and more regular. Ever-improving transportation technology transformed such facilities as the street, Metro, viaduct, and railway station into the very symbols and embodiments of modernity.[4] Similarly, it was the need for transportational efficiency that inspired the first stage of the development of Chang'an Avenue before the Communist revolution.

The power and speed of modern transportation, together with technical innovations in metal and glass construction, revolutionized modern art and architecture in both form and ideology, as represented by such avant-garde movements as futurism and constructionism. In 1925 Le Corbusier proposed his "visionary plan for Paris" to revise the historical center according to his modernist vision, in which the entire historical urban fabric would be erased and replaced with gigantic modern structures located in huge, empty, abstract gardens. This kind of modernist revision of a city's historical center is what Liang criticized in his 1950 Liang-Chen Scheme; the Liang-Chen Scheme failed. Le Corbusier's plan, a modernist utopia in the eyes of many, was never realized. His vision, however, continued to inspire the modernist challenge to the past. Before Le Corbusier, the Eiffel Tower had long been seen as the model of an audacious structure confronting a historical urban context. After him, the Centre Pompidou of 1969–76 and Tour Maine-Montparnasse of 1969–73 continued to reject the prevailing urban fabric in the historic urban center and to arouse controversy over both their height and their style.[5] In 1972 president Georges Pompidou, a modernist who welcomed new urban elements as enrichments of the old city of Paris, argued,

> The modern architecture of the big city leads to towers. The French prejudice, and particularly that of Parisians, against height is, to my eyes, completely retrograde. . . . One cannot be mired in the past. Paris is not a dead city; it is not a museum to maintain. . . . We are the guardians of civilization. The difficulty is to be at the same time the creators. . . . I love art, I love Paris, I love France. I am struck by the conservative character of French taste, particularly of those who call themselves the elite; I am scandalized by the policies of the public powers in matters of art for a century, and that is why I seek to counteract it, with a mitigated success.[6]

This was the same motivation behind the expansion of Chang'an Avenue in the 1950s. Beijing was not a dead city. The best strategy to keep Beijing alive was to develop it according to the new vision of a modernized China. It is not surprising that, in the 1990s, supporters of Paul Andreu's National Grand Theatre project pointed to the success of both the Eiffel Tower and the Centre Pompidou to justify the confrontation the theatre's design presented to the 1959 Great Hall and the centuries-old Imperial City.

Political Power and Via dell'Impero in Rome

The construction of a modern street at the expense of historic buildings, as with Chang'an Avenue, has parallels in the Via dell'Impero in Rome. While new urban life created modern boulevards in Paris, the Via dell'Impero in Rome was intended as a display of the power of a new empire. It was built to link present and past empires, cutting through the imperial fora and connecting the Piazza Venezia in front of the Monument to Victor Emmanuel with the ancient Colosseum. Like Chang'an Avenue, the Via dell'Impero was meant to be a showcase. It was constructed as the main axis of the Esposizione Universale di Roma, Benito Mussolini's ambitious plan for the 1942 event to celebrate the achievements of Fascism. The new capital complex was located on this axis. In 1934 the 1,200-room national Fascist party headquarters was designed to be located at the midpoint of this avenue. Fifty-five hundred units of housing were destroyed to expose the ruins of ancient Rome's imperial fora.[7] While the development of Chang'an Avenue required the demolition of historical areas to make way for modern efficiency, in Fascist Italy, instead of challenging the imperial past, buildings of the recent past were demolished to reveal a more remote and more powerful ancient glory.

Parades of military triumph have a long history in Rome. During the Roman Republic period, from 508 to 44 BCE, triumphal processions lasting for days frequently energized the city. These parades served many time-honored ceremonial functions, including the ritual purification of troops and citizenry contaminated by war, and the appeasement and honoring of the gods associated with their victories. The main purpose of these ancient celebrations, however, was the same as their later incarnations in Rome, Beijing, and Moscow: to justify military campaigns, to display the power of the empire, and to intimidate the nation's enemies. Although Roman triumphs had a strong impact on the city's urban fabric (for instance, in the construction of commemorative arches and the development of fora and theatres), there was no fixed itinerary for the ritual parades, and no single street was designated for these ceremonies.[8] Compared with this ancient counterpart, the impact of twentieth-century ceremonies on urban development was much more self-conscious and purposeful.

A comparison between Mussolini's approach to the historical center of Rome in the 1930s and the Maoist approach to the historical center of Beijing in the 1950s reveals only superficial similarities. Both chose to locate new power centers in the cultural centers of imperial capitals full of historical memories, and both cleared vast amounts of old housing to make way for grand avenues for ceremonial parades. While Mussolini's Via dell'Impero linked the imperial Piazza Venezia with the ancient Roman Colosseum overlooking the imperial fora, Chang'an Avenue cut the Imperial City off from the old administrative center and turned it into a vast public square for mass assembly. While Mussolini's various archaeological projects isolated monuments of the Roman Empire and put them on display in the centers of urban squares, the new Communist Tiananmen Square and Chang'an Avenue marginalized the Forbidden City and the soaring front gates of imperial Beijing, turning them into mere backdrops. Mussolini tried to legitimatize the Fascist regime by establishing associations with a past golden age, the ancient Roman Empire. His various archaeological projects, including those involving the imperial fora (especially the Forum of Augustus), the mausoleum of Augustus, and the Ara Pacis Augustae, were undertaken to equate Fascist Italy with the ancient Roman Empire, and Mussolini, Il Duce, with Augustus.[9] In China, however, Mao did not try to resurrect a past golden age of the Chinese empire. Instead, Mao was concerned with creating an entirely new society, something never attempted by any previous ruler of China, as prophesied in his famous 1936 poem "Snow":

> Alas, emperors Qin Shihuang and Han Wudi
> Were not men of letters;
> Sovereigns Tang Taizong and Song Taizu
> Were short of cultural genius.
> The great monarch
> Genghis Khan was
> Only capable of shooting the big eagles with his bow.
> They are now as nothing:
> Greater and more noble heroes
> Are coming up today.[10]

The propaganda plans for Mussolini's Italy aimed to create "a didactic display of the achievement of the Roman Empire to bolster national pride in the past and inspire loyalty for the present custodians of this exalted tradition."[11] But no regimes in the past four thousand years of imperial history matched Mao's vision for the future of China. Comparing the future development of Beijing with the Fascist refashioning of Rome proves that Mao's scheme was much more forceful and efficient than Mussolini's in terms of the degree to which it fulfilled the political need of a regime. As Spiro Kostof put it in his discussion of Mussolini's project at the mausoleum of Augustus,

Piazzale Augusto Imperatore lacked conviction in its own term; as a consequence, it is unable to impress us today. Its aim as political art had been to use relics of the Augustan age to lend authority to Fascist achievement. The contest, at least in the visual sense, was never really joined. The Fascist side of the balance is too weak: what we are conscious of is the Augustan substance. Our opinion of Augustus is not affected by his association with Mussolini, and our opinion of Mussolini is not enhanced. The Duce yields to the emperor and is lost. The Piazzale, in the end, remains a colossal mistake.[12]

While the glory of the ancient Roman Empire eclipsed Mussolini's Fascist achievements in Via dell'Impero, the development of Chang'an Avenue and Tiananmen Square disconnected and overshadowed the imperial axis and created a socialist showcase to display the power and achievement of New China.

National Identity and Athinas Street in Athens

Like the development of Chang'an Avenue in Beijing, the construction of Athinas Street in Athens was also a governmental gesture aimed at promoting an official ideology of nation building. Immediately after Greece won independence from the Ottoman Empire in 1832, a master plan was made to develop Athens as the capital of the newly independent republic. Athinas Street was created as an axis to link the king's palace and the historical monument of the Acropolis, in an effort to give the long-abandoned capital a new sense of national identity.

Starting at the foot of the ancient Acropolis, Athinas Street is the main north-south axis of the city, cutting through the old city of Athens. However, instead of creating a border between history and modernity, as Chang'an Avenue did with the Forbidden City of Beijing, Athinas Street works more as a link between past, present, and future. Originating at the historic Acropolis, it runs through Omonia Square, which is surrounded by elegant hotels, and extends onward from there.[13]

Unlike Chang'an Avenue, Athinas Street is not the dominant street in the urban fabric of Athens. It is one of three major streets, each representing different aspects of the official ideology and national aspirations of Greece as a new country. Athinas Street was designed to create a strong connection to the classical past. Panepistimiou Street initiated the architectural transformation of Athens into a European-style capital with the Trilogy of Athens: the university, the academy, and the national library. And Mitropoleos Street aimed to promote internal political and cultural unity and national identity with its new cathedral and royal palace. All three streets were designed and constructed in the 1830s shortly after Greece was freed from Ottoman control.[14]

All of the national aspirations embodied in these streets in Athens were focused on forgetting and severing ties with recent Ottoman history in order to construct a new national identity. Here, they served a very similar function to Chang'an Avenue in the Chinese capital. Both embodied modernization in new countries with recent bitter histories.

The Completion of Chang'an Avenue and Chinese Architectural Modernization

Chang'an Avenue shoulders a threefold task in the modernization project of Chinese urban planning and architecture: it is an urban thoroughfare serving the communication needs of a modernizing city, like the Avenue des Champs-Élysées in Paris; it is a national showcase displaying the power of a regime, similar to the Via dell'Impero in Rome; and it is an urban spatial expression articulating a new national identity, along the lines of Athinas Street in Athens. While these tasks are dispersed among different urban elements or different cities in other countries, in China, they are crowded together on Chang'an Avenue. The best example of this is the designation of Beijing as the center for everything. Even after the term "industrial center" was deleted from the definition of the nature of Beijing in the 1990s, an overemphasis on concentration of functions persists. The construction of a socialist capital centered on Chang'an Avenue and Tiananmen Square continues the millennia-long Chinese tradition of building a symbolic center of "all under heaven."

While each period claimed to "roughly complete" Chang'an Avenue according to the targeted "modernity" of the time, the changing and shifting of modernization ideologies constantly created "gaps" for future "completions" to fill. The gaps are measured in terms of the difference between Chinese reality and Western reference, and the Chinese reality is articulated with terms, examples, and theoretical frameworks generated in a Western context.

For the Chinese modernization project, the origin is the West, whose modernity is termed, by Chinese scholars, "early and interior-generated modernization" (*zaofa neishengxing xiandaihua*). Chinese modernity, meanwhile, is considered by Chinese scholars to be "postponed exterior-generated modernization" (*houfa waishengxing xiandaihua*), which means that it was delayed because of historical mistakes and remains immature.[15] Setting aside any so-called historical mistakes, the Chinese modernization process (*xiandaihua zhuanxing*) was also called "staggering" and "twisted."[16] But what is a normal and smooth modernization process? Putting the modernization project in a universal framework, Chinese architecture has forever been looking to the West for future directions.

Instead of challenging the substructure of the modernization project in Chinese architecture, the postmodernist and postcolonial theories recently introduced into China were used by Chinese architects mostly to compete with foreign companies in the design market. The recent rise of nationalism and China's yearning for its glorious past, as represented by the revived development of the central north-south axis of Beijing, is as much a regionalist shadow of the Western-dominated international structure as was socialism in the early decades of the People's Republic of China.

Similarly, the recent movement to restore the character of the ancient capital is as much a response to the dominant Western culture as was the industrialization of Beijing in the 1950s. On one hand, old-style streets are built and proposals are made to raze the "ugly" concrete buildings constructed during the early decades of the People's Republic of China and restore the Old City gate towers; on the other hand, old courtyard housing is torn down to make way for new urban shopping malls, luxury housing, and company headquarters. The former is the erasure of recent socialist memory in order to restore a fake "old Beijing" to appeal to tourism; the latter is the erasure of the memory of an authentic older Beijing to appeal to the world market. While the latter erasure of memory is mourned today, the former is not considered a loss at all. Nostalgia made it a blind spot. Enthusiasm for the north-south axis has revived. The Liang-Chen Scheme proposed to preserve the imperial axis by leaving the Old City intact and constructing a new parallel north-south axis as an administrative center. The most recent city-planning proposal for Beijing, however, calls for strengthening and extending the original north-south axis, just as was done with Chang'an Avenue in the 1950s.

Surface changes should not obscure the visibility of historical repetitions. A Russian commentator recently declared that "China was still just an imitator despite its success in economic fields and rise in international status."[17] This rings true. Far from the optimistic, or pessimistic, prophecy that the twenty-first century will be a Chinese century, the modernization project for Chinese architecture will remain unachievable as long as there is a modernization project at all. The historical continuity formed by the replacement of the present- or past-tense "modern" with the future-tense "modernization" is unself-conscious. It focuses too much on constant updating and forever catching-up, but neglects the intrinsic value of a culture, the subconscious drive that has produced such a replacement. To some extent, the modernization project overemphasizes the significance of the present, which we can experience directly; establishes a definite boundary between past and present where no one can exist; and thus overlooks the continuity of history—the very driving force of Chinese civilization.

Notes

Notes to Introduction

1. Different sections of Chang'an Avenue are specifically defined in this book. For definitions, see the glossary.

2. "Xiang Zhou Enlai zongli yiti gaobie" (Farewell to Premier Zhou Enlai's body), *Wenhuibao* (Wen Wei Po), January 11, 1976 (Hong Kong); "Zhou zongli yiti yisong Babaoshan huohua" (Premier Zhou's body was escorted to Babaoshan for cremation), *Wenhuibao*, January 12, 1976 (Hong Kong).

3. "Quanguo chentong aidao Zhou zongli" (The whole country deeply mourns Premier Zhou), *Wenhuibao*, January 15, 1976. This was the plan as indicated in the newspapers of January 15. Later, however, Zhou's ashes were scattered across the land and seas of China by an airplane, which was, according to Zhou's widow, Deng Yingchao, his final will.

4. Spence, *Search for Modern China*, 649–50.

5. "Relie qingzhu Hua Guofeng tongzhi wei wodang lingxiu" (Warmly celebrate comrade Hua Guofeng becoming the party leader), *Remin huabao* (China Pictorial) (December 1976): 1–23.

6. Esherick, *Remaking the Chinese City*, 1.

7. Wood, *Challenge of the Avant-Garde*.

8. Kuspit, *Cult of the Avant-Garde Artist*.

9. Earlier modernist architects and theorists advocated more formally based definitions of modernity, such as the formal principles of Henry-Russell Hitchcock and Philip Johnson or the space of Sigfried Giedion. Recent scholars have proposed more value-based definitions. Xing Ruan, for instance, defined architectural modernity as faith in common good rather than an overt emphasis on cultural specificity. See Cody, Steinhardt, and Atkin, *Chinese Architecture and the Beaux-Arts*, 153–68.

10. Mao Zedong, "Xin minzhu zhuyi lun," 666–68.

11. Beijingshi Guihua Weiyuanhui et al., *Chang'anjie*, 9.

12. These protests include the May Fourth Movement in 1919, the May Thirtieth Demonstration in 1925, the December Ninth Movement in 1935, and the antiautocratic movement in 1947.

13. Important examples of the anniversary celebrations for the People's Republic of China on October 1 include the founding ceremony in 1949, the first anniversary in 1950, the tenth anniversary in 1959, the thirty-fifth anniversary in 1984 celebrating the reformist regime under Deng Xiaoping, the fortieth anniversary in 1989 shortly after the bloodshed in Tiananmen, and the fiftieth anniversary in 1999 following the reunification with Hong Kong and anticipating the return of Macau to China.

14. Kostof, "Emperor and the Duce," 270–325.

15. Greg Castillo, "Gorki Street and the Design of the Stalin Revolution," in *Streets: Critical Perspectives on Public Space*, edited by Celik, Favro, and Ingersoll et al., 57–70.

16. Zeynep Celik, "Urban Preservation as Theme Park: The Case of Sogukcesme Street," in *Streets: Critical Perspectives on Public Space*, edited by Celik, Favro, and Ingersoll et al., 83–94. For other scholarship on urban streets, Jacobs, Macdonald, and Rofe's *The Boulevard Book: History, Evolution, Design of Multiway Boulevards* offers an overview of the history and techniques in the design and building of modern boulevards, and James Trager's *Park Avenue: Street of Dreams* focuses on cultural influence and sociopolitical milieus in the development of Park Avenue in New York.

17. Meyer, *Dragons of Tiananmen*; Susan Naquin, *Peking*.

18. Strand, *Rickshaw Beijing*.

19. Madeleine Dong, *Republican Beijing*.

20. Hou Renzhi and Deng Hui, *Beijingcheng de qiyuan yu bianqian*; Shi Mingzheng, *Zouxiang jindaihua de Beijing*.

21. Wu Hung, *Remaking Beijing*.

22. Wu Hung, "Tian'anmen Square: A Political History of Monuments," *Representations* 35 (Summer 1991): 84–117.

23. Davis et al., *Urban Spaces in Contemporary China*; Broudehoux, *The Making and Selling of Post-Mao Beijing*.

24. For example, Susan Naquin wrote, "My research was not begun, nor is it now intended to be, an exercise in nostalgia, either for vanished temples or for a lost Peking. Indeed, it is intended precisely to historicize the city's timeless past. Nevertheless, if viewed—just for one moment—against the current destruction of the city, this book reminds even me of a 'record of a dream of a vanished capital.'" Naquin, *Peking*, 708.

25. Wang Jun suggested that Mao personally supported Soviet advisors' opinion to locate the new administrative center in the heart of Beijing; Wang, *Chengji*, 86. Wu Liangyong blamed the strong Soviet influence for the destruction of Old Beijing; Wu, *Rehabilitating the Old City of Beijing*, 18–23.

26. Arnold Hauser, *The Philosophy of Art History* (London: Routledge, 1959), 3–17.

27. Zou Denong, *Zhongguo xiandai jianzhushi*.

28. Zhang Jinggan, *Beijing guihua jianshe wushi nian*.

29. Wu Liangyong, *Rehabilitating the Old City of Beijing*.

30. For example, St. John Wilson, Peter Blundell-Jones, Kenneth Frampton, and Giorgio Ciucci.

31. Sarah Goldhagen, "Something to Talk About."

32. Jianfei Zhu, *Chinese Spatial Strategies*.

33. Rowe and Seng Kuan, *Architectural Encounters with Essence and Form*.

34. Jianfei Zhu, *Architecture of Modern China*.

35. Duanfang Lu, *Remaking the Chinese Urban Form*.

36. Lefebvre, *Production of Space*.

37. The reading of the documents is deconstructionist in the sense that hidden messages and the preconceptions of the texts' writers, intentional or not, are uncovered through such a reading in order to reveal the contradictions and inconsistencies in the discourse of Chinese architectural modernity.

38. Andrew Jacobs, "Confucius Statue Vanishes Near Tiananmen Square," *New York Times*, April 22, 2011; http://www.nytimes.com/2011/04/23/world/asia/23confucius.html

Notes to Chapter One

1. Wilkinson, *Chinese History*, 751–52.

2. Zhongyang yanjiuyuan lishi yuyan yanjiusuo, ed., *Ming Taizu shilu* (Taipei: Zhongyang Yan-jiuyuan, 1962), 295–96, 311–12, 379–80.

3. These nine gates were Xuanwu, Zhengyang, and Chongwen Gates in the south; Chaoyang and Dongzhi Gates in the east; Anding and Desheng Gates in the north; and Xizhi and Fucheng Gates in the west.

4. These four gates were Tiananmen in the south, Di'an Gate in the north, Dong'an Gate in the east, and Xi'an Gate in the west.

5. These four gates were the southern Meridian Gate, the northern Shenwu Gate, the eastern Donghua Gate, and the western Xihua Gate.

6. The Outer City walls were originally planned to encircle the entire Inner City. However, only the southern parts were completed, allegedly due to the enormous time and expense it would have cost. See Pan Guxi, *Yuan Ming jianzhu*, 31.

7. These seven gates were You'an, Yongding, and Zuo'an Gates in the south; Guangqu Gate in the east; Dongbian and Xibian Gates in the north; and Guang'an Gate in the west.

8. These include the Temple of Heaven, the Temple of Agriculture, the Imperial Ancestral Temple, the Altar of Soil and Grain, and Coal Hill.

9. Tiananmen Square during the Republican period refers to the open space to the south of Tiananmen Tower before the socialist expansion. The area was roughly the same size as Imperial Tiananmen Square with some walls removed.

10. This is clearly shown in a map of late Qing dynasty Beijing originally published in 1908 and reproduced in 2002 by China Pictorial Press (Zhongguo Huabao Chubanshe). Some old Beijing people also called the Left and Right Chang'an Gates "the East and West Three-Arch Gates," which has caused much confusion. See also Wang Jun, *Chengji*, 163; Hou Renzhi and Deng Hui, *Beijingcheng de qiyuan yu bianqian*, 111; Beijing Daxue Lishixi Beijing Shi Bianxiezu, *Beijing shi*, 225–26.

11. Also known as the Dynastic Gate, this gate was called Great Ming Gate (Damingmen) during the Ming dynasty and renamed Gate of China (Zhonghuamen) after the founding of the Republic of China in 1912.

12. Wang Yushi, *Tiananmen*, 6–7.

13. Wang Yushi, *Tiananmen*, 27–29.

14. Gao Wei, *Manhua Beijing*, 149–51.

15. Wang Yushi, *Tiananmen*, 32–35.

16. Zhang Fuhe, *Beijing jindai jianzhushi*, 217.

17. Wang Shiren and Zhang Fuhe, "Beijing jindai jianzhu gaishuo," 7–8.

18. Wang Yushi, *Tiananmen*, 36. See also Hou Renzhi and Deng Hui, *Beijingcheng de qiyuan yu bianqian*, 162.

19. For more details about the capital plan in the Zhou dynasty and the section "The Record of Craftsmanship" in *Rituals of Zhou* (Zhouli), see chapter 6. For a French translation of the entire

Zhouli, see Edouard Biot, tr., *Le Tcheou-li ou Rites des Tcheou*, vol. 2 (Paris: Imprimerie Nationale, 1851; repr., Taipei: Cheng Wen, 1975).

20. Liu Zonghan, "Huiyi Zhu Guixin xiansheng," 63–74.

21. Zhang Fuhe, *Beijing jindai jianzhushi*, 216–27.

22. Zhu Qiqian, "Zhongyang gongyuan ji," 113–15.

23. Sun Yat-sen is best known in China as Sun Zhongshan, after Zhongshan Qiao, a pseudonym he took when organizing anti-Manchu revolutions in Japan.

24. Gugong Bowuyuan Zijincheng Bianjibu, *Gugong bowuyuan 80 nian*, 2–61.

25. Beijingshi Difangzhi Bianzuan Weiyuanhui, *Beijing zhi, shizheng juan, yuanlin lühua zhi*, 103–4.

26. The archway was renamed again in 1952: the Memorial Gate for the Guard of Peace (Baowei Heping Fang).

27. Shi Mingzheng, *Zouxiang jindaihua de Beijing*, 273–76.

28. Chang'an Avenue is about 3,800 meters from Bell Tower, the north end of the traditional north-south axis, and about 3,700 meters from its south end Yongding Gate.

29. Although Beijing has served as the national capital of China for most of the last ten centuries, it lost the capital status a couple times, and its name kept changing. During the Yuan dynasty (1271–1368), it was called Dadu (Great Capital). In 1368 the Ming dynasty founded its capital in Nanjing (South Capital) and renamed the former Yuan capital Beiping (North Pacification). In 1403 Emperor Yongle of Ming moved the capital to Beiping and renamed it Beijing (North Capital). The following Qing dynasty (1644–1911) kept both the name and the capital status of Beijing throughout its 268-year rule. After the fall of the Qing Empire in 1912, Beijing continued to serve as the capital of the Republic of China until 1928, when Chiang Kai-shek moved the capital to Nanjing again. Between 1928 and 1937 Beijing was a special administrative city under the former early Ming (1368–1403) name, Beiping. In 1937 the puppet government under the Japanese occupying forces renamed it Beijing again and made it the capital of the "Provisional Government of the Republic of China." In 1945, after the Japanese surrendered, Nanjing was restored as the national capital of the Republic of China and Beijing was again renamed Beiping until 1949. See *Beijing shi*, 75–454. Except for document titles, I use "Beijing" consistently throughout this book, regardless of historical period.

30. Dong Guangqi, *Beijing guihua zhanlue sikao*, 298–305.

31. Zhang Jinggan, *Beijing guihua jianshe wushi nian*, 160. Also Madeleine Dong, *Republican Beijing*, 41.

32. Beipingshi Gongwuju, ed. *Beipingshi dushi jihua sheji ziliao di yi ji*, ii.

33. *Beijingshi jiedao xiangtu* (A detailed map of the streets of Beijing city) (Beijing: Zhongguo Ditu Chubanshe, 1950).

34. Zhang Jinggan, *Beijing guihua jianshe wushi nian*, 161–62.

35. Wang Jun, *Chengji*, 163–69.

36. They were destroyed during the Cultural Revolution (1966–76).

37. Jin Shoushen, "Beijing de dong xi Chang'anjie," 109; Also Zhang Jinggan, *Beijing guihua jianshe wushi nian*, 161–62.

38. Zhang Jinggan, *Beijing guihua jianshe wushi nian*, 161.

39. Zhang Jinggan, *Beijing guihua jianshe wushi nian*, 162.

40. Traditionally, buildings in China were measured by the number of bays. For details about the Chinese system of construction and measurement, see Liang Sicheng, *Chinese Architecture*.

41. Beijing's eastern and western suburbs were already densely built by the mid-1950s, creating heavy traffic in the east-west direction. See Dangdai Zhongguo Bianweihui, *Dangdai Zhongguo de Beijing*, 301.

42. Zhang Jinggan, *Beijing guihua jianshe wushi nian*, 161–62.

43. Wang Jun, *Chengji*, 292.

44. Zhang Jinggan, *Beijing guihua jianshe wushi nian*, 162.

45. Dangdai Zhongguo Bianweihui, *Dangdai Zhongguo de Beijing*, 301.

46. Bridges at Fuxing Gate and Jianguo Gate were built in 1979, Dabeiyao Bridge in 1986, tunnels to the north of Tiananmen Square in 1987, Gongzhufen Bridge in 1994, Muxidi Bridge in 1995, and pedestrian bridges and tunnels have been built along Chang'an Avenue since the 1990s. See Beijingshi Guihua Weiyuanhui et al., *Chang'anjie*, 134.

47. My knowledge of the rules for crossing Chang'an Avenue is mainly from my personal experience in Beijing and from conversations with taxi drivers during late 1990s to the present. I have not found the official published code about traffic control in Beijing.

48. Beijingshi Guihua Weiyuanhui et al., *Chang'anjie*, 134–35.

49. Soviet advisors had been working in China as early as the 1920s, when the Chinese Communist Party was first founded. After the founding of the People's Republic of China, the number of Soviet advisors swelled—mostly in economic and cultural fields—even before the formal agreement was signed. Mao went to Moscow on December 16, 1949, to discuss with Stalin the Soviet aides to China. On February 14, 1950, the PRC foreign minister, Zhou Enlai, and the USSR foreign minister, Andrey Vyshinsky signed the "Treaty of Friendship, Alliance and Mutual Assistance." See Short, *Mao*, 421–25.

50. Liang Sicheng, "Zhi Nie Rongzhen tongzhi xin," 368.

51. For details about Liang-Chen Scheme, see Shuishan Yu, "Redefining the Axis of Beijing."

52. *Chang'anjie*, 48.

53. These projects included the Great Hall of the People, the Museum of Chinese Revolution and History, the Minority Culture Palace, the Minority Hotel, the Military Museum, the National Theatre, Science and Technology Hall, and Xidan Department Store. For details about the Ten Great Buildings, see chapter 2. See also "Guanyu guoqing gongcheng de huibao tigang" (Draft report on the Anniversary Projects), BMA, archival no. 47–1–70.

54. *Chang'anjie*, 78.

55. *Chang'anjie*, 78–79.

56. The list of those institutes gathered to work was similar to that of the 1964 Chang'an Avenue planning, which included the Architectural Design Institute of Urban and Rural Construction and Environmental Protection, the Urban Planning Institute of China, the Tsinghua University Architecture Department, the Beijing Industrial University Architecture Department, the Beijing Architectural Engineering College Architecture Department, the Beijing Urban Planning Institute, and the Beijing Institute of Architectural Design and Research.

57. *Chang'anjie*, 88–90.

58. The key spots to be covered with large green fields are Ziwei Palace, Dongdan Park, the Beijing Hotel, Xinhua Gate, Xidan, the Minority Culture Palace, the Great Hall of the People, and the Museum of Chinese Revolution and History.

59. Dong Guangqi, *Beijing guihua zhanlue sikao*, 400–404; *Chang'anjie*, 90.

60. *Chang'anjie*, 88.

61. *Chang'anjie*, 108.

62. Six architectural and urban planning institutes in Beijing took part in the project: the Tsinghua University Architecture Department, the Beijing Industrial University Architecture Department, the Beijing Architectural Engineering College Architecture Department, the Beijing Institute of Architectural Design and Research, the Beijing Urban Planning Institute, and the Beijing Municipal Architectural Design Institute. See *Chang'anjie*, 4.

63. *Chang'anjie*, 8–10.

64. *Chang'anjie*, 6, 10.

65. *Chang'anjie* 150, 218.

66. *Chang'anjie*, 247.

67. *Chang'anjie*, 247.

68. Gao Han, "Yun dan bi tian ru xi," 222.

69. Zhao Dongri and Chu Ping, "Beijing tian'anmen guangchang dongxi diqu," *JZXB* (January 1993): 2–5.

70. For a detailed discussion on "face," "back," and façade in traditional Chinese architecture, see Wu Hung, "Face of Authority: Tian'anmen and Mao's Tian'anmen Portrait," in *Remaking Beijing*, 51–68.

71. An exception can be found in *pailou* or *paifang*, which are freestanding memorial archways indicating significant passages or boundaries. They were also used in commercial architecture during the imperial era, with the titles of the business inscribed in their horizontal board.

72. Frank Dorn, *Lao Beijing fengsu ditu* (The map of Old Peiking folklore), 1936.

73. Zhang Fuhe, *Beijing jindai jianzhushi*, 62–87.

74. Details on the architectural policies in the 1950s are provided in chapter 2. See also Zou Denong, *Zhongguo xiandai jianzhushi*, 144–45.

75. Brumfield, *History of Russian Architecture*, 487–91.

76. Chinese architects gave such Soviet-style buildings a bantering name because their plans resemble a toad seen from above.

77. Dittmer, *Sino-Soviet Normalization*, 94.

78. Luo Xiaowei, *Waiguo jinxiandai jianzhushi*, 138.

79. Zou Denong, *Zhongguo xiandai jianzhushi*, 191.

80. No Chinese traditional revivalist buildings were built on Chang'an Avenue in early 1950s. However, many appeared elsewhere in the capital—for instance, the Official Living Quarters at Di'an Gate, by Chen Deng'ao in 1954, and the Office Buildings for Four Ministries and One Committee at Sanlihe, by Zhang Kaiji 1952–55. See Zhongguo Xiandai Meishu Quanji Bianji Weiyuanhui, *Zhongguo xiandai meishu quanji*, vol. 2, 4–5; vol. 4, 38–39.

81. Liang Sicheng, "Zuguo de jianzhu," *Gujianzhu luncong*, 104–58.

82. Zou Denong, *Zhongguo xiandai jianzhushi*, 239.

83. Zou Denong, *Zhongguo xiandai jianzhushi*, 231–32.

84. In April 1974, Deng Xiaoping, the head of the Chinese delegation to the United Nations, unveiled Mao's Three Worlds Theory during a UN meeting. According to this theory, the two superpowers—the United States and the Soviet Union—constitute the "first world"; other industrialized countries, Communist and capitalist alike, are viewed as the "second world"; and the rest, the developing countries, are all categorized as the "third world." See Short, *Mao*, 611.

85. Zou Denong, *Zhongguo xiandai jianzhushi*, 285–87.

86. Zou Denong, *Zhongguo xiandai jianzhushi*, 581–84.

87. One of the major causes of such a national identity change was the breakup of the socialist bloc in the 1960s and 1970s. Crisis in Poland and the Hungarian revolt marked the disorder within the socialist bloc as early as 1956. Soviet aides were withdrawn from China in 1960 on Nikita Khrushchev's order, and the Sino-Soviet debate regarding some key issues on the international Communist movement continued until late 1964, when the two countries formally parted. The Soviet invasion of Czechoslovakia to crush the "Prague Spring" in August 1968 and the following military clash on Zhenbao Island in the Ussuri River along the Sino-Soviet border in March 1969 further pushed China away from the socialist bloc. See Spence, *Search for Modern China*. See also Dittmer, *Sino-Soviet Normalization*, 130.

88. Zou Denong, *Zhongguo xiandai jianzhushi*, 326–28.

89. Hitchcock and Johnson, *International Style*, 20.

90. The Chinese American architect for the Jianguo Hotel in 1980–82 was Chen Xuanyuan.

91. Zou Denong, *Zhongguo xiandai jianzhushi*, 372–73.

92. Beijingshi Guihua Weiyuanhui et al., *Beijing shida jianzhu sheji*, 592.

93. Beijingshi Guihua Weiyuanhui et al., *Beijing shida jianzhu sheji*, 138–39, 142.

94. Chinese and Japanese architects cooperated in the design of the Changfugong Center. See Zou Denong, *Zhongguo xiandai jianzhushi*, 440.

95. For more details on the Head Office of the People's Bank of China, see chapter 4.

96. The twelve buildings added to West Chang'an Avenue proper are, on the north side, the Huanan Building (1991), the Propaganda Department of the CCPCC (Chinese Communist Party Central Committee; 1993), the Chinese Industrial and Commercial Bank (1994–98), the Beijing Book Mansion (1994–98), and the Xidan Cultural Square (1998–99); on the south side, the China Education TV Station (1990–96), the Yuanyang Building (1996–99), the International Finance Building (1996–98), the Commercial Building of the Armed Police Department (1999–2003), the Capital Time Square (1995–99), the National Electricity Distribution Center (1998), and the National Grand Theatre (1999–2006).

97. The eleven buildings added to East Chang'an Avenue proper are: the Grand Hotel Beijing (1990), the Oriental Plaza (1997–99), the Ministry of Communication (1992–94), the Xinyuan Building (2002), the National Women's Association Building (1995), the Guanghua Chang'an Building (1994–96) in the north façade; and the Chang'an Club (1990–93), the Guangcai Center (2004), the Beijing Daily Building (2001–2), the Hengji Center (1993–97), and the Zhongliang Plaza (1992–96).

98. Beijingshi Guihua Weiyuanhui et al., *Beijing shida jianzhu sheji*.

99. "Ge" is a multistory building type in traditional Chinese architecture frequently used in gardens and Buddhist temples. For details on traditional Chinese building types, see Liang, *Chinese Architecture*.

100. For details about these buildings using traditional motifs, see "The Chinese Patches and the Foreign Patches" in chapter 5.

101. Beijingshi Guihua Weiyuanhui et al., *Beijing shida jianzhu sheji*, 71.

102. Neolithic altars of the Hongshan Culture are found in modern-day Inner Mongolia Autonomous Region and Liaoning Province, which has close ties with ancient cultures of Northeast Asia and Siberia. The altars usually consist of a series of raised terraces aligned along an axis oriented toward the sun. See Liu Xujie, *Zhongguo gudai jianzhushi di 1 juan*, 87–92.

1. Luo Zhewen, *Zhongguo gudai jianzhu*, 567–612.

2. Sun Dazhang, *Ancient Chinese Architecture*, 532.

3. Zhang Fuhe, *Beijing jindai jianzhushi*, 5–13.

4. Cody, *Building in China*.

5. Some scholars refer to a variety of historicism and eclecticism in architectural design as Beaux-Arts influenced. See Cody, Steinhardt, and Atkin, *Chinese Architecture and the Beaux-Arts*.

6. Pan Guxi, *Zhongguo jianzhushi*, 361–65.

7. In 1937, the Sino-Japanese war broke out. Nanjing was abandoned and the Nationalist capital moved westward to the inland areas, first to Wuhan in Hubei, then to Chongqing in Sichuan Province.

8. Cody, *Building in China*, 173–204.

9. Pan Guxi, *Zhongguo jianzhushi*, 304.

10. Philosophical methods, according to Feng Youlan (Fung Yu-Lan), can be categorized into two major groups: a positive line and a negative line. The positive approach defines the subject or idea directly, that is, by explaining what it *is*. The negative method, on the contrary, defines what is being discussed indirectly by explaining what it *is not*. Feng also argued that classical Chinese philosophy was mainly negative, and Western philosophy mainly positive, and that the future of philosophy relied on the interfusion of the two. See Fung Yu-Lan, *Short History of Chinese Philosophy*, 293–95.

11. Pan Guxi, *Zhongguo jianzhushi*, 348–51.

12. Pan Guxi, *Zhongguo jianzhushi*, 393.

13. Vitruvius Pollio, *De architectura* (Vitruvius: The ten books on architecture), translated by Morris Hicky Morgan (New York: Dover Publications, 1960), 17.

14. Zou Denong, *Zhongguo xiandai jianzhushi*, 132–49.

15. Liang Sicheng, "Minzu de xingshi, shehui zhuyi de neirong," in *Liang Sicheng quanji* 5, 169–74.

16. Mao Zedong, "Xin minzhu zhuyi lun," 666–69.

17. Liang Sicheng, "Zhi zhu de xin," in *Liang Sicheng quanji* 5, 82–83.

18. Liang Sicheng and Chen Zhanxiang, "Guanyu Zhongyang Zhengfu zhongxinqu weizhi," 1950, SAATU, no archival number available, 21–22.

19. Liang Sicheng, *Gujianzhu luncong*, 82–83.

20. Liang Sicheng, "Zhongguo jianzhu de tezheng" (Characteristics of Chinese architecture), in *Liang Sicheng quanji* 5, 179–84.

21. Liang Sicheng, "Zuguo de jianzhu," in *Liang Sicheng quanji* 5, 197–234.

22. *Fashi* literally means "model." It becomes a special term in Chinese architecture, referring to standardized design and construction methods, after the famous Song dynasty construction manual *Yingzao fashi* by Li Jie (Li Mingzhong).

23. Liang Sicheng, "Zuguo de jianzhu," 229.

24. Liang Sicheng, "Zhongguo jianzhu liangbu wenfa keben," in *Liang Sicheng quanji* 4.

25. Liang Sicheng, "Zhi zhu de xin," in *Liang Sicheng quanji* 5, 82–83.

26. Liang Sicheng, "Zuguo de jianzhu," in *Liang Sicheng quanji* 5, 197.

27. Important examples in Beijing include the 1951 Di'an Gate Official Dormitory Buildings, the

1954 Sanlihe Office Buildings for Four Ministries and One Committee, and the 1953 Friendship Hotel. See Zou Denong, *Zhongguo xiandai jianzhushi,* 159–69.

28. Other proposals for the Monument to the People's Heroes included the former drilling ground near Dongdan at the eastern end of historic East Chang'an Avenue, Babaoshan Hill in the western suburb, the top of Tiananmen Tower, and the site of the Gate of China (the Ming dynasty Great Ming Gate and Qing dynasty Great Qing Gate). See Wu Liangyong, "Renmin Yingxiong Jinianbei de chuangzuo chengjiu" (The architectural achievement of the Monument to the People's Heroes), *JZXB* (February 1978): 4–9.

29. For a more detailed analysis of the monument, see Wu Hung, *Remaking Beijing,* 24–50.

30. The number Liang gave in his retrospective report in 1967 was 170–80. According to *Chang'anjie,* it was about 140 designs. See Beijingshi Guihua Weiyuanhui et al., *Chang'anjie,* 57.

31. *Chang'anjie,* 57.

32. Liang Sicheng, "Renmin yingxiong jinianbei sheji jingguo," in *Liang Sicheng quanji 5,* 462–64.

33. Liang Sicheng, "Renmin yingxiong jinianbei sheji jingguo," 462.

34. Beijingshi Guihua Weiyuanhui et al., *Chang'anjie,* 59.

35. Liang Sicheng, "Zhi Peng Zhen xin," in *Liang Sicheng quanji 5,* 127–30.

36. *Ji-nian* can be translated as "memorial," and *bei* means "stele," a stone slab with inscriptions commonly found in traditional Chinese cemeteries, shrines, and temples. However, *bei* is also used to refer to other memorial architecture from the West. For instance, "obelisk" was translated as *fang-jian-bei,* which literally means "square and pointed stele."

37. After the monument was completed in Tiananmen Square, numerous monuments for Communist martyrs were constructed in cities all over China, following its form almost exactly but on a smaller scale.

38. "Structurism" refers to Russian constructivism, which, following Stalin's model, was considered bourgeois in China. See *jiegouzhuyi* in the glossary for further explanation.

39. Yang Yongsheng, *1955–1957 jianzhu baijia zhengming shiliao,* 3–5.

40. Zou Denong, *Zhongguo xiandai jianzhushi,* 198–200.

41. Lu Sheng, a native of Nanjing, was an assistant researcher of Yingzao Xueshe between 1942 and 1944 after graduating from the architecture department at Central University in Nanjing. From 1944 to 1952 Lu taught in the architectural departments at Central University and Beijing University. In 1952 he became an associate professor in architecture at Tianjin University. In 1957 he was classified as "rightist." See Yang Yongsheng, *1955–1957 jianzhu baijia zhengming shiliao,* 6.

42. Lu Sheng, "Duiyu xingshi zhuyi fugu zhuyi jianzhu lilun de jidian pipan," *JZXB* (March 1955): in Yang Yongsheng, *1955–1957 jianzhu baijia zhengming shiliao,* 6–13.

43. Lu Sheng, "Duiyu xingshi zhuyi fugu zhuyi jianzhu lilun de jidian pipan," 11–12.

44. For details on the origin of the basic narrative structure, with Tang represented as the golden age in Chinese architecture, see Shuishan Yu, "Ito Chuta," 57.

45. The movement was formally launched in April and May 1956 during the CCP Central Committee meeting and the seventh supreme State Council meeting.

46. For an explanation of *shijiezhuyi* (worldism), see the glossary.

47. Dong Dayu, "Zai yici chuangzuo taolunhui shangde fayan," in Yang Yongsheng, *1955–1957 jianzhu baijia zhengming shiliao,* 37–38.

48. Jiang Weihong and Jin Zhiqiang, "Women yao xiandai jianzhu," in Yang Yongsheng, *1955–1957 jianzhu baijia zhengming shiliao*, 57–58.

49. "Functionalism" was translated into Chinese as *gongnengzhuyi*. Its linguistic similarity in Chinese with *gonglizhuyi*, which is a philosophical term for "utilitarianism" and implies selfishness, made it a natural pejorative word at the time.

50. Wang Deqian, Zhang Shizheng, and Ba Shijie, "Dui 'women yao xiandai jianzhu' yiwen de yijian," in Yang Yongsheng, *1955–1957 jianzhu baijia zhengming shiliao*, 58–60.

51. Zhu Yulin, "Dui 'dui "women yao xiandai zhuyi" yiwen de yijian' de yijian," in Yang Yongsheng, *1955–1957 jianzhu baijia zhengming shiliao*, 60–62.

52. Many Soviet-aided projects completed before 1955 in China have a full display of the Stalinist Classicist details—for instance, the Beijing Exhibition Hall (originally called the Soviet Exhibition Hall) in 1952–54 and the Shanghai Sino-Soviet Friendship Building in 1955. See Zou Denong, *Zhongguo xiandai jianzhushi*, 182–84.

53. For architecture in Beijing after 1949, supporters for modern architecture often cited Hua Lanhong's Children's Hospital in 1954, Yang Tingbao's Peace Hotel in 1953, and some other buildings as examples. These buildings have asymmetrical plans and clean façades. Not located on Chang'an Avenue, they are not analyzed in this book. For details on these buildings, see Zou Denong, *Zhongguo xiandai jianzhushi*, 108, 120.

54. Yang Yongsheng, *1955–1957 jianzhu baijia zhengming shiliao*, 95.

55. Yang Yongsheng, *1955–1957 jianzhu baijia zhengming shiliao*, 109.

56. Here Liang was referring to 1956–57, when his national form in architecture was criticized as "revivalism" during the Double Hundred Principle movement.

57. Here Liang was referring to the Great Hall of the People and the Museum of Chinese Revolution and History.

58. Liang Sicheng, "Cong 'shiyong, jingji, zai keneng tiaojianxia zhuyi meiguan' tandao chuantong yu gexin" (On Tradition and Creation as Raised by the Policy "Utility, Economy and Beauty if Situation Allows"), in *Liang Sicheng quanji 5*, 307–8.

59. Zhai Lilin, "Lun jianzhu yishu yu mei ji minzu xingshi" (On architectural art, beauty and national form), *JZXB* (January 1955), in Yang Yongsheng, *1955–1957 jianzhu baijia zhengming shiliao*, 93–96.

60. Zhai Lilin, "Lun jianzhu yishu yu mei ji minzu xingshi," 96–97.

61. Mao Zedong, "Maodun lun," 274–312.

62. Zhai Lilin, "Lun jianzhu yishu yu mei ji minzu xingshi," 93–107.

63. Chen Zhihua and Ying Ruocong, "Ping zhai lilin 'lun jianzhu yishu yu mei ji minzu xingshi'" (On Zhai Lilin's "On architectural art, beauty and national form"), *JZXB* (March 1955), in Yang Yongsheng, *1955–1957 jianzhu baijia zhengming shiliao*, 107–14.

64. Zhou Xiangyuan, "Lun jianzhu yishu de neirong—Yu Zhai Lilin tongzhi shangque" (On architectural content—To negotiate with comrade Zhai Lilin), *JZXB* (March 1955), in Yang Yongsheng, *1955–1957 jianzhu baijia zhengming shiliao*, 133–35.

65. Zhai Lilin, "Lun jianzhu yishu yu mei ji minzu xingshi," in Yang Yongsheng, *1955–1957 jianzhu baijia zhengming shiliao*, 102.

66. Chen Zhihua and Ying Ruocong, "Ping zhai lilin 'lun jianzhu yishu yu mei ji minzu xingshi,'" in Yang Yongsheng, *1955–1957 jianzhu baijia zhengming shiliao*, 112–13.

67. Yang Yongsheng, *1955–1957 jianzhu baijia zhengming shiliao*, 124.

68. Yang Yongsheng, *1955–1957 jianzhu baijia zhengming shiliao*, 98.

69. According to Zheng Guangzhong, a professor of urban planning at the school of architecture at Tsinghua University who has participated in all of the major Chang'an Avenue planning after 1949, all of the Anniversary Projects in 1958 were originally to be located on Chang'an Avenue. It was only after the originally planned projects could not be finished in time that buildings located somewhere else were added. Zheng Guangzhong, interview by the author, October 24, 2005, Beijing.

70. "Diqiqu Chang'anjie shulinnei tanfan xu jiwu lianhe ge tanfan juming qingqiu jian zhengdijuan de yuancheng he tanbaishu" (Original petition letter for lowering tax by Xu Jiwu and other vendors and shopkeepers in the woods on Chang'an Avenue in District Seven and their formal confession), August 1949, BMA, archival no. 45-4-29.

71. BMA, archival no. 45-4-29.

72. BMA, archival no. 45-4-29.

73. "Guanyu Chang'anjie gaijian guihua he gaijian jihua buzhou de qingshi baogao" (Report to ask for instructions about the reconstruction plan and strategies of Chang'an Avenue), January 1964, BMA, archival no. 131-*dang* 9-16-139.

74. For instance, the Minority Hotel was added later.

75. The Conference Hall for People's Congress was renamed the Great Hall of the People by Mao after its completion. The popular English translation "Great Hall" will be used in this book.

76. "Military Museum" is used in this book to refer to the People's Liberation Army Museum.

77. "Guanyu guoqing gongcheng de huibao tigang" (Draft report about the Anniversary Projects), February 23, 1959, BMA, archival no. 47-1-70.

78. For details about the social political aspects of the Great Leap Forward movement, see Spence, *Search for Modern China*, 574–82.

79. "Guanyu guoqing gongcheng de huibao tigang," BMA, archival no. 47-1-70.

80. "Remin dahuitang gongcheng shengchan ribao" (Production daily reports on the Conference Hall for People's Congress), February to August, 1959, BMA, archival no. 125-1-1277-1.

81. "Renmin dahuitang sheji gaikuang" (Design outline of the Great Hall), September 1963, BMA, archival no. 47-1-301-1.

82. "Quanguo renmin daibiao dahuitang gongcheng de jiben qingkuang" (Basic facts about the Great Conference Hall of the National People's Congress), August 27, 1959, BMA, archival no. 47-1-92-1.

83. The voices were not unanimous. There were people who were not very interested in the exterior appearance of the building. Some complained about the contrast between such a grand building and the poor living conditions of the common folks. See BMA, archival no. 2-20-101.

84. Beijingshi Guihua Guanliju Shejiyuan Renmin Dahuitang Shejizu, "Remin dahuitang" (The Great Hall), in *JZXB* (September–October 1959): 23.

85. "Remin dahuitang zhengzhi sixiang gongzuo zongjie chugao" (Summary of works on political thoughts in the Great Hall of the People, first draft), October 10, 1959, BMA, archival no. 125-1-1226-1.

86. "Guanyu nongzhanguan, gemin lishi bowuguan gongcheng jiben zongjie he gongren tiyuguan gongcheng yanshou baogao" (Basic summary of the Agriculture Exhibition Hall and Museum of Chinese Revolution and History projects and the acceptance report on the Workers' Gymnasium project), January to March, 1959, BMA, archival no. 47-1-90-1.

87. BMA, archival no. 125-1-1226-1.

88. "1959 nian zuzhi qunzhong canguan renmin dahuitang gongzuo jihua ji jianbao" (Plan and reports for organizing people's visits to the Great Hall), BMA, archival no. 2-20-101.

89. BMA, archival no. 2-20-101.

90. BMA, archival no. 2-20-101.

91. For analysis of the term "mass line" and the ideologies underlying it, see chapter 3 on the collective approach in architectural practice.

92. Pan Guxi, *Zhongguo jianzhushi*, 431.

93. The term *zhushi*, literally "column model," includes the column, its base, and the beams and bracket set on top of it. Trained in Western academic traditions, early Chinese architectural historians in the twentieth century made an effort to combine Chinese and Western architectural systems and terminologies. Liang Sicheng, for instance, translated *zhushi* as "Chinese orders" and made traditional Chinese architectural drawings following the model of illustrations in Sir Banister Fletcher's *A History of Architecture*. See Liang Sicheng, *Chinese Architecture*, 10.

94. BMA, archival no. 47-1-301-1.

95. For more detailed information about the function and design of the Great Hall of the People, see Jayde Lin, *The Great Hall of the People: Defining the Socialist Chinese National Identity through Re-defining the Center*, master's thesis, University of Washington, 2004, 34–57; and Wu Hung, *Remaking Beijing*, 108–26.

96. For a basic introduction to pre-Qin Chinese texts, see Wilkinson, *Chinese History*, 454–79.

97. In addition to these official histories, there are more volumes not compiled by government-sponsored agencies. For a basic introduction to Chinese dynastic historical records, see Wilkinson, *Chinese History*, 483–521.

98. The history of the last dynasty, the Qing, which was compiled by scholars during the Republican era rather than by imperial officials, has never been formally completed in the standard traditional format. This leaves us two different terms, "Twenty-four Histories" and "Twenty-five Histories," depending on whether the last dynasty counts. The title "Draft of Qing History" (Qingshi gao), rather than simply "Qing History" (Qingshi), suggests its less-official status.

99. Liang Qichao, "Zhongguo zhi jiushi" (Old histories of China), in *Liang Qichao wenji* (Selected works of Liang Qichao), edited by Chen Shuliang (Beijing: Beijing Yanshan Chubanshe, 2009), 153.

100. Ma Zhixiang, *Beiping lüyou zhinan* (Tourist Guide to Beiping) (Beijing: Yanshan Chubanshe, 1997), 18–20. See also Zhongguo Lishi Bowuguan, *Zhongguo tongshi chenlie*, cover text.

101. Gugong Bowuyuan Zijincheng Bianjibu, *Gugong bowuyuan 80 nian*, 30–35.

102. "Lishi bowuguan: Guanyu duanmen weixiu" (Museum of History: About repairing Dumen), BMA, archival no. 47-1-673-1.

103. Zhongguo Renmin Geming Junshi Bowuguan, *Zoujin Zhongguo Renmin Geming Junshi Bowuguan*, 7.

104. Zhongguo Renmin Geming Junshi Bowuguan, *Zoujin Zhongguo Renmin Geming Junshi Bowuguan*, 10.

105. For detailed discussion on *jindai*, *xiandai*, *jinxiandai*, and *dangdai*, see the last section of chapter 3.

106. According to Marxism, typical social development was normally experienced as a succession from a primitive society to a slavery society to a feudal society to a capitalist society to a socialist society and finally to a Communist society. In non-Western countries, however, the feudal society was abruptly discontinued by the European imperialist expansion and became colonial society.

Since China was never fully colonized by Western powers, and the central imperial power continued until the capitalist revolution led by Sun Yat-sen, the term "semicolonial semifeudal" society was adopted to characterize Chinese society between 1840 and 1911. The capitalist society in China was extremely short, according to such a theory, only thirty-eight years, from 1912 to 1949, the year the People's Republic of China was founded and the Nationalist regime fled to Taiwan.

107. "Beijingshi wenhuaju, benju dangzu guanyu Beijing lishi bowuguan, ziran bowuguan biangeng mingcheng ji zhongguo geming lishi liang bowuguan choujian qingkuang de baogao" (Report on the changes of names of the Museum of History and the Museum of Nature in Beijing and the founding of the Museum of Chinese Revolution and the Museum of Chinese History), July to September 1959, BMA, archival no. 164-1-31-1, 041.

108. "Guanyu Beijing lishi bowuguan ziran bowuguan liangguan biangeng mingcheng wenti de qingshi" (Application for the change of names of the Museum of History and the Museum of Nature in Beijing), January 7, 1959, BMA, archival no. 164-1-31-1.

109. "Beijingshi wenhuaju, benju guanyu geming lishi bowuguan, gugong bowuyuan san danwei shangjiao wenhuabu lingdao de baogao ji shi renwei bangongting de pifu" (Report on the reorganization of three museums under direct guidance of the Ministry of Culture and the official reply), May 8, 1962, BMA, archival no. 164-1-358-1.

110. In 1927 Nanjing became the capital of the Republic of China. In February 1928 the Technical Specialists' Office for the Design of the National Capital was founded. American engineer Ernest Payson Goodrich and American architect Henry Killam Murphy were hired as engineering consultant and architecture consultant, respectively. The "capital plan" was decreed in December 1929. See Pan Guxi, *Zhongguo jianzhushi*, 321.

111. Pan Guxi, *Zhongguo jianzhushi*, 322.

112. Pan Guxi, *Zhongguo jianzhushi*, 373–83.

113. *Chang'anjie*, 66–67.

114. *Chang'anjie*, 67.

115. "Beijingshi jianzhu shejiyuan, zhongguo geming lishi bowuguan sheji gaikuang" (Summary of the Museum of Chinese Revolution and History Design), September 1963, BMA, archival no. 47-1-301-1, 7–8.

116. "Zhongguo geming he zhongguo lishi bowuguan gongcheng de jiben qingkuang" (Basic facts about the Museum of Chinese Revolution and History project), August 27, 1959, BMA, archival no. 47-1-92-1, 4–5.

117. The practice of scheme collection, which is different from a design competition, during the PRC era will be discussed in chapter 3.

118. *Chang'anjie*, 72.

119. BMA, archival no. 47-1-301-1, 7–8.

120. BMA, archival no. 47-1-92-1, 4–5.

121. Zhongguo Geming Bowuguan, *Zhongguo Geming Bowuguan 50 nian*, 13.

122. "Zhongguo geming bowuguan, Sun Zhongshan xiansheng danchen bainian zhounian jinian zhanlan gongzuo gaikuang" (Summary of the Exhibition in Memory of Sun Yat-sen's One Hundred and Thirtieth Anniversary), March to April, 1966, BMA, archival no. 2-20-456-1.

123. Zhongguo Lishi Bowuguan, *Zhongguo tongshi chenlie*.

124. Zhongguo Renmin Geming Junshi Bowuguan, *Zoujin Zhongguo Renmin Geming Junshi Bowuguan*, 90, 172, 231.

125. Zhongguo Renmin Geming Junshi Bowuguan, *Zoujin Zhongguo Renmin Geming Junshi Bowuguan*, 90, 172, 231.

Notes to Chapter Three

1. "Mass" refers to "people" in the Marxist sense. "Mass-oriented principle" is a translation of the Chinese *qunzhong yuanze*, and "mass line" is a translation of *qunzhong luxian*. Both are standard terms in Chinese socialist ideologies.

2. Mao Zedong, "Zai Yan'an wenyi zuotanhui shangde jianghua," 804–35.

3. Intellectuals were defined as a distinct group in socialist China, referring to the educated population, including artists, writers, and scientists. They were comparable to the bourgeoisie in the West. According to Maoist ideologies, they were to be reeducated by the "mass" to become "cultural workers."

4. Sullivan, *Art and Artists*, 91–112.

5. Spence, *Search for Modern China*, 514–73.

6. Sullivan, *Art and Artists*, 91–155.

7. Chen Zhihua is a professor and architectural historian at the school of architecture at Tsinghua University in Beijing. Chen Zhihua, interview by the author, October 27, 2005, Beijing.

8. See chapter 2 for details on these projects.

9. "Guanyu guoqing gongcheng de huibao tigang" (Draft report on the Anniversary Projects), BMA, archival no. 47-1-70-1, 1.

10. Beijing Jianshe Shishu Bianji Weiyuanhui Bianjibu, *Jianguo yilai de Beijing chengshi jianshe ziliao di 1 juan*, 371–74.

11. BMA, archival no. 131-*dang* 9-16-139.

12. *Chang'anjie*, 78–79.

13. The Design Institute of Industrial Buildings was the predecessor of the later Ministry of Construction Architectural Design Institute, which was the predecessor of the current China Architecture Design and Research Group.

14. "Chang'an Avenue Symposium," group 3, 4th meeting, SAATU, archival no. 64 K032 Z019, 7.

15. "Chang'an Avenue Symposium," group 1, 3rd meeting, SAATU, archival no. 64 K032 Z018, 3.

16. I did not find any document for the guiding principles. These principles were extracted from the discussions of the specialist meetings.

17. Zheng Guangzhong, interview by the author, October 24, 2005, Beijing.

18. BMA, archival no. 2-20-172-1.

19. BMA, archival no. 2-16-371-1.

20. BMA, archival no. 2-16-371-1.

21. BMA, archival no. 2-20-172-1.

22. BMA, archival no. 2-20-172-1.

23. Here I deliberately distinguish between a "meeting" and a "symposium." "Meeting" refers to each separate group discussion, while "symposium" refers to the entire five-day event.

24. Zheng Guangzhong, interview.

25. "Chang'an Avenue Symposium," groups 1 to 3, 1st to 5th meeting, SAATU, archival no. 64 K032 Z016-020.

26. Zheng Guangzhong, interview.

27. Qinghua Daxue Ziliaoshi, *Shoudu Chang'anjie gaijian guihua shuoming, sangao*, July 1964, SAATU, archival no. 64 K032 Z015.

28. Ward (*lifang*) was the basic unit of the ancient Chinese city. A city usually consisted of at least four wards. The city of Tang Chang'an has 108 wards. During the Tang dynasty, a *lifang* was walled and gated for control of urban life. After the Song dynasty, it became more open due to rising commercial activities in Chinese cities. It is not clear what type of *lifang* the Tsinghua schemes were after. In the drawings, these *lifang* units were urban blocks with peripheral buildings and central courtyards, as opposed to a monolithic structure occupying the center of the site.

29. "Chang'an Avenue Symposium," group 3, 1st meeting, SAATU, archival no. 64 K032 Z016, 7.

30. "Chang'an Avenue Symposium," group 1, 2nd meeting, SAATU, archival no. 64 K032 Z017, 13.

31. "Chang'an Avenue Symposium," group 3, 1st meeting, SAATU, archival no. 64 K032 Z016, 2–3.

32. For instance, according to Su Bangjun, a young architect recently graduated from the Tongji University in Shanghai, "[New designs] should consider the present reality of the site. They should not make sharp contrasts with buildings already there. While they should not be too heavy and thus not modernized, they should not be too light and dilute the political atmosphere either. The color scheme should be consistent, with only minor variations." See "Chang'an Avenue Symposium," group 1, 1st meeting, SAATU, archival no. 64 K032 Z016, 11.

33. For instance, Chongqing architect Tang Pu said, "For individual buildings, I think we should think more about modernization. Some look stupidly heavy, with too many decorations. They have great [impact on and] close relationship with modernization ([in terms of] material, design, and construction), [but not good ones]. They do not express modernization enough." "Chang'an Avenue Symposium," group 1, 1st meeting, SAATU, archival no. 64 K032 Z016, 10.

34. See chapter 2 for details of Liang's categorization of architectural styles.

35. "Chang'an Avenue Symposium," group 1, 3rd meeting, SAATU, archival no. 64 K032 Z018, 4–6.

36. For example, see Liang's "Jixian Dulesi Guanyinge shanmen kao" (Research on the Guanyin pavilion and gate at Dule monastery in Ji county), originally published in *Zhongguo Yingzao Xueshe huikan* (Journal of the Institute for Research on Chinese Architecture) 3, no. 2 (1932), in *Liang Sicheng quanji 1* (Complete works of Liang Sicheng, vol. 1), 161–222; "Dunhuang bihua zhong suo-jian de Zhongguo gudai jianzhu" (Images of Ancient Chinese Architecture in Dunhuang Murals), originally published in *Wenwu cankao ziliao* (Reference materials on cultural relics) 2, no. 5 (1951), in *Liang Sicheng quanji 1*, 129–60; "Jianzhu de minzu xingshi" (National forms in architecture), original lecture notes in 1950, in *Liang Sicheng quanji 5* (Complete works of Liang Sicheng, vol. 5), 55–59; "Woguo weida de jianzhu chuantong yu yichan" (Great architectural tradition and heritage of our country), originally published in *Renmin Ribao* (People's Daily), February 19–20, 1951, in *Liang Sicheng quanji 5*, 92–100; "Zhongguo jianzhu de tezheng" (Characteristics of Chinese architecture), originally published in *JZXB* (January 1954), in *Liang Sicheng quanji 5*, 179–84; and "Zuguo de jianzhu" (Architecture of our motherland), originally lecture notes published in 1954 as a monograph, in *Liang Sicheng quanji 5*, 197–234.

37. "Chang'an Avenue Symposium," group 1, 3rd meeting, SAATU, archival no. 64 K032 Z018, 13–14.

38. "Chang'an Avenue Symposium," group 1, 3rd meeting, SAATU, archival no. 64 K032 Z018, 2.

39. "Chang'an Avenue Symposium," group 1, 2nd meeting, SAATU, archival no. 64 K032 Z017, 11; "Discussion Summary," group 2, 2nd meeting, SAATU, archival no. 64 K032 Z017, 4.

40. "Chang'an Avenue Symposium," group 1, 1st meeting, SAATU, archival no. 64 K032 Z016, 5.

41. "Chang'an Avenue Symposium," group 1, 2nd meeting, SAATU, archival no. 64 K032 Z017, 14.

42. "Chang'an Avenue Symposium," group 2, 2nd meeting, SAATU, archival no. 64 K032 Z017, 5; group 3, 2nd meeting, SAATU, archival no. 64 K032 Z017, 1.

43. "Chang'an Avenue Symposium," groups 1 to 3, 1st to 5th meeting, SAATU, archival no. 64 K032 Z016-020.

44. "Chang'an Avenue Symposium," groups 1 to 3, 1st to 5th meeting, SAATU, archival no. 64 K032 Z016-020.

45. "Chang'an Avenue Symposium," group 3, 1st meeting, SAATU, archival no. 64 K032 Z016, 7.

46. "Chang'an Avenue Symposium," group 3, 1st meeting, SAATU, archival no. 64 K032 Z016, 6.

47. "Chang'an Avenue Symposium," group 1, 2nd meeting, SAATU, archival no. 64 K032 Z017, 9.

48. "Chang'an Avenue Symposium," group 2, 1st meeting, SAATU, archival no. 64 K032 Z016, 2.

49. "Chang'an Avenue Symposium," group 2, 1st meeting, SAATU, archival no. 64 K032 Z016, 3.

50. Zheng Guangzhong, interview.

51. "Chang'an Avenue Symposium," group 2, 1st meeting, SAATU, archival no. 64 K032 Z016, 4.

52. "Chang'an Avenue Symposium," group 1, 2nd meeting, SAATU, archival no. 64 K032 Z017, 5; group 2, 2nd meeting, SAATU, archival no. 64 K032 Z017, 11.

53. "Chang'an Avenue Symposium," group 3, 1st meeting, SAATU, archival no. 64 K032 Z016, 5.

54. Liang's original Chinese phrase was *wenzhang nanzuo,* literally, "this article is hard to write." It is a typical Chinese indirect expression, referring to something difficult and troublesome.

55. "Chang'an Avenue Symposium," group 1, 3rd meeting, SAATU, archival no. 64 K032 Z018, 3–4.

56. "Chang'an Avenue Symposium," general summary for 1st meeting, SAATU, archival no. 64 K032 Z016, 10.

57. "Chang'an Avenue Symposium," group 3, 2nd meeting, SAATU, archival no. 64 K032 Z017, 7.

58. "Chang'an Avenue Symposium," groups 1 to 3, 1st to 5th meeting, SAATU, archival no. 64 K032 Z016-020.

59. "Chang'an Avenue Symposium," group 1, 2nd meeting, SAATU, archival no. 64 K032 Z017, 1–2.

60. "Chang'an Avenue Symposium," group 3, 1st meeting, SAATU, archival no. 64 K032 Z016, 4.

61. "Chang'an Avenue Symposium," group 3, 2nd meeting, SAATU, archival no. 64 K032 Z017, 12.

62. "Shoudu Chang'anjie gaijian guihua shuoming, chugao" (Explanation of the Chang'an Avenue Reconstruction Plan, first draft), February 1964, SAATU, archival no. 64 K032 Z013.

63. "Shoudu Chang'anjie gaijian guihua shuoming, chugao," February 1964, SAATU, archival no. 64 K032 Z013.

64. "Shoudu Chang'anjie gaijian guihua shuoming, ergao" (Explanation of the Chang'an Avenue scheme, second draft), April 1964, SAATU, archival no. 64 K032 Z014.

65. "Shoudu Chang'anjie gaijian guihua shuoming, chugao," February 1964, SAATU, archival no. 64 K032 Z013.

66. "Shoudu Chang'anjie gaijian guihua shuoming, sangao," July 1964, SAATU, archival no. 64 K032 Z015, 4–5.

67. "Shoudu Chang'anjie gaijian guihua shuoming, sangao," July 1964, SAATU, archival no. 64 K032 Z015, 9–14.

68. See the section "Symposium Discussions" for details of the criticism about there being too many office buildings.

69. "Shoudu Chang'anjie gaijian guihua shuoming, sangao," July 1964, SAATU, archival no. 64 K032 Z015, 18-20.

70. "Shoudu Chang'anjie gaijian guihua shuoming, sangao," July 1964, SAATU, archival no. 64 K032 Z015, 23–24.

71. "Shoudu Chang'anjie gaijian guihua shuoming, sangao," July 1964, SAATU, archival no. 64 K032 Z015, 25–26.

72. "Shoudu Chang'anjie gaijian guihua shuoming, sangao," July 1964, SAATU, archival no. 64 K032 Z015, 28.

73. "Shoudu Chang'anjie gaijian guihua shuoming, sangao," July 1964, SAATU, archival no. 64 K032 Z015, 37.

74. For details about Imperial Tiananmen Square, see chapter 1.

75. For details about the origins of avant-garde movements in Western arts, see Wood, *The Challenge of the Avant-Garde*; Foster, *The Return of the Real*; Kuspit, *The Cult of the Avant-Garde Artist*; Krauss, *The Originality of the Avant-Garde and Other Modernist Myths*; and Bürger, *Theory of the Avant-Garde*.

76. Having first appeared as marginal practices rejected by institutional art societies, by the 1920s in France such avant-garde movements as impressionism, postimpressionism, fauvism, and cubism were well absorbed into the pantheon of officially sanctioned art. In the German-speaking countries, recently discovered abstraction in form and color provided artists with new modes for psychoemotional expression, such as Viennese symbolism and German expressionism. In Italy, the futurist embrace of speed and machines, though a reaction to the new industrial society, went little beyond the formal aesthetic level. For details, see James Henry Rubin, *Impressionism* (London: Phaidon, 1999); Thomas Parsons and Iain Gale, *Post-Impressionism: The Rise of Modern Art, 1880–1920* (Toronto: NDE Pub., 1999); Sarah Whitfield, *Fauvism* (New York: Thames & Hudson, 1996); Mark Antliff and Patricia Leighten, *Cubism and Culture* (London: Thames & Hudson, 2001); Neil Cox, *Cubism* (London: Phaidon Press Limited, 2000); Colin Rhodes, *Primitivism and Modern Art* (New York: Thames & Hudson, 1994); Charles Harrison, Francis Frascina, and Gill Perry, *Primitivism, Cubism, Abstraction: The Early Twentieth Century* (New Haven: Yale University Press; London: Open University, 1993); Robert Goldwater, *Symbolism* (Boulder, CO: Westview Press, 1998); Shulamith Behr, *Expressionism* (New York: Cambridge University Press, 1999); Max Kozloff, *Cubism/Futurism* (New York: Charter House, 1973); and Richard Humphreys, *Futurism* (New York: Cambridge University Press, 1999).

77. For details about these avant-garde art movements, see Matthew Gale, *Dada and Surrealism* (London: Phaidon Press Limited, 1997); Frank Whitford, *Bauhaus* (London: Thames & Hudson, 2000); George Rickey, *Constructivism: Origin and Evolution*, rev. ed. (New York: George Brazziller, 1995); Richard Andrew, Milena Kalinovska, et al., *Art into Life: Russian Constructivism, 1914–1932* (New York: Rizzoli, 1990); William S. Rubin, *Dada, Surrealism, and Their Heritage* (New York: The Museum of Modern Art, 1968); and Paul Overy, *De Stijl* (London: Thames & Hudson, 1991).

78. Bürger, *Theory of the Avant-Garde*, 35–54.

79. For details about *gandalei*, see chapter 4.

80. Greenberg, "Avant-Garde and Kitsch," *Art and Culture*, 15.

81. See Greenberg, "American-Type Painting," in *Art and Culture*.

82. Kuspit, *Cult of the Avant-Garde Artist*; Bürger, *Theory of the Avant-Garde*, 1–27.

83. Foucault, *Archeology of Knowledge*, 3–17.

84. Krauss, *Originality of the Avant-Garde*, 131–50.

85. Sullivan, *Art and Artists of Twentieth-Century China*, 27–87.

86. Cody, Steinhardt, and Atkin, *Chinese Architecture and the Beaux-Arts*.

87. Foster, *Return of the Real*, ix-xix, 1–33, 127–70.

88. Foucault, *Archeology of Knowledge*, 143.

89. In some cases contemporary history *xiandai* refers to the period between 1919 and 1949, and contemporary history *dangdai* refers to the PRC era (1949–present). For official definitions of *jindai*, *xiandai*, and *dangdai*, see *Xiandai hanyu cidian* (Beijing: Shangwu Yinshuguan, 1986), 592, 1251, 213.

90. Rosalind Krauss, *The Originality of the Avant-Garde*, 170.

91. Lü Peng and Yi Dan, *Zhongguo xiandai yishushi 1979–1989*, 4–6.

Notes to Chapter Four

1. "Mao zhuxi jiniantang jianzhu sheji fang'an de fazhan guocheng" (Design process of the Chairman Mao Memorial schemes), *JZXB* (April 1977): 31.

2. For details, see "Mao zhuxi jiniantang zongti guihua" (The general plan of the Chairman Mao Memorial), *JZXB* (April 1977): 4.

3. Delin Lai, "Searching for a Modern Chinese Monument," 22–55.

4. According to the 1964 Chang'an Avenue planning, no building other than the Monument to the People's Heroes would occupy the center of the square. The southern area of Tiananmen Square adjacent to the Zhengyang Gate was designated a "green square," covered with trees and grass, to contrast with the northern area's vast vacant space for mass assembly. Two monuments had been planned south of the Great Hall and the museum complex, whose specific locations would define an "open," "closed," or "half-closed" Tiananmen Square. For details, see chapter 3.

5. "Mao zhuxi jiniantang zongti guihua," *JZXB* (April 1977): 4–12.

6. "Mao zhuxi jiniantang zongti guihua," *JZXB* (April 1977): 4–12.

7. For details about the principle of "three combinations," see the next section, "Hotels on Chang'an Avenue."

8. "Mao zhuxi jiniantang zongti guihua," *JZXB* (April 1977): 4–12.

9. "Mao zhuxi jiniantang zongti guihua," *JZXB* (April 1977): 4–12.

10. For instance, "the memorial should be practical, firm, solemn, serious, beautiful, and graceful in design; with a Chinese national style, it should be convenient for the people to pay respect to and helpful for the preservation of Mao's remains; the construction and its organization should be wholeheartedly careful." See "Mao zhuxi jiniantang guihua sheji" (The plan and design of the Chairman Mao Memorial), *JZXB* (April 1977): 3.

11. Great effort was also made to achieve a proper image for the Chairman Mao Memorial that took into account the views from Tiananmen Tower, Tiananmen Square, and Chang'an Avenue. See "Mao zhuxi jiniantang zongti guihua," *JZXB* (April 1977): 5–9.

12. "Mao zhuxi jiniantang jianzhu sheji fang'an de fazhan guocheng," *JZXB* (April 1977): 32–33.

13. At this stage, the site was not decided yet. Many designers still envisioned the memorial as a complex either organized around a courtyard or spreading linearly along a passageway. "Mao zhuxi jiniantang jianzhu sheji fang'an de fazhan guocheng," *JZXB* (April 1977): 32–36.

14. "Mao zhuxi jiniantang jianzhu sheji fang'an de fazhan guocheng," *JZXB* (April 1977): 35–37.

15. In total, seven roof types were classified. For each type, multiple schemes were tried out. "Mao zhuxi jiniantang jianzhu sheji fang'an de fazhan guocheng," *JZXB* (April 1977): 39–42.

16. It was widely believed that Mao had scribbled on a piece of paper "With you in charge, I am at ease" and given it to Hua shortly before he died. This was widely propagated during Hua's brief tenure as a major legitimacy for his status as the successor to Mao. See Maurice Meisner, *Mao's China and After*, 427.

17. Yan Zixiang, "Zhongguo jianzhu xuehui di 4 jie daibiao dahui ji xueshu huiyi zongjie fayan" (Summing-up speech at the fourth conference of the Society of Chinese Architecture), *JZXB* (April–May 1966): 21–23.

18. According to Chen Zhihua, professor of architectural history at Tsinghua University, "three combinations" primarily refers to a combination of leaders, specialists, and masses. But Chen also explained that the term varies for different cases and times, especially later in the 1970s when the term "three combinations" simply became a testimony of political correctness while its specific meaning was less important. For instance, it could refer to the combination of old, middle, and younger generations. But when the term was used before 1974, it usually referred to a combination of leaders, specialists, and masses. Chen Zhihua, telephone conversation with the author, March 6, 2006.

19. See all issues of *JZXB* in 1975.

20. Such Westernization tides were abruptly subdued in 1989, as symbolized by the brutal destruction of the statue of the "Goddess of Liberty" on Tiananmen Square during the June Fourth Democratic Movement. After that, the attention of the majority of Chinese were drawn to commercialism and nationalism. See chapter 5 for details on the 1989 event.

21. For details about the concession area in Beijing, see chapter 1.

22. *JZXB* (January 1974): 32.

23. *JZXB* (January 1973): 32.

24. *JZXB* (January 1974): 32.

25. *JZXB* (May 1974): 18.

26. Liu Xinwu, *Wo yanzhong de jianzhu yu huanjing*, 84.

27. Liu Xinwu, *Wo yanzhong de jianzhu yu huanjing*, 87.

28. Hitchcock and Johnson, *International Style*, 20.

29. *JZXB* (January 1974): 33.

30. *JZXB* (January 1974): 33.

31. Zhang Fuhe, *Beijing jindai jianzhushi*, 344–45.

32. The following names basically refer to the same design institution, which had different names during different periods: the Ministry of Architectural Industry Design Institute in the 1950s and 1960s, the Ministry of Construction Architectural Design Institute in the 1980s and 1990s, and the China Architecture Design and Research Group after 2000.

33. According to Beijingshi Guihua Weiyuanhui et al., *Chang'anjie*, published in 2004, renovation design was by the Beijing Architectural Design Institute, led by Zhang Bo, Cheng Delan, and Tian Wanxin. Chinese architecture scholar Lenore Hietkamp told me during a conversation that NBBJ was responsible for the design of part of the revitalization.

34. *Chang'anjie*, 43, 87, 114–15.

35. Spence, *Search for Modern China*, 653–59.

36. See the January to April 1978 issues of *JZXB*.

37. *JZXB* (January 1978): 1–3.

38. *JZXB* (February 1978): 10–12.

39. *JZXB* (February 1978): 13–14; *JZXB* (April 1978): 33–35.

40. *JZXB* (January 1978): 1.

41. *JZXB* (January 1979): 26–30, 56, 59.

42. Hu Dunchang, "Railway Station and Torch: On the Ideology of Architectural Art," *JZXB* (March 1979): 21–22, 48.

43. *JZXB* (February 1979): 38.

44. Bai Zuomin, "The Application of Visual Analysis in Architectural Creation," *JZXB* (March 1979): 9–15, 52.

45. Hou Youbin, "Architecture: The Unity of Opposites of Space and Volume," *JZXB* (March 1979): 16–20.

46. *JZXB* (October 1983): 70–74.

47. *JZXB* (June 1982): 62–67.

48. Feng Zhongping, "Environment, Space, and the New Exploration of Architectural Style," *JZXB* (April 1979): 8–16.

49. Zheng Guangfu, "To Pursue Forms but Oppose Formalism," *JZXB* (July 1982): 38–41.

50. Wang Tianxi, "Architectural Form and Its Status in Architectural Creation," *JZXB* (May 1983): 50–57.

51. *JZXB* (May 1984): 45–49, 50–56.

52. *JZXB* (April 1985): 2–21, 22–26.

53. Bu Zhengwei, "We Should All Have Our Own: The General Trend of Liberation of Individuality in Architecture," *JZXB* (April 1985): 27–31.

54. "Notes of the Symposium on the Designs of Huadu and Jianguo Hotels in Beijing," *JZXB* (September 1982): 21–23.

55. Liu Li, "Impressions and Inspirations," *JZXB* (September 1982): 35–37.

56. *JZXB* (September 1982): 21–23.

57. *JZXB* (March 1983): 57–79; *JZXB* (April 1983): 59–71.

58. *JZXB* (July 1988): 2–9.

59. *JZXB* (July 1988): 9.

60. *JZXB* (July 1988): 9.

61. Yang Yun, "Thoughts after the New Trends in Western Modern Architectural Thinking," *JZXB* (January 1980): 26–34.

62. Mei Chen (Chen Zhihua), "Reading Notes: Advancing and Retreating," *JZXB* (September 1984), 58–62. See also *JZXB* (February 1989): 33–38; *JZXB* (November 1989): 47–50.

63. Qu Zhenliang, "Again on Modern Architecture and National Form," *JZXB* (March 1987): 22–25.

64. Zhang Mingyu, "On Issues of 'National Form' and Others as Inspired by the Evaluations on the National Olympic Gymnasium by Kenzo Tange," *JZXB* (January 1982): 13–15.

65. *JZXB* (October 1987): 17–23.

66. Yang Yun, *JZXB* (January 1980): 26–34.

67. Xu Shangzhi, "On Issues about Architectural Modernization and Architectural Creation of Our Country," *JZXB* (September 1984): 10–12, 19.

68. Luo Xiaowei, "Using Semiotic Analysis to 'Read' Modern African Cities," *JZXB* (May 1983): 44–49.

69. Zhou Puyi, "Craze for 'Contextualism' Appeared in Chinese Architecture," *JZXB* (February 1989): 33–38.

70. Zhang Qinnan, "An Argument for 'Craze for Contextualism,'" *JZXB* (June 1989): 28–29.

71. These symbols were acclaimed as an "expression of the character and the spirit of the time." See Zou Denong, *Zhongguo xiandai jianzhushi*, 569.

Notes to Chapter Five

1. Meisner, *Mao's China and After*, 509–10.

2. Qiu Yongsheng, et al., "Heping cheli, wuren siwang" (Peaceful evacuation, nobody killed), etc., *Renmin ribao* (People's Daily), June 5, 1989; June 9, 1989; June 19, 1989.

3. Meisner, *Mao's China and After*, 509–10.

4. The spring 1989 event in Beijing was referred to in different terms by different political interests. While the Chinese Communist Party called it "political upheaval and anti-revolutionary riot," the Western media called it "the Tiananmen Massacre." I adopt the relatively neutral term "June Fourth Democratic Movement," which was widely used by participators of the events. Most Chinese today simply refer to the event as "June Fourth" (Liusi).

5. Beijing Jianshe Shishu Bianji Weiyuanhui Bianjibu, *Chengshi guihua*, 313; see also Wu Liangyong, *Rehabilitating the Old City of Beijing*, 36.

6. Broudehoux, *Making and Selling of Post-Mao Beijing*, 118–21.

7. Master plan of Beijing city, December 1982, and Master plan of Beijing city (1991–2010), December 1992, in Beijing Jianshe Shishu Bianji Weiyuanhui Bianjibu, *Chengshi guihua*, 270–74, 312–14.

8. Fang Xiangming, "Tell You a True Oriental Plaza," *Women of China* (June 2003); see http://www.rwabc.com/diqurenwu/rw_detail.asp?people_id=468&id=3570; accessed January 9, 2012.

9. Fang, "Tell You a True Oriental Plaza."

10. Broudehoux, *Making and Selling of Post-Mao Beijing*, 118.

11. Broudehoux, *Making and Selling of Post-Mao Beijing*, 123.

12. "Report from the 8th Conference of the National Chinese Political Consultant Committee on Urban and Suburban Construction," Report no. 101, August 17, 1995.

13. Broudehoux, *Making and Selling of Post-Mao Beijing*, 123.

14. Fang, "Tell You a True Oriental Plaza."

15. "Redline" (*hongxian*) is the Chinese urban planning term for the building set-back line.

16. In this book, "standard" or "official" explanation refers to the general introductions of buildings rather than to critical or scholarly discussions. It includes not only introductions for commercial and tourist use but also the self-promoting materials prepared by the designers or sponsors.

17. Although Hong Kong returned to China in 1997, it is still considered an "overseas" territory by the Chinese because its social system is different from that of the mainland.

18. Zhoukoudian is an 18,000-year-old archaeological site near Beijing where the fossil skull of "Beijing Man" was discovered in the early twentieth century.

19. Text from the explanation plaque at the site.

20. Text from the stele on the site.

21. Text from the stele on the site.

22. The texts from the explanation plaque at the site say so. At the time of my visit in 2005, the statues were not there yet.

23. See Sun Xingyan, *Zhouyi jijie* (Collection of annotations to the Zhou dynasty *Book of Changes*) (Shanghai: Shanghai Shudian Chubanshe, 1993), 11, 46.

24. Text from the stele inside Century Hall.

25. The prices given are from 2005.

26. Diane Ghirardo, *Architecture after Modernism* (New York: Thames & Hudson, 1996), 43–62.

27. Beijingshi Guihua Weiyuanhui et al., *Chang'anjie*, 128.

28. *Chang'anjie*, 126.

29. Beijingshi Guihua Weiyuanhui and Beijing Chengshi Guihua Xuehui, *Beijing shida jianzhu sheji*, 116.

30. For instance, the John Fitzgerald Kennedy Library in Boston, Massachusetts, completed in 1979; the Morton H. Meyerson Symphony Center in Dallas, Texas, of 1989; the Warner Building in Washington, DC, of 1993; and the Rock-and-Roll Hall of Fame and Museum, Cleveland, Ohio, of 1995.

31. See Lin Yü-sheng, *Crisis of Chinese Consciousness*.

32. The adjective "grand" was added in the 1980s.

33. Niu Fangli and Huo Jiguang, "Remin dahuitang ce dakeng youwang tianping, guojia da juyuan gongcheng choucuo jianshe" (The big pit next to the Great Hall is hopefully to be filled as the construction of the National Grand Theatre project is being prepared), in *Jianzhu bao* (Architectural News) 635, February 17, 1998.

34. During a 2003 interview by the author in Beijing, Shi Qing, a civil engineering professor at Tsinghua University and professor Li Daozeng's wife, said, "It was a political problem. The design (of the National Theatre) by Mr. Li passed the inspection and censorship of all leaders of the nation, including Chairman Mao and Premier Zhou Enlai. What's more, many suggestions from Premier Zhou were absorbed into the design. It was more a question about the political situation, or more specifically, economic conditions, than a question of artistic solution."

35. See chapter 3 for details.

36. "Chang'anjie guihua shencha huiyi, di 1, 2, 3, 4, 5 ci gezu taolun jiyao" (Discussion summary of the Chang'an Avenue planning evaluation symposium, groups 1 to 3, 1st to 5th meeting), April 1964, SAATU, archival no. 64 K032 Z016-020.

37. Niu and Hou.

38. They were built in the 1920s. See Zhang Fuhe, *Beijing jindai jianzhushi*, 253–57.

39. "Beijing chengshi guihua guanli ju, guanyu zai Chang'anjie liangce jianfang wenti de qingshi baogao" (Beijing Municipal Planning Bureau, on the construction of buildings along Chang'an Avenue), September 28, 1959, BMA, archival no. 131-1-*dang* 10–29 (79).

40. Niu and Hou.

41. Zheng Ping, "Kua shiji de gongcheng: Zhongguo guojia da juyuan gongcheng luochui qianhou" (Project to bridge centuries—before and after the decision to construct the Chinese National Grand Theatre), in *Zhonghua jinxiu* (China the Beautiful) 47 (December 1998), 28–35.

42. The scale of the 1958 National Theatre project was according to the reports on the Anniversary Projects in 1959. See "Guanyu guoqing gongcheng de huibao tigang" (Draft report about the Anniversary Projects), February 23, 1959, BMA, archival no. 47-1-70–1.

43. Niu and Hou.

44. The English translations of these committees generally follow Zhongguo Guojia Dajüyuan Jianzhu Sheji Guoji Jingsai Fang'anji Bianweihui, *Zhongguo Guojia Dajüyuan Jianzhu Sheji Guoji Jingsai fang'anji*, 3.

45. Zhongguo Guojia Dajüyuan Jianzhu Sheji Guoji Jingsai Fang'anji Bianweihui, *Zhongguo Guojia Dajüyuan Jianzhu Sheji Guoji Jingsai fang'anji*, 4, 9.

46. Niu and Hou.

47. Zhongguo Guojia Dajüyuan Jianzhu Sheji Guoji Jingsai Fang'anji Bianweihui, *Zhongguo Guojia Dajüyuan Jianzhu Sheji Guoji Jingsai fang'anji*, 4.

48. Zhongguo Guojia Dajüyuan Jianzhu Sheji Guoji Jingsai Fang'anji Bianweihui, *Zhongguo Guojia Dajüyuan Jianzhu Sheji Guoji Jingsai fang'anji*, 10–11.

49. Zhongguo Guojia Dajüyuan Jianzhu Sheji Guoji Jingsai Fang'anji Bianweihui, *Zhongguo Guojia Dajüyuan Jianzhu Sheji Guoji Jingsai fang'anji*, 4.

50. Zheng Ping, in *Zhonghua jinxiu* (China the Beautiful) 47 (December 1998), 28–35.

51. Arthur Erickson, "My Architectural Career, Works, and Philosophy" (lecture, Department of Architecture, College of Architecture and Urban Planning, University of Washington, Seattle, WA, April 12, 2003). Erickson, one of the foreign jury members, expressed his appreciation for Isozaki's entry in a lecture at the University of Washington in 2003.

52. Zhongguo Guojia Dajüyuan Jianzhu Sheji Guoji Jingsai Fang'anji Bianweihui, *Zhongguo Guojia Dajüyuan Jianzhu Sheji Guoji Jingsai fang'anji*, 4.

53. Zhongguo Guojia Dajüyuan Jianzhu Sheji Guoji Jingsai Fang'anji Bianweihui, *Zhongguo Guojia Dajüyuan Jianzhu Sheji Guoji Jingsai fang'anji*, 4–5, 295–323.

54. Arthur Erickson, lecture, University of Washington, April 12, 2003.

55. Zhongguo Guojia Dajüyuan Jianzhu Sheji Guoji Jingsai Fang'anji Bianweihui, *Zhongguo Guojia Dajüyuan Jianzhu Sheji Guoji Jingsai fang'anji*, 4–5.

56. Zhongguo Guojia Dajüyuan Jianzhu Sheji Guoji Jingsai Fang'anji Bianweihui, *Zhongguo Guojia Dajüyuan Jianzhu Sheji Guoji Jingsai fang'anji*, 5.

57. Zhongguo Guojia Dajüyuan Jianzhu Sheji Guoji Jingsai Fang'anji Bianweihui, *Zhongguo Guojia Dajüyuan Jianzhu Sheji Guoji Jingsai fang'anji*, 29.

58. Original English text from the design program; see Zhongguo Guojia Dajüyuan Jianzhu Sheji Guoji Jingsai Fang'anji Bianweihui, *Zhongguo Guojia Dajüyuan Jianzhu Sheji Guoji Jingsai fang'anji*, 15.

59. For example, scheme 202 by Carlos Ott and Associates, scheme 203 by Wang and Ouyang (Hong Kong), and scheme 404 by Wilhelm Holzbauer (Austria).

60. For example, scheme 107 by the Shanghai Modern Architectural Design Company, and scheme 601 by Design Group (Italy).

61. For example, scheme 401 by Takenaka Corporation (Japan).

62. For example, scheme 102 by Architecture Studio (France).

63. For example, scheme 506 by Central Engineering and Research Institute for Non-Ferrous Metallurgical Industries, and scheme 208 by Zhejiang Building Design and Research Institute.

64. According to its scheme introduction, its red walls were inspired by traditional Chinese architecture, and the golden, black, and red decorations on its three protruding boxes—representing gates—symbolized the golden nails on the doors of the gates in Forbidden City. Zhongguo Guojia Dajüyuan Jianzhu Sheji Guoji Jingsai Fang'anji Bianweihui, *Zhongguo Guojia Dajüyuan Jianzhu Sheji Guoji Jingsai fang'anji*, 142.

65. Scheme 304 by Dennis Lau and NG Chun Man, Architects and Engineers (Hong Kong).

66. Scheme 305 by China Architectural Science Research Institute.

67. Scheme 503 by Shenzhen University, College of Architecture and Civil Engineering.

68. Scheme 506 by Central Engineering and Research Institute for Non-Ferrous Metallurgical Industries.

69. Robert Venturi, *Complexity and Contradiction of Architecture* (New York: Museum of Modern Art, 1977).

70. Christian Norberg-Schulz, *Genius Loci: Toward a Phenomenology of Architecture* (New York: Rizzoli, 1984).

71. Hans Ibelings, *Super-Modernism: Architecture in the Age of Globalization* (Rotterdam: Nai Publishers, 1998), 55–62.

72. Ibelings, *Super-Modernism*, 57.

73. Vittorio Savi and Joseph Ma Montaner, *Less is More: Minimalism in Architecture and the Other Arts* (Barcelona: Actar, 1996), in Ibelings, *Super-Modernism*, 57–62.

74. Ibelings, *Super-Modernism*, 62.

75. I participated in both rounds of the competition of the National Grand Theatre in 1998–99 as one of the designers for the Ministry Institute's scheme. I also worked with Carlos Ott on the collaborated schemes during the first two stages of "modification." Except for the public exhibition of the schemes from the first round of the competition, our knowledge of other participants' successive design ideas was mainly gained through connections with former classmates and friends who were working on the same competition for other institutes. Everyone in the architectural circle was talking about the National Grand Theatre then, during meetings as well as in casual chats.

76. "Si dashi 'zhi' shang tanbing" (Interviews with Four Masters), *Beijing qingnian bao* (Beijing Youth Daily), April 24, 1998.

77. Zhongguo Guojia Dajüyuan Jianzhu Sheji Guoji Jingsai Fang'anji Bianweihui, *Zhongguo Guojia Dajüyuan Jianzhu Sheji Guoji Jingsai fang'anji*, 54.

78. Most of Andreu's projects have been airports. For more than thirty years, he has designed and built dozens of airports all over the world, including the Charles de Gaulle Airport in France (1967–99), the Doha International Airport in Qatar (1976), the Manila Ninoy Acquino International Airport in the Philippines (1981), the Cairo International Airport in Egypt (1986), the Kansai International Airport in Japan (1994), and the Shanghai Pudong International Airport in China (1999).

79. "La porta del Tunnel: Cailais Transmanche Terminal," *l'Arca* 104 (May 1996): 67.

80. Ibelings, *Super-Modernism*, 80.

81. Ibelings, *Super-Modernism*, 79–80.

82. "Opaco trasparente: Abu Dhabi New Terminal," *l'Arca* 125 (April 1998): 37.

83. Paul Andreu, "Borders and Borderers," *Architectural Design* 69 (May–August 1999): 57.

84. Andreu, "Borders and Borderers," 57.

85. Filippo Beltrami Gadola, "Introduction," in Andreu, *Paul Andreu*, 9–13.

86. Yu, "Limit, Passage, and Chinese National Theatre: Interview with Paul Andreu," in *Interior Architecture of China* 15, no. 3 (March 2004): 129–31.

87. Andreu, *National Grand Theatre*, 27–34.

88. According to an article by Paul Andreu in *South China Morning Post*, the true cost of the National Grand Theatre was ¥3 billion. See Andreu, *National Grand Theatre*, 133.

89. See Xiao Mo, *Shiji zhi dan* (The egg of the century), http://www.oldbeijing.net/Article_Special.asp?SpecialID=50, article 5, posted on August 19, 2005; accessed November 22, 2005.

90. Xiao Mo, *Shiji zhi dan*, article 14, posted on August 8, 2005; accessed November 22, 2005, and article 46, posted on August 18, 2005; accessed November 22, 2005.

91. Xiao Mo, *Shiji zhi dan*, article 4, posted on August 3, 2005; accessed November 22, 2005.

92. Dongfang Xinwen, "Renda daibiao cheng guojia dajuyuan sheji fangan hua'erbushi" (Congress Representatives Commented that the Design Scheme for the National Grand Theatre was Pretty but not Practical), http://www.news.eastday.com, posted on March 14, 2000; accessed December 9, 2005.

93. Bandao Chenbao, "Mingri zhongguo guojia dajuyuan jiang zhengshi donggong" (Construction of National Grand Theater of China will Officially Begin Tomorrow), http://www.sina.com.cn, posted on March 31, 2000; accessed December 9, 2005.

94. CCTV, "Wenhuabu buzhang jiu jianzao guojia dajuyuan yishi shou jizhe caifang" (Cultural Minister Interviewed by Reporters on the Construction of the National Grand Theater), http://www.sina.com.cn, posted on March 31, 2000; accessed December 9, 2005.

95. Xiao Mo, *Shiji zhi dan*, article 7, posted on August 3, 2005; accessed November 22, 2005.

96. Xiao Mo, *Shiji zhi dan*, article 10, posted on August 7, 2005; accessed November 22, 2005.

97. Changjiang Ribao, "He Zuoxiu cheng guojia dajuyuan sheji zhong cunzai sida quexian" (He Zuoxiu Commented There Were Four Major Defects in the Design of the National Grand Theater), http://www.sina.com.cn, July 14, 2007; accessed December 9, 2005.

98. Xiao Mo, *Shiji zhi dan*, article 41, posted on August 18, 2005; accessed November 22, 2005.

99. Yangcheng Wanbao, "Qingting butong shengyin, guojia dajuyuan zhanting shigong" (Construction of the National Grand Theater Paused to Listen to Different Voices), http://www.sina.com.cn, posted on July 11, 2000; accessed December 9, 2005.

100. Jiangnan Shibao, "Guojia dajuyuan gongcheng yiyu liuyue yiri qiaoran donggong" (Construction of the National Grand Theater Resumed Quietly on June 1), http://www.sina.com.cn, posted on June 4, 2001; accessed on December 9, 2005.

101. Xiao Mo, *Shiji zhi dan*, articles 41, 42, and 44, all posted on August 18, 2005; accessed November 22, 2005.

102. Xiao Mo, *Shiji zhi dan*, article 45, posted on August 18, 2005; accessed November 22, 2005.

103. Xiao Mo, *Shiji zhi dan*, article 48, posted on August 18, 2005; accessed November 22, 2005.

104. Xiao Mo, *Shiji zhi dan*, article 16, translation by author, posted on August 9, 2005; accessed November 22, 2005.

105. Xiao Mo, *Shiji zhi dan*, article 22, translation by author, posted on August 11, 2005; accessed November 22, 2005.

106. Paul Andreu, interview by the author, September 10, 2003, Beijing.

107. Xiao Mo, *Shiji zhi dan*, article 21, posted on August 11, 2005; accessed November 22, 2005.

Notes to Chapter Six

1. Steinhardt, *Chinese Imperial City Planning*, 154–60.

2. Fu Xinian, *Zhongguo gudai chengshi guihua jianzhuqun buju ji jianzhu sheji fangfa yanjiu*, vol. 1, 10–13.

3. In 1368 the Ming dynasty founded its capital in Nanjing (South Capital) and renamed the former Yuan capital Beiping (North Pacification). In 1403 the Yongle emperor of Ming moved the capital to Beiping and renamed it Beijing (North Capital). For details, see the section "Chang'an Avenue during the Imperial Periods" in chapter 1.

4. Pan Guxi, *Zhongguo gudai jianzhushi di 4 juan: Yuan Ming jianzhu*, 29–32, 104–06.

5. Wang Qiheng, *Fengshui lilun yanjiu*, 26–32.

6. From "Kaogongji: Jiangren" (Record of Craftsmanship), in *Zhouli* (Rituals of Zhou), see Zheng Xuan, *Zhouli zhengzhu* (Annotations of *Rituals of Zhou*) (Taiwan: Zhonghua Shuju, 1965), vol. 41, 14–15.

7. Steinhardt, *Chinese Imperial City Planning*, 72–144.

8. The "Old City" of Beijing in this book refers to the areas previously inside the walls of the Inner City and Outer City during the Ming and Qing dynasties.

9. Wang Jun, *Chengji*, 82.

10. Beijing Jianshe Shishu Bianji Weiyuanhui Bianjibu, *Chengshi guihua*, 147–69.

11. Wang Jun, *Chengji*, 86.

12. For a brief introduction to the life and career of Liang and Cheng, see Shuishan Yu, "Redefining the Axis of Beijing," 580–84. See also Fairbank, *Liang and Lin*; Lin Zhu, *Jianzhushi Liang Sicheng*; Cody, Steinhardt, and Atkin, *Chinese Architecture and the Beaux-Arts*, 56–66.

13. Liang Sicheng, "Zhi Nie Rongzhen tongzhi xin" (Letter to Comrade Nie Rongzhen), *Liang Sicheng wenji 4*, 368.

14. Liang Sicheng and Chen Zhanxiang, "Guanyu Zhongyang Renmin Zhengfu xingzheng zhongxinqu weizhi de jianyi."

15. Lowenthal, *Past Is a Foreign Country*, 4–7.

16. Madeleine Dong, *Republican Beijing*, 304.

17. For a detailed analysis of the Liang-Chen Scheme and its failure, see Yu, "Redefining the Axis of Beijing."

18. Beijing Jianshe Shishu Bianji Weiyuanhui Bianjibu, *Chengshi guihua*, 163.

19. Zhu Zhaoxue and Zhao Dongri, "Dui shoudu jianshe jihua de yijian," 4.

20. Wang Jun, *Chengji*, 234–35.

21. Zhu Zhaoxue and Zhao Dongri, "Dui shoudu jianshe jihua de yijian," 3–5.

22. For more details about the Zhu-Zhao Scheme, see Yu, "Redefining the Axis of Beijing," 589–92.

23. For details on the successive Beijing city master plans and the development of Chang'an Avenue in the 1950s, see Beijing Jianshe Shishu Bianji Weiyuanhui Bianjibu, *Chengshi guihua*, 1–53; and Wang Ruizhi, *Liang Chen fang'an yu Beijing*, 75–112.

24. Zhu Zhaoxue and Zhao Dongri, "Dui shoudu jianshe jihua de yijian," 1.

25. Liang Sicheng and Chen Zhanxiang, "Guanyu Zhongyang Renmin Zhengfu xingzheng zhongxinqu weizhi de jianyi," 4–11.

26. Beipingshi Gongwu Ju, *Beipingshi dushi jihua sheji ziliao di yi ji*, 1947, BMA, archival no. Jia-3.

27. Beipingshi Gongwu Ju, *Beipingshi dushi jihua sheji ziliao di yi ji*, 39–52, 60–61.

28. Beipingshi Gongwu Ju,, *Beipingshi dushi jihua sheji ziliao di yi ji*, ii.

29. Beipingshi Gongwu Ju,, *Beipingshi dushi jihua sheji ziliao di yi ji*, 2.

30. Wang Jun, *Chengji*, 82.

31. Beijing Jianshe Shishu Bianji Weiyuanhui Bianjibu, *Chengshi guihua*, 216, 227.

32. The north gate of the Imperial City Di'anmen was demolished in 1954–55; the south gate of the Imperial City Zhonghuamen (Ming Damingmen; Qing Daqingmen) was demolished in 1959; the south gate of the Outer City Yongdingmen was demolished at the end of the 1950s. See Wang Jun, *Chengji*, 314–16.

33. Yue Jiazao (1868–1944) was a revolutionary-turned-late-Qing-Confucian-scholar, Republican official, and self-trained architectural historian.

34. Yue Jiazao, *Zhongguo jianzhu shi*, 152.

35. See Liang Sicheng, "Tang Dynasty Buddhist Temples and Palaces as We Know Today," originally published in *Zhongguo Yingzao Xueshe Huikan* (Journal of the Institute for Research on Chinese Architecture) 3, no. 1, 1932, in *Complete Works of Liang Sicheng*, vol. 1, 135.

36. For Liang's Beaux-Arts education in the United States, see Cody, Steinhardt, and Atkin, *Chinese Architecture and the Beaux-Arts*, 56–66. For an introduction to the Beaux-Arts influence on modern Chinese architecture, see Cody, Steinhardt, and Atkin, *Chinese Architecture and the Beaux-Arts*.

37. Chen Gan is one generation younger than Liang Sicheng and Chen Zhanxiang. He graduated from the architecture department at Central University in Nanjing in the 1940s. See Chen Gan, *Jinghua dasi lu*, 215–59.

38. Chen Gan, *Jinghua daisi lu*, 23–33.

39. Chen Gan, *Jinghua daisi lu*, 72.

40. The material available does not specify who made these decisions. See Beijing Jianshe Shishu Bianji Weiyuanhui Bianjibu, *Chengshi guihua*, 1–37, 147–233.

41. The Mao era here includes the brief rule of Hua Guofeng, who was the successor chosen by Mao and the leader of China in 1976–78.

42. Beijing Jianshe Shishu Bianji Weiyuanhui Bianjibu, *Chengshi guihua*, 150–52.

43. Beijing Jianshe Shishu Bianji Weiyuanhui Bianjibu, *Chengshi guihua*, 214, 234.

44. Beijing Jianshe Shishu Bianji Weiyuanhui Bianjibu, *Chengshi guihua*, 215–16.

45. The other two were the thoroughfare connecting Guanqu Gate and Guang'an Gate, and the Qiansanmen Street thoroughfare following the southern wall of the Inner City. Beijing Jianshe Shishu Bianji Weiyuanhui Bianjibu, *Chengshi guihua*, 208.

46. Beijing Jianshe Shishu Bianji Weiyuanhui Bianjibu, *Chengshi guihua*, 227.

47. Beijing Jianshe Shishu Bianji Weiyuanhui Bianjibu, *Chengshi guihua*, 237.

48. Beijing Jianshe Shishu Bianji Weiyuanhui Bianjibu, *Chengshi guihua*, 247–51.

49. Beijing Jianshe Shishu Bianji Weiyuanhui Bianjibu, *Chengshi guihua*, 391.

50. Beijing Jianshe Shishu Bianji Weiyuanhui Bianjibu, *Chengshi guihua*, 257–60.

51. Beijing Jianshe Shishu Bianji Weiyuanhui Bianjibu, *Chengshi guihua*, 270–71.

52. Beijing Jianshe Shishu Bianji Weiyuanhui Bianjibu, *Chengshi guihua*, 302–9.

53. Beijing Jianshe Shishu Bianji Weiyuanhui Bianjibu, *Chengshi guihua*, 313.

54. Zhang Jinggan, *Beijing guihua jianshe wushi nian*, 52–56.

55. Gao Wei, *Manhua Beijing*, 108.

56. Beijing Daxue Lishixi Beijing Shi Bianxiezu, *Beijing shi*, 226.

57. Sun Dazhang, *Zhongguo gudai jianzhushi di 5 juan: Qingdai jianzhu*, 46.

58. Chinese officials during the imperial era were divided into nine ranks, called nine *pin*. The first *pin* was the highest, and the ninth *pin* the lowest. Initiated in the third century, the nine-*pin* system in official ranking matured during the Sui-Tang era (581–906) and functioned until the end of the Qing dynasty in 1911.

59. Wang Yushi, *Tiananmen*, 15.

60. Wang Yushi, *Tiananmen*, 27–29.

61. Stories tell of some modern reformers during the late Qing period who were influenced by

Western thought but still couldn't help kneeling down in front of the Hall of Supreme Harmony (Taihe Hall) after walking the imperial north-south axis. See Wang Yushi, *Tiananmen*, 12.

62. Mao Zedong, "On the Draft Constitution of the People's Republic of China," in *Selected Works of Mao Zedong vol. 5*, 129.

63. Wang Yushi, *Tiananmen*, 37–60.

64. *Emperor Kangxi's Inspection Tour to the South*, Wang Hui and others, episode twelve of a hand scroll, color on silk, 67.8 x 2612.5 cm, 30–33rd Year of the Reign of Kangxi (1691–94), Qing dynasty, Beijing Palace Museum.

65. The modern word for parade or procession "youxing" and the traditional word for practicing ritual "xingli" share the same character "xing," which means walking. This might suggest that walking along an axial route used to be the major format of early Chinese ritual performance. The earliest appearance of the word "xingli" is in the "Quli" chapter of the Western Han dynasty (206 BCE–9 CE) collection and annotation of Zhou dynasty (11th century BCE–256 BCE) Confucian works *The Book of Ritual* (Liji). See Wang Meng'ou, *Liji Xuanzhu*, 26. For a detailed Qing dynasty description of imperial "xingli," see *Qingchao tongdian*. For original and extended meanings of the word "xing," see Luo Zhufeng, ed., *Hanyu dacidian* (Chinese dictionary) (Shanghai: Hanyu Dacidian Chubanshe, 2001), 884–85, 922.

66. Foucault, *Discipline and Punish*, 195–228.

67. Beijing Jianshe Shishu Bianji Weiyuanhui Bianjibu, *Chengshi guihua*, 313.

68. Beijing Jianshe Shishu Bianji Weiyuanhui Bianjibu, *Chengshi guihua*, 313.

69. Beijing Jianshe Shishu Bianji Weiyuanhui Bianjibu, *Chengshi guihua*, 218.

70. See Broudehoux, *Making and Selling of Post-Mao Beijing*.

71. Beijing Jianshe Shishu Bianji Weiyuanhui Bianjibu, *Chengshi guihua*, 313.

72. "Beijing City Master Plan (2004–20), January 2005," in *Beijing City Planning and Construction Review* 101, no. 2 (March 2005), 12.

73. "Beijing City Master Plan," *Beijing City Planning and Construction Review* 101, 17–18.

74. "Beijing City Master Plan," *Beijing City Planning and Construction Review* 101, 49.

75. Beijingshi Guihua Sheji Yanjiuyuan, *Qianxin xihui jingcheng lantu*, 77.

76. Beijingshi Guihua Weiyuanhui and Beijing Shuijingshi Shuzi Chuanmei, *2008 Beijing aolinpike gongyuan ji Wukesong wenhua tiyu zhongxin guihua sheji fang'an zhengji*.

Notes to Conclusion

1. Vale, *Architecture, Power, and National Identity*, 20.

2. Evenson, *Paris*, 8–26.

3. Evenson, *Paris*, 38.

4. Evenson, *Paris*, 76–122, 139–41.

5. Evenson, *Paris*, 52–53, 184–92.

6. George Pompidou, "Le président de la République définit ses conceptions dans les domaines de l'art et de l'architecture," *Le Monde*, October 17, 1972. In Evenson, *Paris*, 190–91.

7. Vale, *Architecture, Power, and National Identity*, 30–32.

8. Diane Favro, "Rome: The Street Triumphant: The Urban Impact of Roman Triumphal Parades," in Celik, Favro, and Ingersoll, *Streets*, 151–64.

9. Spiro Kostof, "The Emperor and the Duce: The Planning of Piazzale Augusto Imperatore in Rome," in Millon and Nochlin, *Art and Architecture in the Service of Politics*, 270–325.

10. Translated by Zhao Hengyuan and Paul Woods. See Zhao Hengyuan, *Mao's Poems* (Tianjin: Tianjin Renmin Chubabshe, 1993), 69.

11. Kostof, "The Emperor and the Duce," 287.

12. Kostof, "The Emperor and the Duce," 322.

13. Vale, *Architecture, Power, and National Identity*, 39–41.

14. Eleni Bastea, "Athens: Etching Images on the Street: Planning and National Aspirations," in Celik, Favro, and Ingersoll, *Streets*, 111–24.

15. Pan Guxi, *Zhongguo jianzhushi*, 299.

16. Pan Guxi, *Zhongguo jianzhushi*, 300.

17. *International Herald Leader* (Guoji xianqu daobao), July 11, 2005.

Glossary

The following is a glossary of the most important terms used in the text, giving pinyin romanization, standard Chinese, and the English translation, and explanations when necessary. Please note that personal names are not included, nor are most cities or general historical terms. Except for the "Chang'an Avenue" terms, all terms are listed alphabetically.

Chang'an Avenue (Chang'an Jie) 长安街   The entire east-west thoroughfare of Beijing, including both Chang'an Avenue proper and its east and west extensions. Today this long thoroughfare is referred to as the "Hundred-Li Long Avenue" 百里长街.   Chang'an Avenue is not a static thoroughfare created at one time. Instead, it has grown and experienced many changes over time, and the term "Chang'an Avenue" has been used to refer to different sections of this street in different historical periods. The following naming system is used throughout this book in order to create clear definitions and avoid confusion. The ordering of the terms generally follows the historical development of the avenue, in such a way that the definitions of later terms are built on earlier ones.

historic East Chang'an Avenue (Lishi Dong Chang'an Jie) 历史东长安街 Between Dongdan and Nanheyan Streets. This was the easternmost section of Chang'an Avenue before 1949.

historic West Chang'an Avenue (Lishi Xi Chang'an Jie) 历史西长安街   Between Xidan and Fuyou Streets. The latter forms the western boundary of Zhongnanhai. This was the westernmost section of Chang'an Avenue before 1949.

historic Chang'an Avenue (Lishi Chang'an Jie) 历史长安街   From Xidan to Dongdan Streets (about 3,765 meters in length), including West Chang'an Street and East Chang'an Street during the Ming and Qing dynasties. These are the oldest sections of Chang'an Avenue. During the Republican era, historic Chang'an Avenue included (from west to east) West Chang'an Street, Fuqian Street, East Three-Arch Gate Street (Dongsanzuomen Dajie), and East Chang'an Street. During the PRC era, Fuqian Street merged into West Chang'an Street, and East Three-Arch Gate

Street merged into East Chang'an Street. In a contemporary Beijing map, only historic Chang'an Avenue is specifically labeled as "Chang'an Jie."

Chang'an Avenue proper (Chuantong Chang'an Jie) 传统长安街 From Fuxing Gate to Jianguo Gate (about 6,672 meters in length). This is the stretch of Chang'an Avenue inside the former Inner City walls of Beijing, including Inner Fuxing Gate Street (Fuxingmennei Dajie, from Fuxing Gate to Xidan Street), West Chang'an Street (from Xidan Street to Tiananmen Square), East Chang'an Street (from Tiananmen Square to Dongdan Street), and Inner Jianguo Gate Street (Jianguomennei Dajie, from Dongdan Street to Jianguo Gate). These sections were comprehensively referred to before the 1980s as "Ten-Li Long Avenue" 十里长街.

East Chang'an Avenue proper (Chuantong Dong Chang'an Jie) 传统东长安街 Chang'an Avenue proper, east of Tiananmen Square.

West Chang'an Avenue proper (Chuantong Xi Chang'an Jie) 传统西长安街 Chang'an Avenue proper, west of Tiananmen Square.

Chang'an Avenue extensions (Chang'an Jie Yanchangxian) 长安街延长线 The sections of Chang'an Avenue exclusive of Chang'an Avenue proper, that is, west of Fuxing Gate or east of Jianguo Gate.

East Chang'an Avenue extension (Dong Chang'an Jie Yanchangxian) 东长安街延长线 Chang'an Avenue east of Jianguo Gate, including Outer Jianguo Gate Street (Jianguomenwai Dajie) and Jianguo Road (Jianguo Lu).

West Chang'an Avenue extension (Xi Chang'an Jie Yanchangxian) 西长安街延长线 Chang'an Avenue west of Fuxing Gate, including Outer Fuxing Gate Street (Fuxingmenwai Dajie), Fuxing Road (Fuxing Lu), and Shijingshan Road (Shijingshan Lu).

East Chang'an Avenue (Dong Chang'an Jie) 东长安街 Chang'an Avenue, east of Tiananmen Square.

West Chang'an Avenue (Xi Chang'an Jie) 西长安街 Chang'an Avenue, west of Tiananmen Square.

Baoyuelou 宝月楼 Tower of the Precious Moon

bei 碑 a traditional Chinese stele

Beihai 北海 the northern part of the former imperial garden west of the Forbidden City

Beijing 北京 North Capital

Beiping 北平 North Pacification

bichengxiangmu 必成项目 must-be-completed projects

caihua 彩画 paintings on the wooden frames and ceilings in traditional Chinese architecture

Chang'an 长安 Eternal Peace

Chang'anyoumen 长安右门 Right Chang'an Gate

Chang'anzuomen 长安左门 Left Chang'an Gate

chaohe 朝贺 imperial banquets and receptions

chengshi xingzhi 城市性质 urban nature

chixiandai 迟现代 late-coming modernization

chongyan cuanjian 重檐攒尖 double-eave pointed roof

Chuantong Zhouxian 传统轴线 Tradition Axis

chuantongde 传统的 traditional

chuihuamen 垂花门 a gate type in traditional Chinese architecture, mostly inside a residential courtyard

Chunqiu 春秋 Spring and Autumn Period

cijian 次间 side bays

cuanjian 攒尖 pointed roof without horizontal ridge in ancient Chinese architecture

dabendan 大笨蛋 a big stupid egg

Dadu 大都 Great Capital

dai 代 period, generation, dynasty

Damingmen 大明门 Great Ming Gate

dangdai 当代 the present age

Daqingmen 大清门 Great Qing Gate

dawuding 大屋顶 big roof

ding 鼎 ancient bronze tripod

Dizhi 地支 Twelve Earthly Branches

Dong Jiaomin Xiang 东交民巷 East Jiaomin Alley

Dongdan 东单 East Single Memorial Archway, named after Dongdanpailou 东单牌楼

Dongfang Guangchang 东方广场 Oriental Plaza

Dongsanzuomen 东三座门 East Three-Arch Gate

Dongsanzuomen Dajie 东三座门大街 East Three-Arch Gate Street

dougong 斗拱 brackets in traditional Chinese architecture

Duchayuan 都察院 Imperial Procuratorate

duohui gudu fengmao 夺回古都风貌 take back the style of the old capital

ershiwushi 二十五史 twenty-five dynastic histories

fang 放 open

fang'an zhengji 方案征集 collection of schemes

fang-jian-bei 方尖碑 square and pointed stele

Fangjin Xiang 方巾巷 Fangjin Alley

fashi 法式 model

Fengtiandian 奉天殿 Fengtian Hall

Fengtianmen 奉天门 Fengtian Gate

fu 赋 traditional style of prose most popular in Han dynasty

fuguzhuyi 复古主义 revivalism

fuhao 符号 sign

Fuqian Jie 府前街 Fuqian Street

Fuxing Lu 复兴路 Fuxing Road

Fuxingmen 复兴门 Fuxing Gate; Gate of Revitalization

Fuxingmennei Dajie 复兴门内大街 Inner Fuxing Gate Street

Fuxingmenwai Dajie 复兴门外大街 Outer Fuxing Gate Street

Fuyou Jie 府右街 Fuyou Street

gandalei 干打垒 the application of simple local material and vernacular structure in building construction in Maoist China

ge 阁 a multistory building type in traditional Chinese architecture frequently used in gardens and Buddhist temples

Gongbu 工部 Ministry of Public Works

Gongcheng 宫城 Palace City; also known as the Forbidden City (Zijincheng)

Gongchengzuofa zeli 工程做法则例 *Construction Principles*, a Qing dynasty building manual

Gongli Zhansheng Fang 公理战胜坊 Memorial Archway for the Victory of Justice

gonglizhuyi 功利主义 utilitarianism

gongnengzhuyi 功能主义 functionalism

Gouchengzhuyi 构成主义 Constructivism

goulan 勾栏 balustrade in traditional Chinese architecture

Guanyin 观音 the Chinese bodhisattva of compassion

gudai 古代 ancient history

gudu fengmao 古都风貌 style of the old capital

Guibinlou 贵宾楼 Grand Hotel Beijing

gujia jiegoufa 骨架结构法 bone structure construction method

Guoji Fandian 国际饭店 International Hotel

Guojia Dajüyuan 国家大剧院 National Grand Theatre

Guojia Lishi Wenhua Mingcheng 国家历史文化名城　National Famous Cities of History and Culture

Guomindang 国民党　Nationalist Party

Guoqing Gongcheng 国庆工程　Anniversary Projects

Guozijian 国子监　the imperial education and ceremonial center in Beijing next to the Confucian Temple

guqin 古琴　an ancient seven-stringed Chinese zither

hamashi 蛤蟆式　toad style

Hanlinyuan 翰林院　Imperial Hanlin Academy

Hanren 汉人　Han people

hongxian 红线　red-line width; a standard indicator for the scale of streets in China, it refers to the minimal distance required between the street-front façades of buildings across a street, thus the limit for solid structures in architectural design

houfa waishengxing xiandaihua 后发外生型现代化　postponed exterior-generated modernization

Huagaidian 华盖殿　Huagai Hall

Huangcheng 皇城　Imperial City

Hubu 户部　Ministry of Revenue

Humen 虎门　Tiger Gate

hutong 胡同　traditional alleys

ji 稷　grains

Ji 蓟　an old name for Beijing

Jianguo Fandian 建国饭店　National Construction Hotel

Jianguo Lu 建国路　Jianguo Road

Jianguomen 建国门　Jianguo Gate; Gate of National Construction

Jianguomennei Dajie 建国门内大街　Inner Jianguo Gate Street

Jianguomenwai Dajie 建国门外大街　Outer Jianguo Gate Street

Jianzhu Xuebao 建筑学报　*Architectural Journal*, an official journal of the Chinese Architectural Society

Jiaotaidian 交泰殿　Jiaotai Hall

jiegouzhuyi 结构主义　structurism; the word "structurism" was made up to translate the Chinese pejorative term *jiegouzhuyi*, which refers to Russian constructivism of the 1950s, whose standard Chinese translation now is *gouchengzhuyi*; *jiegouzhuyi* was used to translate "constructionism" in the 1980s, and the misspelled "structurism" was adopted to capture such a discrepancy in the translation of Western terms

Jiegouzhuyi 结构主义　Constructionism

jiejixing 阶级性 class nature

jihui 集会 mass assembly

jindai 近代 the recent past

Jindai Shi 近代史 Recent History

jinghua 精华 cream

Jingshan 景山 Coal Hill

jinian-bei 纪念碑 memorial stele

Jinshendian 谨身殿 Jinshen Hall

jinxiandai 近现代 recent and modern history

Jinyiwei 锦衣卫 Ming dynasty secret police force

Jishu Weiyuanhui 技术委员会 Technical Committee

jiti chuangzuo 集体创作 collective creation

jiti fangfa 集体方法 collective approach

juanpeng 卷棚 a traditional roof style of Chinese architecture, in which the two roof slopes smoothly curve to join each other instead of forming a sharp ridge

jubaopen 聚宝盆 a treasure bowl in folklore that will generate jewels

junshi bowuguan 军事博物馆 military museum

juqi 聚气 the preservation of auspicious energy in feng shui

juyuan 剧院 theatre

Kangxi Nanxuntu 康熙南巡图 *Emperor Kangxi's Inspection Tour to the South*

kou maozi 扣帽子 to label

kun 坤 earth, female, yin

Kunninggong 坤宁宫 Kunning Hall

lang 廊 traditional veranda

laosankan 老三看 old three looks

Liangchen Fang'an 梁陈方案 Liang-Chen Scheme

liangzhou, liangdai, duozhongxin 两轴，两带，多中心 two axes, two belts, and multicenters

Libu 吏部 Ministry of Civil Office

Libu 礼部 Ministry of Rites

lifang 里坊 ward

Lingdao Xiaozu 领导小组 Leadership Small Group

Liubu 六部 Six Ministries

Liusi 六四 June Fourth

longmai 龙脉 dragon vein

Longmen 龙门 Dragon Gate

luodizhao 落地罩 semipermanent wooden space dividers

Mao Zhuxi Jiniantang 毛主席纪念堂 Chairman Mao Memorial

maozi 帽子 a label

meili 美丽 beautiful

miannan er zhi 面南而治 face south to rule

mingjian 明间 central bay

minzu xingshi, shehuizhuyi neirong 民族形式，社会主义内容 national form, socialist content

minzude 民族的 national

minzude, kexuede, dazhongde 民族的，科学的，大众的 national, scientific, and mass-oriented culture

minzuzhuyi 民族主义 nationalism

Nanchang Jie 南长街 Nanchang Street

Nanchizi 南池子 Southern Pool, a place name in Beijing

Nanheyan 南河沿 Southern River Bank, a place name in Beijing

Nanjing 南京 South Capital

neichao 内朝 inner court

Neicheng 内城 Inner City

Neisandadian 内三大殿 Inner Three Halls

paifang 牌坊 memorial archway in traditional Chinese architecture, also called *pailou*

pailou 牌楼 memorial archway in traditional Chinese architecture, also called *paifang*

pin 品 a ranking system for officials in imperial China

qian 乾 heaven, male, yang

Qianbulang 千步廊 Thousand-Pace Corridor

Qianmen 前门 Front Gate; also known as Zhengyang Gate (Zhengyangmen)

Qianmen Dajie 前门大街 Front Gate Street

Qianqinggong 乾清宫 Qianqing Hall

Qiansanmen Dajie 前三门大街 Qiansanmen Street

qichengxiangmu 期成项目 hope-to-complete projects

Qintianjian 钦天监 Imperial Prison

qinwang 亲王 a rank of Manchu princes during the Qing dynasty

que 阙 a traditional Chinese building type with two symmetrical towers on high platforms framing a passageway

queti 雀替 large parallel brackets under the beam

qunzhong luxian 群众路线 mass line

qunzhong yuanze 群众原则 mass-oriented principle

Renmin Dahuitang 人民大会堂 Great Hall of the People

Renmin Yingxiong Jinianbei 人民英雄纪念碑 Monument to the People's Heroes

sanchao 三朝 three main courts

sanjiehe 三结合 three combinations

sanxian jianshe 三线建设 three lines construction

she 社 soil shrine

Shejitan 社稷坛 Altar of Soil and Grain

Shenzhou Diyijie 神州第一街 Number-One Avenue in the Divine Land

shi 实 solid or actual

Shidai Zhouxian 时代轴线 Time Axis

Shidajianzhu 十大建筑 Ten Great Buildings

Shiji 史记 *Records of the Historians*

shijiezhuyi 世界主义 worldism; the word "worldism" was made up to translate the Chinese pejorative term *shijiezhuyi*, which means "internationalism"; in architecture, *shijiezhuyi* more or less refers to the International Style, however, since in Chinese there is another word for "internationalism," *guojizhuyi* (a very positive term in Marxist ideology), the author has decided not to use it in this context

Shijingshan Lu 石景山路 Shijingshan Road

shilang 实廊 a solid or actual corridor attached to the main structure

Shilichangjie 十里长街 Ten-Li Long Avenue

shiyong, jingji, za keneng de tiaojianxia zhuyi meiguan 适用，经济，在可能的条件下注意美观 utility, economy, and, if the situation allows, attention to beauty

shizhou 实轴 a "real" or "solid" axis

shou 收 closed

siheyuan 四合院 traditional Chinese courtyard house

Taihedian 太和殿 Taihe Hall; Hall of Supreme Harmony

Taihemen 太和门 Taihe Gate; Gate of Supreme Harmony

Taimiao 太庙 Imperial Ancestral Temple

Tangrenjie 唐人街 Chinatown

Tiananmen 天安门 Heavenly Peace Gate

Tiangan 天干 Ten Heavenly Stems

tianxia 天下 "all under heaven"; the whole world

tianyuan defang 天圆地方 round sky and square earth

tuichixiangmu 推迟项目 okay-to-postpone projects

waichao 外朝 outer court

Waicheng 外城 Outer City

Waisandadian 外三大殿 Outer Three Halls

waishi gongcheng 外事工程 diplomatic projects

Wangfujing 王府井 a place name in Beijing

wangqi 王气 imperial energy

Wanren Dahuitang 万人大会堂 Grand Conference Hall for Ten Thousand People

Weilai Zhouxian 未来轴线 Future Axis

weimeizhuyi 唯美主义 aestheticism

wenben 文本 text; context

wenfa 文法 grammar

wengcheng 瓮城 protective walls and gates

wudian 庑殿 pure hip roof in ancient Chinese architecture

Wufu 五府 Five Departments

Wujundudufu 五军都督府 Headquarters of the Five Armies

wuxing 五行 five elements

xiandai 现代 modern

xiandaihua 现代化 modernization; modernized

xiandaihua zhuanxing 现代化转型 modernization process

xiandaizhuyi 现代主义 modernism

Xidan 西单 West Single Memorial Archway, named after Xidanpailou 西单牌楼

xieshan 歇山 hip-and-gable roof in traditional Chinese architecture

xiju 戏剧 general term for theatrical performance art

xin xiandaizhuyi 新现代主义 neomodernism

Xingbu 刑部 Ministry of Punishment

xingshizhuyi 形式主义 formalism

Xinhuamen 新华门 Xinhua Gate; Gate of New China

xiqu 戏曲 traditional Chinese operas, sometimes also known as *xiju*

Xisanzuomen 西三座门 West Three-Arch Gate

Xiyanglou 西洋楼 Western Buildings in Yuanmingyuan

xu 虚 void or insubstantial

xulang 虚廊 a void or insubstantial corridor open on both sides

xumizuo 须弥座 high base in traditional Chinese architecture with decorated moldings, originated from the seat in Buddhist statues

xuzhou 虚轴 a "void" or "false" axis

yanchao 燕朝 banquet court

Yangbanxi 样板戏 Model Operas

yangqi 扬弃 selective abandonment

Yezhu Weiyuanhui 业主委员会 Proprietor Committee

Yiheyuan 颐和园 one of the summer palaces of the Qing dynasty in the western suburb of Beijing, popularly known as the "Summer Palace"

Yijing 易经 *Book of Changes*

yimen 仪门 ceremonial gate

Yingzao fashi 营造法式 *Treatise on Architectural Methods*, a Song dynasty building manual published in 1103

Yingzao Xueshe 营造学社 Institute for Research on Chinese Architecture

yishu qinquan 艺术侵权 artist tort

Yongdingmen 永定门 Yongding Gate; Gate of Permanent Stability

yuanbao 元宝 a gold or silver ingot used as money in dynastic China

Yuanmingyuan 圆明园 one of the summer palaces of the Qing dynasty in the western suburb of Beijing, sometimes known as the "Old Summer Palace"

zaofa neishengxing xiandaihua 早发内生型现代化 early and interior-generated modernization

zaojing 藻井 caisson ceiling

zaopo 糟粕 dross

zhengshi 正史 authentic histories

Zhengyangmen 正阳门 Zhengyang Gate; also known as Front Gate (Qianmen)

Zhengyangmen Dajie 正阳门大街 Zhengyang Gate Street

Zhenshan 镇山 Hill to Vanquish Evil Spirits

Zhong'erxin 中而新 Chinese and new

zhonggan zhi yanli yu zuoyou zhi duichen 中干之严立与左右之对称 exactly founded central stem and left-right symmetry

Zhongguo benwei 中国本位 Chinese-oriented

Zhongguo Chuantong Fuxing 中国传统复兴 Chinese Classical Revivalism

Zhongguo chuantong jianzhu 中国传统建筑 traditional Chinese architecture

Zhongguo Geming Lishi Bowuguan 中国革命历史博物馆 Museum of Chinese Revolution and History

Zhongguo Guyou Zhi Xingshi 中国固有之形式 Original Chinese Forms

Zhonghua minzu de weida fuxing 中华民族的伟大复兴 great renaissance of the Chinese people

Zhonghua Qianqiu Song 中华千秋颂 *Ode to the Chinese Millennia*

Zhonghua Shijitan 中华世纪坛 China Millennium Monument

Zhonghuamen 中华门 Gate of China

Zhongnanhai 中南海 the central and southern parts of the former imperial garden, located west of the Forbidden City and north of Chang'an Avenue

zhongyang bangongqu 中央办公区 central office district

zhongzhouxian 中轴线 central axis

Zhouli 周礼 *Rituals of Zhou*

zhuangyan 庄严 solemn

zhuanjia weiyuanhui 专家委员会 specialists committee

zhugao buyu jianguang 柱高不逾间广 the height of a column should not exceed the width of the bay

zhushi 柱式 "column model"; orders of architecture; the column, its base, and the beams and bracket set on top of it in traditional Chinese architecture

Zhushikou 珠市口 a place name in Beijing

Zijincheng 紫禁城 Forbidden City; also known as the Palace City (Gongcheng)

zongluxian 总路线 general line

Bibliography

Abbreviations

BMA   Beijing Municipal Archive

BMAUC Beijing Municipal Archive of Urban Construction

JZXB   *Jianzhu Xuebao* (Architectural Journal)

MIA   Marxist Internet Archive (http://www.marxists.org)

SAATU School of Architecture Archive, Tsinghua University

Andreu, Paul. *The National Grand Theatre.* Translated by Tang Liu and Wang Tian. Dalian: Dalian University of Technology Press, 2008.

———. *Paul Andreu: The Discovery of Universal Space.* Milano, Italy: L'Arca Edizioni, 1997.

Andrews, Julia F., and Kuiyi Shen. *A Century in Crisis: Modernity and Tradition in the Art of Twentieth-Century China.* New York: Guggenheim Museum, 1998.

Bai Hequn. *Lao Beijing de juzhu* [The housing in old Beijing]. Beijing: Beijing Yanshan Chubanshe, 1999.

Banham, Reyner. *Age of the Masters: A Personal View of Modern Architecture.* New York: Icon Editions, Harper & Row, 1975.

Barker, Francis, Peter Hulme, and Margaret Iversen, eds. *Postmodernism and the Re-Reading of Modernity.* Manchester: Manchester University Press, 1992.

Barlow, Tani E., ed. *Formations of Colonial Modernity in East Asia.* Durham, NC: Duke University Press, 1997.

Beijing Chengshi Guihua Guanliju, ed. *Beijing zai jianshe zhong* [Beijing in construction]. Beijing: Beijing Chubanshe, 1958.

Beijing Daxue Lishixi Beijing Shi Bianxiezu, ed. *Beijing shi* [History of Beijing]. Beijing: Beijing Chubanshe, 1999.

Beijing Guihua Jianshe Bianjibu, ed. *Beijing guihua jianshe* [Beijing city planning and construction review]. Beijing: Beijing Guihua Jianshe Bianjibu.

Beijing Jianshe Shishu Bianji Weiyuanhui Bianjibu, ed. *Jianguo yilai de Beijing chengshi jianshe ziliao di 1 juan: Chengshi guihua* [Urban construction data of Beijing City after the founding of the People's Republic of China]. Beijing, 1995.

Beijingshi Difangzhi Bianzuan Weiyuanhui, ed. *Beijing zhi, shizheng juan, yuanlin lühua zhi* [Annals of Beijing, volumes of municipal administration, annals of gardens and parks]. Beijing: Beijing Chubanshe, 2000.

Beijingshi Guihua Sheji Yanjiuyuan, ed. *Qianxin xihui jingcheng lantu: Beijingshi guihua sheji yanjiuyuan youxiu guihua sheji zuopin ji* [Carefully and delicately delineating the capital's blueprints: Excellent planning and design works of the Beijing Municipal Institute of City Planning and Design]. Nanjing: Dongnan Daxue Chubanshe, 2004.

Beijingshi Guihua Weiyuanhui, Beijing Chengshi Guihua Xuehui, and Beijingshi Jianzhu Sheji Yanjiuyuan Jianzhu Chuangzuo Zazhishe, eds. *Beijing shida jianzhu sheji* [Beijing's Ten Great Buildings]. Tianjin: Tianjin Daxue Chubanshe, 2002.

———, eds. *Chang'anjie: Guoqu, xianzai, weilai* [Chang'an Boulevard: Yesterday, today, tomorrow]. Beijing: Jixie Gongye Chubanshe, 2004.

Beijingshi Guihua Weiyuanhui and Beijing Shuijingshi Shuzi Chuanmei, eds. *2008 Beijing aolinpike gongyuan ji Wukesong wenhua tiyu zhongxin guihua sheji fang'an zhengji* [International competitions for conceptual planning and design of the 2008 Beijing Olympic Green and Wukesong Cultural and Sports Center]. Beijing: Zhongguo Jianzhu Gongye Chubanshe, 2003.

Beijingshi Renmin Zhengfu, ed. "Beijing chengshi zongti guihua (2004 nian–2020 nian)" [Beijing city master plan, 2004–2020]. *Beijing guihua jianshe* [Beijing city planning and construction review] 101, no. 2 (2005): 4–51.

Beipingshi Gongwuju, ed. *Beipingshi dushi jihua sheji ziliao di yi ji* [Design data of Beiping urban planning, vol. 1]. 1947. BMA, archival no. Jia-3.

Berman, Marshall. *All That Is Solid Melts into Air: The Experience of Modernity*. New York: Simon & Schuster, 1982.

Boyer, M. Christine. *The City of Collective Memory: Its Historical Imagery and Architectural Entertainments*. Cambridge, MA: The MIT Press, 1994.

Broudehoux, Anne-Marie. *The Making and Selling of Post-Mao Beijing*. New York: Routledge, 2004.

Brumfield, William Craft. *A History of Russian Architecture*. Cambridge, MA: Cambridge University Press, 1993.

Bürger, Peter. *Theory of the Avant-Garde*. Minneapolis: University of Minnesota Press, 1984.

Celik, Zeynep, Diane Favro, and Richard Ingersoll, eds. *Streets: Critical Perspectives on Public Space*. Berkeley: University of California Press, 1994.

Certeau, Michel de. *The Practice of Everyday Life*. Translated by Steven Rendall. Berkeley: University of California Press, 1984.

Chan, Hok-lam. *Legends of the Building of Old Peking*. Seattle: University of Washington Press/Hong Kong: Chinese University Press, 2008.

Chang'anjie guihua shencha huiyi, taolun jiyao [Chang'an Avenue planning scheme evaluation symposium, discussion summaries]. 1964. SAATU.

Chen, Xiaomei. *Acting the Right Part: Political Theatre and Popular Drama in Contemporary China*. Honolulu: University of Hawai'i Press, 2002.

Chen Gan. *Jinghua daisi lu-Chen Gan wenji* [A collection of Chen Gan's writings]. Beijing: Beijingshi Chengshi Guihua Sheji Yanjiuyuan, 1996.

Chen Lüsheng. *Xin Zhongguo meishu tushi 1949–1966* [Pictorial history of new Chinese arts, 1949–1966]. Beijing: Zhongguo Qingnian Chubanshe, 2000.

Cody, Jeffrey W. *Building in China: Henry K. Murphy's "Adaptive Architecture," 1914–1935*. Seattle: University of Washington Press, 2001.

Cody, Jeffrey W., Nancy S. Steinhardt, and Tony Atkin, eds. *Chinese Architecture and the Beaux-Arts*. Honolulu: University of Hawai'i Press/Hong Kong: Hong Kong University Press, 2011.

Cohen, Paul A. *Discovering History in China: American Historical Writing on the Recent Chinese Past*. Translated by Lin Tongqi. Beijing: Zhonghua Shuju, 1989.

Connor, Steven. *Postmodernist Culture: An Introduction to Theories of the Contemporary*. 2nd ed. Oxford: Blackwell Publishers, 1997.

Cooke, Catherine, and Igor Kazus. *Soviet Architectural Competitions, 1920s–1930s*. London: Phaidon Press, 1992.

Cui Yong. *Zhongguo Yingzao Xueshe yanjiu* [Study on the Institute for Research on Chinese Architecture]. Nanjing: Southeast University Press, 2004.

Dangdai Zhongguo Bianweihui, ed. *Dangdai Zhongguo de Beijing* [Beijing of contemporary China]. Beijing: Zhongguo Shehui Kexue Chubanshe, 1989.

Davis, Deborah S., Richard Kraus, Barry Naughton, and Elizabeth J. Perry, eds. *Urban Spaces in Contemporary China: The Potential for Autonomy and Community in Post-Mao China*. Woodrow Wilson Center Series. Washington, DC: Woodrow Wilson Center Press/New York: Cambridge University Press, 1995.

Dirlik, Arif, and Zhang Xudong, eds. *Postmodernism and China*. A Boundary 2 Book. Durham, NC: Duke University Press, 2000.

Dittmer, Lowell. *Sino-Soviet Normalization and Its International Implications, 1945–1990*. Seattle: University of Washington Press, 1992.

Dong, Madeleine Yue. *Republican Beijing: The City and Its History*. Berkeley: University of California Press, 2003.

Dong Guangqi. *Beijing guihua zhanlue sikao* [Strategic thinking of Beijing planning]. Beijing: Zhongguo Jianzhu Gongye Chubanshe, 1998.

Xie Mincong. *Beijing de chengyuan yu gongque zhi zai yanjiu, 1403–1911* [Re-research on the city and palaces of Beijing, 1403–1911]. Taipei: Taiwan Xuesheng Shuju, 1989.

Yang Yongsheng, ed. *Jianzhu baijia huiyilu* [A collection of a hundred architects' memoirs]. Beijing: Zhongguo Jianzhu Gongye Chubanshe, 2000.

———, ed. *Jianzhu baijia shuxinji* [A collection of a hundred architects' letters]. Beijing: Zhongguo Jianzhu Gongye Chubanshe, 2000.

———, ed. *Jianzhu baijia yan* [Collection of a hundred architects' words]. Beijing: Zhongguo Jianzhu Gongye Chubanshe, 2000.

———, ed. *1955–1957 jianzhu baijia zhengming shiliao* [1955–1957 historical documents of a hundred schools contending in architecture]. Beijing: Zhishi Chanquan Chubanshe, Zhongguo Shuili Shuidian Chubanshe, 2003.

———, ed. *Zhongguo sidai jianzhushi* [Four generations of Chinese architects]. Beijing: Zhongguo Jianzhu Gongye Chubanshe, 2002.

Yu, Shuishan. "Ito Chuta and the Birth of Chinese Architectural History." Society of Architectural Historians 64th Annual Meeting, April 13–17, 2011, New Orleans, Louisiana, *Abstracts of Papers*, 57.

———. "Limit, Passage, and Chinese National Theatre: Interview with Paul Andreu." *Interior Architecture of China* 15, no. 3 (March 2004): 129–31.

———. "Redefining the Axis of Beijing: Urban Planning during the Time of Revolution." *Journal of Urban History* 34, no. 4 (May 2008): 571–608.

Yue Jiazao. *Zhongguo jianzhu shi* [History of Chinese Architecture]. 1933. Beijing: Tuanjie Chubanshe, 2005.

Zhang Bo. *Wo de jianzhu chuangzuo daolu* [My architectural experience]. Beijing: Zhongguo Jianzhu Gongye Chubanshe, 1994.

Zhang Fuhe. *Beijing jindai jianzhushi* [A modern architectural history of Beijing]. Beijing: Qinghua Daxue Chubanshe, 2004.

Zhang Jinggan. *Beijing guihua jianshe wushi nian* [Fifty years of the city planning of Beijing]. Beijing: Zhongguo Shudian, 2001.

———. *Beijing guihua jianshe zongheng tan* [A sweeping discussion of the city planning of Beijing]. Beijing: Beijing Yanshan Chubanshe, 1997.

Zhang, Xudong. *Chinese Modernism in the Era of Reforms: Cultural Fever, Avant-Garde Fiction, and the New Chinese Cinema*. Durham, NC: Duke University Press, 1997.

Zhao Dongri and Chu Ping. "Beijing tian'anmen guangchang dongxi diqu guihua yu jianshe" [Planning and construction in the Tiananmen Square area in Beijing]. *JZXB* (January 1993): 2–5.

Zhonggong Zhongyang Wenxian Yanjiushi, ed. *Zhonggong Shisanjie Sizhong Qua-*

nhui yilai lici Quanguo Daibiao Dahui Zhongyang Quanhui zhongyao wenxian xuanbian [A collection of significant documents of the various National Congress plenary sessions of the Central Committee since the Fourth Plenum of the Thirteenth Central Committee of the Chinese Communist Party]. Beijing: Zhongyang Wenxian Chubanshe, 2002.

Zhongguo Geming Bowuguan, ed. *Zhongguo Geming Bowuguan 50 nian* [Fifty years of the Museum of Chinese Revolution]. Beijing: Haitian Chubanshe, 2001.

Zhongguo Guojia Dajüyuan Jianzhu Sheji Guoji Jingsai Fang'anji Bianweihui, ed. *Zhongguo Guojia Dajüyuan Jianzhu Sheji Guoji Jingsai fang'anji* [A collection of design schemes for the International Architectural Competition of the National Grand Theatre P. R. China]. Beijing: Zhongguo Jianzhu Gongye Chubanshe, 2000.

Zhongguo Jianzhu Kexue Yanjiuyuan, ed. *Zhongguo gu jianzhu* [Ancient buildings of China]. Beijing: Zhongguo Jianzhu Gongye Chubanshe/Hong Kong: Sanlian Shudian, 1982.

Zhongguo Jianzhu Yishu Quanji Bianji Weiyuanhui, ed. *Zhongguo jianzhu yishu quanji, 1–24* [The complete works of Chinese architecture, vols. 1–24]. Beijing: Zhongguo Jianzhu Gongye Chubanshe, 1999.

Zhongguo jianzhuye nianjian [Yearbooks of the Chinese construction industry]. Beijing: Zhongguo Jianzhuye Nianjian Zazhi Youxiangongsi, 1984–2003.

Zhongguo Kexueyuan Ziran Kexueshi Yanjiusuo, ed. *Zhongguo gudai jianzhu jishushi* [A history of ancient Chinese architectural technology]. Beijing: Kexue Chubanshe, 1990.

Zhongguo Lishi Bowuguan, ed. *Zhongguo tongshi chenlie* [Chinese history display]. Beijing: Zhaohua Chubanshe, 1998.

Zhongguo Meishu Quanji Bianji Weiyuanhui, ed. *Zhongguo meishu quanji 1–6: Jianzhu yishu bian* [The complete works of Chinese art, vols. 1–6: Architecture]. Beijing: Zhongguo Jianzhu Gongye Chubanshe, 1987.

Zhongguo Renmin Geming Junshi Bowuguan, ed. *Zoujin Zhongguo Renmin Geming Junshi Bowuguan* [Into the Military Museum]. Beijing: Bingqi Gongye Chubanshe, 2003.

Zhongguo Xiandai Meishu Quanji Bianji Weiyuanhui, ed. *Zhongguo xiandai meishu quanji di 1–4 juan: Jianzhu yishu* [The complete works of modern Chinese art, vols. 1–4: Architecture]. Beijing: Zhongguo Jianzhu Gongye Chubanshe, 1997.

Zhongyang Dang'anguan, ed. *Zhongguo Gongchandang bashi nian zhengui dang'an* [Precious archival materials from the eighty years of the Chinese Communist Party]. Beijing: Zhongguo Dang'an Chubanshe, 2001.

Zhu, Jianfei. *Architecture of Modern China: A Historical Critique.* London: Routledge, 2009.

———. *Chinese Spatial Strategies: Imperial Beijing, 1420–1911.* London: Routledge, 2004.

Zhu Qiqian. "Zhongyang gongyuan ji" [Record of the central park]. In *Huoyuan wencun* [A collection of articles of the Huo garden], edited by Beijingshi Zhengxie Wenshi Ziliao Yanjiu Weiyuanhui, 113–15. Beijing: Zhongguo Wenshi Chubanshe, 1991.

Zhu Qiqian, Liang Qixiong, Liu Dunzhen, and Yang Yongsheng. *Zhejiang lu* [Records of sage architects]. Beijing: Zhongguo Jianzhu Gongye Chubanshe, 2005.

Zhu Zhaoxue and Zhao Dongri. "Dui shoudu jianshe jihua de yijian" [Proposal for the urban planning of the capital]. 1950. SAATU, archival no. 212–7301.

Zou Denong. *Zhongguo xiandai jianzhushi* [Modern Chinese architecture]. Tianjin: Tianjin Kexue Jishu Chubanshe, 2001.

Index

Page numbers in boldface indicate illustrations.

National Science and Technology Hall, 82, 107, 120, 204

National Theatre. *See* National Grand Theatre

nationalism, 274, 277, 285; and architecture, 8, 47, 51, 55–57, 139; and Chinese Millennium Project, 179, 186; ideology, 39, 191, and June Fourth Democratic Movement, 179, 304n20

Nationalist Party, 56, 91, 257

NBBJ, 199

Neicheng. *See* Inner City

neoclassicism, 40–42, 73, 86, 136, 138, 164, 231, 295n52

Neumann, Heinz, 214, 216

New Democratic Revolutionary History exhibition, 90

Nikken Sekkei, 47

Nixon, Richard, 159

Nouvel, Jean, 223, 225

Olympic Park, 276, 277

Olympics (2008), 11, 31, 54, 276–77

Opium War, 55, 90, 98, 102, 141; Second, 17, 35

Oriental Plaza, 53, 179–85, **180–82**, 193–94

Original Chinese Forms, 56, 58, 62, 92

Outer City, 15, 126, 181, 246, 288n6, 311n8, 311n32

Outer Jianguo Gate Street, 46, 47

Outer Three Halls, 90, 268

Ouyang Can, **42**

Overseas Chinese Union Building, 82

Pacific Science Center, Seattle, 206

paifang, 63, 291n71. *See also* memorial archway

pailou, 43, 171, 272, 291n71. *See also* memorial archway

Palace City, 13, 245–46, 260

Palace Museum, 20, 89, 92, 100

Palace of Science and Technology. *See* National Science and Technology Hall

Palmer and Turner Group, **182**

Party History display. *See* July First Exhibition

Peace Park, 20, 249

Pei, C. C., **200**, 200–201

Pei, I. M., 46, 170–71, **200**, 200–201, 206, 239

Pei Cobb Freed and Partners, 198, **200**. *See also* Pei, I. M.

Peng Peigen, 235

Peng Zhen, 66, 205

People's Bank of China, 44, 47, **49**, 176

People's Liberation Army (PLA), 101, 149, 179, 192, 296n76

People's Liberation Army (PLA) Museum. *See* Military Museum

People's Republic of China, tenth anniversary of, 3, 90, 92, 104, 112, 204, 231, 265

Plaza of Holy Fire, 187, **187**, 188, 191

Pompidou Center, 239, 280–81

postcolonialism, 238, 285

postmodernism, 140, 173–77, 194–95, 206, 225–26, 285

pure hip roof. See *wudian*

Puyi, 20, 89

qian, 188–92

Qianbulang. *See* Thousand-Pace Corridor

Qianmen Street. *See* Front Gate Street

Qianqing Gate, 268

Qiansanmen Street, 34, 312n45

Qingming Gate, 21

Qintianjian, 17

que, 125, 130

queti. *See* brackets: longitudinal

Research Institute of Architectural Science, 27, 107, **111**, 114

revivalism, 57, 69–73, 85, 174, 176, 295n56

Right Chang'an Gate, 15–17, 18, 22, 130, 132, 268, 288n10

Rituals of Zhou, **247**, 247–48, 313n65

Robert Sobel/Emery Roth and Sons, 47, **48**

roof: double eave pointed, 43; pointed, 52, 63, 66. *See also* "big roof"; *wudian*; *xieshan*

Rossi, Aldo, 194, 225

Roth, Emery, 47, 48

Saint-Simon, Henri de, 134, 136

sanjiehe. *See* three combinations

Sanlihe Office Buildings for Four Ministries and One Committee, **63**

scheme collection, 104–6, 202, 210, 276

Science Palace. *See* National Science and Technology Hall

Shao Weiping, **198**

Shattuck and Hussey, 56

Shejitan. *See* Altar of Soil and Grain